EXPERIENCE AND EMPIRICISM

D1715840

Northwestern University
Studies in Phenomenology
and
Existential Philosophy

General Editor Anthony J. Steinbock

EXPERIENCE AND EMPIRICISM

Hegel, Hume, and the Early Deleuze

Russell Ford

Northwestern University Press
Evanston, Illinois

Northwestern University Press
www.nupress.northwestern.edu

Printed in the United States of America

10 9 8 7 6 5 4 3 2 1

Library of Congress Cataloging-in-Publication Data

Names: Ford, Russell (Russell Clarke), author.
Title: Experience and empiricism : Hegel, Hume, and the early Deleuze /
    Russell Ford.
Other titles: Northwestern University studies in phenomenology & existential
    philosophy.
Description: Evanston, Illinois : Northwestern University Press, 2023. |
    Series: Northwestern University studies in phenomenology and existential
    philosophy | Includes bibliographical references and index.
Identifiers: LCCN 2022024240 | ISBN 9780810145603 (paperback) |
    ISBN 9780810145610 (cloth) | ISBN 9780810145627 (ebook)
Subjects: LCSH: Deleuze, Gilles, 1925–1995. Empirisme et subjectivité. |
    Hume, David, 1711–1776—Influence. | Hegel, Georg Wilhelm Friedrich,
    1770–1831—Influence. | Empiricism.
Classification: LCC B1489.D43 F67 2023 | DDC 146/.44—dc23/eng/20220826
LC record available at https://lccn.loc.gov/2022024240

For Shannon M. Scott
With love and gratitude

Contents

Acknowledgments

This book pursued a meandering path before reaching its final form. It began as an attempt to think through the consequences for contemporary political philosophy of Deleuze's rejection of the traditional concept of subjectivity. Before that question could even gain its footing, however, it was replaced by the question of why Deleuze chose Hume for the subject of his first book. The answer to that question proved to be tantalizingly elusive, necessitating the exploration of a number of rabbit-holes before I was able to satisfactorily formulate the argument of this book.

In my wanderings and spelunking I have benefited from the advice, friendship, and mentoring of a number of people. David L. Levine—who has an uncanny knack for being in the right place, at the right time, and for saying the right thing—encouraged my early philosophical efforts. In graduate school at Penn State, Rich Doyle gave me the courage to pursue my questions and interests and to speak with my own voice, while Charles Scott lent a ready ear and helped me to learn how to listen to the particularities of philosophical problems. Others who have helped me along my professional way include Doug Anderson, Craig Brewer, Andrew Cutrofello, Michael Deere, Namita Goswami, Leonard Lawlor, Rick Lee, Bryan Lueck, Patchen Markell, Carl Mitcham, Ian Alexander Moore, Michael Naas, Jeff Nealon, John Protevi, S. Alan Ray, Alan Schrift, Daniel W. Smith, and H. Peter Steeves. At Elmhurst University I have benefited immeasurably from the friendship and support of my colleagues Chris Travis, Teri Walker, Julie Nosal, Larry Carroll, Scott Matheney, and Nick Behm, as well as the unstinting help of the staff of the A. C. Buehler Library, especially Jennifer Paliatka, Peg Cook, and Julia Venetis.

My former Dean, Alzada Tipton, was a valuable supporter of this project and, together with the EU Center for Scholarship and Teaching, helped facilitate the sabbatical leave that gave it the start that it needed. The Center has also been gracious in providing travel funding so that I could attend conferences where some of the ideas in the following pages were first shared.

Jane Bunker—then at Northwestern University Press—was an early supporter of this project and, along with Trevor Perri, helped it along through its early stages. I am grateful to Faith Wilson Stein for bringing it over the finish line. Additional thanks go to my project editor, Maia Rigas; Anne Strother and the rest of the truly great marketing crew; Paul Mendelson for his outstanding copyediting; and David Robertson for the index.

There were many times when, because of illness, other obligations, or just exhaustion, this project could have fatally fallen apart were it not for the love and support of my mom, Ginny Ford, my brother, Matthew Blazer, and—most of all—my wife, Shannon Scott. And Zelda (of the Chicago Zeldas).

Abbreviations

"EA"   Jean Wahl, "Notes sur quelques aspects empiristes de la pensée de Husserl," *Revue de Métaphysique et de Morale* 57 (1952): 17–45

EHT   Jean Wahl, *Existence humaine et transcendance* (Geneva: La Baconnière, 1944)

ES   Gilles Deleuze, *Empirisme et subjectivité* (Paris: Presses Universitaires de France, 1953)

"HI"   Alexandre Koyré, "Hegel à Iéna (À propos de publications récentes)," *Revue Philosophique de la France et de l'Étranger* 118, no. 9/10 (1934): 274–83

"HK"   Jean Wahl, "Hegel et Kierkegaard" *Études Kierkegaardiennes* (Paris: Fernand Aubier, 1938)

"HM"   Alexandre Kojève, "Hegel, Marx, et le christianisme," *Critique* 1, no. 3/4 (1946): 339–66

II   Gilles Deleuze, *Instincts et institutions* (Paris: Hachette, 1953)

MC   Jean Wahl, *Le malheur de la conscience dans la philosophie de Hegel* (Paris: Presses Universitaires de France, 1929)

"NL"   Alexandre Koyré, "Note sur la langue et la terminologie Hégéliennes," *Revue Philosophique de la France et de l'Étranger* 112 (1931): 409–39

PP   Jean Wahl, *Les philosophies pluralistes d'Angleterre et d'Amérique* (Paris: Félix Alcan, 1920)

RI   Jean Wahl, *Du rôle de l'idée de l'instant dans la philosophie de Descartes,* (Paris: Félix Alcan, 1920)

RP   Alexandre Koyré, review of *Le malheur de la conscience dans la philosophie de Hegel, Revue Philosophique de la France et de l'Étranger* 110 (1930): 136–43

"SR"   Jean Hyppolite, "La signification de la Révolution française dans la 'Phénoménologie' de Hegel," *Revue Philosophique de la France et de l'Étranger* 128, no. 9/12 (1939): 321–52

"ST"   Jean Wahl, "Subjectivité et transcendance," *Bulletin de La Société Française de Philosophie* 37, no. 5 (December 1937): 161–211

"TJ1"   Jean Hyppolite, "Les travaux de jeunesse de Hegel d'après des ouvrages récents," *Revue de Métaphysique et de Morale* 42, no. 3 (1935): 399–426

"TJ2"   Jean Hyppolite, "Les travaux de jeunesse de Hegel d'après des ouvrages récents (suite et fin)," *Revue de Métaphysique et de Morale* 42, no. 4 (1935): 549–78

VC   Jean Wahl, *Vers le concret: Études d'histoire de la philosophie contemporaine (William James, Whitehead, Gabriel Marcel)* (Paris: Vrin, 1932)

"VP"   Jean Hyppolite, "Vie et prise de conscience de la vie dans la philosophie hégélienne d'Iéna," *Revue de Métaphysique et de Morale* 45, no. 1 (1938): 45–61

EXPERIENCE AND EMPIRICISM

Introduction

But what do you know about me, given that I believe in secrecy,
that is, in the power of falsity . . . ?
—Gilles Deleuze, "Letter to a Harsh Critic"

Gilles Deleuze's first book, *Empirisme et subjectivité* (*Empiricism and Subjectivity*), undertakes two linked projects by way of an explication of Hume's empiricism: a conditional extension of the pluralist existentialism of Jean Wahl, and a critical response to the Hegelian rationalism of Jean Hyppolite.[1] While the book is often read by Anglo-American readers in an anachronistic fashion, and mined for elements that will become more prominent in Deleuze's later work, a close reading of the text, coupled with a historical understanding of the major currents that motivated its composition, shows that it is an important philosophical argument in its own right.

The present book argues that Deleuze published *Empiricism and Subjectivity* in 1953 as an intervention in a long-running debate in French academic philosophy. The choice of Hume as a subject was a bold but not an outlandish one. The boisterous postwar political and philosophical debates about what Deleuze then regarded as a defunct subjective humanism, as well as the presence of Hume on the *agrégation* in 1948 (which, in turn, was the likely reason for Hyppolite's course on Hume in the previous year), combined to elevate Hume to a prominence that he had never before enjoyed in French philosophical circles. At the same time, however, Deleuze's book is not a simple explication of Hume. As the book's title indicates—a conjunction of topics with Hume relegated to the subtitle—Deleuze meant to craft his "portrait" of Hume in such a way that it would have contemporary relevance as well as historical interest. Chief among those to whom the book was addressed were Jean Wahl and Jean Hyppolite. For the former, *Empiricism and Subjectivity* offered an example and vindication of the radical empiricism that he had sought in various authors over the previous three decades, even as it rejected Wahl's distinctive subjective account of transcendence. Regarding

Hyppolite, the situation is more complicated, in part because his *Logique et existence* (*Logic and Existence*), a major work in which he would attempt the reconciliation of Hegel's *Phenomenology of Spirit* with his *Logic*, appeared in 1952, only a year before the publication of *Empiricism and Subjectivity* and therefore too close for the latter to address the former in any substantive way.[2] As it pertains to Hyppolite's rationalist Hegel, Deleuze's argument is more negative. From beginning to end, *Empiricism and Subjectivity* is a vindication of empiricism over rationalism and a corresponding rejection of the work of speculative dialectics. What the book retains from Hyppolite is principally a commitment to immanence, but as Deleuze's subsequent development would make clear, his conception of this crucial notion would differ radically from that of his teacher.

Deleuze himself offers few clues for assessing *Empiricism and Subjectivity*. He was educated in the 1940s, during the tumult of the Second World War and the Liberation. As he frequently notes, his most important teachers were Ferdinand Alquié—a Descartes specialist—and Hyppolite. And yet Deleuze is frank about his opinion, if not of his teachers, then of their specializations: "I could not stand Descartes, the dualisms and the Cogito, or Hegel, the triad and the operation of negation."[3] At the same time that his formal education was something of a disappointment to him—but was also, he would later remark, an impetus to do something different, to escape from it—Deleuze found other mentors, each occupying a peculiar place in—and yet also outside of—the narrow confines of professional French philosophy: Jean-Paul Sartre and Jean Wahl.[4]

Sartre is the better known of the two philosophers, but the extent to which the substance of his philosophy exerted a lasting influence on Deleuze is unclear. According to François Dosse's account in *Gilles Deleuze and Felix Guattari: Intersecting Lives*—still the best source of information on the biographical details of the former—Deleuze entered into the French philosophical milieu via his friend, the young Michel Tournier, who brought Deleuze first to the classroom of the medieval scholar Maurice de Gandillac and then, in 1943, to the salon of Marie-Magdalene Davy. In conversation with Dosse, Gandillac recalls that Deleuze made an immediate impression, with other attendees whispering that "he'll be a new Sartre."[5] But it wasn't just a philosophical precociousness that led even Deleuze himself to identify a kinship between himself and Sartre. As a student, again according to the testimony of his peers, Deleuze was deeply absorbed by *Being and Nothingness*.

Given the esteem in which the young Deleuze held Sartre, it is readily understandable how the latter's defining and polemical postwar lecture, "Existentialism Is a Humanism," which Deleuze attended along with Tournier, would have elicited a strong feeling of shock as well as aversion. According to Tournier, their response was immediate and negative: "We were floored. So our master [*maître*] had had to dig through the trash to unearth this worn-out mixture reeking of sweat and of the inner life of humanism."[6] This episode sheds light both on the value of Sartre as a thinker unencumbered by academic trappings—his lecture was to the public rather than an academic audience and was given amidst the turmoil of the formation of the Fourth Republic—and on the distance that Deleuze would come to take from the content of Sartre's work.[7] Humanism would have seemed to philosophically minded auditors like Tournier and Deleuze to be a kind of backsliding from the more engaging and promising theses not only of *Being and Nothingness* but of Sartre's earlier work—especially *The Transcendence of the Ego*. In that work, first published in *Recherches Philosophiques* in 1936–37, Sartre subjects the transcendental elements of Husserl's theory of intentionality to rigorous critique, arguing that they constitute an unnecessary capitulation to idealism.[8]

When Sartre declined the Nobel Prize for Literature in 1964, Deleuze penned a short essay entitled "He Was My Teacher [*maître*]," in which he differentiated Sartre, characterized as a "private thinker," from what he termed "public professors."[9] The former have what Deleuze characterizes as "a double character: a kind of solitude that remains their own in every situation; but also a particular agitation, a particular disorder of the world in which they rise up and speak."[10] Sartre readily fit this description, disdaining any sort of academic position in favor of a multifarious career as a journalist, playwright, novelist, and public intellectual that allowed him to choose his interventions deliberately and to also avoid the burdens and institutional restrictions that come with regular teaching. To the group of Deleuze's "private thinkers," however, can be added a seemingly very different one: Jean Wahl. Deleuze encountered Wahl in the 1940s when he was a regular attendee at Wahl's classes; and according to Dosse, it was "certainly [Wahl] who convinced Deleuze to disinter Hume" and write a thesis on him under the supervision of Hyppolite and Georges Canguilhem.[11] This thesis, which almost certainly also had its source in Hyppolite's course on Hume taught at the Sorbonne in the academic year 1946–47, would lay the foundations for *Empiricism and Subjectivity*.[12]

As a professor at the Sorbonne, Wahl was very much a member of the French academic establishment. His position as a "private thinker" is thus initially somewhat confusing; after all, he was precisely the sort of Sorbonne professor that Deleuze, in his 1964 article, seems to contrast with the private thinker. But at least two factors qualify Wahl for his inclusion alongside Sartre.[13] First, Wahl's work bringing new voices into the world of French academia was unparalleled. It was his 1929 *Le malheur de la conscience dans la philosophie de Hegel* (*The Unhappiness of Consciousness in Hegel's Philosophy*), alongside the important work of Koyré and Kojève, that would lead to the explosion of interest in Hegel in France. Along with Gabriel Marcel's 1927 book *Journal métaphysique* (*Metaphysical Journal*), Wahl's 1932 *Vers le concret* (*Toward the Concrete*) was a founding work for French phenomenology and existentialism.[14] While Wahl was teaching courses on Plato's dialogues in his official capacity at the Sorbonne, his work in the 1930s on Kierkegaard almost singlehandedly served to make the Danish thinker necessary reading for the existentialists. In addition to his philosophical work, Wahl was an accomplished poet who did much to facilitate encounters between philosophy, poetry, and the arts generally (both in France and while he was in exile in the United States during the Second World War).[15] Perhaps more important than his published work—and more characteristic of a "private thinker"—were the various conferences that Wahl organized outside of the official academic establishment. These include the conferences he organized at Mount Holyoke College during his exile in the United States and, most importantly, his creation after the war of the Collège Philosophique, an extra-institutional venue for intellectual exchange that hosted thinkers ranging from Emmanuel Levinas to Bertrand Russell. Deleuze is perhaps thinking specifically of Wahl when he writes, in "He Was My Teacher," "even the Sorbonne needs an anti-Sorbonne."[16]

The central moment of Wahl's own philosophical trajectory was his 1937 lecture "Subjectivité et transcendance" ("Subjectivity and Transcendence"), presented to a meeting of the Société Française de Philosophie. Wahl invited philosophers from across Europe—including Heidegger and Karl Jaspers—and intended to use his address to mark out the positions and disagreements surrounding the various strains of existential philosophy, as well as to argue for his own distinctive position. Wahl's remarks were brief, but he published a considerably expanded version of them as *Existence humaine et transcendance* in 1944, and after the Second World War this text would serve as the basis for an important discussion of the fortunes of existentialism at the Club Maintenant—the second such lecture at the club, following the success of Sartre's "Existentialism Is a Humanism."[17]

To find Deleuze's "private thinkers" in such temporal and spatial proximity is perhaps not so surprising. The shattering effects of the Second World War on the relatively concentrated world of French academic philosophy is virtually impossible to calculate. After the Liberation, its reconstitution was an affair both intellectual and political. As mentioned above, Sartre's lecture was both philosophical and political, aiming to garner adherents to his distinctive definition of existentialism at the same time that it sought to stake out a position relative to the elections contemporaneous with the address. Similarly, what Levinas referred to as Wahl's "famous communication" of 1937, and the works that immediately followed it, while without an overt political purpose, sought to organize a number of disparate philosophical projects that all somehow bore on lived experience or, in Wahl's terms, the concrete. However important Sartre was as a figure for the young Deleuze, it was Wahl's project that would hold his philosophical interest not only in his first book but even as late as 1990, when he would write to Jean-Clet Martin on the occasion of the publication by Martin of a book about Deleuze's philosophy: "I have only one thing to say to you: do not lose the concrete, return to it constantly. Multiplicity, refrain, sensation, etc. are all developed in pure concepts, but are strictly inseparable from the passage from one concrete to another."[18]

Outline of the Argument

The first three chapters of this book trace, through the works of Wahl and Hyppolite, as well as others, the origins of the problem that Deleuze responded to with *Empiricism and Subjectivity*. Chapter 1, "Jean Wahl and the Problem of Transcendence," elaborates the development of Wahl's thought beginning from his thesis work and continuing through his remarkable 1944 book *Existence humaine et transcendance* (*Human Existence and Transcendence*). Already in his encyclopedic *Pluralist Philosophies of England and America*, Wahl begins to formulate what will become the problem of the concrete. For Wahl, the question to be asked is: how can human thought adequately respond to the demand it feels to conceptualize the particulars of its experience without occluding those very particulars behind the generality of concepts? He accepts the movement of human thought toward the transcendent, but he argues that this pursuit must be thought in conjunction with the experience that grounds, spurs, and justifies it. As the thinker of the Whole, Hegel occupies the position of Wahl's chief antagonist from the opening lines of *Pluralist Philosophies* in 1920 through *Le malheur de la conscience dans la philosophie de Hegel* at the end of the decade. In Hegel, Wahl finds a dialectic between partial and complete human knowledge. The lived, working struggle to bring this dialectic to an end and thereby obtain a complete system of knowledge, a knowledge of the Whole, is for Wahl the source of the particular and particularly essential unhappiness of human consciousness. However, rather than following Hegel and seeing an end to this dialectic, Wahl sees the struggle for knowledge of the Whole to be insurmountable by philosophical or intellectual work.

Much of the work on Hegel's philosophy in the 1920s (and, to some extent, even prior to that) had been Christian in nature, and Wahl's treatment of Hegel is substantially informed by that prior work. In *Le malheur* Wahl argues that the aim of Hegel's philosophical project is to accomplish philosophically the theological "reconciliation" that is "the essential idea of religion."[19] Such a reconciliation is achieved by a consciousness that has worked through the mediations of concrete difference, and that has endured the unhappiness of what Wahl calls "the moment of infinite difference."[20] In a striking passage, Wahl writes that it is "very similar to the wrath of God . . . an infinite pain, and the burning flame of this necessary pain is necessary for spirit to become conscious of itself."[21] For Hegel, the becoming-conscious of itself of spirit is the completion of history and the achievement of human destiny. It is the very definition of happiness. However, Wahl is troubled and ultimately dissatisfied with this conclusion. He sees in Hegel a religious aspiration to a mystical synthesis of the concrete, but in this aspiration Hegel is forced to mask the qualitatively different upsurge of feeling that grounds his work. His failure is nonetheless the greatest effort to overcome and resolve the dialectic of pluralism and monism in favor of the latter, drawing the transcendent completely into the bounds of the immanent.

Chapter 2, "Koyré's Hegel and Wahl's Kierkegaard," discusses the impact of Wahl's momentous book as well as his own shifting interests in the 1930s. Wahl did not write his book on Hegel in order to offer a historical answer to the problem of the unhappiness of consciousness. Rather, Hegel's system serves as a kind of apotheosis of the problem— one that, for Wahl, necessarily fails. But not all of Wahl's contemporaries were convinced that Hegel did fail and chief among these was Wahl's friend and colleague, Alexandre Koyré. Wahl and Koyré had been colleagues for a brief time at the beginning of the 1920s, so it was no doubt with pleasure that Koyré agreed to review his friend's book in the *Revue Philosophique de la France et de l'Étranger*.[22] But Koyré's review is more than just an account of Wahl's argument in *Le malheur*; it is both an appreciation and a sustained criticism of it and—together with Wahl's book—it marked the beginning of the serious scholarly reception of Hegel in France. For Koyré, the young and theologically inclined Hegel was someone that Hegel himself overcame in his work. Koyré therefore reverses the order of value that Wahl applied to Hegel and argues that what is distinctive and valuable in Hegel's work is not the persistence of a youthful infatuation with religious mystery and irrationality, but the creation of a philosophical system. What Wahl has done in *Le malheur*, as Koyré memorably phrases it, is to prioritize the "lovable Hegel," the ardent, impassioned, youthful Hegel, at the expense of the philosophical achievement of the more mature Hegel. "The middle-aged Hegel," Koyré writes, "is not lovable." Even more strikingly, Koyré contends that "Hegel's greatness lies in his inhuman coldness" (*RP*, 142).

Chapter 3 will return to Koyré's work, but the remainder of chapter 2 follows Wahl in the 1930s and 1940s as his work gradually moves away from Hegel. In 1932 he published *Vers le concret* (*Toward the Concrete*), a book that was highly influential and at the same time elicited little explicit response, in part, no doubt, to Wahl's characteristically couching his own arguments within presentations of three other philosophers: William James, Alfred North Whitehead, and Gabriel Marcel. While Wahl had touched on empiricism throughout *Pluralist Philosophies*, the preface to *Vers le concret* is decisive for understanding the philosophical elements that Deleuze took from his "private thinker." Wahl distinguishes two kinds of empiricism: a first-degree empiricism that ignores the problem of the givenness of being—that simply accepts or asserts this givenness—and a second-degree empiricism, a "meta-empirical empiricism," in which being is a feeling, not an idea, and is known as felt. Wahl, of course, aligns himself with this second-degree empiricism, in which he finds an affirmation of the qualitative difference of the concrete. This qualitative difference neither persists nor can it be comprehended by reflection.

The year 1933 would find Wahl engaged with the same set of problems but having shifted figures—presenting a paper on "Hegel and Kierkegaard" to a meeting of the Hegel Congress in Rome. Like Hegel in the 1920s, Kierkegaard in the 1930s was a novelty on the French philosophical scene, and Wahl's work on him did much to bring Kierkegaard to the center of existentialist debates. Looking back on *Le malheur*, Wahl now argues that the early Hegel seems to be more "pre-Kierkegaardian than pre-Hegelian."[23] What obstructs any agreement or reconciliation between the mature Hegel and the melancholy Dane is that, in Hegel, the *Logic* brings with it a "sense of victory" over the trials and tribulations of finite life whereas, in Kierkegaard, there can be no such triumph. This irreconcilability is figured by Wahl in terms of a Hegelian *Weltanschauung* of "the day," and a Kierkegaardian *Weltanschauung* of "the night." Wahl's choice is clear: transcendence, the world of the night, cannot be eliminated. Finite subjectivity is never satisfied; never happy. Hegel's philosophical achievements are not without their charms, but the admiration they evoke is inevitably accompanied by "a feeling of collapse."[24] For Wahl, the choice for the second hypothesis is one for "the world of problems, ruptures, and failures, where, gaze fixed toward a transcendence that only they can see, [individuals] remain a problem for themselves, they remain full of irreducible multiplicities and ruptures."[25] Wahl's empiricism of the "second degree" does not take being as given, but recognizes the "thickness" or the "shock" of the immediate. In *Vers le concret* (*Toward the Concrete*) this empiricism is ascribed specifically to Hume, who "penetrates his empiricism of the first degree to find that of the second degree."[26] It is precisely this empirical thickness that Koyré argues is overcome and conceptualized by the process and progress of Hegel's dialectic.

In the mid-1930s Koyré left France for Cairo, but his arguments concerning the development of Hegel's thought were largely taken over by a young Jean Hyppolite. Chapter 3, "Hyppolite and the Promise of Immanence," therefore turns from tracing the development of Wahl's intertwined notions of empiricism and transcendence to Hyppolite's work in the 1930s and 1940s, showing how his particular reading of Hegel continued Koyré's work and, in so doing, moved into a particularly fruitful tension with Wahl's work.

Koyré argued in favor of the mature Hegel from philosophical premises: the philosophical achievement of the *Logic*, the triumph of speculative thought, is what gives it—and Hegel—the claim to philosophical greatness. Hyppolite takes a different tack. Drawing from an impressively broad range of sources that had become available primarily since the beginning of the twentieth century, Hyppolite argues with Koyré that Hegel's mature works are philosophically more significant than his youthful writings, but he does so not solely on the basis of the superiority of speculative thought, but on a close reading of the development of problems internal to Hegel's work. This genealogical approach remained a prominent feature of Hyppolite's engagement with Hegel throughout his work in the late 1930s—when he completed his translation of the *Phenomenology of Spirit*—as well as during the 1940s, when he published his magisterial *Genése et structure de la Phènomènologie de l'esprit de Hegel* (*Genesis and Structure of Hegel's Phenomenology of Spirit*. Throughout these works, Hyppolite develops a consistent project that aims to show the way that Hegel's early concerns for the particularities and struggles of finite life—the very things that Wahl argues are irreducible—never depart from Hegel's work, but are instead caught up and transformed by the speculative work of the dialectic. For Hyppolite, then, it is Hegel's achievement not merely to have conceived the *Logic*, but to have struggled through the earlier phases of his thought and to have brought to philosophical fruition that experience of struggle. As Hyppolite will later remark, with Hegel's mature system, "immanence is complete."

Transcendence has not merely been set aside or overcome, it has been thought through without remainder.

Like the projects of so many other philosophers, the trajectories of Wahl and Hyppolite were decisively altered by the outbreak of the Second World War. During the war years their fates differed sharply: Hyppolite continued to teach in occupied Paris while Wahl, captured and imprisoned for a time, barely escaped occupied France with his life and spent the remaining years of the war in the United States, characteristically presiding over gatherings of intellectuals and artists at Mount Holyoke College. Chapter 4, "The Second World War and Its Aftermath," surveys the state of Wahl's and Hyppolite's projects immediately after the war and also brings the young Gilles Deleuze onto the stage. Hyppolite's star was in the ascendant after the war, with the late 1940s belonging to him or, perhaps more properly, to Hegel. In 1947, Raymond Queneau published an edited collection of notes taken in Alexandre Kojève's seminar in the 1930s. The sharp disparity between Kojève's reading of Hegel—best summarized in his lengthy 1946 critical review of Henri Niel's 1945 book *De la médiation dans la philosophie de Hegel* (*Mediation in Hegel's Philosophy*)—and Hyppolite's more historically sensitive work led to a number of critical assessments of the French interpretation of Hegel.

By the end of the 1940s and the beginning of the 1950s, some clarity had begun to emerge. Hyppolite was recognized as the leading commentator on Hegel. Phenomenology, chiefly through the work of Merleau-Ponty, was again a field of active interest that would only grow with the publication of Husserl's *Experience and Judgment*, as well as Trân Duc Thao's attempted synthesis of Marxism and Husserlian phenomenology in his 1951 *Existentialisme et dialectique materialisme* (*Existentialism and Dialectical Materialism*). Wahl, too, continued to articulate the ineradicable transcendence proper to human finitude across the range of his activities, both professional and extramural. It was in this milieu that Deleuze emerged, having completed his formal studies shortly after the war and passed the *agrégation* in 1948. The importance of Deleuze's education cannot be underestimated in taking stock of his early work. As much as he was later inclined to belittle his education and to portray himself as a kind of philosophical maverick, there is a relatively clear trajectory from his student years through his first writings in the 1950s. Chapter 5, "Empiricism between Immanence and Transcendence," clarifies this trajectory.

Hume had never enjoyed a wide readership in France, either at the time of his works' initial publication or after. That Deleuze should write a book devoted to Hume in 1953 is therefore somewhat strange. However, several factors—Hume's presence on the 1948 *agrégation*, the increasing attention given to humanism (and Deleuze's early rejection of it), Wahl's emphasis on the empiricist aspects of Husserl's thought in his recently published *Experience and Judgment*, and Hyppolite's course on Hume in 1946–47—all contributed to the rationale behind the topic of Deleuze's *Empiricism and Subjectivity*.[27] Chapter 5 considers these factors, but also analyzes Deleuze's intervention in terms of a pair of philosophical problematics: Wahl's contention that transcendence is an irreducible aspect of finite existence, and Hyppolite's contention that the achievement of Hegel was to have abolished the impulse toward transcendence through the work of speculative negation. From Wahl, Deleuze takes the call for an empirical philosophy faithful to the differential elements of experience even as he rejects the insistence on an impulse to transcendence. From Hyppolite, Deleuze takes the immanentization of human experience, but rejects the negating reflection that abolishes qualitative difference. Far from merely being a book "on" Hume, *Empiricism and Subjectivity*, as its title indicates, is an intervention into debates that dominated and shaped French philosophy in the early 1950s.

Chapter 5 discusses *Empiricism and Subjectivity* in its historical context and also analyzes its opening chapter, which is the most conventional one insofar as it deals with Hume's epistemology. Chapter 6, "Hume, Empiricism, and the Primacy of the Practical," considers the central sections of Deleuze's book. Deleuze hews closely to Hume's texts even as he sets them to work within a contemporary context. As Deleuze insists throughout *Empiricism and Subjectivity*—and even beyond it—Hume is first of all a practical philosopher, and his epistemology is only a part of a larger practical thinking. As chapter 6 shows, in the second and third chapters of *Empiricism and Subjectivity*, Deleuze argues for an empirical practical philosophy that ultimately privileges the work of the imagination. It is reflection in the imagination, not reflection via speculative negation, that will preserve both immanence and the concretely and differentially real. Chapter 4 of *Empiricism and Subjectivity*, "God and the World," gives Deleuze a special kind of "test case" for the reading of Hume he has elaborated in the first three chapters of the book. In the thoughts of God and the World—thoughts of totality, of the Whole—human beings find that they cannot renounce what are ultimately fictions. Here we see Wahl's problematic at work, but whereas Wahl sees human beings drawn to transcendence by intimations of the Whole, Deleuze offers a reading of Hume in which the Whole—God and the World—is simply an outgrowth of the operation of the faculty of the imagination.

Finally, chapter 7, "Empiricism Vindicated," considers the concluding chapters of *Empiricism and Subjectivity*, in which Deleuze distances himself slightly from Hume in order to more pointedly position his read-

ing in relation to the problematics of Wahl and Hyppolite. Of key importance here is the effort to, in William James's and Wahl's terms, go *round*
Kant.[28] Far from turning on the question of whether knowledge begins
from experience or not, empiricism and critical rationalism—Hume and
Kant—can be distinguished according to whether one begins with a "methodically reduced" plane of analysis in which the subject and the given
are present and the question is that of their relation, or whether one
proceeds purely "immanently" and asks how the subject is constituted
in the given. The latter is, for Deleuze, the procedure open to Humean
empiricism when it is compelled to offer a response to the transcendental
critique of Kant.

The key concept that Deleuze draws from his reading of Hume as
an answer to the challenge of Kantian rationalism is "intentional finality." Again, the very language indicates the phenomenological as well
as Hegelian milieu in which Deleuze is working. Deleuze argues for a
worldly conception of finite existence that would retain its ability to
create wholes, worlds, but would forever remain impotent to determine
the Whole. If this seems to place Deleuze firmly in the camp of Wahl, he
insists—along with Hume—on the multiplicity of finite existence rather
than a constituted self. Such experiences are, a later Deleuze might argue,
experiences of becoming that do not so much open a constituted subjectivity to something other as recast subjectivity itself as multiplicitous.

1

Jean Wahl and the Problem of Transcendence

> True intelligence is, above all else, a craving after the concrete
> and the particular.
> —Jean Wahl, *Pluralist Philosophies*

"Nous autres, civilisations, nous savons maintenant que nous sommes mortelles."[1] The poet Paul Valéry's somber words, with which he opened the first letter of his "The Crisis of the Mind," sketched in sharp relief the awesome horror that confronted Europe as the smoke of war began to recede.[2] The letters appeared first in the British journal *Athenaeum*, less than six months after the November 1918 armistice. The Treaty of Versailles was being negotiated. Dark trenches still ran across the blasted landscape of northern France like so many gaping wounds. Shakespeare's prince, invoked by Valéry, "hardly knows what to make of so many skulls."

This is an "intellectual Hamlet," however, and the bones he muses over are the traces of an exemplary past now bleached of their power to secure a future. The question of the passage from war to peace—"darker and more dangerous" than its reverse—is urgent: "no one can say what will be dead or alive tomorrow." And this liminal moment is made even more dangerous, more serious, by the situation that prevailed in Europe before the war. Looking back, Valéry sees "nothing . . . and yet an infinitely potential nothing." Like the Danish prince who serves now as its posthumous avatar, the chief characteristic of European modernity was a dangerous diversity of conflicting possibilities and, like that same prince, its luxuriating confines—in which all manner of thoughts could be earnestly entertained—which precipitated a bloody actuality: the heat death of Europe.

> The physicists tell us that if the eye could survive in an oven fired to the
> point of incandescence, it would see . . . nothing. There would be no
> unequal intensities of light left to mark off points in space. That formi-

dable contained energy would produce invisibility, indistinct equality. Now, equality of that kind is nothing else than a perfect state of *disorder*.

In his second letter, Valéry turns to the admittedly false perspective—but "every point of view is false"—of the contribution that the intellect might make to the establishment of peace. He finds the problem to be "a threatening conspiracy of things," a conspiracy of global scope in which the qualitatively rich but quantitatively dwarfed "cape" of Europe, appended like a geographical afterthought to the mass of Asia, is in danger of being swamped by its own prodigious achievements and inventions. Unable to examine the qualitative element and character of Europe "in detail," Valéry is nonetheless able to put forward his "basic theorem": that the standardization of the arts and sciences, as well as the parallel diffusion of culture, will inevitably invert the scales. Whatever it is that constitutes Europe's greatness, its worldly preeminence, will not be balanced by the work of others; it will be overcome and subordinated. Liquidated. But "intellectual physics" allows for the physically miraculous: the reemergence of wine from the water that diffused it. And so the mind is stirred to that peculiar possibility, hope, which affirms the power of "freedom" against the deathly expanse of sheer undifferentiated energy. "We must for a time give up considering groups," Valéry concludes, "and study the thinking individual in his struggle for a personal life against his life in society."[3]

***

Jean André Wahl was 26 when the First World War broke out and 32 when, one year after the publication of Valéry's essay, he submitted the two theses for his *doctorat d'état: Les philosophies pluralistes d'Angleterre et d'Amérique* (*The Pluralist Philosophies of England and America*) and the shorter *Du rôle de l'idée de l'instant dans la philosophie de Descartes* (*On the Role of the Idea of the Instant in Descartes' Philosophy*).[4] Across a career that would span more than half of the twentieth century and bring him into contact with a dizzying number of thinkers in France and abroad—as a teacher, commentator, translator, editor, organizer, and critic—Wahl would elaborate and pursue several of the ideas first broached in these early works. He was anything but a one-note thinker, however. Indeed, one of Wahl's persistent skills was his ability to introduce foreign philosophers and philosophical works into French academic debates. More than just introducing these figures—which included William James, Hegel, Kierkegaard, Heidegger, and Nicolai Hartmann, as well as lesser-known thinkers such as Jules Lequier—Wahl often became a champion for them, drawing their work into dialogue with contemporary problems in order to explore the products of these encounters and collisions. Wahl's friend Emmanuel Levinas hit upon an apt characterization of his style when, in a 1976 memorial address, he described his late friend's prose as "scintillating."[5] Indeed, Wahl's texts often give the impression of skipping through several voices. They are marked by an almost frenetic pursuit of questions and concepts through texts both poetic and philosophical, but they also manifest a steady purpose, driving Wahl's interlocutors toward the problem of what he would come to call "the concrete." It is this idea more than any other that defines Wahl's influence and importance. With it, he gave succinct and substantial form to Valéry's spectral question.

The shattering effect of the First World War led many in Europe—politicians, writers, artists, and others—to attempt to revivify and renew the search for—and the question of—the possibility of a meaningful Whole. Frederick Brown describes Andre Breton's 1924 "Surrealist Manifesto" as "a prescription for rebirth of the spirit. It would work the magic that doctrinaires vested in nationhood and priests in communion. It would unlock the true life."[6] Running through such formulations is an often unspoken conviction that the war was a kind of "mis-fire" and that the disastrous project which aimed to "unlock the true life" was one that needed to be repeated more than rethought. A contrary strain of thought, with which Wahl's work harbors a deeper affinity, questions and rejects the idea that progress is an unproblematic movement toward Wholeness. Although it gives the initial impression of being simply a historical survey of a particular philosophical lineage, the thesis of Wahl's *Pluralist Philosophies* decisively turns away from narratives of progress.

Across the full historical breadth of the European philosophical tradition—from Plato and Descartes through Hegel, Anglo-American pluralism, and including the work of his contemporaries in both France and Germany—Wahl's encyclopedic knowledge was set to work against the drive to dissolve the individual into the group, to rationalize and conceptualize even the most intense experiences, and to render immanent the transcendent.[7] This conflict between immanence and transcendence which informed all of Wahl's work would come to a head in the debates that followed the Second World War. Amidst the discussions—political and philosophical—that continue to be inadequately gathered under the heading of "the Humanism Debate," Wahl's defense of transcendence figured prominently.[8] The chaotic fruitfulness of those debates underwent a significant homogenization in the early 1950s. The reasons for this are many—and a discussion of some of them forms the subject of chapter 4 of this book—but even before the transformative arrival of structuralism, Jean Hyppolite was able to succinctly articulate the completion of an epochal philosophical movement in his book *Logic and Existence*: the equation of Nietzsche's declaration of the death of God with the achievement of absolute knowing through Hegel's System is the definitive overturning of Platonist metaphysics.[9] In a phrase that would echo through a subsequent generation of French philosophy— and which spoke directly counter to Wahl—Hyppolite announced that "immanence was complete."[10]

Wahl's interwar work was an important resource for Hyppolite, but the two were working in parallel during the war years and immediately after, when a young Deleuze encountered them both as teachers. During the war and the German occupation, Hyppolite taught in several lycées around Paris and produced several works that would both excite and anchor the postwar interest in Hegel: his translation of Hegel's *Phenomenology of Spirit*, his brief *Introduction à la philosophie de l'histoire de Hegel* (*Introduction to Hegel's Philosophy of History*), and his massive *Genesis and Structure of Hegel's Phenomenology of Spirit*.[11] *Genesis and Structure* did more than provide a commentary on Hegel's text. As will be discussed in chapter 3, Hyppolite's interpretation emphasized the importance of the development of Hegel's thought prior to the composition of the *Phenomenology*—the topic of a lively debate in France during the 1930s between Alexandre Koyré and Jean Wahl.

Wahl's experience during the Second World War was starkly different from Hyppolite's. Soon after the French defeat, Wahl was forced from his position at the Sorbonne and, after a harrowing imprisonment at Drancy, was able—through the help of friends in France and abroad—to make his way first to Morocco and then to New York.[12] The catastrophe of the war interrupted the preparations to publish *Human Existence and Transcendence*, an important and uncharacteristically direct statement of Wahl's philosophy that expanded on remarks given at an important meeting of the Société Française de Philosophie in 1937.[13] *Human Existence and Transcendence* was finally issued by a small Swiss publishing house in 1944—a short note indicated that "circumstances" had prevented Wahl from reviewing the page proofs—and develops what Wahl terms a "transcendental empiricism."[14] He argues that there is a subjective experience of transcendence that cannot be eliminated, that philosophical reflection never completely reduces the concrete to immanence, and that this insistent transcendental reality must be investigated as real. The key to this "source of philosophy" is a pre-conceptual intuition most vividly exhibited by "poet-thinkers" such as "Rimbaud, Van Gogh, and Nietzsche" whose lives are evidence of an ineradicable transcendence that is both an impetus for philosophical thought and its irreducible remainder.[15] The works of such poet-thinkers express the transcendence that eludes philosophy, and Wahl's discussion of language in *Human Existence and Transcendence*, as well as his 1947 *Poésie, pensée, perception* (*Poetry, Thought, Perception*), to be taken up in chapter 4, offers a striking counterpoint to Hyppolite's elevation of philosophical language in his *Logic and Existence*.[16]

Pluralist Beginnings

The two parts of Wahl's 1920 *doctorat d'état* are the obverse and complementary sides of the problem that would preoccupy him over the next three decades. Harkening to Valéry's call for sociological and anthropological analysis to be set aside in favor of a renewed attention to individual existence, Wahl begins to formulate what he will come to call the "problem of the concrete": how can human thought adequately respond to the demand it feels to conceptualize the particulars of its experience without occluding those very particulars behind the generality of concepts? Wahl's initial philosophical work pursues this problem in three ways. First, he identifies the dialectical structure of human thinking, a dialectic that is visible at the beginning and the end of modern philosophy: in the coupling of mortal and divine knowledge in Descartes, as well as in Hegel's dialectic. Describing this dialectic as one that cannot be reduced to any quantitative opposition, as one between qualitatively different terms, Wahl's own thought develops the neutral monism of Bertrand Russell and G. E. Moore, in which the externality of relations and terms is a rejection of any attempt to derive a particular whole from the essential nature of the partial.[17] Every dialectical synthesis of the diversity of experience is therefore a creative one, not the revelation of a final and total truth, and Wahl thus sides with a Jamesian pluralism against the various strains of neo-Hegelianism. Pluralism, realism, and an insistence on the fruitlessness of the inevitable dialectic of finite thought: these are the distinctive preoccupations of Wahl's early works, and they will continue to ramify throughout his career. In his 1976 essay "Jean Wahl: Neither Having nor Being," written in memory of Wahl, Emmanuel Levinas borrows his friend's terminology to describe Wahl's philosophical project as that of "building a house of flame."[18] The architectural metaphor is a pervasive one in Descartes and post-Cartesian philosophy, but Levinas's phrase succinctly highlights Wahl's mischievous subordination of its aspirations to totality and completion. His project aims to account for the imperative to systematization without losing its restless, unhappy origin.

The touchstone for Wahl's philosophy is Hegel. It was Hegel who not only formed the basis for the philosophical problematic of the nineteenth century but also, by corraling all thought into his System, claimed to fulfill the aspirations of modern philosophy. Wahl compares this systematizing drive to a kind of "Don Juanism," a quantitative amalgamating whose ensemble is qualitatively transformed in an act of intellectual alchemy.

> It is Hegel who has made possible the setting out of the problem. The work of Hegel is the most powerful effort that has ever been made in order to yield a global philosophy, where everything is explicated by the idea.[19]

There is another philosophical inclination, however, and another tradition—represented by, among others, Russell and Moore—that is not organized by a drive toward Wholeness. The problem can be summarized as thought's struggle to think the qualitative diversity of experience, or what Wahl calls "the concrete," a concept that would be decisive for two generations of French philosophers.[20] It would come to serve as a kind of banner, a rallying cry, that represented a choice for the particular over the general, rupture over continuity, subjectivity over totality, night over day, and ultimately, for Wahl, transcendence over immanence. "The qualitative dialectic [of Kierkegaard] will be a protestation against the Hegelian dialectic, against the ideas of immanence and continuity."[21] Before Kierkegaard, however, it was Anglo-American pluralism and the Cartesian theory of time that offered Wahl resources for a philosophical thought that eschews closure and completion. Though often placed in its vanguard, the work of Wahl was also a potent counter-force to the distinctively French Hegel of the twentieth century.[22]

Wahl's *Du rôle de l'idée de l'instant dans la philosophie de Descartes* appeared alongside but also appears to be quite different from *Pluralist Philosophies*. The former clocks in at fewer than fifty pages and narrowly considers the work of a single philosopher, while the latter is more than five times as long and ranges across dozens of thinkers. At the heart of Wahl's analysis of Descartes is a confusion that arises from the latter's unwitting employment of two different conceptions of time without either reconciling them or discerning their conflicts.

> Descartes' work here consists in profoundly uniting to the idea of continuous creation, as it is presented in Scholasticism, the idea of discontinuous time, as it was formulated in the mechanics and the physics of the Renaissance. (*RI*, 18)

This unification anticipates and could even be said to distantly engender the nineteenth-century debates between monism and pluralism.

Descartes's project aims to secure both personal and scientific knowledge, to firmly ground and thereby obtain the status of indubitable truth for human knowing. The cause of human errors—theoretical and moral—is that every chain of reasoning implies time: "the weakness of human beings comes from the fact that they are forced to have recourse to memory" (*RI*, 2).[23] The cogito, uniquely indubitable, is not the product of a chain of reasoning, nor is its certainty something that is remembered: "The *Cogito* is the affirmation of an instantaneous certitude, a judgment, a reasoning, collected [*ramasse*] in an instant" (*RI*, 5). This instantaneous certainty is the ground upon which the edifice of worldly scientific knowledge will stand, and it also serves as a warrant for the ultimate unity of that knowledge. Systematic reflection analyzes things into essences, which in turn allows for the deduction of actual worldly diversity. At the same time, among the innate ideas of the human mind Descartes finds the idea "of infinity, of unity" which, by definition, cannot be derived from the diverse and discontinuous (*RI*, 11). Once apprehended, this thought comes to be identified as that of God, of the cause of the continued existence of the world, of eternal truths, and of the cogito itself (*RI*, 13). The idea of God is an underived idea of the continuous, always acting cause of thinking and is also the unifying principle for Descartes's mechanistic world; "it is actual infinity [in act]" (*RI*, 14–15).

The difference between the infinite continuity of God and the finite diversity of things leads Wahl to shift his discussion from the *Meditations* to the *Principles of Philosophy*, where he uses Descartes's example of a candle flame to analyze the unity of a transcendent God with the immanent mechanism of the physical world. On the one hand, the flame is a single entity burning over the course of a particular period of time. On the other hand, however, this selfsame flame is consumed in each instant and a new flame takes its place (*RI*, 19). This contradiction is insurmountable for the cogito, which attempts to conceive of the persistence of the flame as "a chain of creations" that differ from the flame's ignition only by their ordinality, by not being designated as "first." From God's perspective, however, the ignition and the burning of the flame are combined in a "simple and unique" activity, an instantaneous action; but it is an instant, Wahl notes, "that is beyond time and instants" (*RI*, 19). The flame shows that continual creation is more than "a kind of myth" deployed by Descartes to safeguard God's omnipotence; it is also the symbol of the "union of movement and stability that characterizes the world of Descartes" (*RI*, 19, 40). It is a figure of God's instantaneous certainty, of the unity of the diverse in a knowledge that apprehends an unchanging truth in the particular elements of experience, and it is precisely this knowledge that lies beyond every human effort while nonetheless constituting its ideal.

> We find ourselves therefore ceaselessly before this same tendency, this same effort: to see things in the instant. The continuity of the action of God, the unity of the mind, the continuity of space—the fact that God creates without ceasing, that the soul always thinks and that space is full—the theory of intuition as the theory of the creation of essences and existences and of God by God himself, that of light and of *conatus* are only completely explained if one gives an account of the Cartesian theory of time. (*RI*, 44)

Instantaneous knowledge is knowledge of and in the unity of time. It is a knowledge that is not just other than but is opposed to the diverse and differentiated knowledge of human beings: the Cartesian God counters the diversity of nature—natural differences are gradually diminished by the common divine action that creates them (*RI*, 29).[24] At the same time, beginning as early as Descartes, the trajectory of modern philosophy appears to Wahl to be inextricable from a demand, rooted in human temporality, to confront and to think the persistent irruption of these differences.

In sharp contrast to *Du rôle de l'idée de l'instant*, Wahl's *Pluralist Philosophies* is a sprawling, encyclopedic account of the development of a dizzying number of strains of Anglo-American thought over the course of the nineteenth and early twentieth centuries. Indeed, its readers could be forgiven for thinking of it as merely a survey of philosophers and philosophical movements. It begins *in medias res*: "It is particularly since 1870 that the philosophical teaching in English universities has been inspired by the idealist monism of German Idealism" (*PP*, 1). And only with the book's conclusion does the reader learn that its exhaustive—and exhausting—litany of names and theories reflects a deliberate and calculated strategy: "it is perhaps appropriate to study the pluralists in this scattered way, in bits and pieces, according to one of James' favorite expressions" (*PP*, 239). There is no pluralism properly speaking, Wahl insists, only many pluralisms allied in their diverse opposition to what he calls "monism" and "monadism," the intertwined claims for an abstract unity subtending a world of essentially identifiable individualities. The provocation for pluralism is the unification of monadism with "temporalism"—a combination that echoes *Du rôle de l'idée de l'instant*—which yields "every real possibility" (*PP*, 240). In 1870, monism meant the philosophy of Hegel, and the philosophical work that contested and rejected it was not the pursuit of a new system so much as the rejection of the very idea of system; in its inception, pluralism was an "experience and adventure of thought" (*PP*, 254).

These two philosophical approaches, which for Wahl have the character of philosophical *temperaments*, play off of one another in a dialectic that repeatedly promises to disclose an underlying order (*PP*, 255).[25] This historical dialectic is inevitable because each philosophical attempt to conceptualize reality inevitably falls short, and this insufficiency motivates theoretical reconceptualization. Nonetheless, Wahl sides with pluralism. The experience of the individual subject is the philosophical starting point for Wahl, but from this beginning, philosophical thought, especially over the course of the previous century, is drawn into speculative reflection that aims at unifying experience within a transcendental totality. Wahl's interest in pluralism, and his later insistence on remaining attentive to the concrete, is a reaction—echoing Valéry's—to this drive toward totality. *Pluralist Philosophies* sides with pluralism in order to counterbalance the flight into monism, and Wahl takes from his analysis two important facets of pluralism that will continue to inform his subsequent work: the distinction between a quantitative and a qualitative logic, and the neo-realist separation of relations and their terms.

William James is, for Wahl, exemplary of pluralism—to such an extent that, in his 1921 review for the *Journal of Philosophy*, the American philosopher Sterling Lauprecht notes sardonically that "if it were not for the concluding section of M. Wahl's work, the book might well have been entitled 'The Philosophy of William James, its motivations, sources, and influence'"—but James's radical empiricism does not exhaust its possibilities.[26] The pluralist "affirms both the diverse and the temporal character of things, and also affirms that these two characters mutually imply one another; however, the pluralist also does not prejudge that these characters will always remain real, and does not necessarily deny the unity toward which the world may appear to tend, and which, at this very moment, is perhaps already immanent in its diversity" (*PP*, 241). Pluralism is a kind of speculative agnosticism about wholeness or totality. It doesn't reject Hegelian monism—the pluralist resists any prejudgment—so much as it insists on the present reality of the diversity of worldly experience and the different senses of that diversity, including the sense that gives it a teleological form. It resists the urge to gather this real diversity into the unity of abstract categories even as a historical dialectic beckons pragmatism, offering comfortable closure at the end of a chain stretching from the monist's assertion of an encompassing rational unity, to the pluralist's assertion of real and irreducible difference, to the seductive assertion of "a dialectical process at work in experience itself" (*PP*, 249). The oscillation of James's thought is thus read by Wahl as exemplary of a more general philosophical development: "Everywhere [in Anglo-American philosophy] we find ourselves before the same vortex of thought . . . Monism appears behind pluralism; or pluralism behind monism" (*PP*, 255). This persistence of the possibility of the immanent unity of the experientially diverse even leads Wahl to don the mask of the monist and muse that "James seems to go from Hegel to Hegel, as a Hegelian might say" (*PP*, 249).

The common themes of a half-century of Anglo-American philosophy lead the monist to assert "that the succession of doctrines is perhaps more rational than it at first seems, that an order is realized in this disorder" (*PP*, 255). The vortex of negating and self-negating philosophies may be "the origin of a dialectic that would lead us out of pluralism" (*PP*, 256). The pluralist, on the other hand, refuses the metaphysical postulate of unity: for the pluralist, "the world is a great incomplete thing which goes on endlessly completing itself, without ever being completed" (*PP*, 240). Thinking perpetually finds itself drawn into well-worn teleological grooves, and the challenge for pluralism is to stay with as-yet incomplete experience and not surreptitiously appeal to the idea of completion. One of pluralism's most fruitful efforts is the (neo-)realism of G. E. Moore and Bertrand Russell, in which "the development of contemporary English and American philosophy is linked to the development of the problem of the exteriority of relations" (*PP*, 251).[27] The theory of the externality of relations—whose core is the claim that there is no property of a thing from which its relations can be deduced—strikes directly at an equally central tenet of monism: that knowledge of any part implies knowledge of the whole (and vice versa).[28] For the pluralist, experience can only ever be known empirically; for the monist, the structure of experience, at the very least, can be deduced from any experience by analyzing the relation of its constituent elements. The denial of such a deduction is a similar kind of intellectual experiment to the denial of the parallel postulate that yields non-Euclidean geometry: it cannot be a question of proving either the interiority or the externality of relations, one can only follow the explication of each choice.[29] As Wahl notes, Russell identifies his realism with pluralism by noting that "instead of being shut in within narrow walls, of which each nook and cranny could be explored, we find ourselves in an open world of free possibilities, where much remains unknown because there is so much to know" (*PP*, 248). In this complex world, simple entities enter into an array of different complexes, and their different relations, both mental and physical, must be studied empirically.

Wahl himself is not, however, content to adopt the position of the neo-realists. "Pluralism calls itself a philosophy of the parts; monism is a philosophy of the whole . . . [and] . . . the ideas of whole and of parts have no meaning except through each other" (*PP*, 258). The empiricism of James and the other pluralists remains stuck at the level of "the plane of quantity," from which comes a language of "parts" that inevitably draws the idea of the "whole" in its wake, precipitating a dialectic (*PP*, 258). But before being determined as a part or element of some unified world, every experience has a qualitative unity: "[that unity] is sensation, it is the feeling itself. It is not abstract unity; it is the concrete totality. The concrete is the particular seen as a whole" (*PP*, 259). *Pluralist Philosophies* is thus the first text in which Wahl deploys the central notion of "the concrete," a term that will secure him a place at the center of the debates concerning existentialism both before and after the Second World War. Here, the concept still remains elusive (ironically). According to Wahl, pluralism often errs when it endeavors to think different particular experiences because it either arrays them side by side or it subsumes some to others. Both such attempts bring a kind of unity to experience by deploying a qualitatively undifferentiated "intellectual space" (*PP*, 259). In order to be "a philosophy of the purity and the separation of things," however, the radical empiricism of the pluralist ought to maintain that "the object is continuous, and it is discontinuous" (*PP*, 256).[30]

Closing his book, Wahl emphasizes the commonalities of pluralism and monism: for both there is a denigration and mistrust of the abstract, a conviction that experience outstrips every effort of the discursive intellect, and an insistence on the qualitative aspect of experience (*PP*, 270). Summarizing James's position, Wahl notes that for his radical empiricism "the object is immanence and transcendence at the same time . . . The relation between subject and object is no longer finally thinkable . . . here, strictly speaking, there is no relation, there is a presence" (*PP*, 257).[31] There are experiences that rupture the thoughtful relation of the subject and the object, that frustrate any ability to conceive of their relation, and that thereby threaten an interjection of transcendence into immanence. Wahl challenges philosophy to cleave to such experiences, to remain with this "presence." To do so is to prospect for a pluralist thinking that outstrips thought's discursive tendencies, one that is qualitative not quantitative: "beyond the logic of quantity exists a logic of quality that negates it, . . . experience is not additive, but intensive, . . . the Absolute is revealed by an act of thought" (*PP*, 270). Even Wahl's "beyond" here threatens a return to the quantitative. Together, transcendence and immanence are the ineradicable aspects of Wahl's concept of the concrete: "the particular that is closed back upon itself [*se referme sur lui-même*], that becomes a separate life" (*PP*, 259).[32] Puzzling as this statement is with its apparent invocation of a kind of solipsism, Wahl is choosing his language carefully. There are experiences that cannot be conceived discursively but that are *nonetheless experienced* and experienced intensively, in a way that marks their qualitative difference. Such experiences leave objects to themselves, and the thinker in awe before their alterity or in frustration as they slip the grasp of every concept.

The discovery of the concrete reveals the common spur, the problem that motivates and provides a mutual anchor for the opposed projects of monism and pluralism. It also permits Wahl himself to formulate a kind of philosophical program: the affirmation of the immanence of the transcendent, he concludes,

> should not be a negation of pluralism, it should recognize the irreducibility of phenomena, it should be both a realism and a dialectic, it should feel the presence of the object and the creative act of the mind [*l'esprit*] simultaneously, and it should retain that empiricism, that voluntarism and that mysticism, that sense of the concrete particular that typically characterizes the pluralist doctrine and gives it its value. (*PP*, 271)

The Challenge of Hegel

Du rôle de l'idée de l'instant and *Pluralist Philosophies* gather an immense amount of material around a relatively succinct question: how can the qualitatively different moments of human experience be adequately rendered by thought? This is the problem of the concrete. Wahl's pursuit of this problem over the course of the next ten years is signposted by two texts. The first of these, a 1926 monograph on Plato's *Parmenides*, was well received but unexceptional. The second, however, on Hegel's *Phenomenology of Spirit*, would profoundly reshape the philosophical landscape in France. In *Le malheur de la conscience dans la philosophie de Hegel*, Wahl presents a Hegel whose concern for historical and lived experience overturned decades of French readings that had largely prioritized Hegel's logicism and monism.[33] Wahl's Hegel, drawn in large part from a study of his recently published youthful writings, seems to be an ally of pluralism. However, as when he appeared on the stage of *Pluralist Philosophies*, Hegel will prove to be a disappointment, his dialectic unable to capture the concrete reality of qualitatively different experiences. Although the concern for the concrete guides Wahl's investigation, *Le malheur* also provoked another significant debate. Wahl insists that philosophical thought must remain attentive to the subjective experiences that give rise to it. But what is the force of this injunction? Might the worth of philosophy not be precisely its ability to extricate itself from the subjective and particular and attain to the level of the universal? This is one of the central questions running through the varied discussions of Hegel in France in the 1930s, and those discussions quickly come to focus on the nature of Hegelian mediation as the essential structure of ideal relations (to borrow a description from the neo-realists). The account of mediation becomes a cipher for the task and purpose of philosophy.

Wahl was not the only one drawn to Hegel and German idealism amidst the scientific and moral uncertainty that followed the First World War. His work and interests brought him into contact with other like-minded intellectuals in France, notably the Philosophies group.[34] The Philosophies were a motley group of intellectuals, poets, and philosophers who took up the gauntlet cast down by Valéry and, determined not merely to stew in the anxiety provoked by the war, set about the task of finding a solution to the "crisis."[35] Initially, this solution took the form of a new mysticism, a renewed spiritualism that implicitly rejected Valéry's judgment that the barbarity of the First World War rendered any such program misguided and dangerous. In the early 1920s, however, the Philosophies group was introduced to Hegel by the Surrealists whose chief exponent, André Breton, literally thrust Hegel's *Logic* into the hands of a somewhat bewildered Henri Lefebvre.[36] At the time the Philosophies were, in the words of one of their most prominent members, Georges Politzer, "searching for a spiritual father" and hoped that such a figure might be found in German idealism.[37] In 1926, the Philosophies published Politzer's translation of Schelling's *Philosophical Inquiries into the Essence of Human Freedom*, and in his introduction, Lefebvre echoed Wahl in describing Schelling as a "concrete metaphysician" for whom consciousness provided the requisite unification of the diversity of experience.[38] That same year, in the inaugural issue of the short-lived journal of the Philosophies group, *L'Esprit*, Wahl published the first French translation of the "Unhappy Consciousness" passage from Hegel's *Phenomenology of Spirit*. It appeared without any framing discussion, although he followed it, in 1927, with a "Commentary on a Passage from Hegel's *Phenomenology of Spirit*" in the more staid *Revue de Métaphysique et de Morale*.[39] In *Pluralist Philosophies* Hegel had been largely a foil for Wahl's genealogical account of pluralism. Wahl's subsequent work on the "unhappiness of consciousness" brings the status of the dialectic to center stage, highlighting the Hegelian innovation that allows him to move from the concrete to the rational without remainder. The dialectic thus provides the central, distinct problematic through which the much larger issues of monism and pluralism, difference and unity, and immanence and transcendence can be worked through. Reviewing the trajectory of his earlier work in *Études Kierkegaardiennes* (*Kierkegaardian Studies*), Wahl highlights Hegel's status as arch-provocateur:

> There is a qualitative logic completely different from this cult [of the drive to assess all the particulars in order to integrate them into a whole], quantitative despite everything, of the whole of space and time. From there the revolt of James, pluralism. From there the revolt, more profound, of Kierkegaard. But it is Hegel who has made possible this setting out of the problem.[40]

Le malheur, which collects Wahl's translation and commentary on the unhappy consciousness and also situates it within a significantly expanded discussion, is undoubtedly what brought Wahl and his work to the attention of the larger French philosophical community. Wahl did not pluck Hegel out of thin air—in addition to the Philosophies group, other French academics were finding a strange and attractive Hegel in the pages of the *Phenomenology*, including Alexandre Koyré, whose 1926–27 course on German speculative mysticism at the École Pratique des Hautes Études featured a section on Hegel.[41] As with Politzer and the Philosophies group, Koyré linked the unhappiness of consciousness to an experience of destitution, to a loss of normative bearings. This is a laicized version of the sinful consciousness—free but weighed down by anxiety—and is a negative moment in the evolutionary progress of the mind, one in which religious belief has vanished but its absence is still felt as a loss.[42] Koyré believed that Hegel's *Phenomenology* could serve as a kind of textual Virgil, leading consciousness along a dialectical path not into a new mysticism, but into the rational clarity of Absolute Knowledge. Wahl was less sanguine about the ability of finite knowledge to reach the paradise of truth.

Beginning with Koyré's largely positive review of Wahl's book in the *Revue Philosophique de la France et de l'Étranger* in 1930—he described it as "an effort to apprehend the life and blood of the system behind and beneath its abstract formulas, which are only its pale and distant expressions"—the positions and partisans of a new debate began to take shape that would serve as a major axis of French philosophy throughout the 1930s.[43] The discussion between Koyré and Wahl was an important part of a wide-ranging academic engagement with Hegel that included the first International Hegel Congress held in The Hague in 1930, articles in journals such as *Recherches Philosophiques* (founded by Koyré) and *Revue*

Philosophique de la France et de l'Étranger, and in several important books.[44] The discussion would last until Koyré departed Paris for Cairo in the mid-1930s and, at roughly the same time, Wahl's work began to focus more and more on Kierkegaard. By then Hegel had attained the status of a "master thinker" in France and new problems—and new protagonists—were beginning to emerge. For Wahl and Koyré, the chief point of contention was the relation between Hegel's youthful writings and his mature philosophical system: was he able to surpass the Romanticism of his youth and articulate a fully conceptualized knowledge? Or is his Absolute Knowledge achieved only through the sacrifice of the experience that it claims to grasp? The answer to these questions hinges on the work of mediation, on the dialectic.

Wahl, like Koyré, utilizes Hegel's *Philosophy of History* and his *Philosophy of Religion* to describe the unhappiness of consciousness in his 1927 "Commentary" as "religion insofar as it remains at the moment of transcendence without perceiving that it has implicitly surpassed this moment."[45] Two years later, Wahl would reprint this "Commentary" as the central section of *Le malheur,* but he follows the religious explication of the unhappiness of consciousness with a section "On the Formation of the Hegelian Theory of the Notion." Together, these two sections highlight the contrast between the youthful and religiously oriented Hegel's aversion to the sterility of rational conceptualization and the mature and systematic Hegel's embrace of the concept as the "concrete universal," as a kind of "Aristotelian entelechy" (*MC,* 194). At the time, the transformation of the panlogicist and systematic Hegel into someone who spoke to the palpable issues of contemporary lived reality must have seemed a work of philosophical alchemy.[46] For Wahl, Hegel's signal achievement was the phenomenological dialectic whose movement is the movement of reality, its concrete development. The dialectical surpassing of the unhappy situation of consciousness, of the loss of religious and moral certainty, would therefore be not merely *a* solution to Valéry's crisis—whose very contingency would prolong the crisis—but *the* solution, a securing of the human spirit to its proper ground. With this solution, what initially appeared as transcendent becomes immanent: "religion is first transcendence, one could say, in the sense that its content always escapes and remains in the distance. . . . But when it is interiorized, it then appears as essentially mediated" (*MC,* 136–37). For Wahl, however, any completion of immanence is also the elimination of qualitative difference, of intensive feeling, and a retreat into monism. *Le malheur* is thus a book about the essential but instructive failure of Hegel.

What drove both Wahl and Koyré to Hegel, as it drove other contemporary thinkers to Marxism, neo-Kantianism, phenomenology, vitalism, or any number of other contemporaneous projects, was the specter of Valéry's "crisis" with its tension between the ineliminable diversity of the world and the arbitrary character of any unification. These loom like Scylla and Charybdis over interwar philosophical work, which is also obligated to reject any sort of mystical resolution. The urgent philosophical task is, for Wahl, either to discover the means to articulate the immanent rationality of concrete existence or to show the incoherence of the problem. His work on the dialectic of pluralism and monism leads him to the latter option; the restless unhappiness of consciousness is a constitutive feature of its existence.[47] The value of Wahl's reconstruction of Hegel's intellectual itinerary is, however, not merely negative. Hegel's philosophical development is important because his pursuit of a unified rational System is *an exemplary case* of the struggle of consciousness with its unhappiness—a struggle that, for Wahl, has no resolution. Koyré, however, will argue contra Wahl that Hegel's dialectic allowed him to overcome the limitations of his youthful formulations. For Koyré, a sharp line can be drawn between the earlier and later works; in his mature System, Hegel achieves a conceptual systematization of the concrete by mobilizing the philosophical capacities of language against the mystical and poetic.

The value of Hegel's early writings, for Wahl, is that they describe an experience of thought that thought itself is essentially motivated to surpass. The young Hegel's experience of this inner limitation of thought imbues mortal existence with a tragic character, but it also serves as an impetus for that "adventure of thought" whereby reason, incited by a feeling for the implicit unity of empirical diversity, attempts to apprehend that diversity in a unified thought. As Wahl writes at the outset of *Le malheur*, the interest of the section of the *Phenomenology of Spirit* on the unhappiness of consciousness is less the role that it plays in Hegel's philosophy and more the way that Hegel poses the problem of this fundamental and essential experience (*MC*, vi). *Le malheur* is not, then, a book about the *Phenomenology*.[48] Like *Pluralist Philosophies* and *Du rôle de l'idée de l'instant*, it is a book concerned with a particular attempt to resolve the question of how to think the unity of the diverse.[49]

From the first lines of his preface, Wahl explicitly rejects interpreting Hegel's philosophy as an abstract monism; Hegel's thought "cannot be reduced to some logical formulas" (*MC*, v). There are three reasons for this. The first concerns the dialectic, which "before being a method" is a movement and experience of thought: "the dialectic . . . is an experience by which Hegel passes from one idea to another" (*MC*, v). It is not a preconception; the passage from one idea to another is motivated by the ideas themselves.

> There is not on one side essence and on the other something which is
> not essence, there are not two things of which each is a beyond [*Jen-
> seits*] in relation to the other.
>
> There is a thought which goes from one to the other, and which fur-
> thers [*assiste á*] this play that it creates and that creates it.
>
> Said still otherwise, abstract forms are not true and real things. It
> is the movement that goes from one to the other which is the true.
> (*MC*, 2)

Secondly, there is an experience of this concrete passage: "negativity is
the very movement of a mind by which it always goes beyond what it is"
(*MC*, v). Again, Wahl emphasizes that the dialectic is not the application of logical negation to experience, but is rather the recognition of
negation as a structure of experience. The final reason that Wahl gives
for rejecting the panlogicist reading of Hegel is the Romantic, Christian Hegel revealed by his youthful writings: "it is in part reflection on
Christian thought, on the idea of a God made man, that led Hegel to the
conception of the concrete universal. Behind the philosopher, we discover the theologian, and behind the rationalist, the romantic" (*MC*, v).
The incipient knowledge that is human thought is stimulated by a sense
that the diversity of experience has an intrinsic order—such is the upshot of the opening sections of the *Phenomenology*—and the struggle to
make this sense explicit is reflected in the historical progress of religion:
"Abraham and Moses, David, Christ, can be taken as the symbols of the
relation between the general and the particular" (*MC*, 129).[50] In *Le malheur* it is God, but a tragic God, that stands at the beginning and end of
the adventure of thought, securing its unity. The dialectic, negativity,
and God—the Christian divinity as the exemplary instance of the "concrete universal"—are the tools with which Hegel attempts to explicate
the unity of the diverse.

The aim of Hegel's philosophical project is therefore to accomplish
philosophically the "reconciliation" that is "the essential idea of religion"
(*MC*, 112). Such a reconciliation is a thought that has worked through
difference, a consciousness that has endured the unhappiness of "the
moment of infinite difference" and has thereby explicated its immanent
unity (*MC*, 112). Dialectical negation is the incomplete aspect of every
dynamism that makes such reconciliation possible. The heart of Hegel's
dialectical reconciliation, the idea of negation is "the immanent pulsa-
tion of the spontaneous movement of vitality," and as Hegel describes
it in an earlier "philosophical and lyrical variation," it is "very similar
to the wrath of God . . . an infinite pain, and the burning flame of this

necessary pain is necessary for spirit to become conscious of itself" (*MC* 94, 107). God is the divination of the negative, the unifying dynamism of the proliferating diversity of nature, but there is also self-consciousness, self-possessing substantial consciousness, "a heart that calls to the heart" whose unhappiness—the struggle to unify nature—is the same as God's (*MC*, 108). The apotheosis of this single, synthesized unhappiness is the promise of a "speculative Good Friday" in which duration and eternity, difference and unity, are "reunited in the conception of a duration, of a change, in the eternal" (*MC*, 109). This ultimate synthesis achieves the reconciliation of finite time and eternity that bedeviled Descartes: "such is again the flame insofar as it constantly changes its substance and conserves it in its permanent form" (*MC*, 110).

The dialectic wielded so adroitly by Hegel had been pushed to a point of crisis by Fichte and Schelling—a crisis whose analysis structures both *Faith and Knowledge* and *The Difference between Fichte's and Schelling's Systems of Philosophy* and which Hegel experienced as a lived crisis as well as a philosophical one.[51] The bad infinity of Fichte's Ego, the indifference of Schelling's Absolute, are aspects of the rending that moves thought and that remains unconsoled in their opposition. Hegel's genius is to have begun with the diagnosis of this play of forces, to have grasped that "there is a thought that goes from one to the other [thing and essence], and that fosters [*assiste à*] this play that it creates and that creates it. In other words, abstract forces are not something true and real. The true is the movement that goes from one to the other" (*MC*, 2). And if unhappiness is the reversal and collapse of each one into the other, then apprehension of the movement which is the true ground of which each pole is only an aspect "becomes happiness" (*MC*, 3). The discovery of reason as negativity is an individuated happiness, and precisely as such, is a happiness that Hegel is not yet happy with. In his early theological writings, Hegel was anxious to join the freedom of reason with "something that is both infinite and objective," and he figures this as love, then as being, and then as life, a progress of thinking that ends in "a profound irrationalism" (*MC*, 155, 169).

Reason is the self-identification of unhappy consciousness; it differentiates itself, *in the whole*, and thereby transfigures its unhappiness into happiness (*MC*, 110). The self-differentiation is not a relation between two different beings but is—and this is Hegel's advance over both Fichte's pluralism and Schelling's monism—the substantial relation whose dynamism yields different beings: the movement of the concept is "a matter of creating self-consciousness from substance, and from self-consciousness a substance" (*MC*, 113). The exhaustive analysis of this instantaneous happiness whereby light suffuses the whole without dissolving its elements, flashing out as these elements themselves—"Every person is light and burning flame"—is not enough to persuade Wahl (*MC*, 111).

> Far from believing that the philosophy of Hegel is a purely rational philosophy, we would say that it is an effort toward the rationalization of a ground [*fond*] that reason cannot attain. Despite what Hegel sometimes tells us, there are no purely transparent symbols for reason; light shines in the darkness; the symbols exist, with an opaque and resistant existence, lights come to be projected onto them, which makes them burn with a dark glare. (*MC*, 108)

Reflection cannot pass into reason without remainder. In Hegel's words, the importance of the idea of the unhappy consciousness is "the affirmation of the fact that from an affirmation the spirit goes towards what is contrary to the preceding [thing]."[52] On the one hand, then, Wahl's reading overturns the panlogical interpretation of Hegel's concrete universal as a logical totality that precedes and determines thinking, and follows Hegel in finding totality in the structured, logical movement of the thoughtful apprehension of the concrete. Thinking's discovery of its own dynamism, the dialectical differentiation of the concrete, allows reason to attain a foothold and for the unhappiness of consciousness to be superseded. The evanescence of the moments of consciousness into one another is an exchange that the unhappy consciousness constantly makes with itself:

> In this stage the spirit must perpetually triumph in order to go toward a happier consciousness. The principle of the antithesis is necessary to the elevation toward synthesis, and synthesis is happiness; in order to reach this happiness, it is necessary to traverse unhappiness. The two ideas are rejoined under another form in the idea of negativity. (*MC*, 8)

The movement of the unhappy consciousness is composed of two rational processes: a thought of opposition that goes from thesis to antithesis, and a thought of (re)union, of completion and finality, in which the movement of thought acquires wholeness by attaining to a more complete thesis (*MC*, 3). The unhappy consciousness itself is a precipitate of the perpetual return of the first of these processes: "it is an aspect of the dialectic immanent to the spirit. We can say that it is the dialectical element separated, insofar as it can be, from the speculative element, or if one wants, the negative dialectic insofar as it is separated from the positive dialectic" (*MC*, 93–94). Unhappiness is produced by "the opposition of objectivity," the confrontation of consciousness with what is not consciousness: "consciousness as a subject before an object" (*MC*, 115).[53] The two available options in this confrontation seem to be either a subjective and idealist monism—the reduction or incorporation of the object into the subject—or an objective and materialist pluralism—the elimination of the subject within an engulfing objectivity. Any happiness won by either of these recourses is merely provisional, however, because the negative moment, the oppositional confrontation of the subject and the object, recurs. For happiness to win out over unhappiness, reason must negate the oppositional separation in which reason itself has become lost (in the as-yet unthought opposition of thinking and object), thereby finding itself again by working through its destitution. "Abstraction is synonymous with unhappiness; the concrete universal will be, for the spirit, joy . . . The knowledge that first appeared as falsification and separation is revelation and union" (*MC*, 115).

Christianity offers the key to conceptualizing the victory of reason. "At the beginning of his life, as toward the end, Hegel declares himself [*s'affirme*] a theologian," but he is a Christian one, which allows him to employ the divinity of Christ and the doctrine of the Trinity to conceive of the positive dialectic as other than the transcendental and logical imposition of an objectivity onto finite consciousness (*MC*, 14). Negation is the immanent appearance of truth, of the eternal but also eventual triumph of reason produced by the immanent work of the "concrete ideal of the *Aufheben*" (*MC*, 97).[54] In Hegel, reason as the salvation of the individual unhappy consciousness is one moment of the larger reconciliation of God and the world, and it is the judgment of God that secures the concrete universal amidst the destruction of reflection carried out by the positive action of the dialectic:

> In uniting opposed terms, in negating itself as opposed, reason destroys these terms [those opposed by reflective thinking, by unhappy consciousness] and at the same time maintains them; their disappearance in the absolute assumes their appearance. One understands that the law of reflection is its own destruction. (*MC*, 181)

Le malheur is concerned with evaluating Hegel's deployment of mediation to bring consolation to the unhappy consciousness.[55] According to Wahl, the tensions within the idealisms of Fichte and Schelling—as well as the tension between these idealisms—were not just thought by Hegel, they were for him a feeling of being rended (*déchirée*) and torn. The thought emerging from and motivated by this existential tear is born not from Socratic wonder but from dissatisfaction. Such is the true beginning for both philosophy and religious belief, and its end, its accomplishment, is synthesis, the attainment of the feeling of happiness (*MC*, 8). The feeling of unhappiness has a lengthy philosophical pedigree—it is "the accord of the discordant, to take up the terms of Heraclitus"—but Hegel's invention of the dialectic, the discovery of the force and power of negation, promises to finally put it to rest (*MC*, vii). The light of reason shines in the darkness of the world of objects, and for Hegel, the reflection of this light is harmonized and stabilized in the concepts of absolute knowing, in the truth. But for Wahl, concepts, the symbols of reason, flash with a dark glare—the noise of the world disrupting the signal of thought.

Hegel's dialectical development of thinking beyond its negative moment is motivated by the theological concerns apparent in his youthful writings. There, the path to happiness is a trial, a willed undertaking; the moment of synthesis cannot be simply mechanically generated by the play of opposed determinations: "one must not represent in too schematic a fashion this march from thesis to antithesis and then to synthesis that is produced in Hegel's mind. Perhaps the analogies, though first brought to light by Hegel, between his way of grasping things and those of Fichte or even Schelling, have misled the historian of philosophy a bit on this point" (*MC*, 3).[56] The moment of synthesis is the most valuable innovation of Hegel's philosophy, resolving the unhappiness of reflective thought by discovering in the dynamism of that unhappiness an order that "brings thought back to its point of departure" (*MC*, 4). This order, by which Hegel sought "to transform the ideal of his youth into a form of reflection, into a system," is secular Destiny (*MC*, 170). It is ultimately the consciousness that being has of itself, of its unity as something hostile to the plurality of individualities that nonetheless *are being*, and with which it can therefore be reconciled. "In its first form, it is opposed to the individual, as the ruse of the universe that tends to oppose him; in its second form, it is the unity of the individual and the universe" (*MC*, 171). Separately, the two processes of Hegel's philosophy, the movement of negation and that of synthesis, lead nowhere, devolving into an indefinite process that can never soothe consciousness. Hegel's *Phenomenology*, however, is the narrative of reason, an account of the complete trajectory of thinking as it works out of its unhappiness.

> In order to be sure that it contains nothing more that is contrary to itself, it is necessary for life to have exteriorized bit by bit all of its contraries; in order for it to assimilate the entire universe, it will be necessary for it to have left room for all those similar lacks that are in it. The reflection, the possibility of separation prevents the first synthesis of complete being; for there to be the second, it is necessary

that this possibility of separation itself be integrated. The momentary disequilibrium must find its place in the final equilibrium. Separations, limitations, reflections, developments, are necessary so that the rich plenitude of life can be found anew, life fully explicated and unlimited. (*MC*, 5)

These stages are so many "ways of life," Wahl notes, anticipating his work on Kierkegaard, and "it is thus that the opposition of thought and being, that of the essential and inessential are not projected onto an abstract plane, but, on the contrary, are studied in the way in which they are felt, lived by humanity" (*MC*, 7). For Hegel, the completion of history, the achievement of human destiny, is happiness, but for Wahl, the element of lived experience, of the willed overcoming of torn consciousness, is ineradicable. Happiness, synthesis, is forever incomplete: aspiring to a mystical synthesis of the concrete, Hegel is forced to mask the qualitatively different upsurge of feeling that grounds his work. His failure is nonetheless the greatest effort to overcome and resolve the dialectic of pluralism and monism in favor of the latter, drawing the transcendent completely into the bounds of the immanent. Recoiling from this effort, Wahl will turn to Kierkegaard, to radical empiricism, and, ultimately, to his own distinctive re-valorization of transcendence, to "transcendental empiricism."

2

Koyré's Hegel and Wahl's Kierkegaard

The defense of a rational and systematic Hegel against Wahl's passionate crypto-theologian would fall to Alexandre Koyré, whose substantial review of *Le malheur* appeared in 1930.[1] Koyré had been an important voice in the French reevaluation of Hegel that began in the mid-1920s. A former student of Husserl at Göttingen, Koyré came to Paris just before the First World War and saw combat in France and Russia as a member of the Foreign Legion. After the war Koyré returned to Paris, completing his thesis in 1922 and, in 1929, his *doctorat d'état*. In 1922 he became a faculty member at the École Pratique des Hautes Études where he would teach—in addition to posts at the University of Cairo, Johns Hopkins University, and several other institutions—for forty years. Although now largely recognized for his contributions to the philosophy of science, both Koyré's teaching and scholarship were pivotal for the interwar debates over not just Hegel but, through Hegel, the distinctive task of philosophy. Like Wahl, Koyré looked to the recently published Jena writings both for clues to understanding Hegel's mature project and in order to legitimate Hegel's place in the socially and practically oriented discussions of the interwar period.[2] However, where Wahl argued that there was a continuous development from Hegel's earlier work to his mature writings, Koyré insisted that there was a decisive and important break and that the value of the later, philosophical Hegel lay precisely in its difference from the earlier work. This debate characteristically reflected the philosophical commitments of its participants: Wahl arguing that the lived anguish that motivated the youthful, "theological" Hegel could not be completely overcome by philosophical reflection, and Koyré arguing that Hegel's discovery of the dialectic facilitated a transformation of the religious problematic and its philosophical resolution.

The Unlovable Hegel

The prominence given to Hegel in Koyré's 1926–27 course on German mysticism would appear to have inclined Koyré to a favorable review of

Le malheur. However, Koyré's clear admiration for Wahl's book is coupled with an equally strong rejection of its thesis. Wahl's reading of the *Phenomenology* asserts the primacy not just of Hegel's early, religious writings, but of the religious pathos that inspired them. The later, more systematic works are then tethered to the earlier works by Wahl's interpretation, which insists that those later works be interpreted according to the problematic of the earlier ones. The resulting philosophical system is thereby reduced to a lived and tragic experience of attempting and failing to adequately conceptualize its original motivating religious feeling. In Wahl's idiom: Hegel's dialectic is an ultimately vain attempt to apprehend the concrete in thought, to formulate a logos adequate to its originating pathos. "But," Koyré muses, "isn't such a failure characteristic of every philosopher?" (*RP*, 141). Reversing Wahl, Koyré argues that what is distinctive and valuable in Hegel's work is not the persistence of a youthful infatuation with mystery and irrationality but the creation of a philosophical system—one which Hegel had formulated as early as 1800 "in his head"—which superseded that infatuation. Wahl, Koyré avers somewhat cheekily, prioritizes the "lovable Hegel," the ardent, impassioned youthful Hegel; "the middle-aged Hegel," by contrast, "is not lovable" (*RP*, 142). Even more strikingly, he contends that "Hegel's greatness lies in his inhuman coldness" (*RP*, 142).

To dismiss the unlovable Hegel would be to discard what he himself claimed to be his primary philosophical achievement: not the "rhythm of mystical thought" but "the eternal cyclical movement of thought" (*RP*, 142). The work of the young Hegel reveals the problem that Hegel surpasses, not the hidden key to his philosophy. Koyré thus to some extent returns to the earlier French interpretation of Hegel as a panlogicist, a monist, in order then to emphasize what is distinctive and non-Romantic in Hegel's mature philosophy. "What is true for Hegel, what HEGEL is, is the *Logic*" (*RP*, 142). From the standpoint of the *Logic* there is no tragic pathos; the final victory has always already been achieved. In the completed and eternal movement of the absolute there is no tragedy, no despair, no unhappiness. If something of the tragic does persist, it is transformed: "it is a tragedy thought, not a tragedy lived" (*RP*, 142). This echoes the interpretation of Victor Delbos, for whom the synthesis of the *Begriff* is a cause of itself, present at the beginning and the end of the dialectic as what prevents it from falling into the void.[3] "Hegel needs conflict, oppositions, and sufferings in order to nourish the movement of spirit; but the tragic, which is real for man, is not at all real for God. For God—and also for Hegel—the tragedy is already surmounted" (*RP*, 142). Thus, Koyré asks rhetorically: how could Hegel be anything other than an optimist?[4] Hegel's specifically philosophical greatness is to have reconceived what he first called "love" as "notion," not to have surreptitiously pursued the former under cover of the latter (*RP*, 143).

In 1931, just a year after his review, Koyré published a substantial article on Hegel in the *Revue Philosophique de la France et de l'Étranger* entitled "Note sur la langue et la terminologie Hégéliennes" ("A Note on Hegelian Language and Terminology").[5] In his review of Wahl's book, Koyré had argued for the primacy of logos over pathos, the primacy of Hegel's mature philosophical System over his impassioned religious ideas. Wahl, of course, had argued the reverse: that there is an opaqueness to concrete lived experience that spurs but also frustrates conceptual reflection. In "A Note on Hegelian Language" Koyré takes up precisely this problem. One of the questions that emerged from the first International Hegel Congress was how to smooth the various frictions between the startling number of different approaches to Hegel without limiting the prospects for further innovative research. Hegel's idiosyncratic language, which was foreign to most of his readers—including native German speakers—was itself troublesome enough that Charles Andler suggested somewhat pedantically that it might be necessary to create a "Hegel dictionary."[6] This would be, Koyré's article argued with characteristic boldness, to invite a vicious circle: after all, the creation of a dictionary first required a secure understanding of Hegel's philosophy.[7] More significantly, however, Hegel himself eschewed the all-too-common philosophical recourse to neologism, and according to Koyré, his distinctive philosophical achievement is importantly tied to his use of everyday language. Echoing Wahl, Koyré averred that philosophy has no need for an abstract, specialized, artificial language: "the language of philosophy must be living and concrete, because its thought must be living and concrete" ("NL," 412). However, abjuring abstract expression does not entail lapsing into intellectual vagueness; what it does mean, for Hegel, is that philosophy ought to disavow "every strictly and artificially limited [*arrêtée*] terminology, every effort to establish a univocal and reciprocal relation between a term and its signification" ("NL," 413). There is a dynamic force in language with which philosophical thought has a unique and distinctive affinity. Philosophical thought "dies" when it is "separated from the spiritual values and from the spiritual life incarnated in language," when it is separated from history, from temporality ("NL," 414).[8] Koyré is clearly quite close to Wahl here. The remaining difference between them is their respective prioritizations of the System and its elements: Koyré begins with the sense of the whole incarnated in historical language, with Hegel's philosophical discovery of immanent dialectical unity, while Wahl begins with the youthful Hegel's fascination with the struggle of particular historical individuals (including himself) to express the sense of transcendent experience.

The promise and lesson of Hegel's philosophy is, of course, that these opposed points of origin are ultimately joined in and by absolute thinking.

> Hegel says quite clearly: "terminology" arrests thought. But, on the other hand, the usage of the terms of a living language, precisely to the extent that these terms have different significations, invites thought not to become fixed; on the contrary, in passing from one of these significations to the other, [thought may] discover internal relations between apparently entirely different things, [it may] discover—or rediscover—in place of the dead and rigid identity of the abstract, the living identity of the concrete. Actualizing the relations suggested by language, thought is set into motion, progresses, is deepened, and the fixed notions of the understanding thereby come to be transformed into living concepts of reason. ("NL," 414)

Although speech and language are discussed only "incidentally" in the *Phenomenology*, Koyré argues that any reckoning with Hegel's text requires close attention to its linguistic expression: "for Hegel, language is Spirit realized; the evolution of Spirit is incarnated and translated in the evolution of language; spirit is inconceivable outside of it and thought is impossible outside of speech" ("NL," 415–16).[9] The enriching and deepening of language in the development of the *Phenomenology* is "the same process" as the enriching and deepening of Spirit: "language [is] the stages of the incarnation [of spirit] and, at the same time, of spirit's acquiring consciousness of itself [*prise de conscience de soi*]" ("NL," 421). Everything that thought finds and expresses in the logos of the philosophical proposition, "everything that it has conquered was, in some way, already there in the spiritual experience of humanity, and notably in language" ("NL," 423). Hegel's work challenges its interpreters to *recognize* the truth *already contained* in language; the "naive speculation" of language is a clue to the discovery of the "true speculation" of reason ("NL," 424). Truth is not timeless, however. As Koyré emphasizes, Hegel's wordplay, his "popular etymology," certainly shows the marks of his "milieu," but his philosophical use of language is not a method to reach what a term means "at bottom" ("NL," 427). The unity of Hegel's system is a *historical* unity: "all of the stages that spirit goes through . . . form the whole experience of spirit, and in this whole experience they are all conserved [*conservées*] in memory" ("NL," 428). To the unhappy and suffering individual of Wahl's forward-looking tragic interpretation, Koyré counterposes the essentially happy retrograde movement of history as the memory of spirit. It is the priority of history, of time viewed from and gathered into the future, that gives Hegel "his anti-Romantic optimism in the assurance of the victory eternally won [*remportée*] by spirit" ("NL," 429). This priority does not render history extrinsic or inessential—Hegel's drama, the becoming of the finite, is no comedy—because "time alone allows for the realization of dialectical development, since, being negation and death, only it is a source of movement and life" ("NL," 429, 430).

In Wahl's interpretation, the intensity of concrete experiences is indissociable from their presence and so must be ineluctably lost in the becoming-whole of conceptualized time. Following the mature Hegel's prioritization of the future over the present, Koyré argues that time is "the incarnation, so to speak, of the being-there (*Dasein*) of the dialectical movement itself," or, in the words of the *Encyclopedia*, time is "the becoming-object of intuition" ("NL," 431). The confluence of terminology here is striking. Koyré, the former student of both Husserl and Bergson, is linking the novel ontological phenomenology of Heidegger to the more familiar concern for intuitive knowledge. The achievement of the *Phenomenology* is to show that every "phenomenon is birth and disappearance . . . which itself is neither born nor perishes, but is in itself and constitutes the reality and the movement of life and truth" ("NL," 434). It is "a bacchanal in which no one is sober," and the totality of this dynamism, Koyré emphasizes, is *the judgment of time* (Chronos) according to which the finite and determinate moments of spirit and thought become positive in the passing of their presence, in their negativity.[10] Philosophical thought achieves the consolation sought by the unhappy consciousness whose present is always already a becoming-past, an incipient memory whose recollection is the task of a properly philosophical use of language. The vagaries and vagueness of everyday language indicate this passing of presence, and in Hegel's philosophical dialectic "time is, in effect, the being-there of the *Aufheben* itself" ("NL," 434).

At the very end of *Le malheur*, Wahl had noted that there are "primitive elements," particular temporal and finite elements and experiences whose concrete specificity threatens to "shatter the armature of the system," and he even ventures that these elements are "perhaps more precious than the system" (*MC*, 194). For him, Hegel's philosophical system is a project born of lived distress, personal struggle, and although it aims to bring this struggle to a close it cannot do so. The concrete cannot be exhaustively conceived because, Wahl emphasizes, the concrete is not exhausted by the conceptual. The present harbors an irreducible kernel of feeling that eludes every retrospective grasp. For Koyré, however, in the very language mobilized by Hegel's philosophical project is the conceptual grasp of the whole that secures existence against sheer temporal dispersion. This turn to language, which will have such a decisive impact on subsequent French philosophy, differentiates philosophical language, *logos*, from the everyday finite language of *pathos*.[11] Koyré argues that the language of Hegel's system is the dialectical synthesis of the temporal and the eternal; the Hegelian concept is the linguistic construction of history, the triumph of life over death, and the "integration of past forms in the present."[12] Returning to the challenge of finding a reliable and objective reference for navigating Hegel's text, Koyré concludes his essay by archly suggesting that the best commentary on Hegel would be "a good *historical* German dictionary" ("NL," 439; emphasis in the original).

Kierkegaard and the Other Dialectic

In 1932, one year after Koyré's essay on the importance of language in Hegel, Jean Wahl published a major work that would help him secure, in 1936, a position at the Sorbonne. The book's title—*Vers le concret* (*Toward the Concrete*)—immediately became a slogan and rallying cry for a diverse array of philosophical projects, including the then-nascent existentialist philosophy.[13] The success of the book validated Wahl's claim that its odd conjunction of James, Whitehead, and Gabriel Marcel is not forced but fated by "a vast movement directed 'toward the concrete'" (*VC*, 41). For all of the excitement and attention that it garnered, however, Wahl's book did not foster any new surge of interest in James or Whitehead— and Marcel, Wahl's peer and friend, had already established himself independently as an important French philosophical voice.[14] Even Wahl appeared to turn away from these central figures as he devoted much of his immediately subsequent work to Kierkegaard—who appears only briefly in *Vers le concret*. Like Hegel, Kierkegaard studies had undergone a renaissance in Germany in the 1920s, and new translations of his work were beginning to appear in France that allowed for a fresh appraisal of his philosophical contributions.[15] For all of its importance in the wider philosophical community, *Vers le concret* is a transitional work in Wahl's oeuvre; although he is more willing to interject his own voice into the discussion and to develop his own points, the terms of the debate remain set by others. This will continue throughout his work on Kierkegaard and Kierkegaard's relation to contemporary thinkers such as Heidegger and

Jaspers. Only at the end of the decade will Wahl venture his own original philosophical contribution, first in a conference convened in 1938 and then, in 1944, in *Human Existence and Transcendence.*

Vers the concret is composed of three substantial essays—one each on William James, Alfred North Whitehead, and Gabriel Marcel—preceded by a short and programmatic preface which provides Wahl's justification for gathering his three subjects together.[16] Without mentioning Koyré by name, Wahl analyzes the discussion of language in the Sense-Certainty section of the *Phenomenology* in order to challenge the claim that the immanent dialectical power of language is capable of capturing the concrete. According to Hegel, the fact that the statement "now is night" is true when it is first written but becomes false with the subsequent dawn is evidence of the "non-reality of the concrete" (*VC*, 31). The true is the temporal, expressed in the sense of language, not the fragmentary present. The lesson that Hegel draws is that the concrete can only ever be the object of "purely subjective intentions," of a romantic "indefinite aspiration" whose partiality is recouped in the truth of language. However—and here Wahl plays upon the dialectic itself by insisting on an equally possible converse lesson—"should we not say instead that language, far from revealing the real, is itself revealed, but as powerless?" (*VC*, 31). Wahl's dialectical phrasing is important here—the conflict is no mere opposition of dogmatic interpretations. A central issue of *Vers le concret* is the character of the dialectic itself.

Hegel's discussion of language and the concrete shows that idealist metaphysics is neither blind to—nor ignorant of—the concrete. For idealism, however, the concrete is real only insofar as it provides a point of departure for reflection (*VC*, 30). Realism, with which Wahl aligns both himself and the three authors that he considers in *Vers le concret*, insists on the contrary: that there is a positive valence to the "shock" that the concrete offers to thought; shocks and events, or, better, "contact, participation, communion . . . form the tableau that is the sensible world" (*VC*, 30 and note 1). For the realist, subjectivity inheres in the world, and this entails both that the world is presented prior to being fully explicated and that this presentation cannot be reduced to a negative moment in a more expansive trajectory of thought. This postulate of realism allows Wahl to gather his triumvirate under the banner of a particular kind of empiricism. While every empiricism affirms the given and asserts the non-deducibility of being, Wahl identifies two different strains or degrees of empiricism that develop out of this initial assertion: a first-degree empiricism that ignores the problem of the givenness of being—that simply accepts or asserts this givenness—and a second-degree empiricism, a "meta-empirical empiricism" in which being is a feeling, not an idea, and is known as felt.[17] Wahl aligns himself with this second-degree empiricism in which he finds an affirmation of the qualitative difference of the concrete. This qualitative difference neither persists nor can it be comprehended by reflection. It is, however, repetitive, a felt experience of transcendence that is seemingly constitutive of subjective experience.[18] When it turns toward this concrete, "thinking encounters the object but as something that it cannot fully comprehend" (VC, 36).

Wahl's meta-empirical empiricism recognizes a dialectic between immanence and transcendence but also insists on its incompletion: the object is both present to—and a beyond for—the subject (VC, 34). This incompletion is not negative, however. Returning to the discussion of quantity and quality in *Pluralist Philosophies*, Wahl differentiates its moments from "spatial" transcendence, on the one hand, and from the material "indistinction" of immanence on the other. Both kinds of dialectical closure entail the quantitative suppression of quality. Meta-empirical empiricism, on the other hand, unapologetically asserts the reality and value of the non-quantitative; there is a "higher immanence" which is the community of minds, and there is a "higher transcendence" which is the "God of the priests," but also the God or source of the moral conscience (VC, 37–38).[19] The dialectic of such an empiricism moves from an assertion of the immanence of the subject and the object to an assertion of the transcendence of the object in relation to the subject, and then back again. This is a dialectic that Wahl attributes to Kierkegaard, not Hegel, and one that "does not suppress oppositions, but holds them before itself" (VC, 45).[20] In dialectics such as Hegel's, the experience of difference is too quickly harnessed and reduced by the work of negation. The experiential distinctiveness of the positive concrete is generalized in order to facilitate the self-absorption of thinking (VC, 46). Hegel's philosophy makes clear this perennial philosophical project, but Wahl argues that there is another tradition, made visible by Kierkegaard's criticism of Hegel, that includes "theologians and philosophers close to theology," as well as novelists like D. H. Lawrence, and which insists on a transcendent dimension of experience that cannot be rendered immanent (VC, 46). For that tradition, the privileged experience of transcendence is the same as what captivated the young Hegel: love, both human and divine (VC, 46). What divides the two traditions is whether this love is a promise of synthesis or an infinite longing.

***

In 1933, the year that Hitler became chancellor of Germany, the year the first concentration camps were established, the year that Heidegger joined the Nazi Party and then became rector of Freiburg University—in such a year Hegel's system must have seemed almost unbearably anachronistic. And even more so at a conference in the capital of Mussolini's Italy. Wahl's address to the 1933 Hegel Congress in Rome is entitled "Hegel and Kierkegaard."[21] At the time, Kierkegaard was almost entirely unknown in the French philosophical community. The first French translations of his work were less than a decade old—several fragments had been published in 1927, and a full translation of the *Diary of a Seducer* appeared in 1929—but many more would appear during the 1930s.[22] Alongside these translations, Wahl published several essays on Kierkegaard and his influence on contemporary philosophers in both France and Germany, helping to cement Kierkegaard's philosophical importance. The persistent unhappiness of consciousness in Hegel's mature system now manifests a "disinterestedness," an "ennui," that no dialectics can overcome. Every attempt to introduce dynamism into objectivity is ultimately hobbled by the true aim of Hegel's thinking: "the System wants the identical" and the identical is the static, the unchanging.[23] Although, Wahl admits, these critical claims—which reprise those of *Le malheur*—remain "external" to Hegel's philosophy, they nonetheless highlight what initially attracted Kierkegaard to Hegel: the felt urge to unify the real diversity of existence without thereby eliminating that very diversity. For Kierkegaard, the universality and objectivity with which Hegel's dialectic secures "the concept at the heart of the phenomenon" is also what destroys the distinctive and qualitative difference of the phenomenon itself.

"Hegel and Kierkegaard" proceeds in a series of overlapping deepenings or unmaskings of Kierkegaard's difficult and complex relation to Hegel. What draws the two thinkers together initially is a problem now recognizable as Wahl's own: "the effort to grasp the concept at the heart of the phenomenon without destroying the reality of the phenomenon, through the idea of concrete reason, through this sense of the totality that makes both the essence of the universe and the essence of the individual understood" ("HK," 159). Kierkegaard, of course, rapidly became disillusioned with the "universality and objectivity" of Hegel's philosophy because he judged that its universality was achieved only through a distinctive kind of temporal conservatism ("HK," 161). As Koyré emphasizes, the philosophical answers to the questions of experience are attained by incorporating events within their immanent historical development. Action is to be guided by—and finds its meaning only within—history, and this entails that the present be granted a certain priority over the possible as well as the aspirational: "for Hegel, a great philosophy is the incarnation of the spirit of the age; for Kierkegaard, it is a protestation against the spirit of the age" ("HK," 160). This opposition is made clear by the uses to which each philosopher puts Christianity. Kierkegaard judges Hegel's conceptualization of Christianity to be its elimination ("HK," 161). The essential elements of Christianity—faith, sin, and salvation—are individual relations to a transcendent divinity that cannot be explained because any explanation involves a legitimation and generalization. To annul faith's essential secrecy and make it public would be to abolish the work of grace. Kierkegaard's "hero of belief," Abraham, exemplifies the paradox that every effort of conceptual thought to suture the "abyss" at the heart of Christian faith devolves into a "scandal of reason," its bankruptcy before the grace of God ("HK," 161). Hegel's attempt to overcome the abyss through conceptual mediation is, Wahl argues, premised upon the subordination of the particular to the general, the individual to the species; "for Kierkegaard," on the other hand, "the re-vindication of the rights of religion is essentially the protestation of the individual against his subordination [*asservissement*] to the species" ("HK," 162). This protestation shifts the quarrel between Kierkegaard and Hegel from the ability of a purely immanent universality to account for the qualitative diversity of the concrete—a problem that engages Hegel's philosophy only externally, in terms of its conclusions—to the narrower but more fruitful question of the dialectical development of subjective thought and experience.

For Hegel, the concrete universal is the real, particular, and effective agent disclosed by philosophical thought. Before the completion of the philosophical work of Spirit, it is an amalgam of individual and species, of finite time and history, but it becomes reconciled and unified through philosophical dialectic. Kierkegaard, on the other hand, understands the concrete universal as an irreducible juxtaposition of the individual and the whole, of mortality in the face of eternity, that is only ever joined by a graceful act of God. Impassioned existence, the sensible, worldly life of the individual filled with "concrete spiritual movements," admits of no general knowledge. "There is no 'sin in general'" ("HK," 163). For the Christian Kierkegaard, it is the paradigmatically private experience of sin that marks the insuperable abyss between thinking and being, between thinking and existence. Sinfulness is the feeling of subjectivity confronted with transcendence, with its radical destitution. It motivates reflection, which is also thereby an effort at reassurance and consolation. Thought wants the truth but is always confronted with a decision. In the inevitable "leap from thought to being," the attempt to secure truth in order to decide correctly, thought is precipitated into an always insufficient dialectics. Such is "the fever of thought," the tragic character of existence ("HK," 164). The feeling of sin persists as the irreducibly present in the dialectical reconciliation of finite subjectivity and the world in which it inheres. There is no language for the irruption of transcendence. Indeed, the "absolute is a glaive, not an amalgam. The internal is not external, reason is not history. The absolute makes heterogeneities appear, for it is transcendence" ("HK," 164).

In retrospect, the young Hegel now seems to Wahl to be more "pre-Kierkegaardian than pre-Hegelian." His account of God as "the being-one of two natures" anticipates Kierkegaard's "paradoxical synthesis," and his depiction of Christ as the one who "addressed himself to individuals, not to nations" anticipates Kierkegaard's own formulation ("HK," 166). What bars their reconciliation, however, is the "sense of victory" in the mature Hegel's philosophical system; what Koyré highlights as the function or action of rational judgment. Like Wahl, Kierkegaard insists resolutely on the unhappiness of consciousness. It does give rise to a dialectics, but one that cannot develop. In this persistently discontinuous, frustrated dialectic, finite thought runs up against the transcendent and thereby discovers its own specific difference; thinking "never completely rejoins being, it does not agree with it [*ne se fond pas avec lui*]" ("HK," 165). Kierkegaard's unhappy consciousness, ineluctably tragic finitude, is a subjectivity which, "refusing to be integrated into the System, . . . thinks that, without following the detours of the evolution indicated by philosophy, it can, from the place where it is, pursue [*parcourir*] the difficult path that will lead it straight [*droit*] toward God. Kierkegaard's work is," Wahl writes, "Romanticism's revenge against the System" ("HK," 167). However, for all that he finds appealing in Kierkegaard's work, Wahl rejects his Christian framework and concludes his essay by identifying contemporary atheist existentialism as a continuation of Kierkegaard's work.[24] The transcendent, God, is not partially present for Kierkegaard; "what is present is the empty and void place where God would be" ("HK," 167). This empty place of the transcendent is what Wahl elsewhere calls the qualitative differentiation of the concrete, and in "Hegel and Kierkegaard" he emphasizes its importance for both Heidegger and Jaspers. Heidegger here is mentioned only in passing—Wahl notes that the shallow thinking and chatter of *das Man* is a purely intellectual effort that blinds the existent human being to the depths of its own being—but Wahl finds a philosophical ally in Jaspers.[25] Wahl writes that Jaspers "has discerned the feeling for existence as separation and aspiration toward that from which it is separated. And, in his own philosophy, he wants to bring to light these two feelings created by their reciprocal tension: a feeling of subjectivity and a feeling for being, or, as he says, a feeling of existence and of transcendence" ("HK," 169). Like Valéry, the rejection of the possibility of a unifying conceptual system leads Jaspers to the practical question of how to formulate adequate beliefs and values that might rightly guide worldly action, while, like Wahl, Jaspers wants to "bring to light" the two "feelings" of existence and transcendence without resolving them; he wants to exhibit them in their irresolvable tension. For Jaspers, transcendence is the thought of the "antinomic relations" that constitute existence, a thought that engenders "the flux and reflux of feelings: hope-despair, challenge-humility" that is the fate of finite consciousness ("HK," 170). It engenders existential dread, anxiety, which admits of no intellectual overcoming. These "failures" to secure an adequate and unifying conception of the concrete "lead us to affirm transcendence; they are explained by the absolute *other*, impervious to our reason and to our acts. These failures, they are our blows at the gate of transcendence; they show us that there is a gate" ("HK," 170; emphasis in the original).[26]

To the *Weltanschauung* of Hegel, of "the day," then, Wahl opposes the *Weltanschauung* of "the night," and, citing his monograph on the *Parmenides*, he closes his essay by gathering the debate between Kierkegaard and Hegel, its resumption in contemporary existentialism, and his own philosophical project together under the banner of a metaphysical choice—coextensive with the Western philosophical tradition—between two hypotheses of the One: the infinitely multiple One of the Hegelian hypothesis, of the day, and the absolutely One of the Kierkegaardian hypothesis, of the night ("HK," 170–71). Wahl's choice is clear: transcendence, the world of the night, cannot be eliminated. Hegel's philosophical achievements—like those of other partisans of the first hypothesis—are not without their charms, but the admiration they evoke is inevitably accompanied by "a feeling of collapse . . . ; achieved art is quite close to decadence, triumph is the beginning of failure, and perfection contains the germs of decline, but imperfection contains the germs of the life of perfection; in the failure of the still clumsy primitive [*primitive encore malhabile*], do we not sometimes feel—in the most lively way—the truest triumph?" ("HK," 171). For the existentialist Wahl, the acknowledgment of absolute transcendence returns the philosophical problematic to subjectivity. The partisans of the second hypothesis choose "the world of problems, ruptures, and failures, where, [with their] gaze fixed toward a transcendence that only they can see, they remain a problem for themselves, they remain full of irreducible multiplicities and ruptures, but perhaps they thereby feel, in a more intense fashion, both themselves and their relation with the *other*" ("HK," 171; emphasis in the original).

"Hegel and Kierkegaard" and the other essays collected in *Études Kierkegaardiennes* show that across Wahl's trajectory from Hegel, to the empiricists of *Vers le concret*, to Kierkegaard, a core problem drives his thinking: how to philosophically account for the qualitative experiences that give rise to—but which cannot be incorporated into—a rational dialectic. What is distinctive in his work on Kierkegaard, however, is that Wahl now focuses his attention—as he had begun to do in *Vers le concret*—on the differences between two dialectics. Kierkegaard and Hegel share a common problem: "the attempt to grasp the concept at the heart of the phenomenon without betraying the reality of the phenomenon," the problem of "concrete reason." For both thinkers, this experience gives rise to a dialectic. However, the Hegelian dialectic overcomes unhappiness through the speculative reconciliation of the Absolute with itself, a kind of auto-immanentization of the transcendent that ultimately synthesizes every otherness, as the dialectical moment of negation, into a conceptualized positivity. Against such a positively immanent totality, however, Kierkegaard argues for a dialectic of subjective existence that culminates not in synthesis, but in a mystical negation that is irreducible to Hegelian negativity.[27] The negative union that characterizes Kierkegaard's thought, according to Wahl, is "the union of a restless [*s'exaspère*] subjectivity and an affirmation of transcendence," a union unattainable by a subjectivity that is created and sustained by the love of God.[28]

The affirmation of transcendence that Wahl adopts from Kierkegaard is striking and exemplary of the distinctive importance of Wahl's philosophy. At a time when French philosophy seemed generally to be moving more and more toward a fully immanent account of experience, Wahl argues precisely the contrary: that there are elements of existence that cannot be reduced to immanence. It is no longer a question of merely adjudicating the relative priority of subjective experience and knowledge. In his work on Kierkegaard, Wahl extends the claim made in *Le malheur*—that there is a qualitative aspect of experience that dialectical thought can never apprehend—not by demonstrating the failure of monism, but by arguing for the philosophical coherence of an existential pluralism. His debate with Koyré threatened to issue in a kind of willful choice between contrary dialectical emphases: either of subjective experience or of objective conceptualization. Kierkegaard's work gives Wahl the opportunity to insist on the irreducibly paradoxical transcendence of the concrete, on an experience that rules out every positive dialectic, leaving only the naked encounter of thought and its other.[29] Hegel had utilized Christianity in order to escape the aporias of idealism and achieve the tranquil and complete conceptualization of his philosophical system. But Kierkegaard takes the side of the younger Hegel and denies the legitimacy of the use to which the mature Hegel sets Christianity.[30] Christ is "the unmediatable mediator" for Kierkegaard; his very existence is a "scandal of reason" that tempts philosophy—as it tempted Hegel, here cast as a kind of intellectual Adam—into the original sin of "the divinization of the human," the auto-immanentization of the transcendent.[31]

Wahl emphasizes what he calls two "feelings" that testify to this scandal: the feeling for the secret and the feeling for existence. Both of these feelings are textual as well as biographical issues in Kierkegaard. Just as Wahl interprets the trajectory of Hegel's thought through, in part, his youthful personal struggles, so he finds the feeling for the secret in Kierkegaard's observation of his father's melancholy shame and, above all, in Kierkegaard's own refusal to marry Regine Olson.[32] These negative manifestations, however, belie the secret's positive essence. It is the mark of the essential and insuperable difference between the internal and the external, between subjective experience and the necessarily generalized expression of this experience in language. The secret is, by definition, what is not shared.[33] For Kierkegaard, however, the secret is known to God, and the individual experiences this divine knowledge as both the consciousness of sin and as the promise of grace. To reconcile sin and grace, to explain and justify their relation dialectically or otherwise, is to blaspheme, to simultaneously exalt humanity and humble God. The secret is every human being's unique mark of finitude that temporalizes and isolates them. Just as a marriage to Regine would have brought Kierkegaard's love into the ambit of the common and universal, so any conceptualization of the secret would evacuate its decisive intensity. Here is Kierkegaard's rejoinder to Koyré: divine love defeats all language.

The secret marks an experience. Turning again to the issue of linguistic quantification and its distortions, Wahl insists that Hegelian mediation relies upon degrees of difference whose quantification allows them to be pushed to a limit, precipitating their contraries.[34] Kierkegaard's insistence on the experience of the secret—"the secret of Kierkegaard's existence"—attests to a dimension of human existence that can never be sublated because it is limitless. "For Kierkegaard, the antithesis must subsist, must remain armed and active. Uncertainty remains at the heart of belief, like an unceasingly new goad; sin persists in faith."[35] This essentially theological experience is generalized by Wahl into a description of the instantaneous presence—the intensity—of experiences that frustrate any conceptualization. Kierkegaard is a thinker for whom "there is no system of existence"; like the neo-realists, every relation is formed within an existence replete with "radical heterogeneities" and "qualitative differences."[36] Every exclusively unifying system, even Hegel's, fails. No dictionary—German or otherwise—can index or exhaust the sense of existence.

Subjectivity and Transcendence

On December 4, 1937, Leon Brunschvicg opened a meeting of the Société Française de Philosophie with the sad news of the death of Henri
Delacroix the previous day. Delacroix's 1900 essay, "Søren Kierkegaard,
le Christianisme absolu à travers le paradoxe et le désespoir" ("Søren
Kierkegaard: Absolute Christianity through Paradox and Despair"),
had been decisive for introducing Kierkegaard into French academic
philosophy.[37] Delacroix's passing was made even more poignant by the
topic that Wahl chose for his remarks to the meeting: "Subjectivity and
Transcendence."[38] After almost a decade of close work on Kierkegaard,
Wahl was now presenting something like the upshot and synthesis of this
work—work which also drew upon themes and issues that extended back
as far as his doctoral theses. What's more, Wahl attached a great deal of
importance to this meeting and apparently hoped that it would be an occasion for crystallizing various philosophical positions and approaches
to what he identified as the most pressing contemporary philosophical
issues. Prior to the meeting, he circulated a written invitation that also
included a brief resumé of his topic, linking Kierkegaard to contemporary German philosophy (principally Heidegger and Jaspers) via "the two
essential ideas"—subjectivity and transcendence—"that, from a philosophical point of view, characterize the thought of Kierkegaard."[39] In
addition to those able to attend the meeting, several of the recipients of
Wahl's letter—including both Heidegger and Jaspers, but also Levinas,
Raymond Aron, Karl Löwith, and others—replied with written remarks
that were published in 1938 together with Wahl's replies.[40] All of this
material—the resumé, the more substantive remarks that Wahl delivered at the meeting, the discussion following the lecture, and the written comments to those unable to attend—is vital for understanding the
preoccupations of French academic philosophy on the eve of the Second
World War, and the central role Wahl played in shaping the direction
of its debates. Rhetorically, in "Subjectivity and Transcendence"—and
in *Human Existence and Transcendence*—Wahl is shifting from the indirect style of his earlier work, in which his voice is often almost entirely
masked behind those of others, to a more direct elaboration of his own
philosophical project. Wahl would remain an important author of philosophical commentaries until the end of his career, but his work just before
the war's outbreak foregrounds the philosophical commitments which,
until then, had been largely confined to the margins.[41] The core of these
commitments—an insistence on the irreducibility of transcendence—is
a claim that will fall more and more out of fashion in the decade after
the war.[42]

The title "Subjectivity and Transcendence" announces the theme of Wahl's remarks, but it also creates a retrospective frame for the central preoccupations of his previous work. The analysis of Descartes's instantaneous knowledge, memorably figured by the flickering light of a candle's flame; the preference for pluralism over monism that guides *The Pluralist Philosophies*; the perennial scope of this opposition, according to Wahl's reading of the *Parmenides*; its dialectical character figured by the unhappiness of consciousness in Hegel's *Phenomenology of Spirit*; Kierkegaard's account of the tragic persistence of this unhappiness against all philosophical and (positive) theological attempts to overcome it; and the contemporary efforts of philosophers such as Heidegger and Jaspers to elaborate a non-Christian formulation of this unhappy situation—all of these engagements are drawn into Wahl's argument. Its focus is Hegel's philosophical discovery, the tool by which the unhappiness of consciousness can be overcome and the means by which transcendence can be made immanent: philosophical dialectic. At the end of the preface to *Vers le concret*, Wahl had written that the dialectic "is explained by what surpasses [*depasse*] it"; the dialectical succession of ideas "is explained by what is beneath [*au-dessous*] them, by the non-relational ground that they are forced to explain, but which always preserves its implicit character" (*VC*, 42, 43). Philosophical dialectics accounts for the necessity of its development by appealing to the essential character of the dialecticized elements: the unhappiness of consciousness is not overcome willfully, but through the development of its own nature. Wahl's insistence on the separation of material and relations requires dialectics to either justify its claim to arise solely from material or to admit that it is one relational account among others.[43] The question, then, is not whether a particular dialectical account is correct or not, but is instead: what gives rise to dialectics? For Wahl—and here he follows Hegel and Kierkegaard—dialectics arises from a subjective experience of transcendence. There is first a feeling that draws attention to a distinctive present, to what feels and seems different, and which thought then works to integrate dialectically, by establishing relations, finding commonalities, and minimizing differences (*VC*, 45).

The dialectical apprehension of concrete experience has, for Wahl, a kind of inevitability to it—consciousness is ineluctably unhappy—but it is nevertheless capable of two modulations: one, the Hegelian, negates the positivity of the concretely real, surpassing it by making transcendence the false apprehension of immanence; while a second one is the Kierkegaardian, which Wahl terms the dialectic of "negative ontology," according to which the positivity of the dialectic is negated by the real (*VC*, 45). This second modulation does not deny or suppress the work of reason, but it limits it by refusing to obliterate the feeling that motivates it. Returning to Valéry's apprehension, Wahl notes that the only possible resolution for the dialectic of negative ontology seems to be some kind of mystical experience. This, finally, brings him to the contemporary work of Jaspers and Heidegger. Wahl understands both philosophers to have taken Kierkegaard's problematic and stripped it of its theological trappings. More broadly, such ontological efforts point to the possibility of a non-mythical ontology (VC, 45–46). In Wahl's formulation of this ontology, subjectivity undergoes concrete experiences of transcendence that irresistibly propel it into a dialectics. Hence the twofold problematic of his lecture: subjectivity and transcendence.

What remains unquestioned by Wahl is subjectivity, and his humanism is no doubt one of the reasons why Wahl's philosophical star rose and fell with the fortunes of existentialism. The experience of transcendence is a human experience, indexed by irreducibly human feelings such as awe, passion, and love. Even as he pushes to dissolve any essential connection between relations and their elements, Wahl—perhaps retaining here a kernel of his early work on Descartes—does not consider subjectivity itself as a relation. The cogito, human thinking, is a given. Heidegger's objections to existentialism—both to Wahl and then to Sartre—are decisive in this regard. Ontology requires that subjectivity as a philosophical problem of the first order be abolished; it, too, is a particular relation. As will be shown, one of the most innovative aspects of Deleuze's philosophy—already at work in his earliest publications—is a criticism of Wahl's humanistic adherence to a philosophical subjectivism.[44]

Wahl begins his oral remarks to the conference by differentiating two oppositions at the root of Kierkegaard's account of anxiety: an ontological one between the finite individual and an infinite transcendent God, and an ethical opposition, provoked by "the presence of evil" in the world. Both of these oppositions lead the individual subject to question the nature of the transcendent as well as his relation to it ("ST," 161). How can a perfectly good and all-powerful God allow wickedness and injustice? And if God does allow these things, how can that God be a source of precepts for the conduct of a righteous life? While the ontological source of anxiety figures prominently in Wahl's work on Kierkegaard throughout the 1930s, the priority given to the discussion of evil here is distinctive and further highlights the particular shape of Wahl's problematic.

The anguish occasioned by the experience of the transcendent is experienced as a suspended judgment—a raised gavel—whose contours are utterly unknown. There is an inherent superiority in transcendence to which the existent is, for Wahl, unavoidably subject.

> The existent is anguished because it does not know what it is faced with, whether it is before a beneficent transcendence or a maleficent transcendence, the face of God or a demonic force, whether the movement that it accomplishes is a movement of "transascendence" or "transdescendence." ("ST," 161)

According to Kierkegaard, whose account of anxiety Wahl is following closely, the radical unknowability of God produces a moral problem vividly exemplified by the story of Abraham: how does he know—if the transcendent is unknowable—whether it is a beneficent God that righteously demands the sacrifice of Isaac? How does Kierkegaard's religious stage avoid devolving into an ethical relativism? This question reprises Descartes's doubt in a moral register, and Wahl provides only an indication of a possible resolution: perhaps, stripped of its theological trappings, transcendence is neither necessarily good nor necessarily evil; perhaps it is simply "nature" ("ST," 162). And, Wahl asks, is that any less "mysterious" than the idea of God? ("ST," 162). Divesting Kierkegaard's account of transcendence thus seems to end in a moral naturalism. Turning to Kierkegaard's contemporary inheritors, Wahl argues that both Heidegger and Jaspers engage this problem. Their work remains "in the interior of our world," Wahl emphasizes, "refusing to follow Kierkegaard when he seeks 'repetition' in the beyond" ("ST," 162).

Both Heidegger's conception of being-in-the-world and Jaspers's concepts of communication and history—the latter, Wahl notes, present already in Kierkegaard—are secular philosophical formulations of the immediate subjective experience of transcendence. However, the chief stumbling block to any attempt to laicize Kierkegaard's thought is, of course, sin: the subject's feeling of insufficiency before the transcendent. In Heidegger, the fallen character of *Dasein* and its absorption in the world of "*das Man*" seems to express this experience, while Jaspers, whose work Wahl judges to be "more profound" than Heidegger's, identifies sin with subjective limitation ("ST," 162). However, even this account threatens to devolve into yet another dialectics which would thereby also surreptitiously readmit the corresponding idea of totality. Jaspers is alert to this problem and attempts to preempt it, but, Wahl notes, any attempt to laicize repetition seems to result— "like all theories of the instant or of eternal return," he remarks, implicitly critiquing his own earlier work— only in "an *Ersatz* idea of eternity" ("ST," 162).[45] These problems are, for Wahl, definitive of the contemporary philosophical situation, and his brief overview of the deficiencies of the work of two of his most prominent peers leads him to the pivotal question: can a philosophy of existence be formulated that is both utterly secular, divested of all religious overtones, and that refuses the temptation of totality, that does not culminate in "a general theory of existence"? ("ST," 162). Wahl believes that it can, and he concludes his remarks by encouraging his audience to turn their attention to the "philosophies of existence" not espoused but embodied or enacted in the exemplary lives of individuals like "Rimbaud, Van Gogh, or Nietzsche" ("ST," 163).

Wahl's friend Gabriel Marcel opens the subsequent conversation by posing a series of questions and objections concerning the concept of transcendence and, specifically, Wahl's neologisms "transascendence" and "transdescendence." He begins by expressing dissatisfaction with Wahl's use of the terms "good" and "bad" in connection with these two terms. What is Wahl's frame of reference for his evaluative terms: are they used in relation to a "bio-energetic" notion of power? If so, Marcel argues, then the Nietzschean claim that the good is whatever amplifies the power of an individual is simply a "truism" ("ST," 173–74). But if Wahl means to employ the terms within the "spiritual tradition of humanity," then he has not successfully justified his distinctive interpretation ("ST," 173). This leads Marcel to the heart of his objection: for him, there can be no laicized concept of transcendence; it is impossible to separate the concept of transcendence from its theological elements ("ST," 179). Moreover, he contends, such a philosophy of existence would "degenerate" into an account of "pure facticity" ("ST," 175). The importance of the existential philosophies that Wahl appears ready to discount is that they not only indicate but also *explicate* the value of exemplary lives like those of Rimbaud, Van Gogh, and Nietzsche. Marcel ends his intervention by observing laconically that each of these names represents "a failed philosophy" ("ST," 181). In his response, Wahl seems to recognize Marcel's objection to a laicized concept of transcendence as decisive, and he appeals to Herbert Spencer's concept of the Unknowable for an example of a nontheological conception of transcendence ("ST," 177).[46] Marcel, however, is unswayed and dismisses this comparison, noting that Spencer uses the Unknowable to speak exclusively of the "infra-objective" world.

This exchange leads to an important intervention by another religious philosopher, the Christian existentialist Nicolai Berdyaev, who draws an interesting distinction between "existential philosophers" (such as Kierkegaard and Nietzsche) who value lived experience, and "philosophers of existence" (such as Jaspers and Heidegger) for whom existence is an object of philosophical reflection ("ST," 187). He then notes that there are two different ways of surpassing subjectivity: objectification and transcendence. In the former movement, presumably exemplified by

Spencer's conception of scientific progress (although Berdyaev does not make this claim) and by the work of Heidegger and Jaspers, philosophical reflection and explication gradually replace the subjective with the objective; however, in the latter movement, of "existential philosophy" properly called, the emphasis is not on reflection but on transcendence itself, a movement that is not "toward" anything but is simply the ecstatic existence of concrete subjectivity ("ST," 187–88). Wahl repeatedly expresses his agreement with this distinction and, in conclusion, quotes with approval Nicolai Hartmann's remark that transcendence "is the movement of what is transcended toward that which transcends it," a definition that avoids reifying the referent of the term ("ST," 192).[47]

* * *

The violent interruption of the Second World War threw everything into chaos. The French academic community fragmented amidst the upheaval of the Occupation as some professors joined the Resistance, others acquiesced to the Vichy regime, and still others, especially Jewish academics, fled for their lives to the United States and elsewhere. This fragmentation meant that the period immediately following the war was a time of reconnection and for the discovery of the results of several different avenues of thought that had been pursued in diverse contexts during the war years. Wahl himself returned to France immediately after the war, in 1945, and resumed his teaching at the Sorbonne with a class on Heidegger.[48] In 1947 he created the Collège Philosophique, an organization that was intended to provide a noninstitutional space for the exchange of philosophical ideas and which would play an important role in the development of postwar French philosophy, hosting lectures by Sartre, Levinas, Bertrand Russell, and others.

The record of Wahl's publications after the war also shows his interest in surveying and assessing the various strands and strains of French philosophical thought: *Tableau de la philosophie française* (*An Overview of French Philosophy*) appeared in 1946, *Petite histoire de l'existentialisme* (*A Short History of Existentialism*) appeared in 1947, and Wahl wrote an essay on "The Present Situation of French Philosophy" ("La situation présente de la philosophie française") for a volume of essays that appeared in the 1950 anthology *Philosophic Thought in France and the United States*, edited by Marvin Farber.[49] All of this work ensured that Wahl's influence on subsequent generations of thinkers was both extensive and substantial, but despite this influence, the project of a philosophy of existence, a philosophy that maintains "that there are views of reality which cannot be completely reduced to scientific formulations," went into decline in the postwar years and never again enjoyed the privilege and attention that it previously had.[50]

For Wahl, the problem of the absolute, the problem that generated the dialectical shape of human existence, also fated subjectivity to oscillate, and perhaps to choose, between "the transcendent immanence of perception and the immanent transcendence of ecstasy."[51] What is unquestioned in Wahl's work is the character of human existence itself; for him, subjectivity is a given. During the war years, the question of the transcendental constitution of the subject led to a growing divide between existential accounts of the primacy of an active subject—the magical genius of Novalis, the transcendental subject of one branch of phenomenology, and so on—and a developing group of thinkers arguing that the subject is itself constituted. This latter possibility entailed that the subject could be studied by the sciences, a fact that facilitated the distinctively French combination of dialectical materialism and phenomenology in the late 1940s and 1950s.[52] The passive constitution of subjectivity offered the possibility of the conclusive incorporation of the transcendent into the immanent.

Hegel's work remained a central resource for this debate, ironically in large part due to the work of Wahl. But where prewar debates had occurred without access to a complete French translation of the *Phenomenology*, and so relied exclusively on fragmentary translations and on the commentaries of interpreters such as Koyré, Wahl, and Kojève, the postwar discussions were able to avail themselves of Jean Hyppolite's masterful translation—published in two parts, in 1939 and 1941—and his commentary, *Genesis and Structure of Hegel's Phenomenology of Spirit*, which appeared in 1946. Taking up many of Koyré's insights, but no less attentive to Wahl's arguments, Hyppolite's work presented a Hegel in which the absolute structure of the logos of the System, which at first appears to transcend subjectivity, is, in fact, as thinking comes to discover, its immanent genesis. As Koyré argued, the greatness of Hegel is to have surpassed the dimension of partiality, of antinomic heterogeneity, by finding in thought a unity that finite life is denied. Absolute thought is the happiness of unhappy consciousness, thought but never lived.

In 1952, Hyppolite further secured his interpretation with *Logic and Existence*, which details the relation of the System of the *Logic* to the dialectical development of the *Phenomenology*. "Immanence is complete," Hyppolite can conclude at the end of *Logic and Existence*; and Wahl's existentialism, the dialectic of qualitative intensity, is decisively rejected. But if Wahl and the other existentialists had accepted subjectivity as a given, thereby opening themselves to a materialist critique, Hyppolite's absolute immanence also shares an existential premise: the negativity that is the source of the dialectic. This assumption would attract the interest of the young Deleuze, who would begin his philosophical career by challenging the unquestioned persistence of this supposition, and he would find the resources for his critique in Wahl. Where Wahl's positive account of transcendental empiricism is succeeded by ecstatic transcendence, itself a product of the negativity essential to the dialectical characterization of human existence, to subjectivity, Deleuze will argue that such an empiricism is only ever distorted by the return of transcendence. To appreciate this intervention, it is necessary to return to the 1930s and follow the development of Hyppolite as he entered the philosophical lists.

3

Hyppolite and the Promise of Immanence

> Dilthey wants to find in this work [Hegel's *System-Fragment* of 1800] a philosophy of nature and a philosophy of religion. He finds the general meaning of the text in what he calls Hegel's "mystical pantheism."
> —Jean Hyppolite, "Hegel's Youthful Works in Light of Recent Works"

A generation younger than Wahl, Jean Hyppolite rose to philosophical prominence in the midst of the existentialist debates of the 1940s through a fortuitous combination of ability, interests, and timing. After completing his *khâgne* and *hypokhâgne* preparatory classes at the lycée Henri IV, Hyppolite entered the École Normale Supérieure in 1924, just as Wahl began teaching in various lycées and was beginning his work on Hegel in the company of the Philosophies group.[1] At the École Normale Supérieure, Hyppolite was one of a distinguished group of students that included Sartre, Raymond Aron, and Simone de Beauvoir, as well as Merleau-Ponty, with whom he would share a deep friendship until the latter's untimely death in 1960.[2] Hyppolite placed third on the *agrégation* in 1929—before a jury that included Wahl and which awarded first and second place to Sartre and Beauvoir, respectively. Throughout the 1930s, Hyppolite taught in several "different obscure lycées in the French countryside," famously teaching himself German by reading the *Phenomenology of Spirit*.[3] He was perhaps apprised of Kojève's famous seminar which began in 1933—Sartre, Aron, and Merleau-Ponty were all in regular attendance at this course which presented Hegel to a "limited but important public"—but made no attempt to follow it.[4] While Kojève and the intellectual aristocracy of Paris met for their heady discussions, Hyppolite steadily published articles on Hegel while simultaneously preparing the first full French translation of the *Phenomenology of Spirit*. His translation appeared in two parts, in 1939 and 1941, just before and just after the jarring defeat and surrender of France. 1941 was also the year that Hyppolite returned to Paris to take up a teaching post at the lycée Henri IV, where his students included both Gilles Deleuze and Michel Foucault. Hyppolite's monumental thesis for his *doctorat d'état*, *Genesis and Structure of Hegel's Phenomenology of Spirit*, appeared just after the war, in 1946, while he was teaching alongside Georges Canguilhem in Strasbourg.[5] In 1948 Hyppolite took up a position at the Sorbonne where he taught until 1954, when he returned to the École Normale Supérieure as its director. Finally, in 1963, he was elected to succeed Martial Gueroult at the Collège de France, titling his chair the Chair of the History of Philosophical Thought (supplanting Gueroult's Chair of the History of Philosophical Systems) and teaching there until his untimely death in 1969.

While principally known for his later work on Hegel, Hyppolite's first essays—published during the 1930s—are important not only for the light they shed on his development but, here more importantly, for the way that they take up and extend Koyré's position in the debate with Wahl. Unlike Koyré, there seems to have been little or no direct correspondence or interchange between Hyppolite and Wahl (at least until later in the 1950s). However, Hyppolite's project in these essays is the same as Koyré: ascertaining the relation between Hegel's youthful work and his more mature philosophy. The stakes remain the same: either Hegel's youthful work retains a truthful and transcendent element unassimilable by the later work—and perhaps by philosophy itself—as Wahl would have it, or the later, dialectical Hegel achieved an immanent conceptual capture of the concrete diversity of finite life.

The Historical Approach to Hegel

The historical development of Hegel's thought is at first glance a somewhat surprising topic to find at the center of French philosophical debates in the 1930s.[6] However, the ground for this discussion had been laid as early as the turn of the century, when works by Dilthey and Nohl challenged the prevailing panlogicist interpretation of Hegel which had dominated late nineteenth-century interpretations of his work. The first edition of Dilthey's *Die Jugendgeschichte Hegels* (*The Young Hegel*) (1905) gave a systematic interpretation of Hegel's early work that emphasized its Romanticism. Two years later, Herman Nohl published a large selection of Hegel's early works under the title *Hegels Theologische Jugendschriften* (*Hegel's Youthful Theological Writings*), thereby enabling Dilthey's interpretation to be critically assessed against Hegel's actual texts. Following the First World War, a series of studies appeared in Germany that emphasized the influence of Hegel's intellectual and cultural milieu on his philosophical development.[7] Finally, a particular concern with the significance of Hegel's early works again emerged in the late 1920s and early 1930s—now in both Germany and France—with the most notable books being those by Haering and Wahl.[8] This phase of the debate was further enriched by the 1931 publication of Hegel's Jena writings (1803–06) and by Appelin's publication of the so-called "Tübingen Fragment" in 1933.[9] The French interest in Hegel that becomes so conspicuous in the late 1920s, and which continued for the next several decades, thus reflected the internationalization of discussions of Hegel rather than a "French discovery."

Dilthey's revolutionary and revelatory reinterpretation of Hegel was certainly one important cause of the chain of major works on Hegel at the beginning of the twentieth century, but it was certainly not the only one. In France prior to the First World War, Bergsonism had positioned itself opposite Brunschvicg's neo-Kantian rationalism precisely by allocating to itself the mantle of a philosophy attuned to and engaged with concrete life. Hegel's philosophy, now augmented by the religious and practical concerns of his early work, became an important resource both for prewar Bergsonians and then for postwar philosophers trying to distance themselves from what was sometimes dismissed as a bankrupt mysticism. Coupling the clearly rationalist aspirations of the *Logic* with the concretely practical concerns of his youthful writings made Hegel and, more generally, German idealism an invaluable resource for Wahl, Koyré, the Philosophies group, and anyone else who hearkened to Valéry's urgent call to attend to the "crisis of the mind." In addition to staking a position on the relation between Hegel's various texts, the interpretations by Wahl, Koyré, and Hyppolite, also address broader philosophical issues such as the relation of the practical to the theoretical, the concrete to the conceptual, and the phenomenal to the Absolute. Disagreements over the meaning and relevance of Hegel's youthful writings were thus in part proxy battles in a larger debate concerning the relation between philosophical conceptualization and worldly life. For Wahl, the philosophical aspiration to think the concrete culminates in the ek-static experience of transcendence, or what Bruce Baugh has aptly characterized as a game of "loser wins" in which the recognition of its inadequacy demonstrates philosophy's truth.[10] Both Koyré and, following him, Hyppolite, reject Wahl's persistent appeal to an unthinkable transcendence and argue that Hegel's philosophical achievement is the elimination of any such transcendence. Hegel's philosophy has shown that the "loss" that precipitates the mind's inescapable unhappiness is only ever phenomenal, and is perpetually rewon by the *immanent* work of philosophical Spirit in language and history.

In addition to already existing work, several additional factors contributed to the discussions of Hegel's development in France in the early and mid-1930s. Hegel's youthful works were the focus of Wahl's *Le malheur* as well as Theodor Haering's two-volume *Hegel, sein Wollen und sein Werk* (*Hegel: His Aims and Work: A Developmental History of His Thought and Language*). The First International Hegel Congress that was convened in The Hague is 1930 allowed for the exchange of ideas across national boundaries. In 1932, Hegel's Jena writings—from the years 1803–1806—were published by Johannes Hoffmeister, and these provided still more material with which to discern Hegel's intellectual development. They also were particularly important for assessing Hegel's pre-*Phenomenology* ethical and political philosophy. Finally, Aspelin's *Hegels Tübinger Fragmente, eine psychologisch-ideengeschichtliche Untersuchung* (*Hegel's Tübingen Fragment: A Psychological-Historical Study*) appeared in 1933, seemingly offering a glimpse into some of Hegel's earliest philosophical thinking. Koyré took stock of these publications—especially in his 1934 essay "Hegel à Iéna" ("Hegel in Jena")—but this would be his last word on Hegel. At the time, Koyré was in the midst of his work with Fuad University and had recently handed over to Kojève his seminar at the École Pratique des Hautes Études. However, the impact of Koyré's article was extensive, and it had a particularly formative effect on the first works of Hyppolite.

Ehrenberg, the first editor of Hegel's Jena writings and the coauthor of *Hegels erstes System* (*Hegel's First System*) in 1915, had argued that there is a "caesura" between the youthful writings collected and published by Nohl in 1907—a publication that Koyré emphasizes "has dominated every modern interpretation of Hegel"—and the subsequent Jena writings.[11] Wahl's reading of Hegel followed Ehrenberg, portraying the shift as one from a concern for the subjective experience of consciousness to a concern with the universality of that unhappy and negative existence. For Koyré, however, "there is no caesura between them [the Jena writings] and the *Phenomenology* or even the *Encyclopedia*. Hegel in Jena is already Hegelian, already master of his method, already a virtuoso of the dialectic, already in possession of a system" ("HI," 276). The "unlovable" middle-aged Hegel is already at work in the "dry and boring" Jena writings; these writings are not only difficult to read, but are thematically concerned with the philosophy of nature, and if Hegel's system is "certainly dead," then his philosophy of nature is the deadest part of a dead system ("HI," 276). Koyré, however, is not interested in conducting a necroscopy, and he insists on the important connections between Hegel's philosophy of nature and his philosophy of spirit. The philosophy of nature is properly concerned neither with an obstacle to spirit nor with the mere matter for spirit's incarnation; Koyré argues that, for Hegel, nature is "alienated spirit, lost in the other of itself, plunged into unconsciousness and sleep" ("HI," 277). Already in his 1802 course, Hegel emphasizes that spirit *is* only in and as the act of self-discovery and therefore, Koyré notes, nature is neither ontologically nor temporally *prior to* spirit but is an eternal and essential moment *of* spirit ("HI," 277). As an act of self-discovery, spirit is the unity of the movement by which it returns to itself from out of *its own* alienation, and this movement is infinite. Citing the *Jena Logic*, Koyré emphasizes that "the dialectic is nothing other than the application of infinity to concepts. A passage to the limit that breaks them and transforms them into their contraries, which brings to concepts the disquiet and the mobility of being" ("HI," 278). It is this dialectical character of Hegelian infinity, its incorporation of negation, that enables Hegel to surpass not only Lessing and Fichte, but also Schelling, with whom he was especially close during his time in Jena ("HI," 278–79).[12] Hegel's conception of infinity ensures the vitality of his philosophy of nature; it is at once the positing of finitude over against a sterile and dead infinity and the infinite self-disclosure of infinity in the negation of the opposition of the finite and infinite. "The discovery of the dialectical character of infinity," Koyré emphasizes, "provides Hegel with the solution he was looking for" ("HI," 279).

Installing negativity at the heart of the absolute allows the absolute to be productive, and the productive and dialectical infinity is, then, the formal schema of time: "the being that is insofar as it is not, and is not insofar as it is." To the dialectic of infinity there "responds the dialectic of the instant" ("HI," 279). The philosophy of nature elaborated in Jena is therefore not a philosophy of actually existing concrete nature, nor is it a mere conception of nature; it is already a phenomenology. The Jena philosophy of nature tells the story of the dialectical clarification of spirit, not objects. It is the exposition of the phenomenological "scaffold" that subtends any philosophy of nature ("HI," 280). This "reduction" of philosophy to phenomenology that is the supreme achievement of Hegel's work also fosters its greatest danger ("HI," 281). Koyré concludes his essay by turning to a "decisive moment" in the "history of the self-constitution of spirit": the advent of language, the moment when nature ceases to be merely subjective experience and becomes objective nature—nature proper—through the act of "conferring names" ("HI," 281–82). With language, the world of subjective images becomes a world of objective things, of objects whose names allow them to be known truthfully. For Hegel, language *is* spiritual reality. Koyré cautions, however, that "there is no "language." There are only *languages*" ("HI," 283; emphasis in the original). For there to be a true language, for a single language to be the language of spirit, it would have to be spoken by the proper agents; and these agents, who together constitute a "true people," would require a proper politics. Thus, Koyré concludes, "the philosophy of Spirit degenerates into a philosophy of the State" ("HI," 283). In Jena, Hegel still retained his youthful anticlericalism—the Church must bow to the secular sovereign—but "from Jena [Hegel] was—in spirit—in Berlin" ("HI," 283). Koyré wrote these closing lines in 1934, and few readers in France could fail to hear their contemporary sound.

The different trajectories of their scholarly work carried both Koyré and Wahl away from Hegel after the early 1930s. Wahl retained Hegel primarily as a foil for his work on Kierkegaard and, to a lesser extent, his work on existentialism; and Koyré began his well-known work on modern science, publishing *Galilean Studies* in 1939. Even as Wahl and Koyré began to turn away from Hegel, however, Hyppolite began to publish his own work, taking up the debate where Wahl and Koyré left off.[13] Hyppolite's work cannot, however, be squared neatly with either earlier protagonist. With Wahl, he contends that Hegel's philosophy did arise from his youthful religious questions and problems but, with Koyré, he agrees that Hegel's philosophical achievement is to have overcome his youthful sentimentalism and to have thereby broken through the impasses of his early writings and attained a distinctively philosophical level.

Hyppolite on Hegel's Development

Hyppolite's first published contribution to the discussion of Hegel, "Les travaux des jeunesse de Hegel d'après des ouvrages récents" (1935; "Hegel's Youthful Works in Light of Recent Work"), pays close attention to Hegel's method—a distinctive characteristic of all of Hyppolite's subsequent work but also one that echoes, at certain points, Koyré's discussion of the key concept of infinity—and states that Hegel's continuing importance is due to something more than simply "the idealist form of the system."[14] Like Koyré, Hyppolite contends that even as a young man, Hegel never fell entirely under the sway of Romantic irrationalism and that he was always in search of a *philosophical* reconciliation of the unhappiness of consciousness. Sketching the itinerary of his article, Hyppolite writes: "We will see Hegel, beginning from a very concrete problem, that of the meaning of a 'positive religion,' enlarging his problem more and more, leading up to a general conception of all spiritual phenomena, to the idea of a dialectical structure of all life during the Frankfurt period" ("TJ1," 16). Again, Hyppolite insists that it is Hegel's dialectical method that secures his importance and continuing relevance and that also provides a guide for tracing the development of his mature philosophy.

Hyppolite's article divides Hegel's early work geographically as well as temporally: a Tübingen period (1788–93) is followed by a Berne period (1783–96) and then a Frankfurt period (1797–1800), after which Hegel will join Schelling in Jena. Already as a seminary student in Tübingen, Hegel, along with his close friends and fellow students Hölderlin and Schelling, were deeply impressed by Rousseau and, like him, longed for the kind of robustly humanistic society represented (for them) by classical Greece. Hyppolite emphasizes that for Hegel and his colleagues spiritual life was "supra-individual," and they gave a theological formulation to the question of how the Greek world differed from their own: "under what conditions is a religion living?" ("TJ1," 405, 409). For Hegel, the answer to this question requires thinking through the opposition between religion and reason. Juxtaposing the practice of Jesus with the rationalist criticism of arbitrary institutional authority, he reformulates the opposition of religion and reason as the "more concrete" opposition between "subjective and objective religion" ("TJ1," 407). Subjective religion is not "mysticism" but is rather the outgrowth of free willful action, which Hegel contrasts with the objective prescriptions of religious institutions ("TJ1," 407, 408). Behind subjective freedom is the freedom of love, so important to the young Hegel, which is "the empirical manifestation of a reason that surpasses individual reason." It is "supra-individual" but not irrational ("TJ1," 408). The consequent difficulty is understanding how objective religion cannot just be aligned with—but can itself be a facet of—love, of the freedom of each individual subject. Contemporary religious life is bedeviled by two oppositions: "its concrete character is opposed to the abstractions of the understanding, and its authoritative and exterior character is opposed to religious life" ("TJ1," 411). A living religion must reconcile its immediate concrete practice with the institutional and ceremonial practices that ensure its historical identity.

In Berne, Hegel transforms the abstract question of how to reconcile the opposed aspects of religion into the question of how over time a living and concrete religion can degenerate into a dead one, whose force comes from a compulsive authority. This transformation is characteristic of the work of that "fully armored" Hegel which Koyré championed over against Wahl's tragic thinker: the opposed meanings of positive religion are thought together as the aspects or facets of a single true meaning that is neither beyond nor beneath their temporal movement but *is* that very temporal movement. Hegel's investigation of the life of Jesus is exemplary of this method; it is an "anthropological analysis of consciousness" showing how an exemplary individual—one who "united the sensible and universal"—could institute and be memorialized by Christianity ("TJ1," 416).[15] Such an investigation yields conclusions not just about Christianity but, more importantly, about "human nature" ("TJ1," 414). At the same time, it runs up against the problem of the irrational, of that "part of reason that surpasses the rational" ("TJ1," 415). Perhaps addressing Wahl's interpretation of Hegel's early work, Hyppolite stresses that Hegel's concern is with the question of whether or not religious life arises out of the concrete life of a group of people or is a mere form of life imposed on them from without. Irrationality is an aspect of religious experience, but it is not determinative of the religious life of a community ("TJ1," 418).[16] While he was in Berne, Hyppolite emphasizes that Hegel's works often obscure their philosophical import behind their manifest concern with concrete historical changes. Hegel analyzes several different problems in these works—the transition from paganism to Christianity, the work of memory and the unconscious activity of the soul, the relation between the fractured I and God—and these historical analyses will become, in the *Phenomenology*, moments of consciousness ("TJ1," 420, 422, 423–24). Hyppolite's analysis thus serves as a detailed textual justification of Koyré's thesis: Hegel's system is already at work in his early writings. Moreover, Hyppolite's account of Hegel's development shows that his system is not a fixed object or form—a dead artifact—but is the living and conceptual action that unites and thereby reconciles human history. Hegel's system is concrete and temporal.

In Frankfurt, Hegel develops further the element of negativity and strife that animates his system, the "splintered consciousness," but also the movement of opposition and reconciliation that suffuses spiritual life ("TJ2," 549). Hegel's unhappy stay in Frankfurt was a time for him to study several of his contemporaries—notably Schelling, but also Schiller and Kant—and the question of the dominant influence on Hegel during the years immediately preceding his mature work was an important and lively one in the 1930s. Hyppolite is largely in agreement with Haering's thesis which rejects the interpretation of Dilthey, Erdman, and Kroner, who all incorporated Hegel's development into a larger arc that begins with Kant, Fichte, and Schelling ("TJ1," 400–403). Although Hegel certainly read Schelling's work while in Frankfurt, Hyppolite asserts that the differences between them are "more profound than the resemblances" ("TJ2," 550). However, the works of Schiller and Hölderlin, concerned with the "dialectics of life, love, and destiny," appear to have had a significant effect on the development of Hegel's later thought ("TJ2," 551).

In "The Spirit of Christianity and Its Destiny," the principal text Hegel authored in Frankfurt, the dialectics of life, love, and destiny are explicated by the historical development of Christianity in which love reconciles Christ, the exemplar of "living religion," and destiny ("TJ2," 551). It is this dialectical development that will prove indispensable for

Hegel's mature system. "Love is, for Hegel, a concrete example of synthesis . . . the model of every living relation" ("TJ2," 558). "The Spirit of Christianity and Its Destiny" argues that Christ's message of love reconciles duty and inclination, thereby overcoming the fractured consciousness marring Judaism ("TJ2," 561). However, for Hegel, love "has a tragic destiny. Either it is limited to a small community, and it is opposed to the rest of the world; or it is indefinitely extended, and it becomes superficial, purely thought and not lived." But love's destiny, the "immanent dialectical structure" of the world, yields neither a pessimism nor any kind of teleological utopianism ("TJ2," 565). As the "*pleroma* [in Greek in Hyppolite's text] of the law," love clarifies history as the immanent development of absolute spirit without reducing history either to a series of contingent particularities or to the consequence of an extraneous purpose or end.[17] Love is the conjoining of the self and its community, of inclination and law ("TJ2," 561).

Hegel's absolute spirit can already be discerned in the *System-Fragment* of 1800. In the *System-Fragment*, Hegel's "essential preoccupation" is with "relations of spirit to spirit, the relation of human being to human being, of individual to nation, of lover to beloved, of man to God" ("TJ2," 567). The remarks on nature that open the *System-Fragment* are, Hyppolite asserts, "only a more universal expression of this structure of all spiritual phenomena" ("TJ2," 569). Hyppolite here stresses his agreement with Wahl that "the unhappy consciousness is at the heart of the Hegelian system," but contrary to Wahl, he further contends that the dialectic of the unhappy consciousness is governed by Hegel's distinctive conception of negation, and even if it is a lived experience for consciousness, it cannot be reduced to individual suffering ("TJ2," 567).[18] Hegel's conception of negation arises out of his work on the central problem posed by religious history: how to reconcile and join unity and separation, "the two dialectical moments that express religious life" ("TJ2," 570). The struggle to think the relation of man and God, which is also found in Wahl's contemporaneous work on Kierkegaard, is precisely this problem, and it is the foundational importance of this struggle for Hegel that marks his difference from both Schelling's naturalist intuition and Hölderlin's aesthetic intuition. The relation between man and God is not a unique intuition but must be thought according to *the* dialectic, "according to the same requirements of all spiritual life" ("TJ2," 570).

The "new" element in the *System-Fragment* is Hegel's concern for matter, the assertion not just of its relevance for spiritual life but its necessity: "the deduction of matter means nothing else, here, than the place of matter in the life of spirit and the necessity of an objectivity for spirit itself" ("TJ2," 572). Before Hegel joined Schelling in Jena, his thinking was exclusively concerned with questions of religion and religious history, while Schelling's was concerned with material nature. "Yet," Hyppolite asserts, "their methods are identical." It is Schelling's influence that leads Hegel to apply his dialectical conceptualization of religion to nature; Hegel never studied them separately ("TJ2," 574). Working in close proximity in Jena, both Schelling and Hegel wrestled with "the problem of the Spirit-Nature synthesis, but each placed their respective emphasis on the other term."[19] For Schelling, the problem is resolved by conceiving Nature as an inferior form of Spirit; for him, Nature develops into Spirit.[20] For Hegel, however, the problem is resolved by recognizing and valorizing the indispensable work of the negative. Drawing from his studies of religious life, Hegel begins not with identity—Schelling's starting point—but with "opposition, the unhappy consciousness" ("TJ2," 577). The decisive importance of Schelling for Hegel's thought is therefore to have provoked him to expand his previous work on the dialectical structure of religious life into a "dialectical method."[21]

Hyppolite's "Hegel's Youthful Works" ends with the *System-Fragment* of 1800 and Hegel's departure from Frankfurt to Jena. His subsequent essay, "Vie et prise de conscience de la vie dans la philosophie hégélienne d'Iéna" (1938; "Life and Consciousness of Life in Hegel's Jena Philosophy"), traces the further development of Hegel's thought during his time in Jena (1801–07). In this essay Hyppolite argues that in Berne and Frankfurt "Hegel was interested less in philosophical speculation than in *a description of the human condition*" ("VP," 46; emphasis in the original). Hegel's subsequent reorientation was, for Ehrenberg, one of his first interpreters, "a mystery," but, following Koyré—whom he cites—Hyppolite argues that Hegel's early work on religious life had a clear existential character: "Hegel lived the passage from the finite to the infinite" ("VP," 47). In Jena, it was precisely this lived experience that became the object of reflection.[22] The challenge was to find a mode of thinking, a method, adequate to the living and concrete diversity of the world. Hegel begins by rejecting Schelling's philosophy of nature, and conceives nature not as biological but, echoing his studies of Christianity, as primarily given for human consciousness. Nature is a moment of conscious life. It is not, however, the object of a mystical intuition; nature is the occasion for the elaboration and experience of human, spiritual relations. The strife that produces natural diversity is preserved as a unity because it is a spiritual unity whose content is nothing other than its concrete and worldly historical experiences. "The grasp of consciousness has in the Hegelian dialectic a creative and motive role; Hegel already said in the first system of Jena that spirit is 'what is discovered,' and nature only that which allows spirit to be rediscovered" ("VP," 47). The key to Hegel's ability to transform the historical insights of religious history into a pervasive dialectic of life, to construct a phenomenology of spirit, will be his analysis of infinity in the *Jena Logic*.

Human life, relation, and infinity are three equivalent terms for Hegel. Human life must be thought; when thought, it is relation; and infinity is what allows thought and relation to be conceptualized.[23] Hegel's discussion of infinity is a cornerstone of his logical dialectic and represents his original contribution to the defining problem of modern philosophy: that of relation.[24] For Hegel, "infinity is the very life of relation, the dialectical means that allows the dialectical development of each term of a relation to be conceived" ("VP," 51). Infinity is, in the *Jena Logic*, an anticipation of the negation of the negation in the *Phenomenology*: each related term is the negation of the other, and their relation is the redoubled negation of these negations. Furthermore, relation is ubiquitous: "everything is life and movement in relation, as infinite." "Dialectic is the life of content, and thought is not an empty form. *All living relations have their particular structures that must be thought as such.* In order to think a relation, one must grasp each term and the relation itself in infinity. *Infinity is then the middle term that makes life thinkable and relation living, that by which the problem of knowledge and the problem of life are identified*" ("VP," 51; emphasis in the original). Wahl had argued that this dialectical relation defeated every attempt at conceptualization because the unity "thought" transcended every particular determination. Hegel's innovation, as Hyppolite emphasizes, is to reject any attempt to situate infinity beyond the living relations in which each finite and determinate thing is determined via its negative relation to its determinate other. Infinity is the act of transcending, which incorporates differences, not transcendence, which abolishes them.

Hyppolite notes that the "biological dialectic" of Hegel's Jena writings reflects his earlier account of Abraham. The dialectical relation between the living individual and the totality of life is conceivable starting from either term, but Hegel chooses to begin from the position of the individual confronting its hostile surrounding world. The work of that individual transforms the world into one organized for the existent's purposes, but this transformation is also a transformation of that existent from organic thing into action. It is a development that culminates in the "mutual penetration" of the individual and the universal "translated by the logical idea of the power of the negative" ("VP," 54). Hyppolite emphasizes that this is not a translation performed or enacted *by* consciousness, it is the translation of *life* into (self-)consciousness—a translation of infinity into history, where history, "the system of shapes assumed by consciousness," according to the *Phenomenology*, "is the middle term between universal spirit and its individuation or sense-consciousness" ("VP," 56).

The philosophical concept (*Begriff*) is not merely an epistemological implement applied to some concrete content; "for Hegel, the concept is the act of intellection itself" ("VP," 57). In the Jena writings Hyppolite finds Hegel at work developing his mature philosophy of spirit: "concrete dialectic, [which] should surmount intuition, and become a philosophy of the history of spirit, as development of itself by itself" ("VP," 59). Although the concern for the concrete may seem to echo Wahl, Hyppolite's detailed account of the way that the concept comes to supplant intuition—a problematic that echoes the debate between Bergson and Brunschvicg—implicitly sides with Koyré and the rejection of any transcendence that would defeat conceptualization.

The final article that Hyppolite published before the outbreak of the Second World War, "La Signification de la Révolution Française dans la 'Phénoménologie' de Hegel" ("The Meaning of the French Revolution in Hegel's *Phenomenology*"), appeared in the *Revue Philosophique de la France et de l'Étranger* in 1939. Having traced the historical progress of Hegel's philosophical development in order to justify a particular interpretation of Hegel's mature work, Hyppolite's 1939 essay is an important moment of his own philosophical itinerary for a couple of reasons. First, and primarily, it illustrates the stark differences between Hyppolite's Hegel—developed in close dialogue with the work of an international community of scholars and interpreters—and Kojève's, expounded contemporaneously in his famous Paris seminars and far more idiosyncratic.[25] After the war, Kojève would declare that any reading of Hegel was a political act, and the theme of Hyppolite's essay marked his explicit intention to link his work on Hegel to the turbulent political affairs of the 1930s—affairs that reached a point of crisis just as it appeared in print.[26] Finally, "The Meaning of the French Revolution" in many ways serves as a kind of prelude to Hyppolite's translation of Hegel's *Phenomenology* as well as his own *Genesis and Structure*.

Drawing from his extensive elaboration of Hegel's philosophical development, Hyppolite begins by cautioning his reader that "the interpretation of passages of the *Phenomenology* is particularly delicate. It is a context where concrete or singular events are inextricably mixed with universal ideas." The method that Hegel develops and deploys in order to conceptualize this mixture "is precisely what constitutes the originality of this work, the greatest effort ever attempted in order to connect the singular and the universal which for common consciousnesses are juxtaposed without interpenetrating [*se penetrer*]" ("SR," 322). The young, pre-*Phenomenology* Hegel was a "realist," attentive to the news and events of the present, whose diversity furnished him not merely with grist for a preferred conceptual mill, but with the real movement of history whose meaning required philosophical clarification but not imposition. Key to the early Hegel's ethical thought is a tension between a conception of human freedom whose fullest achievement and fulfillment is found in "its worldly work," and another conception in which at least some part or aspect of human freedom is essentially outside of and refractory to citizenship. Although Hyppolite opens his essay by noting that "in the Preface to the *Phenomenology*, Hegel characterizes his time as an era of transition to a new period," he also cautions that Hegel's letters show him to be a reformer but not a revolutionary ("SR," 326). Hegel's political optimism leads him to clamor for the birth of progressive political minds out of the conflict between "what ought to be" (*Sollen*) and what is in fact the case. But Hegel's fondness for tumult—as pregnant with what "ought to be"—proves to be short-lived, and it is soon replaced by an attempt to conceptualize fate, "destiny." Summarizing the evolution of Hegel's political philosophy up to the *Phenomenology*, Hyppolite writes that he moves "from a reformist attitude to a contemplative attitude toward what "ought to be" (*Sollen*), to "the comprehension of what is" ("SR," 329). This passage recapitulates the "preparation" for the French Revolution described in the *Phenomenology*, those historical events whose dialectic precipitated the Revolution as their necessary outcome.

The *Phenomenology* fascinated interwar France in no small part because of the feeling of crisis, rupture, and incipient change that gripped philosophy and then the world during those decades. It was Valéry's *pharmakon*. As Pierre Macherey aptly notes, "for Jean Hyppolite [too], the *Phenomenology* . . . responds to the needs, to the urgent necessities of a singularly trans-temporal philosophical actuality."[27] These necessities, the restless stirrings of the absolute, are never fully quieted, and truth only ever becomes a matter of urgency in times of crisis—as Napoleon strides through Jena, as the Wehrmacht descends upon Warsaw, and then Paris. Hegel's *Phenomenology* is "the development and the formation of natural consciousness and its progression to science, that is to say, to philosophic knowledge, to knowledge of the absolute."[28] It is the story of how freedom clarifies itself as fate by disclosing the meaning of its temporal activity, its history. Hyppolite's Hegel, like Koyré's, can only ever be optimistic. For Hyppolite, the *Phenomenology* proper is comprised only of "the first three moments of the book, that is, consciousness, self-consciousness, and reason."[29] In these three moments Hyppolite marks the difference between the *Phenomenology* and the *Logic*, an issue that he will later take up in *Logic and Existence*—distinguishing phenomenology from both noumenology and ontology and describing it as the self-criticism of phenomenal knowledge by which that knowledge surmounts its own limitations to attain truth.[30]

Hegel has "a distinctively realist mind" that enables him to resist inventing a schema, a rack upon which to stretch history ("SR," 323). The phenomenological method pursues the story, the history, of how consciousness surmounts its limitations and learns that it is always the history of a particular becoming. The lessons of the French Revolution cannot be generalized. "For Hegel, then, it is a matter of rediscovering the forgotten path that has led the human spirit to this turning point in its history, and of explicating this moment by the anterior becoming" ("SR," 322). Indeed, Hyppolite's account of the development of Hegel's own attitudes toward the French Revolution prior to 1807 forms an important part of the larger developmental history of truth. Hyppolite's Hegel is no abstract dreamer, but neither is he a quietist, and Hyppolite's own concrete situation periodically flashes forth from his exegeses as when, closing his discussion of Hegel's commentary on Württemberg, Hyppolite writes: "the patience of men must finally be transformed into courage and daring in order to modify what is; if not they will flee into dream, eternal solution of the German mind" ("SR," 327).[31] In his youthful works, Hegel passes from a reformist attitude through a contemplative study of *Sollen* to, finally, the "comprehension of what is," and according to Hyppolite, these attitudes are reprised in the account of the French Revolution in the *Phenomenology* ("SR," 329). The outcome of the battle between religion and the Enlightenment, the Terror with its unprincipled utility, is "quite ambiguous." Hyppolite notes, however, that "after Robespierre, there is a name that is unspoken, but which must necessarily be read between the lines: Napoleon." What Napoleon means for Hegel is a reconstituted State that expresses not the "merely apparent will of its citizens, but their destiny" ("SR," 348). Then, with the Restoration, the tyrant too must exit the stage. Is the history of revolutions the story of the progressive reconquest of self-alienated spirit, culminating with historical agents acting as universal spirit? Hegel seems to shy away from this view—an avoidance or hesitation that Hyppolite likens to Luther's denial of the possibility of Heaven on earth—and instead describes the ultimate failure of the French Revolution as a historical fact whose positive outcome is the transfer of Spirit to another country: Germany, the land of dangerous dreamers, where Romanticism will theorize what the French sought to incarnate ("SR," 361).

The full import of Hyppolite's contributions not only to the French study of Hegel but to philosophy generally would have to wait for the end of the war to gain recognition and acknowledgment.[32] In the meantime, what discussion there was concerning Hegel was largely centered around the famous seminar of Alexandre Kojève and then, following its conclusion, the existential and phenomenological work of Merleau-Ponty and

Sartre.[33] While these were important for subsequent philosophical developments, what is more relevant for the present argument is the direction in which Wahl's work developed. As has been noted earlier in chapter 2, Wahl's 1937 address to the Société Française de Philosophie was the culmination of over a decade of work in which, through the exploration of a wide range of thinkers, he sought to defend the finite and concrete human experience of transcendence against conceptual appropriation. Without having ever organized them as such, Wahl's work marshals a constellation of nineteenth-century "poet thinkers"—Kierkegaard foremost, but also Nietzsche, Rimbaud, Novalis, Van Gogh, and others—that marks a historical rupture with the more orthodox philosophical work of Hegel. The experiences of these "poet-thinkers" will serve as evidence for the irreducible and transcendent yearning of concrete human existence.

Philosophy's Essential Failure

In June 1944, the same month as the Normandy landings, the Swiss publishing house Éditions de la Baconnière published Wahl's strange and difficult little book, *Human Existence and Transcendence*. In many ways the culmination of the work that began with his thesis on Descartes and *The Pluralist Philosophies, Human Existence and Transcendence* lays out Wahl's unique account of transcendence. Part of its difficulty is certainly due to the violent interruption of the war, or, as a note appended to the front of the book states, to "the circumstances" that prevented Wahl from reviewing the proofs prior to the book's publication. These "circumstances" had made of the 1937 conference which should have marked a "turning point" a kind of conclusion, and Wahl's book was thus isolated by both circumstances and preoccupations. The very structure of the book also presents a challenge. The first chapters of the book exhibit a marked stylistic contrast with Wahl's earlier work; the "scintillating" and encyclopedic citational style of his previous works remains, but now other thinkers and theories are arrayed around Wahl's own account of transcendence, augmenting or situating his claims, whereas in previous works the situation was the reverse. The later chapters of *Human Existence and Transcendence* return somewhat to that older style, however, and it concludes with chapters on Descartes, William Blake ("Poetry and Metaphysics"), and two chapters on Novalis ("Magic and Romanticism" and "Novalis and the Principle of Contradiction"). In previous works, Wahl had sought resources and responses to Valéry's "crisis" in other philosophers; in *Human Existence and Transcendence* he responds much more in his own voice.

In his 1937 "Subjectivity and Transcendence," Wahl had indicated the importance of "existential philosophers"—in Berdyaev's distinctive sense—for elaborating an account of concrete experience that was attentive to the qualitative difference of transcendent experiences and which refused any closure of experience, whether dialectical or theological. In the preface to *Human Existence and Transcendence,* Wahl cites with approval Karl Löwith's claim that philosophy was dramatically altered in the nineteenth century, that Hegel was the last philosopher.[34] However, the subsequent work of "poet-thinkers" such as Kierkegaard and Nietzsche was not, contrary to the claims of Jaspers and others, a radically new phenomenon. These poet-thinkers have a venerable, if subterranean, lineage—Wahl invokes Pascal, Dante, and even Plato and Socrates as precursors—that serves as a sort of counter-movement to "perennial philosophy" and everything that it entails.[35] Using the terms that organized *Pluralist Philosophies,* monism and pluralism, Wahl differentiates these lineages according to their respective ways of thinking the absolute. The absolute, in turn, is thought according to the Platonic formulation of the *Parmenides:* "Being is, and non-being is not."[36] The simplicity of this thought, its unity, is immediately subject to philosophical critique: apprehended by thought, the absolute is "refracted," resulting in two versions of the absolute: one immanent and the other transcendent (*EHT,* 57).[37] The nineteenth-century poet-thinkers and their antecedents, however, eschew both of these alternatives—as does Wahl—and insist that the lived experience of the absolute cannot be resolved into one of these options.

The distinction between thinking and feeling emphasized by Wahl's stress on lived experience does not imply a preference for one over the other. The value of the lives of individuals such as Rimbaud, Van Gogh, and Nietzsche is not that they offer privileged access to the absolute. None of these lives, nor any combination or portion of them, offers anything like the "truth" of the absolute. Each life is rather one facet of the inevitably multiple, "rended" (*déchirée*) thought of the absolute. Against the intellectual facets of the immanent and transcendent conceptual reductions of the absolute—the absolute unity of the diverse (pluralism) and the unitary absolute other beyond the diverse (monism)—Wahl sets the poet-thinkers' nonintellectual apprehension of the absolute by feeling, and this sensible apprehension is refracted as well. On the one hand, in Novalis and Romanticism, the sensible absolute is described as a feeling of "fusion." But in the works of Max Scheler, D. H. Lawrence, and Gabriel Marcel, the absolute is a feeling of "love, where [separate beings] are present, but present face to face with each other, rather than present in each other." No expression of the absolute enjoys any preeminence: the refracted and rended absolute "is at the same time an absolutely absolute unity" (*EHT*, 58).

The early twentieth-century interest in these poet-thinkers, in existential philosophy, had created what Wahl characterizes as a kind of philosophical confusion about the sensible absolute. Kierkegaard and Nietzsche begin from the experience of the death of God, an experience that "places man before an abyss." The feeling of this experience gives rise to two different conceptual paths: "[Nietzsche] posits an immanence that, if we allow ourselves to be crushed, is just as capable of crushing us as transcendence; [Kierkegaard posits] a transcendence that frightens and consoles us" (*EHT*, 9). In both thinkers, the sensible experience of transcendence gives rise to a conceptual effort toward the absolute, to "a search for eternity in the instant, in the instant of repetition and resurrection" (*EHT*, 8). The absolute is thus a limit of human existence toward which it stretches, drawn to ecstatically abandon its very finitude, and from which it falls back to find itself changed and enriched. The "scintillating" attraction of the instantaneous apprehension of the absolute is, however, ineradicable. The existent can neither give up this frustrated desire, nor can it satisfy it. The experience of transcendence cannot be clarified because, by its nature, it is a feeling that is other than the conceptual grasp of language and thought; the instant is the presence to thought of the "unsayable" (*EHT*, 23–24). "And through [*par*] this limit, at this frontier, a light beckons [*miroite*] of which one cannot say if it comes from thought, or from the Other, or from the nameless Thing" (*EHT*, 24). What, then, can thinking retain of the transcendent as transcendent, as the unconceptualized and unsayable absolute, in its conceptualized thought and language: "returning to immanence, can one avoid losing transcendence?" (*EHT*, 24). For Wahl, this question presents a kind of false problem.

> Since Plato [the instant] has haunted the mind of philosophers and writers. From the instant of the third hypothesis to the instantaneous pleasures of Aristippus, taken up again by Walter Pater and André Gide, to the theological instant (the instant of the incarnation, the instant of the resurrection, the instant of the final judgment *in ictu oculi*), to that of Kierkegaard, to that of Dostoevsky, to the Nietzschean eternal return that sanctifies the instant, to Rimbaud's eternity, one could follow the course of these meditations in search of eternity lost [*a la recherché de l'eternite perdu*], and found again in the instant, and ask oneself if the instant is not for the modern thinker a consoling myth rather than a

> reality, a substitute for eternity; and nevertheless it is reality, existential
> reality endlessly offered, endlessly lost. (*EHT*, 24)

The sensible absolute is a *real* feeling; but its reality is its existence as feeling. The existential philosophy exemplified by Kierkegaard and Nietzsche only ever gives expression to the dialectic of transcendence and immanence that arises from this feeling. The simultaneity of the thought of the unitary and rended absolute requires that this thought be dialectical: "The absolute is divided, and the thought of the eternal takes time" (*EHT*, 59). Contrary to Hegel's account, however, the dialectic is perpetual and inescapable. Its dream is to transcend transcendence, to work through the refractions of the absolute and ultimately grasp its pieces together with its unity in an absolute thought. This "hopeless," perhaps even mad dream is that of thinkers from Novalis to Proust: Kierkegaard and Nietzsche, Heidegger and Jaspers are all working to formulate the idea of the instant, the idea of an eternally repeating eternity (*EHT*, 60). That idea, Wahl declares, is a myth; there is no thought on the other side of the dialectic; human finitude ensures the irreducible temporal pluralism of thinking.

Transcendence is the experience of an "absolute [that] exists only in our relation with it" (*EHT*, 61). At its root, it is the feeling of a tension between the individual and the absolute that pushes thinking into dialectical movement. The apparent inescapability of dialectics leads Wahl to contrast an "existential dialectic," one that aims at "an accord of the discordant" with two other dialectics: the Hegelian and the Platonic (*EHT*, 9).[38] The Platonic dialectic insists on the transcendence of the whole, on another truthful realm of full or whole being beyond the finite and partial. Conversely, the Hegelian dialectic perpetually overcomes the negative moment of discordant otherness with a synthetic moment, a return of the whole, by which the partial is revealed to be only an inadequately thought element of the whole.[39] In one dialectic, the diverse is secured in its diversity, and thus rendered truthful, by something different from it; in the other, the partial is adequately thought only as part *of a whole*. Both dialectics reveal an attempt to close the movement of transcendence in some kind of completed dialectic—transcendent or immanent—which, for Wahl, is the "consoling myth" of the instant of intellectual apprehension.

Like Hegel and Plato, Wahl's dialectical description of existence begins with its essentially intentional character; subjective consciousness is between worldly experience and the apprehension of experience by thought. "Concrete existence is always existence before a work, in an action, or before another being. An existence is relation with something other than itself" (*EHT*, 29).[40] Here and elsewhere in his work from the 1930s and 1940s, Wahl avails himself of Heidegger's account of being-in-the-world as the irreducibly ek-static structure of human existence, of *Dasein*.[41] Transcendence is not the action or accident of a subject set over against an object; the transcendental character of human existence is both "the bringing to light of the subjective in what is most objective, and of the objective in what is most subjective" (*EHT*, 14).[42] The dialectic of transcendence is lived as a subjective tension; the absolute can be experienced, but always only partially. All of the attempts to privilege one facet over another—whether it is the objective other of science, the subject, the dialectical movement from the subject to the object, or even the tragic feeling of this ceaseless movement—fail; existence flees from itself (*EHT*, 32).

Echoing still another poet, Wahl avers of subjectivity: "if we want to rediscover paradise lost, we must lose ourselves in paradise regained; this is even a condition for rediscovering it. Consciousness takes place between this loss and this rediscovery, it is necessarily unhappy" (*EHT*, 23). As Wahl stressed to Marcel in 1937, this is why the lives of individuals such as Nietzsche, Van Gogh, and Rimbaud are philosophically important: they are not "failed philosophies," they are the exhibition of philosophy's essential failure. They show "the source of philosophy," what gives rise to reflection and conceptualization, and in themselves, in their partiality, they offer an explication of transcendence whose persistence in excess of every philosophical explanation is not a deficiency but the very sustenance of thought. The existential dialectic is a self-rending, a breaking and a multiplying of the individual (*EHT*, 10). In this fragmentation, philosophical reflection initially appears as an effort at suturing and mending consciousness. However, the lives of existential philosophers such as Nietzsche, Van Gogh, and Rimbaud are testaments to subjectivity's irreducibly heterodox existence; "if one attains transcendence, consciousness disappears; it can be attained only in the unconsciousness of itself and of transcendence" (*EHT*, 36).[43] The lived experience of transcendence is therefore both an accomplishment—a victory—and a defeat: a defeat because the sensible experience of transcendence vanishes in the face of its reification by conceptual thinking, but also an accomplishment insofar as the impetus for this conceptual apprehension is the persistent sensible experience of the concrete other. For Wahl, there is no philosophical thought without the other; the experience of transcendence is the origin of philosophy.[44] The unhappy negativity of dialectical subjectivity carries with it "a [not simply negative] need that the being feels to annihilate its own thought in an attitude of submission to this domination of transcendence" (*EHT*, 23).[45] This feeling is impossible to explicate. "To exist absolutely," to reconcile without reduction transcendence and subjectivity, is to experience a kind of joy that does not abolish unhappiness, it

> is to be conscious of this ground impervious to consciousness. The absolute is the tension, what grounds it in me, and what resists it outside of me, and the passage toward the exterior with the help of what is most internal in us. And at the same time, it is the destruction of these distinctions. (*EHT*, 62)

The dialectic of transcendence has still another facet: "if truth is in judgment, reality is in the sphere of the non-conscious" (*EHT*, 22). Truth is the proper character of the relation that overcomes the distance between subjectivity and what provokes experience, and Wahl's claim that this overcoming is never sufficient undercuts the traditional goal of philosophical reflection. Of what use is reflection if every attempt at the absolute collapses in failure? As Wahl noted in *Vers le concret*, the failure of philosophical reflection is linguistic; the irreducible silence of sensibility marks not the falsity of the concrete, but the impotence of language. Wahl here returns to the terms of his decade-old debate with Koyré concerning the specific character of Hegel's achievement—an achievement that had since been developed in important ways by Hyppolite. The language of Nietzsche and Rimbaud—and the images of Van Gogh—are not the language of the absolute, they are the concrete source of that language. Wahl praises Schelling for having grasped that poetry is the unity of the subjective and the objective, of consciousness and the unconscious (*EHT*, 78). The former becomes dominant in philosophical conceptualization, the latter in poetry, but the limit-point of each is marked by silence.

The existential dialectic that persists with the plurality of the subjective and the objective is therefore not an extended chain of thought but "a short dialectical chain between two moments where dialogue—at least apparent dialogue—ceases, in order to leave speech, if I may say, in silence." The tension of the existential dialectic exists "at every moment," between the concrete presence of things in perception and the ek-static union of the mind and the world; it persists in an intensity "that defines existence situated between the transcendent immanence of perception and the immanent transcendence of ecstasy" (*EHT*, 10–11). If the conceptual dialectic of transcendent immanence—exemplified by the dialectics of Plato and Hegel—is the organizing force of the dominant philosophical tradition, championed by Koyré and Hyppolite, the work of the nineteenth-century poet-thinkers now joins that tradition with a dialectic of sensibility. Beginning from perception, one moment of this dialectic is what, citing Schelling, Wahl calls a "transcendental empiricism [that seeks] the conditions in which experience is, we do not say possible, but real" (*EHT*, 18). It is an empirical realism that joins the poetic project of a Rilke with the phenomenological project of a Husserl, but it is not a "surface realism" because it begins with, and never abandons, perception:

> Remaining at the stage of our perception, not decomposing this perception following the articulations of something other than it, it will present to us concrete things not artificially concretized, but born of a natural knowing: things. (*EHT*, 21)

Transcendental empiricism aims at an untranslated exposition of the concrete and real conditions of experience. It explicates transcendence without interpretation in a positive dialectic of feeling, a "logic of quality," that is irreducible to the extensive and quantitative logics of totality characteristic of philosophical conceptualization (*EHT*, 11). "The problem of existence, then, will not be resolved theoretically, but rather practically; by the feeling a human has of being able, to a certain extent, to reconcile their past, their future, and their present" (*EHT*, 33). This practical resolution is experienced as a kind of ecstasy.

Even the ek-stasis of transcendental empiricism does not soothe the urge to transcendence, however, and Wahl does not advocate a simple rejection of philosophical thought in favor of poetic expressions of feeling.[46] Such expressions give better approximations of the absolute but they do not give the absolute itself. "Consciousness is always distance," it is always ek-static, which means that even in apprehending sensibility there is a difference between sensing and the sensed. There is an essential "negativity that 'calls the tune' of the antitheses," that cannot be overcome and that ultimately grounds transcendence itself; there is no ek-stasis without a fracture or gap (*EHT*, 22–23). To the philosophical dialectic of thinking there corresponds a sensible dialectic of feeling. This is the unity of sensible diversity, an ecstatic plenitude that is a "point of arrival situated beyond consciousness just as perception is situated before it" (*EHT*, 22). However, the absolute unity of the sensible would be the utter negation of consciousness, the negation of ek-static existence in the suture of the differentiating fracture of the sensible. Feeling, too, is unhappy; enduring ecstasy is a myth. This sensible unhappiness must therefore be motivated by a deeper negativity, a desire for self-annihilation as the necessary complement to the fulfillment of transcendence, to the attaining of the absolute (*EHT*, 23). Like the failure of philosophical dialectics, whose positive result is the disclosure of the dimension of the sensible, the failure of sensible dialectics is not, despite its collapse, merely futile or absurd. Its collapse exposes the occluded feeling of the absolute that is Wahl's own "critical" conception. To the "classical" conception of the absolute which envisions it as the conjoining of immanence and transcendence in the conceptual apprehension of the whole and its parts, Wahl opposes a thought of the absolute that persists "in the intense feeling for the partial and the ephemeral," an absolute also found in William Blake's "*minute particular*," in Jakob Boehme's *Grund*, and in D. H. Lawrence's "*dark god*" (*EHT*, 61–62).[47]

Wahl's critical conception of the absolute is the distinctive achievement of *Human Existence and Transcendence*. It is in some ways a choice, almost a personal preference—Wahl emphasizes this aspect of his critical conception of the absolute when he stresses that it is "ours"—but it is also a manifestation of the spirit of the age, one that breaks with the "classical" conceptions of the absolute, and its selection is a response inseparable from the contemporary sense of crisis (*EHT*, 22). It is a familiar and strange response—familiar insofar as the plea to turn to the intensity of the ephemeral, to the "element where I realize myself by destroying myself," is echoed by several thinkers between the wars, notably the Surrealists and Acéphale, both groups with which Wahl was affiliated (*EHT*, 62).[48] It is also a strange invocation, however, made even more so by Wahl's turn to the Romantic poet Novalis in order to elucidate it. Here again, after surfacing to speak with his own voice in favor of a particular conception of the absolute, Wahl returns to his earlier style of grafting his own thinking onto the carefully cultivated body of another thinker's work. More indicative than explicative, Wahl's discussion of Novalis stresses the latter's conception of the "magical" activity of intellectual intuition as the creative co-production of the world and the subject: "[we are] personified and all-powerful points. The individual is a magical principle" (*EHT*, 98). The magic of human existence is then to be able to conceive and follow the dialectical play of contradiction in thought, as well as to apprehend the point at which these "fecund contradictions" exceed the resources of thinking. Where thought breaks down, at the point of ecstasy, Novalis sees "the highest task of the highest logic: to destroy the principle of contradiction" (*EHT*, 107). This task, achieved by the mind as "a tool for linking completely heterogenous terms," is magical; its expression is poetry (*EHT*, 108–9). Like the other poet-thinkers favored by Wahl, Novalis's genius-poet would surpass the human, but not by finding the whole in the instant; the genius-poet conjoins partial but intensive, ecstatic, sensible experiences. Descartes's flame thereby acquires a new interpretation:

> The act of leaping over itself is, everywhere and always, the highest act, the original point, the genesis of life. The flame is nothing other than an act of this kind. Thus philosophy begins where the philosopher philosophizes himself, that is to say is simultaneously consumed, determined, and satisfied. (*EHT*, 112)[49]

The ideal flame has become an empirical one.

4

The Second World War and
Its Aftermath

> Apart from Sartre . . . the most important philosopher in France
> was Jean Wahl.
> —Gilles Deleuze, "On the Superiority of Anglo-American
> Literature"

"J'ai pitié de nous tous, ô tourbillons de poudre!"[1] So resounds the voice of
Valéry's Clotho in 1946, sharply echoing the poet's own words from 1919.
Valéry himself was dead, having lived long enough to see the Liberation
and the near-miraculous reprieve of Paris, and to greet the official end of
the war in Europe. But at the end of July 1945 in Paris there seemed little
reason for hope. The continent was a blasted disaster zone parceled out
to uneasy occupiers. The monstrous horror of the extermination camps
cast an ineradicable shadow over any sense of victory. August would bring
Hiroshima, and then Nagasaki. Looking back, it is no longer as "striking" as Hyppolite believed that the reflexive crisis of conscience that
gripped Valéry's *man of spirit* should have become "constitutive of Existence."[2] Existence had become dust: granular, common, lifeless, and gray.
    When Hyppolite's "Note sur Paul Valéry et la crise de la conscience"
("Note on Paul Valery and the Crisis of Conscience") appeared in the
Catholic journal *La Vie Intellectuelle* in 1946, Hyppolite justified his topic
by noting that it "offers, before the extension of this crisis [of conscience]
to all humanity in general, a particularly pure form of that pessimism that
today appears to extend to all of us."[3] The "crisis" of the mind that Valéry
had revealed to a previous generation's leading lights has become the
very condition of self-conscious existence in the existential philosophy of
Sartre and others.[4] It could be formulated succinctly in a phrase of Rimbaud's that is both pithy and profound: "the true life is absent."[5] But how,
Hyppolite asks, is this absence to be interpreted? "It is despair because
it is the negation of vital spontaneity . . . We can no longer believe in life
because we surpass it, and because consciousness of life is consciousness
of its unhappiness. But is this negation, so tragic for human races at the
apex of their culture, truly the loss of all hope? Is this nothingness only

nothingness, an always-future emptiness [*creux toujours futur*], or is it the sign of a transcendence?"[6] Against existential despair, Hyppolite sets a Christian philosophy of hope in which finite life is suspended between the "lost paradise of the unconscious" and the hope of grace, of a transcendental reconciliation.[7] Hyppolite does not, however, simply adopt this solution. If existentialism asserts that being-for-oneself can only issue in the bad faith of atheism or in the philosophically impossible faith of Christianity, Hyppolite questions the finality of this oscillation or choice. "Must it [consciousness] not rediscover either nature or grace, or perhaps the one through the other?"[8] This is the promise of Hegel: the ultimate reconciliation of nature and grace, of the opposed tendencies of consciousness, and of finite freedom and its concrete world. For Hyppolite, the task of Hegel's philosophy—the task of *philosophy*—is to discover the conditions of and for the true work of freedom, a task that requires the sentimental fog of existentialism to be swept aside by the light of conceptual knowledge.[9] As it was for Koyré, Hegel's philosophy is for Hyppolite not a closure but a remarkable kind of opening; at the end of the *Phenomenology*, freedom is no longer "a freedom for death, or a vain engagement in nature, an engagement always repeated and always refused."[10]

Today Hyppolite is principally known and remembered through the work of several brilliant students who credit his reading of Hegel—propounded in his classes as well as in publications—for its acumen, its insight, and also for delimiting the problems and prospects of postwar French philosophy.[11] Speaking after Hyppolite's death on the occasion of his elevation to the Collège de France, Foucault remarked that Hyppolite was the thinker who "tirelessly explored, for us, and ahead of us, the path along which we may escape Hegel, keep our distance, and along which we shall find ourselves brought back to him, only from a different angle, and then, finally, be forced to leave him behind, once more."[12] Deleuze remembered Hyppolite as a teacher who had "a powerful face with unfinished features," who "rhythmically beat out Hegelian triads with his fist, hanging his words on the beats."[13] However, as has become clear, Hyppolite was far more than an interpreter of Hegel. At the very least, his work came to represent a particular Hegel, a logicist and immanent Hegel set over against the anthropological Hegel of Kojève in the aftermath of the war. Even more than Wahl, Hyppolite pursued his own project—the elimination of transcendence—through a close engagement with Hegel's work. This is the reason why Deleuze would attach such importance to Hyppolite's 1952 *Logic and Existence*. Far from being a simple "commentary" on Hegel that solves the problem of the relation between the *Phenomenology* and the *Logic*, it attempts the definitive surpassing of empirical knowledge by speculative knowledge.

Wahl's distinctive conception of transcendence was a central element of his own philosophical project and was also a point of orientation in the postwar debates that convulsed French academic philosophy. However, Wahl's habit of couching—even concealing—his own thought within extended engagements with other thinkers makes his voice difficult to discern. Again, Levinas's description of his friend's style—a kind of philosophical pointillism—helps to show that what in detail looks like a series of summaries and commentaries becomes, within an expanded scope, a method of intervention. The upheaval of the Second World War was devastating for such a project—as it was for so many others—not only making the connections between Wahl's works more difficult to see and trace, but interrupting the publication of his own attempt to synthesize and present his work in *Human Existence and Transcendence*. After returning to Paris from the United States he published three short works in rapid succession—*Tableau de la philosophie française* (1946; *An Overview of French Philosophy*), *Introduction à la pensée de Heidegger* (1946; *Introduction to Heidegger's Thought*), and *Petite histoire de l'existentialisme* (1947; *A Short History of Existentialism*)—which sought to crystallize several different strains of philosophical thought around Wahl's own distinctive formulation of existentialism.[14] As he notes at the conclusion of the brief text that opens *A Short History of Existentialism*,

> We are observing a whole philosophical movement which dislodges previous philosophical concepts, and which tends to make more acute our subjective understanding at the same time as it makes us feel more strongly than ever our union with the world. In this sense, we are witnessing and participating in the beginning of a new mode of philosophizing.[15]

Within this mode are two distinctions that form "the dilemma of existentialism."[16] There is the recent existentialism of Heidegger and Sartre which "goes from a consideration of existence proper to a study of Being with the help of the idea of existence," and there is the existentialism exemplified by Kierkegaard, who was entirely uninterested not only in ontology but in formulating a philosophy at all.[17] *A Short History of Existentialism*, like the other two texts, initially seems to be concerned principally with elaborating the work of others and with providing a kind of orientation to the contemporary philosophical field in France after the war. However, all three texts are equally—and perhaps even primarily—an exposition of Wahl's distinctive conception of existentialism, which demonstrates "that the origins of most great philosophies, like those of Plato, Descartes, and Kant, are to be found in existential reflections."[18]

In the summer of 1945, Koyré wrote to Wahl that, in Paris, "everybody is an existentialist!" But even as the appellation spread, there also proliferated a wide range of attempts to circumscribe the bounds of this new form of thought.[19] Moreover, the question of the proper meaning of existentialism was, as Hyppolite's "Note on Valéry" implies, a personal and political question as much as a philosophical one. Issues of individual and collective responsibility were neither academic nor occasional in the years immediately following the Liberation, and questions of ethical agency, human worth and dignity—including, but not limited to, the well-known "question of humanism"—and social values were at the forefront of the reintegration of Resistance members and citizens of the Third Republic who now were forced to work together to create a Fourth Republic. When Sartre presented his lecture "Existentialism Is a Humanism" to a packed auditorium in Paris in late 1945, he spoke as much to the electorate and the new National Assembly, elected only eight days before, as to the mandarins wrestling over the question of whether existentialism was properly atheist, socialist, or Christian. Extra-academic matters bore significant consequences for existential theory: the increasingly appalled shock at Heidegger's Nazism; the political fortunes of the French Communist Party (PCF), including its relations to Lysenkoism and Stalinism; the institutional valorization of the sciences, the scientific method, and objectivity, all closely linked to the creation of UNESCO and to the distribution of Marshall Plan funds; and even the alternately mundane and horrifying personnel questions that confronted various academic institutions dealing with faculty who had been deported, driven into exile, executed, or who had collaborated with the German occupying forces—all these shaped and decisively influenced what can appear in retrospect to be a purely academic debate.[20]

The relatively quick demise of existentialism can hide this array of debates and problems that animated French philosophy after the war. The most familiar and common explanation for its demise is that existentialism is irrational, that it obstinately persists at the level of sentiment, thereby inevitably lapsing back into subjectivism or even solipsism. This customary explanation for existentialism's demise, however, misses the extent to which existentialism struggled against the very hazards that its critics warned against. Wahl's work in particular stresses the importance of Heidegger's being-in-the-world, with its indication not of an inward-directed subjectivity but of an intra-worldly existence. Existentialism's most prominent figures—Beauvoir, Sartre, and Camus—were widely known less for their theoretical work than for their literary and journalistic work, their plays, and, especially in the case of the latter, their work with the Resistance, all of which were well-known to their contemporary readers and provided ample evidence of existentialism's concern for concrete worldly existence.[21] The debates within existentialism—not just the now-familiar debates between Sartre and Camus, or between Sartre and Merleau-Ponty, but also those between atheists and Christians, between liberals and socialists—did not so much bear political implications as they were immediately political. Existentialism's relatively brief postwar apex was a time of both tumult and consolidation.

Existentialism in Postwar France

Like Wahl and others, Hyppolite was an active participant in the efforts to take stock of the postwar fortunes of existentialism, which were for him and others tied to criticisms of Bergsonism and to the practical realities of a radically altered postwar world. In "Du bergsonisme à l'existentialisme" (1949; "From Bergsonism to Existentialism"), Hyppolite notes that while the grounds were laid for existentialism prior to 1939, "one must situate its emergence in the historical context of the world war, of the Occupation, and of the threats that today weigh on human destiny."[22] Hyppolite understands himself as part of the existentialist upsurge, often naming both Sartre and Merleau-Ponty as his fellow travelers, which makes his essay at least in part an exercise in self-description.[23] Violently shaken by the war, the problems of existentialism were importantly connected to the problems of the prewar generation of French philosophers; "to understand the success of existentialism," Hyppolite writes, one must analyze the criticisms that the existentialists make of Bergsonian philosophy.[24] Valéry's call for intellectuals to work out a practical and worldly response to the "crisis" of post–World War I Europe depicted Bergsonian philosophy as an ineffectual and dangerous mysticism, at best inadequate to Valéry's challenge, at worst complicit in the disaster that necessitated it.[25] Hyppolite states this central inadequacy succinctly: "Bergson's philosophy is a philosophy of life before being a philosophy of human history."[26] Bergson himself emphasizes this anti- or non-human vocation in *The Creative Mind*, flatly stating that "philosophy should be an effort to surpass the human condition."[27] The murder of over 100 million people in a matter of decades makes such a claim appear alternately farcical and monstrous. It was a real failure, a failure to address its historically determinate and determined world, that rendered Bergsonism a naive and even mystical optimism, "a philosophy of serenity." For Hyppolite, however, this failure issues dialectically in an equally determinate philosophical renewal.[28] Existentialism refuses to ignore or to turn away from the human anguish that Bergsonism seemed to ignore in its haste to take flight from the world, its seeming scorn for real human needs and crises, and existentialism thereby forges the two paths of a "spiritual itinerary":

> Every existentialist begins from the anguish that Bergsonism rejects, *some* [Sartre] show that human reality—despite its fundamental project of being God—cannot achieve this impossible transcendence . . . others discover a transcendental hope behind the failure of the human adventure, revealable only in a cipher (Jaspers), or in a mystery to whose threshold a reflection on reflection can lead us (Marcel). In either case, philosophy cannot surpass human existence; either it disappears in action, or it ends in faith.[29]

Bergsonism topples into the problem of transcendence. Wahl's work makes this clear, and Hyppolite tacitly appeals to it when he emphasizes that while, for Bergson, human anguish was thought solely as a moment of the larger movement of life, it need not be entirely reduced to that moment: "in [*On the*] *Two Sources* [*of Morality and Religion*], Bergson shows how the conscious intelligence of man, first made in order to prolong the movement of life and to participate in the creative force, tends to turn back against life. This idea of a *consciousness of life* which goes *against life* was at the origin of what Hegel called *unhappy consciousness*: 'The consciousness of life,' he wrote, 'is the consciousness of the unhappiness of life.'"[30] For Bergson, action-crippling anguish is undone by the intuitive work of fabulation, whose myths revivify human finitude by reconnecting and re-situating it within the larger movement of life.[31] Extending the link to German idealism—which also displayed a marked interest in myths and fiction—Hyppolite notes that such a solution echoes the work of the Romantics, and he declares flatly that "today it is this serenity of a nature foreign to man that we are no longer capable of comprehending."[32] It is an ethical and political incomprehension as much as a philosophical one.

According to Hyppolite's analysis, the existentialist critique of Bergsonism issues in the problem that attracted Wahl, the problem of transcendence, of the sense of "going beyond" human existence, which issues in two philosophical trajectories: the Sartrean analysis of existence as a failed transcendence, and the contrary analysis of thinkers like Jaspers and Marcel for whom transcendence is not willed but is to be hoped for. Both strains push any final consolation or serenity beyond the bounds of human existence and thereby produce "a crisis of philosophy itself."[33] The aim of philosophy has traditionally been the apprehension of a transcendental truth from whose perspective the errors and injustices of finite life are annulled or dissolved. Existentialism, however, forecloses

any philosophical or rational appeal to transcendence: "so-called vertical transcendence is accessible only to faith" and faith, after Valéry, after
the horrors of two wars, can only ever be the dereliction of thought. "We
can no longer seek to become more lucid about [*sur*] this human reality
that we ourselves are and that we ourselves make; a philosophical system
that would allow us to surpass this existence, to refer it to something
other than itself, seems impossible."[34] For Wahl, however, the value and
upshot of this discovery is that it reveals the limitations of conceptual
philosophical thinking; the impossibility is not absolute, but is instead
particular to conceptual thought and philosophical language whose drive
to systematize is frustrated. But human thought has other resources, and
at the point where conceptual systematization breaks down, poetry can
succeed in expressing the concrete in its diversity.[35]

Hyppolite is less ready than Wahl to draw a sharp line around traditional philosophical projects. Faced with the perpetual failure of philosophy to secure the present or future legitimacy of human thought and
action, Hyppolite—evincing here a kinship with Bergson—appeals to a
thinking of the past, of history. If transcendence is no longer philosophically viable, Hyppolite writes at the conclusion of his article, then "there
remains . . . the meaning of the historicity of this [human] existence, and
the enlargement of this historicity in(to) history [*l'élargissement de cette his-
toricité en histoire*]. How can we understand the link between [*des*] human
existents: historical becoming? How can we envisage the problem of the
meaning of this history which in some ways is given to us, but which also
constitutes us? Today the ultimate problem where existentialists, Marxists, and Christians come into conflict appears to be that of this '*meaning* of history.'"[36] The problem of the meaning of history is not merely
a problem *of* history. It is the problem of the truthful efficacy of human
action, of how we ought to live.

One of the chief reasons why Hyppolite's work on Hegel proved
so fundamental for postwar French philosophy was because it identified
and addressed precisely this question. In *Genesis and Structure*, Hyppolite
argues that although the *Phenomenology of Spirit* should not be mistaken
for a history of the world, there is "nonetheless a certain relation between
phenomenology and the philosophy of history."[37] This relation is twofold, and each facet is a necessary component of absolute knowledge.
On the one hand, the *Phenomenology* is the account of the development
of empirical knowledge into objective and scientific—philosophical—
knowledge.[38] On the other hand, this development can only be achieved
insofar as empirical consciousness "simultaneously becomes aware of a
certain history of the spirit, without which absolute knowledge is inconceivable. This act of becoming aware is not a pure and simple return to

the past; in its retrospective apprehension it justifies the past and determines its meaning."[39] The necessity of this second historical task is Hegel's greatest philosophical innovation. The aim or purpose of philosophy *as such*, the phenomenological achievement of truth through the surpassing of merely empirical knowledge, requires individual consciousness to overcome its partiality through the mediation of history. In the meaningfulness of its experience of the past, individual consciousness teaches itself the nature or essence of its own time—this is what Hegel means when he speaks of culture as a moment of the absolute.[40] To become educated in this way, to become cultured, requires that the past be found meaningful, justified, but it also requires as a correlative condition that the present be understood as the justified meaning *of that past*, as its necessary outcome and consequence. The present is then lived as a time of hope, since it too will be found meaningful and justified. There is a path open to existentialism other than the destitution of Sartre, the aporias of Jaspers and Marcel, or the poeticizing transcendence of Wahl: in Hegel's phenomenology, consciousness discovers both nature and grace in the meaning of history, in the past that is as objective as nature, and in the future of that past which consciousness now understands as *its own*.

Reflecting the influence of Heidegger, Hyppolite's analysis of the fortunes of existentialism stresses the problem of temporality over the more familiar problems of human existence and experience. The philosophical interest in time—indissociable from the work of Heidegger—was, in postwar France, also an inheritance from Bergson, and it recurred in almost every area of culture touched by Valéry's call to arms. Reflecting on the development of existentialism and, specifically, on the importance of Hegel for that development, Wahl notes that although Heidegger's influence is clear in Kojève's reading of Hegel, it was Alexandre Koyré's article—presumably "Hegel in Jena"—that emphasized the importance of time for Hegel's philosophy.[41] As shown above, Koyré contends that the distinctive achievement of Hegel's philosophical language—the logos—is that its truth character arises from the dialectical synthesis of the temporal and the eternal, from the "integration of past forms in the present."[42] Koyré's essays—and his debate with Wahl—were of central importance for Hyppolite as he developed his own distinctive account of Hegel's philosophy through the several articles that he published in the 1930s.[43] Like Koyré, Hyppolite argues for the central importance of Hegel's account of time and temporality; where he differs from Koyré is in his prioritization of the past, of history. As Wahl notes, Koyré emphasizes the importance of the future, but for Hyppolite, anxious to avoid the aporias of Christian existentialism, such a prioritization, without a correlative insistence on the importance of history, risks relapsing into a sterile optimism that is all too similar to Bergsonism. By joining a future-oriented philosophy of freedom to a past-oriented philosophy of culture—thereby fulfilling Hegel's demand that subject become substance and substance become subject—Hyppolite's work made Hegel's philosophy, as a philosophy of the contemporary meaning of history, the inescapable touchstone not just for existentialism but for virtually every strain of postwar French philosophy.[44] If Hegel was unavoidable, there were nonetheless a number of guides to his thought other than Hyppolite. What differentiated Hyppolite and contributed to his success—in addition to his singular influence as a teacher—was his oft-stated aim of being a kind of honest broker, of letting Hegel's texts speak for themselves without weighing them down with foreign claims and concerns. In this he followed the tradition of historians such as Émile Bréhier and Martial Gueroult.[45]

Hyppolite and the "Ambiguity" of Hegel

After the prewar essays analyzed in the previous chapter, and Hyppolite's translation of Hegel's *Phenomenology of Spirit*, he published, in 1946, *Genesis and Structure of Hegel's Phenomenology of Spirit*. In truth, Hyppolite's translation of the *Phenomenology* had already been the presentation of a distinctive and distinctively rational Hegel. With his brief "Translator's Preface" but above all with his voluminous notes that situate Hegel's text in relation to both his own philosophical context and the context of twentieth-century philosophy, Hyppolite created a remarkably contemporary Hegel, one that spoke to present-day concerns without ceasing to be historically distinct, and one sensitive to the anguishing vicissitudes of mortal life who still found a philosophical way to surmount them.

Hyppolite's analysis of the reasons for the philosophical shift from Bergsonism to existentialism offers important insights into why Hegel was a particularly important touchstone and resource for a variety of philosophers and philosophical projects that otherwise seem incommensurable. Hegel's philosophy does not provide a solution to Valéry's existential crisis; it is, for Hyppolite, "*ambiguous.*" Is the absolute idea "which is immanent to history . . . an end of history in which man as man will be realized, or is it the *Logos*, that which is said in the errancy of history, of which man is only the bearer or guardian?"[46] The former interpretation, Hyppolite contends, is the one pursued by "humanism."[47] Hegel himself, however, without ever quite eliminating the ambiguity, seems to favor another path which doubles the question of "the meaning of history." It is a matter not only of the humanist question of the meaning produced *by* history, it is also the question of the meaningful production *of* history. Hyppolite had already broached this question in 1937 when he wrote that "human life interprets itself, and this self-interpretation—forgetting, return, future—is history itself."[48] The meaning of history is not outside of history, waiting to be discovered in some transcendental structure or entity; it is always already there in the meaningful production of history achieved through the linguistic work of human beings. "To speak Being, this appears to be man's task, the proper meaning of consciousness that thereby becomes the universal self-consciousness of Being."[49] The *Phenomenology of Spirit* narrates the itinerary of consciousness by which it attains to spirit—Hyppolite likens it to an "earthly *Divine Comedy*"—by which consciousness becomes the universal self-consciousness of Being, and to the distinctively philosophical task of a "transcendental logic."[50]

The suspension and refusal of such a judgment is a theme common to Hyppolite and Wahl and had a decisive and lasting impact on Deleuze. For Wahl, judgment was broken by a return to the concrete and by an insistence on the truth-character of nonconceptual and ecstatic existence, communicable by poetry. In his 1962 "Projet d'enseignement d'histoire de la pensée philosophique" ("Project for Teaching the History of Philosophical Thought"), Hyppolite indicates the decisive point on which his project diverges from one such as Wahl's. The discovery of the transcendental is the constitutive moment of the history of metaphysics, it is what enables metaphysics to be delimited from every other form of human inquiry.[51] Wahl argues that existentialism is a new way of posing this problem—one that, rightly understood, ought to pursue investigations of distinct and exemplary existents (Nietzsche, Van Gogh, Rimbaud, etc.) rather than impossible conceptualizations of such existents—and while Hyppolite shares Wahl's concern for the experience of transcendence, he draws a philosophical lesson from it. "There is [in the history of metaphysics] a genesis and a structure of an original style, where an intentional sense engulfed in thought must be rethought and reactivated. The history of philosophical thought therefore offers us a fundamental history, which requires a proper method, and attempts to reconcile genesis and structure."[52] Wahl affirms genesis by affirming the philosophical value of the lives of different existents, but denies the possibility of any reconciliation with conceptual structures. Hyppolite's project, on the contrary, explicitly "refuses both the philosophical nonsense of a purely empirical history and the impotence of a non-historical rationalism."[53] In his "Project," Hyppolite succinctly outlines his distinctive path through and beyond existentialism, accepting the value and importance of concrete experience, of existence, while also insisting on the philosophical task of formulating the concepts and structures of this experience in language, of formulating its logos. Echoing the titles of his two major works—and thereby providing something of a bridge between them—Hyppolite writes that "the genesis and structure of philosophical thought lead to the problematic of logic and existence."[54]

Hegel Contested

When the Second World War began in 1939, Hyppolite was teaching the hypokhâgne course at the lycée Lakanal, just outside Paris. During the war and Nazi Occupation, he moved from Lakanal to the more prestigious lycée Louis-le-Grand and then to the lycée Henri-IV, where he taught from 1941 to 1945 and where his students included both Foucault and Deleuze. Unlike many of his contemporaries and colleagues, Hyppolite seems to have taken no part in the Resistance. Leon Brunschvicg, who had been forced to give up his chair at the Sorbonne and to flee Paris during the Occupation, died in 1944, and after the Liberation Martial Gueroult was named as his replacement. Hyppolite then assumed Gueroult's post in Strasbourg, where he joined Georges Canguilhem. Only a few years later, however, Hyppolite himself was appointed to the Sorbonne, where he would remain until leaving to direct the École Normale Superiéure in 1954.[55] After the war, Hyppolite rapidly rose in prominence in French philosophical circles as a result of his distinctive work on Hegel. As both Alphonse de Waelhens and Émile Brehier noted in their reviews of Hyppolite's *Introduction to Hegel's Philosophy of History*, one of Hyppolite's primary interests during his professional coming-of-age was the problem of teleology, especially as it arises in Hegel's philosophy.[56] During the war, Hyppolite had participated in a series of discussions organized by "three Christian intellectuals": Maurice de Gandillac, Marie-Madeleine Davy, and Marcel Moré.[57] As Étienne Fouilloux has shown, a frequent and important topic of these discussions, and one that intersected with Hyppolite's work on the meaning of history, was the eschatological element in Christianity.[58] The problematic issue of eschatology differentiates Hyppolite's project sharply from three of the most important trajectories within the complicated tangle of postwar Hegel scholarship in France: some authors'—such as Beauvoir and Sartre—utter rejection of eschatology, exhorting human beings to create their own meanings and values; Wahl's work, arguing that existence ought to be investigated in its concrete and empirical contingency; and that of Alexandre Kojève whose prewar lectures were published in 1947, and who put forth a stridently eschatological reading of Hegel.

In 1946 Kojève published a lengthy review of *De la médiation dans la philosophie de Hegel* (*Mediation in Hegel's Philosophy*) by Henri Niel, a Catholic professor at Lyon whose work is exemplary of the religious interpretation of Hegel.[59] Kojève's review, "Hegel, Marx, et le christianisme" ("Hegel, Marx, and Christianity"), is a fascinating blend of criticism and praise that also comprehensively displays the "anthropological" reading of Hegel which was the major competitor for philosophical recognition in postwar France. On the one hand, Kojève argues that Niel, "who finds in Hegel the Christ of the Gospels," inverts the true sense of Hegel's work.[60] It is rightly Hegel that should be found in Christ since, in theological terms, Hegel's God is the post-historical achievement of Man, and his Christ is "the dyad Napoleon-Hegel" ("HM," 39). This comment shows the extent to which Kojève reads Hegel not merely as a philosopher but as the truth—a point he makes at the conclusion of his article when he challenges Niel's own conclusions regarding Hegel's "failure" ("HM," 40ff.). However, on the other hand, Kojève praises Niel for recognizing mediation as Hegel's key philosophical innovation: "to say Mediation is to say Dialectic. [And] . . . Dialectic is the very structure of concrete reality itself . . . To analyze Mediation (i.e., Dialectic) in Hegel's philosophy is therefore to analyze that philosophy itself in its whole concrete content." Niel's book therefore has the rather striking character of being "a perfectly correct summary of the dialectical philosophy" while simultaneously misunderstanding the central notion of mediation ("HM," 21). This somewhat paradoxical situation leads Kojève to significantly expand the scope of a typical book review, since Hegel's "radically atheistic philosophy" can only be saved from Niel's religious misreading through a detailed account of the concrete work of mediation ("HM," 22).

For English-speaking readers who know Kojève primarily or exclusively through the material collected from his 1930s seminars and published in the abridged *Introduction to the Reading of Hegel*, his complex elaboration of Hegel's philosophy, and the command of its diverse parts on display in his review, is both jarring and fascinating. Here is the author who infamously reduced all of Hegel to the relation between the master and slave, ranging over the entirety not only of the *Phenomenology* but of the *Logic* and the *Encyclopedia* as well. Kojève's summary of Hegel's philosophy is organized according to what he calls its three "planes": the ontological, the metaphysical, and the phenomenological. Although the young Hegel initially discovered "the fact of dialecticity" on the phenomenological plane, as love, Kojève's review begins from the other end of Hegel's philosophy ("HM," 28). Where Hyppolite and Wahl agree in prioritizing Hegel's development in terms of a deepening refinement of earlier problems and issues that were never completely abandoned, Kojève agrees with Koyré and insists on the distinctive philosophical achievement of Hegel's mature systematic philosophy. Accordingly, Kojève's review begins its exposition of the Hegelian dialectic not with the phenomenology of the master and slave but rather on the "ontological" plane, with the dialectic of Being ("HM," 22–24). Strikingly, Kojève characterizes the ontological dialectic in terms of the "thesis-antithesis-synthesis" scheme that Hyppolite utterly rejects. "Hegel expresses this 'dialectical' (= trinitarian) conception of real concrete Being also by saying that this Being is not only *in itself* (*an sich*; = Thesis or Identity), but also *in and for itself* (*an und für sich* = Synthesis or Totality)" ("HM," 23). Negativity here effects mediation by temporizing Being, or rather, since Negativity is the temporization of Being and not some external agent, Being is mediated by Negativity, and as so mediated, is the unity of Being and thought that Hegel calls Absolute Knowledge.

From this ontological account Kojève "descends to *the metaphysical plane*." It is unclear what motivates this descent and what relation the two "planes" have to each other, but on this metaphysical plane, "real-concrete-Being is objective-Reality (*Wirklichkeit*)." If the ontological problem is that of Being coming-to-be as Totality, the metaphysical problem is that of Spirit coming-to-know-itself "as it reveals itself to itself" ("HM," 24). Textually, the metaphysical plane aligns with the arguments of the *Encyclopedia* and the later sections of the *Phenomenology*, and it is important to note again that Hyppolite argues that the passages following "Reason" and concluding with "Absolute Knowing" were outside the scope of the initial plan of the *Phenomenology*. For Kojève, the resolution of the metaphysical problem is the work of humanity: "Man in his objective reality is Action. That is to say, he is only real to the extent that he really or 'objectively' *negates* natural reality. And this means," Kojève continues, "that he is *transcendent* with respect to nature" ("HM," 25; emphasis in the original). This transcending Action is the work of meaning which gives value to the world, and in so doing, correlatively shows Action to be Man-in-the-world. The work of meaning reaches its limit—the infamous end of history—when human beings no longer *want to negate* ("HM," 27). This limit is marked by the advent of the Wise Man who comprehends the objectivity of human work. The solution of the metaphysical problem brings Kojève to the third plane: the phenomenological, where the problem is the development of true knowledge by and through "empirical Existence (*Dasein*)." The solution to the phenomenological problem is found in the dialectic of recognition. According to Kojève, this dialectic of recognition replaced the young Hegel's dialectical account of love as Hegel struggled to account for history during the years 1800–1806.[61] Phenomenologically speaking, historically acting human beings are agents who acquire recognition through their transformative—

and therefore negative—actions, a recognition that, when it becomes universal, "constitutes the concrete content of universal history" ("HM," 30). Here a familiar Kojève returns, insisting that

> the evolution of Hegel's thought is completed at the very moment when he discovers (1800) the dialectic of Recognition (*Anerkennen*) or of Action (*Tat*), which he immediately substitutes for the dialectic of love. From that day on, for the remaining 32 years of his life, Hegel did nothing but set forth the diverse complementary aspects of the dialectic, the general schema of which he discovered at the end of his juvenile period. He begins by describing the totality of the phenomenological aspect in his *Phenomenology*. Then, in the *Logic*, he completely analyzes the ontological aspect. Finally, the whole metaphysical aspect is given to us in the *Encyclopedia*. As for later publications, Hegel simultaneously describes in them the phenomenological, metaphysical, and ontological aspects of the various "constitutive elements" (*Momente*) of this same total dialectic which realizes itself and reveals itself as universal history; elements that are political, legal, aesthetic, religious and, finally, philosophical. ("HM," 30–31)

Universal recognition is achieved when the struggle for recognition is resolved by each human being becoming satisfied as "a recognized citizen of a *universal and homogenous State*" ("HM," 34; emphasis in the original). This State has arrived, for Hegel—and for Kojève—with the Napoleonic Empire ("HM," 37). Napoleon completes and thereby brings history to an end, and Hegel, whose philosophy merely thinks the concrete reality of human history, completes and justifies the achievement of Napoleon. It is the philosophical work of Hegel, as historical actor, that completes the work of knowledge by thinking through, knowing, and thereby reconciling the diverse totality of history.

Does the banal observation of the continuation of historical time after Hegel offer an easy refutation of his philosophy? This is Niel's claim, but Kojève is quick to reject it. Nothing—in action or in theory—has occurred since Hegel that is new in the sense of being other and opposed to the historical figures worked through in his philosophy. What has arisen in Hegel's wake is an opposition between two interpretations *of Hegel*—a "leftist" one and a "rightist" one—whose phenomenal action is the concrete chronicle of human activity from Hegel to Kojève writing in postwar France ("HM," 41). The opposition between these two interpretations is a continuation of the struggle for universal recognition, for the satisfaction of universal citizenship, waged now under the banners of liberalism and communism (or Marxism). Hence, according to Kojève's famous conclusion, every interpretation—even one that attempts to be as nonpartisan as Hyppolite's—takes sides in this struggle and thereby is inevitably a piece of political propaganda. And because they are programs for action, these pieces of propaganda place Hegel's texts and their interpreters in the vanguard of present historical action.

The Humanism Debate

On October 28, 1945, less than six months after the end of the war in Europe, and barely a year after the Allied liberation of Paris, Jean-Paul Sartre took to the podium at the Club Maintenant. The crowd was electrified. A vote to create a new national government had taken place only a week before and there was a general sense of optimism, of coming change, of a decisive end to the horrors of the Second World War. Sartre had catapulted to academic fame in 1943 following the publication of *Being and Nothingness*, his magnum opus that would secure his place at the center of French philosophical life. He was also—and perhaps better—known for his fiction and for his plays. Apart from his intellectual and academic prominence, Sartre had also been a member of the Resistance during the German occupation of France, helping to found the Socialisme et Liberté organization and regularly writing for Camus's journal *Combat*.[62] The original title for the lecture according to Beauvoir, "Is Existentialism a Humanism?" reflected Sartre's concern—stated in the opening lines of the essay—to "defend existentialism."[63] This defense is to be made against several quite different criticisms, but two preeminently: those of the communists, who rejected existentialism for its subjectivism which inhibits solidarity, and the Catholics, who rejected existentialism for, in Sartre's words, "denying the reality and validity of human enterprise" and thereby "relativizing all values."[64]

The great majority of Sartre's essay is therefore comprised of an account of the particular features of "atheistic existentialism," and it is only quite late in the essay that Sartre turns to an explicit consideration of humanism.[65] Transforming rather than rejecting the positions of the communists and Catholics, Sartre's essay closes by asserting that "existentialist humanism" is fundamentally intersubjective and that it is in transcending what Sartre earlier called the "human situation" that action becomes hopeful.[66] "Existentialism Is a Humanism" thus attempts to turn the tables on Sartre's critics by appropriating their own term. In his response to the objections made by the Catholics and communists, Sartre shows that, far from existentialist humanism being "bourgeois" or "despairing," its critics' versions of humanism are the dangerous ones—the proximity of Fascism and "failed" versions of humanism in the essay underlines this point.

In the political context of postwar France, Sartre's text was significant not so much for its claim that existentialism is, in fact, a humanism—although, as Sartre notes, in *Nausea* he had been critical of humanism, but there it was precisely that particular kind of humanism which took human beings as "an end and supreme value"—but for its claim that the humanism of atheist existentialism "was both philosophically atheistic and politically communist."[67] Sartre's assertion that his own version of existentialism was a humanism was not so much an attempt to thread a needle between two competing camps as it was the establishment—the throwing down of a gauntlet—of a new position that remedied the deficiencies of both the communist and Catholic positions. It thereby staked out the only proper political position. The result was immediate and forceful: the humanism of atheist existentialism, equally alien and disagreeable to both camps, became a highly visible target for their attacks.[68]

The Catholic philosophical rejoinder to Sartre was relatively slow in coming, primarily academic, and built on an established tradition.[69] The communist response was more popular and more overtly political. Immediately following the Liberation, France was governed by the Provisional Government, which was dominated by a threefold alliance between the French Communist Party (PCF), the socialists, and the Christian democrats (an alliance known as *tripartisme*). Among the most important tasks for the Provisional Government was the organization of a popular vote to elect a National Assembly and a national referendum to allow the Assembly to draft a new constitution. The election and the referendum took place on October 21, 1945, just eight days before Sartre's lecture. An overwhelming voter turnout brought the Third Republic to an official end, gave the *tripartisme* alliance a majority in the new Assembly, and authorized the creation of a new national constitution. This unanimity almost immediately began to fray, however, with Charles de Gaulle resigning from the government in January 1946 (following disagreements with PCF ministers), and the referendum on a draft constitution failing in May. A new National Assembly was elected in June and, following a narrow victory in a referendum on October 13, the constitution of the Fourth Republic was officially adopted. In 1947, the PCF was expelled from the governing coalition in France—in part due to disagreements over policies toward French Indochina and Madagascar, but also in part due to the need for a still impoverished France to avail itself of the funds available through the Marshall Plan, which required the expulsion of all communists from the government.[70] Politically, the expulsion of the PCF from the *tripartisme* governing coalition in 1947 and their subsequent exclusion from the *troisième force* of the Fourth Republic allowed the communists to assume a more directly oppositional stance to the policies of the French government. The cataclysm of the war and the communists' violent resistance to the Fourth Republic's policies (which was encouraged by Stalin) meant that the rhetoric of human rights and the rational goodness of humanity, which were embraced by the Fourth Republic in its alliance with the United States against the Soviet Union, was a particularly vexed point of contention. Practical and political debates surrounding the Universal Declaration of Human Rights, and UNESCO's activities in Europe, as well as more intellectual debates concerning the necessity and moral justification of violence, were all opportunities for the PCF to counter the "bourgeois" and "idealist" humanism of the French government.

At the same time, Catholic politicians and thinkers sought to provide an absolute and transcendental guarantee for the emerging humanism. Between the wars, Catholicism had been an important and vibrant part of French philosophical debates and could count among its adherents major figures such as Jacques Maritain, Gabriel Marcel, and Henri de Lubac, as well as fellow intellectual travelers such as Simone Weil and Jean Wahl, whose work on Kierkegaard placed him in close proximity and conversation with Catholicism. Stefanos Geroulanos has characterized "the fundamental tenet" of prewar French Catholic philosophy as "the idea that no conception of human dignity is complete without a recognition of a spiritual and transcendental dimension to human nature, a dimension that necessarily entails (in the sense of *presupposes*) a recognition of God."[71] This idea is at the center of de Lubac's *Drame de l'humanisme athée* (*The Drama of Atheist Humanism*), published in 1945, the same year that Sartre delivered "Existentialism Is a Humanism." De Lubac's book shares several intellectual touchstones with Sartre's essay—Dostoevsky and Comte, notably—but their confrontation was staged by Gabriel Marcel in his review of *The Drama of Atheist Humanism*, a review which appeared in the Catholic journal *La Vie Intellectuelle* only weeks after Sartre's lecture.[72] The Catholic suspicion was that existentialism—even Sartre's—dispensed with ethical universals and, also, with God. The major touchstone around which the Catholic discussion of humanism revolved was Heidegger's reply to Sartre, the "Letter on Humanism." This discussion was slow to materialize, for political as well as philosophical reasons, and only fully emerged in the mid-1950s, roughly coinciding with the controversial Cerisy colloquium on Heidegger.[73]

Again, the slow development of the Catholic philosophical response to Sartre contrasted sharply with the immediacy and energy of the communist response. The French Communist Party, and communism generally, enjoyed a prestige in France during and after the war that is sometimes difficult to understand, given the relative disregard into which communism has fallen over the last few decades in the industrialized West.[74] At the beginning of the Second World War French communists were divided. The Molotov-Ribbentrop Pact led to the proscription of the PCF by the French government and the communists were directed by Stalin and the Comintern to remain neutral and antiwar, a stance that largely persisted even after the invasion of France and the subsequent installation of the Vichy government. Communist neutrality came to an end with the German invasion of the Soviet Union in 1941, again following the orders of Stalin and the Comintern. Aided by their experiences in the Spanish Civil War, the communist Resistance became a formidable military as well as intellectual force over the remaining years of the war and, bolstered by this notoriety, the postwar PCF adopted the moniker "Le parti des 80K fusillés" ("The party of 80,000 shot") and fared well in the elections of 1945.

If Sartre's lecture was given in the midst of a debate over the proper sort of humanism for French communism to embrace, beginning in late 1947 the debate would shift radically.[75] Articles in the Marxist journal *La Pensée*, contemporaneous with the political expulsion of the PCF from the national government, ceased arguing for a particular "correct" humanism and instead indicted all humanism as bourgeois ideology. In 1948 the communist journal *La Nouvelle Critique*, which advocated a distinction between bourgeois and proletarian science, was founded and provided a space for intellectuals to perform self-criticism.[76] Two of the most prominent participants in the humanism debate with Sartre, Henri Lefebvre and Roger Garaudy, were among the first to undertake this self-criticism and took the occasion to explicitly disavow their former embrace of the now-poisonous term "humanism."[77] The inextricable combination of humanism and bourgeois liberalism was also prominently featured in Lukács's 1948 *Existentialisme ou marxisme* (Existentialism or Marxism?) and in Merleau-Ponty's 1947 *Humanisme et terreur* (*Humanism and Terror*).[78]

Phenomenology, Genesis, and Empiricism

Alongside the humanism debate, another philosophical discussion, begun before the war, was assuming increasing importance. The principal figure in this discussion was Edmund Husserl, whose work was central to the early work of Levinas and Merleau-Ponty, among others. Husserl's

work was particularly esteemed for its rigor, and a number of French philosophers, including Levinas and Merleau-Ponty, but also Jean Cavaillès
and Trân Duc Thao, found in Husserl's work a scientific cast of mind that
was more promising than the work of "existentially inclined" philosophers
such as Heidegger and Jaspers. After the war, in the late 1940s and early
1950s, a window opened into which Husserl's work entered, assuming a
new relevance as the different dominant strains of existential humanism
threatened to descend into irrationalism. Looking back, Jean-François
Lyotard's 1954 *Phénoménologie* (*Phenomenology*), would describe the split
as one between a scientific, rational phenomenology and a distinct but
also all-too-closely-bound irrational, subjective phenomenology.

Lyotard's *Phenomenology* is an important document for assessing the
status of phenomenology—and especially Husserlian phenomenology—
at the beginning of the 1950s. It begins with the programmatic statement that "philosophy must not only be grasped as event . . . but worked
through as thought—that is, as problem, genesis, give-and-take movement of thought."[79] Lyotard writes that phenomenology displays two
"faces": "a strong faith in the sciences drives its program of solidly establishing their underpinnings, and of ultimately stabilizing the whole edifice and heading off a future crisis. But to accomplish this, it must leave
even science behind, and plunge into matters 'innocently.' A rationalist
bent leads Husserl to engage himself in the pre-rational; yet an imper-
ceptible inflection can turn this pre-rationality into an irrationality, and
phenomenology into a stronghold of irrationalism."[80] Phenomenology is
properly philosophy, then, because it most rigorously engages the event
of thought: this is the problem of genesis. The presentation of Husserl
that forms the first part of the book is a careful analysis of the way that
intentionality is discovered by Husserl as "an answer to the question,
'How can there be an object in itself for me?'"[81] This question leads to the
familiar problem of transcendental solipsism and the "lifeworld" in the
later writings of Husserl. Lyotard notes briefly the presence of Wahl in
these debates and characterizes Wahl's position as one that takes "the last
aspect of Husserl's phenomenology . . . as empiricist."[82] For Husserlian
phenomenology, there is an "ineffable belief at the heart of the "passive
presentation" that places the rational recovery of its ineffable ground out
of reach.[83] Lyotard closes with a description of phenomenology as "the
defeat of philosophy, of logos" (in its Husserlian sense), since the origin
is never grasped as such: the ineffable, pre-reflective is, for Lyotard, the
location of the problem of genesis, of grounding.

In the same year that Lyotard published *Phenomenology*, Louis Althusser would ascribe his observation of "the increasingly clear abandonment of existentialism and the 'return to Husserl,' to his [Husserl's]

rationalist theses and to his theory of science."[84] Althusser's judgment is particularly important because, after completing his studies at the École Normale Supérieure in 1947 and passing the *agrégation* in 1948, he returned to the École Normale as an *agrégé répétiteur* and would remain at the École for the rest of his professional life, exercising an outsized importance on the intellectual development of several generations of France's elite thinkers. Althusser was a member of both the Catholic group Jeunesse Étudiantes Chrêtiennes, which he joined in 1937, and the PCF, which he joined in 1948, thus occupying both poles of an intellectual debate at the height of their hostilities (he would resign from the Jeunesse Étudiantes Chretiennes in 1952).[85] Althusser's strong sympathies for the rationalist Husserl were doubtless an important force in the shift of fortunes experienced by various phenomenologists, as evident in their presence in—or absence from—the exposés and theses of the Normaliens at the time. As documented by Edward Baring, these exposés show a sharp increase in references to Husserl—who was absent entirely from the exposés of 1948—in the 1950s alongside a decline in references to Sartre, a downward trend which would continue through the rising interest in Heidegger that accelerated in the mid-1950s.[86]

Lyotard's and Althusser's concerns to some extent reflected a bifurcation in Husserl studies after the war. On the one hand was the strain of French Husserl scholarship that was anchored in works such as Levinas's 1930 *La theorie de l'intuition dans la phenomenologie de Husserl* (*The Theory of Intuition in Husserl's Phenomenology*) and Eugen Fink's pivotal 1933 essay "Die phänomenologische Philosophie Edmund Husserls in der gegenwärtigen Kritik" ("The Phenomenological Philosophy of Edmund Husserl and Contemporary Criticism") a strain that was pivotal for philosophers such as Jacques Derrida who were to engage with the idealist elements of Husserl's phenomenology. On the other hand was a lineage anchored this time by Ludwig Landgrebe, Husserl's assistant prior to Fink, and oriented around Husserl's text *Experience and Judgment*. While the lineage grounded in Fink and privileging the problem of genesis has been fruitfully explored by scholars such as Leonard Lawlor, Paola Marrati, and Edward Baring, similar investigations of the project and reception of *Experience and Judgment* have been lacking.[87] The first printing of *Experience and Judgment* was made in Czechoslovakia just after the death of Husserl in 1938, but it was almost entirely destroyed when the publisher closed in the following year. The book wasn't reprinted until 1948.[88] Its reappearance was greeted with two significant publications by Jean Wahl: "Notes sur le première partie de *Erfahrung und Urteil* de Husserl" ("Notes on the First Part of *Experience and Judgment*") in 1951, and "Note sur quelques aspects empiristes de la pensée de Husserl" ("A Note on Some Empiricist Aspects of Husserl's Thought") in the following year. For "notes," these essays are impressively substantive—each running to more than two dozen pages.[89]

As Landgrebe states in his "Editor's Foreword to the 1948 Edition," Husserl's *Experience and Judgment* is principally concerned with presenting the analytic-descriptive investigations that "contribute to" the phenomenological foundation of logic, and so forms a pair with *Formal and Transcendental Logic*—published in 1929—which was concerned with the "inner sense" of logic generally.[90] *Experience and Judgment* is therefore concerned with pre-predicative experience, the world of passive *doxa* that is prior to the world of *episteme*, of knowledge and cognition.[91] In an essay contemporaneous with the two "notes" devoted to *Experience and Judgment*, "The Present Situation of French Philosophy," Wahl discusses Merleau-Ponty and Levinas, two thinkers who represent the "culmination" of French phenomenological philosophy, and stresses that their work is "directed toward vital and original, concrete and metaphysical conceptions of the real" and that, at least in the case of Merleau-Ponty, this work is "a continuation of Husserl's work in *Experience and Judgment*."[92] In his 1951 "Notes" essay, Wahl characterizes one of the central concerns of Husserl's text as the idea that the necessary intentionality of judgment is a founded intentionality, an intentionality that is founded on a sphere prior to judgment.[93] On the one hand, Husserl argues that, in the pre-judgmental sphere, the "explicative synthesis" is, upon reflection, understood by the distinction between "substrate" and "determination," a distinction that pre-judgmental explication makes possible.[94] This distinction is relative, however, since any determination can itself become a substrate for another explication. However, Husserl then argues "from the genetic point of view" about the operations of experience and finds that there are "absolute substrates" that close off the infinite regress of substratifications in an experience that is immediately explicable.[95] These absolute substrates are absolute not for all possible experience, but for the particular experience of an individual intentional consciousness. The paradigmatic sort of substrate that can be determined as absolute is therefore bodies as "objects of external sensuous perception."[96] In this way, Wahl notes, Husserl's investigations offer "a phenomenological justification for empiricism."[97]

The discussion of explication seems to lead to a division between the passivity of explicative contemplation by which an intuited object is itself explicated, and the activity of relational contemplation by which an intuited object is co-given with its objectively co-present surroundings in what Husserl calls a "plural unity of the affecting."[98] However, Wahl observes that Husserl troubles this easy distinction by noting that the external horizon is conjoined with "the horizon of typical preacquaintance in which every object is pregiven."[99] Wahl characterizes this as a domain that is "intermediary between the passive and active domains, which could be called the domain of active pre-constitution."[100] This domain is that of relational contemplation, of the associative temporal unity of memory and perception, which Husserl characterizes as the relationality of "free imagination."[101] Wahl further notes that Husserl's emphasis on a unity that is prior to judgment brings phenomenology together with the (radical) empiricisms of F. H. Bradley and William James.[102] Having worked through the foundation of predication and judgment, Wahl spends the rest of his essay sketching the several ways that *Experience and Judgment* clarifies the relation between Husserl and Heidegger, while also posing several questions that are raised by *Experience and Judgment*.[103] Ultimately, Wahl notes, Husserl risks "losing the precious acquisitions of ante-predicative realism" in his analysis of the "productive spontaneity" of consciousness, of the cogito, which threatens a return to "constructive idealism."[104] Husserl, Wahl cautions, must not forget the concrete.

In a letter to Wahl, Landgrebe distills to four the numerous questions that Wahl raises quickly in the final pages of his essay.[105] First, Landgrebe affirms Wahl's overall reading and emphasizes a difference between the "idealist program" of texts such as *Ideas* and *Cartesian Meditations,* and the "results of [Husserl's] detailed analyses" that diverge from that program.[106] And he goes on to write that the "historical function" of Husserl's phenomenology could be said to be *"the triumph of idealism over itself through the efforts to think to the limit a theory which had, as its starting point, the subject."*[107] From these global remarks Landgrebe turns to particulars. To Wahl's assertion that the absolute substrate provides a "phenomenological justification for empiricism," Landgrebe replies that this "sensuous Hyle"—which, he notes in parentheses, are "the descendants of Humean impressions"—is "phenomenologically verifiable" to the extent that "all experience is founded on . . . what is encountered," but that accepting hyletic givens as the ultimate elements of sensibility results in a phenomenologically untenable "principle of dissociation" rightly criticized by Erwin Straus and by Merleau-Ponty.[108] The problematic status of the absolute substrate also causes the ambiguity in Husserl's concept of world. On the one hand, the world is conceived idealistically by Husserl as the totality of appearances given to a consciousness, and its concept is the belonging together in unity of all individual beings; it is therefore an absolute substrate since every existent, as such, is "non-independent" in relation to the unity of the world.[109] The world is also immediate presence, however, the horizon of all possible experience, and as such it cannot be rendered as an idealist concept. Landgrebe emphasizes that the sensualist concept of sensibility, according to which the elements of experience are irreducible and absolute, is what prevents the world as horizon from decisively overturning Husserl's idealist concept of world. Finally, Landgrebe defends Husserl's account of deception as the ground of negative judgment against Wahl's assertion of the converse. Negation is not a negative predicative judgment since negation is the experience of a being in the world, which is the experience of a being "menaced by nothingness," an experience that is "the presupposition of the possibility of deception which, in its turn, makes possible the negative judgment." In conclusion, Landgrebe notes that, for Husserl, there is an absolute difference between activity and passivity, and he differentiated between perception as the activity of receptivity and simple affection as "pure passivity."[110]

It is unclear whether Landgrebe's letter reached Wahl prior to the composition of his subsequent essay on *Experience and Judgment*, published in 1952. However, Landgrebe's response provides a useful guide for understanding the significance of Wahl's empirical reading of Husserl's phenomenology. At bottom, it is a question of the absolute substrate. From there, it is a question of the world. Subsidiary to these questions are the questions of negation and of the distinction between activity and passivity.

Wahl's "A Note on Some Empiricist Aspects of Husserl's Thought" begins by acknowledging that Husserl's phenomenology is ordinarily conceived and presented as a theory of essences; in other words, as an idealism. Wahl wants to set aside all idealist presuppositions and instead trace the consequences of the realist presuppositions, the consequences of the realist postulate and the empiricist postulate that it contains. In contrast to Wahl's essay of the previous year which contented itself with a single work which he opposed to the rest of Husserl's corpus, the 1952 essay extends the conclusions of the earlier essay beyond *Experience and Judgment* to Husserl's work generally. Taking up the task of pruning Husserl's idealism, Wahl proceeds from the disclosure of the pre-predicative in *Experience and Judgment* to the articulation of a realist empiricism within Husserl's phenomenology. He begins with the Husserlian exposition of the domain prior to judgment on which intentionality is founded.[111] The realism of phenomenology arises from the demonstration that every mode of consciousness is an intentional modification of an original givenness, the intuition of which phenomenology strives to attain. From this realism arises an empiricism, and Wahl's empirical postulate entails that all judgments are founded on pre-predicative syntheses, on experience as an originary kind of evidence ("EA," 203). Determination is therefore doubled: first, a passive pre-constitution, then an active constitution. Pre-predicative syntheses threaten an infinite regress which Husserl avoids by asserting the presence, "here and now," of the objects of perception (a presence that distinguishes them as such from, for instance, objects of the imagination) ("EA," 204). The "return to things themselves" is therefore the move from *episteme* (judicative knowledge) to the originary apprehension of beings in their originary self-givenness (*doxa*). The pre-predicative is thus discovered by the genetic tracing of pre-predicative evidence back to experience (non-predicative evidence) ("EA," 205).

Evidence and intentionality are indissociable, and Husserl's realism is found by Wahl in his assertion that, in reflection, non-reflective experiences are understood as experiences that were actually had by intentional consciousness ("EA," 205). The pre-given appears not as one or several distinct objects but as a field, the world as a horizon of familiarity from which objects stand out ("EA," 206). Wahl asserts that the priority of passive genesis is gradually developed in Husserl's work but that it appears particularly clearly in *Experience and Judgment.* Moreover, activity and passivity cannot be rigidly distinguished, but their respective roles must be discerned through concrete analysis. Are the ideas of passivity and the unconscious merely limit-concepts for phenomenology? ("EA," 207). The phenomenological sense of evidence is not the same as the scientific one—the *Ideas* makes clear that there is a type of evidence peculiar to each region of being—and the idea of evidence is enlarged by Husserl through an integration of empirical experience as well as affectivity ("EA," 208–9). This broadening is linked to a reflection on Hume's theory of belief, Wahl notes ("EA," 209).[112] There are three consequences of the preceding for the theory of truth. First, the nature of perception entails a fundamental inadequacy according to which the judgment of perception never contains the state of affairs that it designates ("EA," 209). As evidence, truth is always becoming, and the second consequence is therefore that truth is the lived temporality of constituting consciousness. Finally, the truth of judgment, adequation, is distinguished from "veritable being" ("EA," 210).

Wahl next turns to the empirico-real idea of the world. The world is that in which we always already live and act, an absolute substrate that provides the ground for all active cognition. The world is a spatiotemporal horizon that makes everything determinable in space and time without thereby determining them in a particular spatiotemporal system. Thus there is a "pre-world" prior to the formed or categorical world ("EA," 211). And in this world are other egos. This pre-world is the subject of the analyses of *Experience and Judgment* which show that relations are included within experience, a point on which phenomenology agrees with James's radical empiricism. Because the objectivities that are intended in perception are "real, are meant as enduring contemporaneously, objectively," objective time belongs to them as objects ("EA," 212). This will move the investigation from perception to the opposition of perception and memory and to the lived experiences of memory ("EA," 213). Spatial determination arises between the indeterminability of primordial experience and the full determination of scientific knowledge ("EA," 214). Temporal determination is found in protention and retention, the latter being the primary remembrance in which the lived-through is retained in the present and which grounds memory, and the former being the equally primary dissolution of the present as it passes away ("EA," 215). The present is a "streaming present," but it must be completed by the principle of the unity of recollection and the principle of omni-temporality ("EA," 216).

What of the ideas of negation and possibility? Wahl first notes a tension between the phenomenological claim that the domain of consciousness does not have the same diverse perspectives as the world of things and the claim that every variety of reflection is a modification of consciousness ("EA," 216). Negation is something that arises from the pre-predicative and is a modification that presupposes the belief in the world. Similarly, hesitation is the pre-predicative origin of possibility, just as deception is the pre-predicative origin of negation ("EA," 217). The study of reflection, of the activity of the mind, also leads to the study of objects as the unitary objective correlates of unities of cognition. The idea of substance arises from the idea of a substrate in general, every particular substrate being itself relative. Things are then the result of unifying syntheses of perception in the stream of consciousness which grasps objects intentionally as really being there ("EA" 218). The theory of the thing leads to that of the particular thing that is the body of the perceiving consciousness—an existent thing that is a "founded object" insofar as its perception is grounded on the existent soul of another— and then to the idea of nature in which the body of perceiving consciousness is found ("EA," 219). Within nature are found others which allow for the natural determination of objects of culture. Does this idea of the world lead to transcendence, to the idea of God? Wahl wonders. One sense of transcendent indicates that the object of cognition is not contained in the act of cognition, it is "real," immanent. A second sense of transcendent applies to all non-evident cognitions that posit something objective but do not intuit it. This is opposed to a second kind of immanence that is synonymous with self-givenness. Wahl emphasizes that in *The Idea of Phenomenology*, lectures given in Göttingen in 1907 but only published in 1950, Husserl had argued that all transcendence is immanent to transcendental subjectivity ("EA," 220). From the *Cartesian*

Meditations, then, come two ideas: the distinction between the two tran-
scendences (and the assertion of a philosophical confusion between the
psychological given and the transcendent as unclear in itself) and the
idealist affirmation of immanent transcendence ("EA," 221). Finally, in
Formal and Transcendental Logic, perception is defined as the self-giving
of the transcendent. There thus seems to be a dual tendency in Husserl
by which he brings to light the element of transcendence in perception,
only to try then to bring it back to immanence. Wahl voices the characteristic worry that the stress on the pre-predicative might be lost if the
immanence of transcendence is preferred to the empirico-realist results
that make us "respect the phenomenon," that make us apprehend what
is beyond consciousness ("EA," 221).

As Landgrebe writes in his 1952 letter, Wahl's essays are the first
works that do more than just comment on or summarize the arguments
of *Experience and Judgment;* Wahl "pushes further" the problems posed by
Husserl.[113] And Landgrebe was not the only one to respond immediately
to Wahl; in a long note at the beginning of Wahl's first essay, he refers to
certain reservations that Walter Biemel expressed to him via letter concerning Wahl's contention that in *Experience and Judgment* one finds a
"realist" character. It is this contention, that *Experience and Judgment* can
be characterized by "a realist affirmation [that] seems to dominate from
the beginning," that is both the most controversial claim made by Wahl
and the key movement in developing an empirical rather than dialectical
solution to the problems of phenomenology.[114]

Empiricism and Subjectivity

Despite the violent interruption of the Second World War, the foregoing
analysis of Wahl's and Hyppolite's projects in the postwar years shows
each of them reconstituting their projects while also taking account of the
ruptures engendered by the war. For Hyppolite, the postwar years were
a time of increasing notoriety as *Genesis and Structure*—along with scholarly appreciation of his translation of Hegel's *Phenomenology*—became a
textual anchor for those interested in a more faithful, less idiosyncratic
approach to Hegel than that offered by Kojève. At the same time, in his
teaching and his research, Hyppolite was beginning to think through
the problems that would lead to his next great work, *Logic and Existence,*
which appeared in 1952. While teaching classes on Hume, Bergson, and
Kant in the late 1940s, Hyppolite was developing his account of the link
between Hegel's *Phenomenology* and the *Logic,* the link between existence

and its self-apprehended sense which, in contrast to those of other think-ers, Hegel's dialectic was to render entirely immanent.

Wahl's postwar work also largely continued the pursuit of prob-lematics that he had at least begun to develop before the war. The inter-rupted publication of *Human Existence and Transcendence*, coupled with the rapid development of existentialism (in its many guises) during the war meant that one aspect of Wahl's postwar work was the continuation of the conversation that he had sought to begin with his 1937 address: a defense of an existentialism that firmly placed transcendent experience at the heart of any attempt to theorize existence. Wahl's characteristically heterodox interests also made him a central figure in the intellectual re-constitution of France—a role for which his wide-ranging philosophical expertise was well-suited—both at the Sorbonne and through the crea-tion of the Collège Philosophique. These interests also led him into the midst of the renewed interest in Husserl, and Wahl's articles devoted to *Experience and Judgment* show him again championing empiricism—and this time, Hume explicitly—against the ideal reduction of experience.

The debate between Hyppolite and Wahl would not be renewed by them until Wahl's extensive review of *Logic and Existence*, "Une Inter-pretation de la *Logique* de Hegel" ("An Interpretation of Hegel's *Logic*"), which appeared in 1953.[115] That same year, Gilles Deleuze would publish *Empiricism and Subjectivity*. The foregoing has laid the groundwork for reading Deleuze's book not only as a book on Hume, but more properly as an intervention in the debate between Wahl and Hyppolite.[116] Deleuze does not, however, simply choose sides. Although Hyppolite maintains the dialectical account of the development of subjectivity, Deleuze is drawn to his elimination of transcendence. Similarly, where Deleuze finds common cause with Wahl's insistence on the irreducibility of concrete experience, he is considerably less sanguine about the latter's resort to transcendence. The title of Deleuze's book therefore lays out a program: an investigation of empiricism as a philosophical method that resists dia-lectical appropriation, coupled with an investigation of the empirical sub-ject, a non-Cartesian subject, that rejects the insistence on experiences by which the subject is drawn to an unreachable transcendent Whole.

5

Empiricism between Immanence and Transcendence

> So, after the Liberation, the history of philosophy tightened
> itself around us—without our realizing it—under the pretext of
> opening up a future of thought, which would also be the most
> ancient thought.
> —Gilles Deleuze, "A Conversation"

During an interview conducted near the end of his life, in the midst of
a lengthy account of the dissatisfaction that quickly emerged in postwar
France with the phenomenological account of the subject, Michel Foucault abruptly states: "We should also talk about Deleuze. . . . He was interested in empiricism, in Hume, and again in the question: Is the theory of
the subject we have in phenomenology a satisfactory one? He could elude
this question by means of the slant of Hume's empiricism."[1] During his
student years, phenomenology had two faces for Deleuze: the immanent
and dialectical one represented by Hyppolite's reading of Hegel, and
the transcendent and mystical one represented by Wahl's philosophy. As
Foucault indicates in his description of *Empiricism and Subjectivity*—a sly
reference to Deleuze's fondness for Lucretius and the latter's concept
of the *clinamen*—Deleuze sought a way out of the very *problem* posed by
Wahl and Hyppolite.[2] Put another way, *Empiricism and Subjectivity* is something of a graft onto the organ of French academic philosophy—one that
would cut deeply enough into it to obtain an original growth or movement of thinking. The language of the graft is especially pertinent, given
Deleuze's implication within the various apparatuses of French academic
culture.

Gilles Deleuze was born in 1925 and came of age amidst the violence
and disorientation of the Second World War.[3] He spent almost the entirety of the war in Paris, finishing at the lycée Carnot in 1943 and then attending the prestigious lycée Louis le Grand for his *hypokhâgne* and *khâgne*

courses from 1944 to 1946. According to François Dosse, Deleuze subsequently failed the entrance exam to the École Normale Supérieure—not having prepared for one of the subjects of the exam—but was awarded a scholarship to study at the Sorbonne. There he completed his *diplôme d'études supérieures* with a project on Hume that was jointly supervised by Jean Hyppolite and Georges Canguilhem.[4] In 1948, Deleuze took and passed the *agrégation*—placing highly in a distinguished group that included Louis Althusser (who placed second), François Châtelet, and Gilbert Simondon.[5] Throughout his philosophical education, Deleuze availed himself of the myriad opportunities presented by the philosophical community in Paris. In addition to classes and conversations with his generational peers, Deleuze also attended the regular conversational gatherings at Marcel Moré's apartment, as well as events organized at the estate of Marie-Magdalene Davy.[6] He attended the classes of a range of thinkers, including Jean Beaufret, Ferdinand Alquié, and Martial Gueroult, as well as Hyppolite and Wahl.

As discussed above, Wahl had been forced to flee France during the German occupation, and from 1942 to 1945 he taught in the United States at Mount Holyoke College, where he presided over an annual multidisciplinary symposium modeled on the *Décades* held at Pontigny before the war.[7] Upon his return to Paris immediately after the war, Wahl resumed his teaching at the Sorbonne with a course based largely on one of Heidegger's courses taught in Freiburg in 1928–29.[8] Wahl also taught courses on British philosophy and pre-phenomenological existentialism which, according to Deleuze's friend Olivier Bevault d'Allonnes, they both attended regularly.[9] Significantly, it was most likely in part due to Wahl's urging that Bertrand Russell delivered his 1947 lecture at the Sorbonne on "The Principle of Individuation," a topic that would inform Deleuze's work throughout his career.[10]

Just as Wahl's attempt to gather the leading philosophers of Europe around the common question of subjectivity and transcendence in 1937 was violently upended by the war, so too were Hyppolite's professional activities caught up in the larger events of the war. During the war Hyppolite taught in various lycées in and around Paris, including the lycée Henri IV, where he taught the *hypokhâgne* course from 1941 until 1945—which Deleuze attended. In 1945 Hyppolite received an appointment at Strasbourg, but he taught several courses at the Sorbonne over the next several years, including seminars on Hume in 1946–47, on Kant in 1947–48, and on Bergson in 1948–49.[11] Deleuze's presence in the latter two classes is impossible to confirm—indeed, the course on Bergson took place after Deleuze had passed the *agrégation* and taken up his first teaching position in Amiens—but it is doubtless the case that Deleuze took the Hume class and that it formed the basis for his *diplôme*.[12]

Hume in France

Despite Foucault's confident claim, it is difficult to know why Deleuze chose to write and publish a monograph on Hume, given the context of French postwar academic philosophy. However, this choice was, of necessity, a product of both personal choice and institutional factors, chief among them being the *agrégation*. As Alan Schrift's work has shown, the *agrégation* exerted enormous pressure on the intellectual trends, research programs, and debates of French academic philosophy throughout most of the twentieth century.[13] Although the precise reasons for the presence of a particular author or work on the *agrégation* are impossible to specify, as is the extent to which inclusion on the *agrégation* influences scholarly production, it is certain that a philosopher's appearance on the *agrégation* entails an inclusion of that philosopher in the general milieu of the contemporaneous philosophical discussion. Students preparing for the exam must be offered the opportunity to take advanced classes on the included authors. Moreover, those charged with teaching those classes often incorporate the authors into their own work. Introductory texts appear; and, for non-French authors such as Hume, appearing on the *agrégation* often occasions new translations of their works.[14]

Although he had appeared on the *agrégation* previously, Hume enjoyed a noteworthy run of appearances from 1946 until 1959, roughly corresponding to the tenure of the sociologist Georges Davy as the president of the jury for the *agrégation*.[15] During those years, Hume's *Treatise of Human Nature* was the text assigned for the (English) oral exam, and in 1946, 1947, 1950, 1951, 1958, and 1959 Hume's work was also assigned for the written portion of the exam (which required familiarity with the work of Hume as a whole). In 1946, both books I and III ("Of the Understanding" and "Of Morals") of the *Treatise* were required for the oral exam, in 1947 book II ("Of the Passions) was added, and then, from 1948 until 1959, the first three parts of book I ("Of Ideas in General," "Of the Ideas of Space and Time," and "Of Probability and Knowledge," omitting the fourth part, "Of Skepticism") were required. Hyppolite's course on Hume, offered at the Sorbonne in 1946–47, would almost certainly have required Deleuze to become familiar not only with all three books of the *Treatise* but with Hume's other works as well.

Empiricism and Subjectivity is an example of the consequent effects of the inclusion of a philosopher on the *agrégation*. This is not to say that Deleuze's philosophical interest in Hume was forced on him by his academic preparation, but rather that Deleuze's professionally necessary study of Hume provided him with a ready vehicle for beginning his own philosophical work. Hume's persistent presence on the *agrégation* ensured that work on his philosophy possessed a certain contemporary currency, since he became a figure drawn into the orbit of the ever-developing milieu of philosophy not only in Paris, but also in lycées throughout France. Understanding Deleuze's reasons for focusing on Hume is a complicated task that requires us to look beyond his own text and consider it in its relation to the philosophical circumstances and debates that formed the context of its publication. However, *Empiricism and Subjectivity* itself can serve as something of a guide for such an investigation insofar as its own arguments and claims situate it, more or less explicitly, in relation to other debates and lines of inquiry.

At first glance, *Empiricism and Subjectivity* appears to maintain only a tenuous relation with other French Hume scholarship of the twentieth century—and seems to have entirely different philosophical concerns from the dominant philosophical debates in postwar France. Instead of engaging with that tradition, *Empiricism and Subjectivity* engages three mutually ramifying but distinguishable philosophical problematics: the problem and project of a science of man which Deleuze inherits through Hyppolite's reading of Hegel, but which also connects to larger debates within French phenomenology and, in particular, with the renewed interest in Husserl that followed the war; the existential critique of rationalism and other debates occasioned—directly or indirectly—by Wahl's work on transcendence; and, finally, the problem of ontology—ultimately traceable to Heidegger's prewar influence—which Deleuze inherits from both Hyppolite and Wahl, but which will emerge as a central concern only in the "Conclusion" of *Empiricism and Subjectivity*. This concern with ontology would become much more important in Deleuze's work immediately subsequent to *Empiricism and Subjectivity*—both the two essays that he published on Bergson in the 1950s, and his course on "What Is Grounding?"[16] It is a concern that helps make sense of the shifting orientation of Deleuze's thought in the 1950s as he turns from a "science of man"—the term with which he concludes his review of Hyppolite's *Logic and Existence* in 1954—to a theory of what human beings, as natural beings, can do.[17]

The preceding has made it possible to sketch the various institutional forces and influences that shaped *Empiricism and Subjectivity*; the polemical focus of the book is Hyppolite's presentation of Hume and empirical knowledge. Although Hyppolite's course notes are lost, the substance of his account of Hume can be gleaned from the extensive discussion of empiricism and empirical knowledge in Hyppolite's 1952 *Logic and Existence*. There, the "empirical" is explicitly contrasted with the "speculative." According to Hyppolite, empirical judgment is restricted to the mere observation of a state of affairs, while speculative thought is able to think the content of a judgment in its "passage" in a way that facilitates and permits the mutual identification of logos and subject. Although Hyppolite does not limit his analysis of empiricism to Hume, it is with explicit reference to Hume that he contrasts the empirical judgment and its work constituting empirical subjectivity with the speculative judgment and its constitution of the judgment that "the Logos is nature."[18]

> By means of the negative judgment, empirical thought negates merely itself; it negates the objectivity of its connections. It leads to the empirical subjectivity of experience, such as Hume brought to light. There are connections, but they lack significance; they are subjective, contingent, and always susceptible to being negated. But this negation of empirical thought is reflected merely into empty tautology: A is A, B is B. This thought, which is given the content, cannot engender it, cannot think mediation, which is the genesis of being as the self. Empirical thought observes, it does not comprehend passage; it indicates merely in this oscillation between affirmative and negative judgment what is required of speculative thought, the reconciliation of the empirical connection, which is rich in content but without reflection (affirmative judgment), and of the tautology, which is indeed reflection but reflection without content (negative judgment).[19]

This account of empiricism is challenged, as discussed in chapter 3 above, in Wahl's preface to *Vers le concret*. In the *Phenomenology of Spirit*, what Wahl calls the "concrete" is argued to be the most empty and vacuous sort of thing; "the most general and abstract." However, Wahl is quick to note that this dismissal is famously accomplished only by way of language: when I write 'now it is night,' the empty falsity of this statement is revealed with the subsequent dawn. But there is another interpretive course that can be followed here: perhaps Hegel's example shows not the emptiness of the concrete, but rather the impotence of language to engage with it.[20] What is common to both the idealist and the realist is what Wahl calls the "shock" of the concrete or, later, following James and Whitehead, the "thickness" (*épaisseur*) of the world. For the idealist, this shock is one that activates the intelligence, spurs scientific inquiry, and ultimately fashions a scientific whole from discrete parts.[21] For the realist, however, the world is not to be analyzed into the terms or parts grasped by the intelligence, but is rather to be allowed to be apprehended in its complexity by thinking. The realist, thus un-"shocked" by the world, is thereby capable of thinking the world without intellectual apprehension—in the double sense of grasp and anxiety.

The realist is therefore an empiricist, in Wahl's terms, insofar as the thought of the given renounces the knowledge of the whole as the *terminus ad quem* of the knowledge of the parts of the world. These parts may be parts of wholes, but there is no totalizing Whole that would be explicated by them. One degree of empiricism takes from rational idealism the thought of the Whole as a kind of necessary and unquestioned presupposition for any empirical study. But in Hume—and this is one of the few mentions of Hume in all of Wahl's work—there is an empiricism of a "second degree" in addition to that of the first.[22] This second degree or meta-empiricism insists on the irreducible density of the given while at the same time abolishing the very notion of the Whole. The result, Wahl insists, is a realism that is both immanent and transcendent. It is transcendent insofar as there is a pull toward a totalizing sense of the given—a Whole—and it is immanent in its equally strong pull toward distinct but non-atomic parts. In terms of the discussion of Hume in chapter 1 of *Empiricism and Subjectivity*, the immanent character of second-degree empiricism is most clearly found in the understanding whose principles determine every perception as a distinct existence and cannot find any evidence in perception for any connection between them. This is Hume's atomism. But to this atomism is joined an associationism; the mind which has become subject orders experience according to principles. This associationism acquires a transcendent character when the freedom of the imagination is harnessed to purposeful determination. Hume does not posit a Whole but, Deleuze will insist, human beings act with what he calls a "finality," or purposiveness.

Deleuze's first published work on Hume was not *Empiricism and Subjectivity*, but rather a book coauthored with André Cresson and entitled *David Hume: Sa vie, son oeuvre, avec un exposé de sa philosophie* (*David Hume: His Life, His Work, with an Explanation of His Philosophy*). This book was published in 1952 as part of a series of introductions to philosophers written by Cresson for a series edited by Émile Bréhier. As published, much of the book appears to have been completed by Cresson before his death in 1950, but two sections of the book—"L'Oeuvre" and "Complément sur l'oeuvre"—appear to be exclusively or primarily authored by Deleuze.[23] While these sections offer little in the way of discussions or arguments that might enhance or extend the much more substantial text of *Empiricism and Subjectivity*, published one year later, the text does include Deleuze's distinctive formulation of Hume's chief philosophical problem: "How does the human imagination become a human nature?"[24] The formulation of this problem serves to distinguish Deleuze's *Empiricism and Subjectivity* from other French scholarship on Hume, as well as enabling Deleuze to use his text to intervene in philosophical discussions of immanence and transcendence.

When *Empiricism and Subjectivity* was published in 1953, there was relatively little contemporary work on Hume published in France—much of the academic oxygen having been sucked up by phenomenology. Hume's work itself had had little impact on philosophical debates in France at the time of its publication in the eighteenth century, and in the first half of the twentieth century there were only a few books and articles devoted to the Scotsman's work.[25] Perhaps most significantly, especially for Deleuze, Hume was only infrequently mentioned by Wahl, an absence made doubly significant given Wahl's interest in Anglo-American philosophy generally. In *Pluralist Philosophies*, Hume earns only a glancing mention within a larger quotation from William James: "The true direction of philosophical progress," writes James, "lies, in short, it seems to me, not so much *through* Kant as *round* him to the point where now we stand." Continuing on in the voice of the pluralists, Wahl writes that "Hume does not fully satisfy us nowadays; but if we must correct him, let us do so while we remain his disciples."[26] Thus Wahl notes the signal importance of Hume for recent philosophical initiatives, while at the same time funneling him—as he does so many philosophers in his book—into the stream of ideas that pours forth in James's pluralism. Wahl's mention of Hume is emblematic of a pattern: when Hume did appear amidst the philosophical debates of pre- and postwar France, it was generally insofar as his work was an influence on another philosopher of greater importance—as was the case with Gaston Berger's 1939 essay, "Husserl et Hume." Monographs on Hume in French were virtually nonexistent prior to the publication of Cresson and Deleuze's introductory text and André-Louis Leroy's more significant 1953 book, *David Hume*, which appeared in the Presses Universitaires de France's "Les Grands Penseurs" series.[27] Leroy had worked extensively on Hume for decades. In 1929 he published *La Critique et la religion chez David Hume* (*Critique and Religion in David Hume*), and during the 1940s he completed several modern translations of Hume's work, including the first complete translation into French of the *Treatise of Human Nature* in 1946.

Empiricism and Subjectivity appeared in the same year as Leroy's study *David Hume*, and while both are centrally concerned with Hume, Leroy's book is a work about Hume, whereas Deleuze's book is an attempt to utilize Hume for specific philosophical ends. Significantly, *Empiricism and Subjectivity* includes virtually no references to texts other than Hume's own—a trait that would become something of a feature in Deleuze's work on historical philosophical figures and can serve to obscure the influences at work in them. Nonetheless, the preceding argument has made clear that Deleuze was not composing his work in a vacuum. Animated by the divergence between his teachers Wahl and Hyppolite, Deleuze turned to Hume's empiricism as—in James's words—a way to go *round* not just Kant but the entire post-Kantian tradition, especially the various strains of idealism that could be traced back to Hegel. Deleuze's distinctive use of Hume can be assessed by noting how it intersects, to greater and lesser degrees, with Leroy's more conventional exposition.

Leroy's *David Hume* appeared in a different series of the same publishing house (Presses Universitaires de France) as *Empiricism and Subjectivity*.[28] It is a comprehensive and detailed monograph—no doubt of immense help to students studying for the *agrégation*—and its purpose is clearly to articulate Hume's philosophy as comprehensively and accurately as possible. A brief consideration of the structure of its presentation of Hume's philosophy can thus serve to differentiate Deleuze's own approach to Hume. Leroy's book is considerably more extensive in its discussion of Hume, and of its four parts—bracketed by introductory material and a concluding chapter on Hume's relation to contemporary philosophers and philosophical issues—Deleuze's own book seems to most closely track the first part: "Activities and Elementary Structures of Human Nature."[29] Both Deleuze and Leroy emphasize in their opening lines that Hume's project is the constitution of a new science of man, and both emphasize that Hume's project is fundamentally moral or practical in character. However, where Deleuze rapidly converts the project of the science of man first into "the substitution of a psychology of the affections of the mind for a psychology of the mind" and then into the question: "How does the mind become a human nature?" Leroy's presentation models Hume's own method and follows an order drawn from Newton's method in his *Principia* (to which Leroy explicitly analogizes Hume's *Treatise*): "First separating the forces of nature through an analysis of phenomena in order then to demonstrate, from these forces, the still unobserved phenomena, but with laws that are expressed in useful mathematical formulas . . . The first two books of the *Treatise* study the supports [*resorts*] of human activity, passions, and understanding; the third exhibits the concrete spectacle of the moral and political world."[30] This method leads Leroy first to analyze the progression of Hume's philosophy from perceptions through the imagination to custom and judgment, and then on to finality before applying the results of this analysis to "customs and human institutions" in the fourth part of his book.

Deleuze's question, one that is not given as such in Hume's texts, leads him to immediately contrast morality and knowledge in each of his first four chapters before turning to the distinctive character of his own concern with Hume in chapters 5 and 6 and concluding his book with the same topic that closes Leroy's first chapter: finality.

In comparison with Leroy's more conventional presentation of Hume, it becomes apparent that *Empiricism and Subjectivity* is not merely a different *presentation* of Hume, but something other than simply a book *on* Hume. As the preceding chapters have made clear, Deleuze's book—and this is signaled already by its title—is an intervention into the debate between Wahl and Hyppolite, principally concerning the constitution of the subject. For the former, human experience ineluctably yields experiences of transcendence that proffer either an ineffable and mystical experience of union with a Whole (*transascendence*) or an equally ineffable ecstasy (*transdescendence*) of the sole and sovereign individual, freed from every external yoke. For Hyppolite, on the other hand, the transcendent impulsion of the individual exhibits an internal structure, manifest in language and governed by negativity, which permits the rational reconciliation of the individual and the Whole—a reconciliation that is accomplished in the properly philosophical speech or logos of Hegel's logic. *Empiricism and Subjectivity* shows that Deleuze is disquieted by both of these alternatives. His question—which animates the entirety of *Empiricism and Subjectivity*—is whether experience and, with it, human nature, can be constituted without a negative moment or element that precipitates the subject into transcendence of one kind or another. The vindication of empiricism as a secure ground of human knowledge obviates the necessity of its rational recuperation. The status of the empirical—and of empiricism as a philosophical project—lies at the crux of Deleuze's concerns.

Going Round Kant

Deleuze, who would later become famous for his "portraits" of various philosophers, already shows a concern for how to approach the work of another philosopher in *Empiricism and Subjectivity*. The opening section of chapter 6, "The Principles of Human Nature," makes two intertwined arguments. The first is a justification for an argument made at the end of chapter 5: that the "fundamental claim" of empiricism is that there is no theoretical subjectivity, that the two different kinds of principles that together constitute the subject ultimately resolve into the priority of one kind of principle (the practical) over the other (the theoretical) (*ES*, 117). This resolution is achieved by recourse to finality—"the agreement of the subject and the given"—which will be the focus of the final sections of *Empiricism and Subjectivity* (*ES*, 126).[31] There, the identification of finality as the unity of the principles of association and the principles of passion will also be shown to determine it as a distinctive feature of empiricism generally. Hence, the second argument that Deleuze makes at the outset of chapter 6 concerns how one can distinguish empiricism from rationalism. The groundwork for this argument is the determination of the terms by which a philosophy may be questioned and critiqued. Although in later works Deleuze will offer various overlapping accounts of how to properly address the work of another philosopher, it is important to avoid anachronism and to pay strict attention to what he specifically says in *Empiricism and Subjectivity*.

According to Deleuze, there are two erroneous ways of criticizing a philosophy: by criticizing it as the intention of its author or by criticizing it as the response to a particular set of problems. The former is a psychological error. It begins with a "fictional psychology" of the author, and it mistakes their philosophical project for the product of a personal wish (*ES*, 119). Although it appears to critically engage a philosophical project, this approach in fact is no more than a kind of game whose consequences are at best unclear and at worst null. Simple-minded assertions such as: Hume "wants to pulverize the given," beg the question: supposing this is true, what follows? This sort of psychological criticism is therefore not so much wrong as empty; to stop at the criticism of the intentions of a philosopher never digs further down in order to expose the situation or the conditions that motivated specific philosophical choices. The second erroneous way of criticizing a philosophical project amounts to an attempt to remedy the defects of the first approach precisely by providing an account of the problems to which the theory is a response, and therefore not a subjective preoccupation. Deleuze calls this a "scientific error" (*ES*, 119). To say that a philosophical project is motivated by particular problems is to establish a historical relation: such and such a philosophical project arises because certain problems had arisen and were prominent at the time of its composition. Establishing the historical antecedents of a philosophical project is a kind of scientific undertaking, but it does not establish what is properly philosophical in the project. To say that there are historical problems with which Hume is engaged and which he is attempting to resolve with his philosophy is a historical assertion that may shed some light on Hume's project, but according to Deleuze, this approach fails to engage with Hume in a properly philosophical manner.

Given these negative depictions of philosophical criticism, one may well ask: what then, for Deleuze, makes for a proper philosophical criticism? His answer to this question has two parts. First, he asserts that "a philosophical theory is a developed question and nothing else." Clearly this echoes the second, erroneous, approach to a philosophical project—that of the scientist, who asks after the historical problems that motivated the development of a particular philosophical theory.[32] What the historian leaves to the side, however, is the way that any philosophical project or system, *as philosophical*, is a subordination and determination of what Deleuze rather vaguely expresses as "things." Every philosophical theory is a conceptualization of the thinkable. It unfolds not across a given that is thinkable but *as* a given that is thought; the given is determined according to the question that roused thinking to action. Deleuze thus conjoins to the first aspect of philosophical criticism a second aspect: the critique of a question and the development of that question are "one and the same" (*ES*, 119). If, as Deleuze insists, a philosophy or philosophical system is not to be taken as an attempt to solve a problem or problems, but rather as an effort to develop a question as far as possible, then that philosophy contains its own critique insofar as it thinks the given in terms of *its* originating question *rather than according to another*. A philosophical question "subordinates and submits" the given to itself, and through this submission, the elements of the given "reveal an essence, a nature." A different philosophical question, forced by a different problem, would reveal a different essence, a different nature. A philosophical project's degree of rigor can thus be measured by the distinctiveness of its revealing submission of the given to its question.

Deleuze illustrates this polemical and abstract definition of philosophical critique with a relatively brief account of Descartes's philosophical project. This selection is not by chance. Descartes is the paradigmatic figure of the French philosophical tradition, and was much more familiar to Deleuze's readers than was Hume. He is also, however, the acknowledged forefather of contemporary rationalism and, especially, phenomenological rationalism. The capsule description of Descartes offered in implicit contrast to the depiction of Hume is therefore also a description of the difference Deleuze sees between the rationalist question and the empiricist question. Descartes's question is: how can knowledge be certain? This problematizes the given by recasting it as doubtful. The *cogito* is then developed out of the original question and also becomes a tool or path for its development, which, "at its limit," states the conditions of the problem to which it responds in the form of doubt (*ES*, 119). Less tersely, Deleuze is arguing that what distinguishes Descartes's philosophy, what makes it valuable or interesting, is that Descartes uses his question (how can knowledge be certain?) to craft a tool by which he obtains a refashioning of the given that provoked the original question. Philosophical thought does not emerge fully formed from the idle musings of the philosopher; it emerges in the midst of a world that has always already been determined in certain, sometimes multiple, ways. The force of philosophical thinking activates and motivates a question that reconceptualizes the world according to different determinations. The outcome of any philosophical questioning is therefore not an absolute determination of the world—because such an "answer" would imply both an objective or absolute existence of the question and, correspondingly, an ability of the question to get outside itself—but a *useful* and therefore *practical re-determination*; one that, at a minimum, reconceptualizes the previous determination of the world. Every philosophical question, every philosophical system or theory worthy of the name, undertakes such a re-determination of the world.

In the case of Descartes, this re-determination attains the limit of its question in doubt. What makes doubt the limit of Descartes's question? Because Descartes's question is about certainty, about the elimination or at least containment of doubt, the methodical deployment of doubt defines his philosophical system by marking the frontier within which knowledge can be cultivated and preserved. Doubt facilitates the division between knowledge and the unknowable as well as all the attendant determinations of this division. The establishment of this frontier is immediately problematic—and thus subject to criticism—according to the very question that motivates it, then, because doubt shows the conditions of the question and so exposes the possibility of another equally rigorous question.

This account of philosophical practice and critique allows Deleuze to justify what had been, at the beginning of *Empiricism and Subjectivity*, merely an assertoric or postulated characterization of Hume's philosophy. Empiricism is, first of all, the philosophical attempt to account for knowledge without recourse to anything other than the given. It is, therefore, first of all a dualism. The world is given—as what occasions thinking—and so is the subject who not only knows this world, but whose thinking determines the world in a manner other than the way that the world is given as determined. "The empirical duality is between terms and experience, or more exactly between the causes of perceptions and the causes of relations, between the hidden powers of Nature and the principles of human nature" (*ES*, 122).[33] The psychological and sociological conditions for Hume's question are foreclosed to inquiry. They are impossible to determine, since such a determination would allow for any number of empirical philosophical systems. However, it is possible to distinguish empirical from rationalist philosophies: the essential feature of the latter is the assertion that "*relations are derived [decoulent] from the essence of things*" (*ES*, 123; emphasis in the original). The two most prevalent characterizations of empiricism, atomism and associationism, both of which account for the given in such a way that relations are *not* derived from the essence of things, are then nothing but the "implications" of Hume's empiricist question.

Such a definition of empiricism requires that the traditional distinction between empiricism and rationalism be rethought, and here Deleuze takes up James's advice, echoed by Wahl, to go *round* Kant. According to the "classical definition proposed by the Kantian tradition," Deleuze writes, empiricism is distinguished by the fact that it argues that knowledge both begins from and is derived from experience (*ES*, 121). Applied to Hume, however, this interpretation immediately encounters two problems. First, Hume argues that knowledge is only ever the means to some practical activity; the epistemological question is a subsidiary, secondary question. The second problem with the Kantian account of empiricism is that, for Hume, experience is not constitutive. In Hume, the term "experience" refers either to a collection of distinct perceptions (and these are the effects of principles) or to conjunctions of past objects, in which case experience functions as a principle but not as the source of principles (*ES*, 121). In whatever way the Kantian definition of empiricism is specified, it fails to identify the distinctive cast of Hume's question, which inquires into the way the given comes to be known: how is the subject constituted in the given?

According to Deleuze, one of the signal achievements of Kant's critique of empiricism is to have engaged Hume's philosophy precisely at the level of the problem of the agreement between the principles that determine the given and the principles that determine the subject who knows the given. The question of the determination of the mind as a subject is the question of how the imagination becomes a faculty. What is it, though, that justifies this substitution of the imagination for the given? In Hume, the imagination is not a faculty of the mind, nor is it a kind of predetermined mental space that ideas occupy; the imagination is the name of the undetermined ensemble of ideas.[34] Hume's question requires that the given be determined merely as determinable and ideal (made up of ideas), but neither determined nor systematized (since this is what Hume's question is seeking to explain). According to Hume's empiricism, then, the given, imagination, becomes a faculty—that is, it becomes determined and systematized—when "a law of the reproduction of representations, a synthesis of reproduction, is constituted under the effect of principles" (*ES*, 124). In other words, the given becomes a known world when it is lawfully synthesized in and along with a determinate subject.

Deleuze notes that Kant's Critical philosophy also begins from the given, from the determination of the undetermined but determinable imagination.[35] Where Hume's question was determined by the need to explain the way that two different things (subject and given) could exist in a relation, Kant's question in effect argues that any such dualism that begins from the separation of the subject and the imagination makes their accord conceivable only as an "accident," as something occasional and not at all systematic (*ES*, 125). To remedy the apparent impasse of such a dualism, Kant's critical rationalism begins from the determination of the given as "a set of phenomena . . . that can be presented as a nature only by means of an *a priori* synthesis. . . . This is why criticism [*le criticisme*] is not an empiricism" (*ES*, 125). For the rationalist, the lawfulness of subjective, worldly knowledge arises not from the fortunate accord of different principles, but rather from a transcendental synthetic activity that secures the accord of thinking and the imagination.

Kant's critical rationalism is developed into the absolute idealism of Hegel, and Deleuze would have learned this development in the teaching of Hyppolite. But he also learned of another "resolution" to the problems of empiricism from Wahl, who, as discussed earlier in chapter 4, was closely engaged with Husserl's *Experience and Judgment* at roughly the same time that Deleuze was preparing *Empiricism and Subjectivity* for publication. Husserl, like Kant, proposes a rationalist solution to the problem of the determination of the lawfulness of the given world. In an appendix to *Experience and Judgment*, he offers a phenomenological solution to what he regards as Hume's empirical skepticism.[36] According to Husserl, this skepticism is not only the result of an inability to obtain valid judgments of causality about relations of fact; it also reflects dissatisfaction with any psychological explanation and justification of such judgments. Since psychology is itself a science, and hence reliant upon judgments that can only be validly grounded philosophically, Hume does not resort to psychologism. In *Experience and Judgment*, Husserl offers a rationalist solution to Hume's problem by rehabilitating the status of principles of probability and arguing that, phenomenologically, they have a status equivalent to relations of ideas, not facts. "[Hume's] failure here was inevitable because he did not make clear to himself the essence of purely phenomenological analysis in opposition to the psychological and, in connection with this, because he did not clarify the nature of the rational justification which is possible in the phenomenologically realizable domain of the relations between ideas."[37] Within the limited scope of the probable, Husserl argues that judgments are made not on the basis of psychological formations or laws, but on the basis of the given itself.[38] Phenomenologically, then, empirical skepticism is overcome through the phenomenological reduction that insists on the rationality of the given and thereby avoids the danger of lapsing into the psychologism to which empiricism seems prone.

In this regard, the quote from Hume with which Deleuze introduces his discussion of Kant's critique of empiricism is especially important. Deleuze writes that for Hume reason is an "instinct [that] arises from past observations and experience," but he wonders further *"why past experience should produce such an effect, any more than why nature alone shou'd produce it?"* (*ES*, 121–22; emphasis in the original). For Husserl, the retention of the past is rationally given, but, Deleuze writes, Hume notes that this very givenness must be explained and therefore concludes that, since it can't be, the operations of reason should be understood not as transcendental causes but as effects. The genetic analysis of the operations of reason is either rationally undecidable or it reduces to a psychological problem. This enables Deleuze to assert that empiricism is not interested in the phenomenological problem of genesis (*ES*, 122).[39]

Just as the debate between Wahl and Hyppolite provides the problem that orients *Empiricism and Subjectivity,* so the debates surrounding phenomenology that were contemporaneous with its writing provide its context—especially with regard to the problem of subjectivity. Deleuze does not engage directly with the postwar wave of Husserlian phenomenology in France; however, the problem of psychologism and the particular, non-transcendental way that Hume's philosophy avoids it, would have been—for its author as well as its readers—a problem indissociable from the problematic of postwar phenomenology. Deleuze's approach to Hume, perhaps influenced by the work of Gaston Berger and Wahl, is concerned with the problem of psychologism from the outset, but is careful to map out an approach to the problem—beginning in the very first paragraph of the book—that steers away from the phenomenological justification of objective knowledge and science.[40] Similarly, Deleuze's book will close with a chapter on finality which has as its backdrop the phenomenological privileging of intentionality.

Setting Hume to Work: The Opening of *Empiricism and Subjectivity*

Stylistically, there is an interesting and telling tension in the first chapter of *Empiricism and Subjectivity.* There is no preface or introduction to the text, leaving the first chapter to fill the role of orienting the reader to the problem or problems that will be taken up by the book. And, indeed, the first chapter seems to perform this duty admirably, guiding the reader through its points by way of a series of explicitly stated questions, a series that begins with the second sentence: "What is his [Hume's] fundamental project?" At the same time, however, the apparent disjunction between the text and the dominant contemporary philosophical debates in France makes it unclear *for whom* these questions are questionable. Is the book intended to introduce its reader to Hume? To critique Hume's philosophical system? Or to critique one or more of its themes? In fact, in a way similar to Wahl's works on other philosophical figures, *Empiricism and Subjectivity* obliquely introduces Hume's philosophy into an already existing philosophical problematic. The preceding considerations of the chief philosophical problems prior to and contemporary with the book's composition—those problems with the most academic relevance at the time of the publication of *Empiricism and Subjectivity*—provide an indispensable guide to answering the question: *for whom* is the problem developed in *Empiricism and Subjectivity* a relevant and important line of thinking? Briefly: the one who follows the questions laid down by Deleuze, beginning from the one that asks about Hume's fundamental project, is the one who takes seriously the possibility of a counterclaim to the project of phenomenology.[41] And, by extension, this counterclaim is an intervention in the larger debate between Wahl and Hyppolite concerning the necessity of transcendence in any account of human nature. No phenomenologists are cited anywhere in *Empiricism and Subjectivity*. Hume, however, is not an unknown figure in debates concerning human nature: Berger's work notes his importance for Husserl, empirical knowledge and judgment are important for Hyppolite's exposition of speculative knowledge and judgment, and—on Wahl's reading—Hume is an important precursor for the pluralism of William James.

Deleuze defines Hume's fundamental project as a *psychological* one that nonetheless makes possible a *science* of man. *Empiricism and Subjectivity* begins with the problem of the psychological in order to elaborate a *non*-phenomenological resolution that nonetheless makes possible scientific knowledge. Deleuze implicitly asks if phenomenology might go astray precisely in the way that it rejects psychologism, a way that leaves unquestioned the claim that the mind is the object of a possible scientific philosophy. The substitution of a psychology of the mind's affections by Hume makes such a scientific understanding possible by providing a definite and consistent field for thought. At the same time, this reorientation of philosophical thought away from the Kantian or idealist question of the a priori constitution of the knowing human being distinguishes empirical philosophy from its rationalist rivals.

Empiricism and Subjectivity opens with an assertion: "Hume proposes to make a science of man" (*ES*, 1). Indeed. The same assertion opens the first chapter of André Leroy's contemporaneous introduction to Hume.[42] But Deleuze immediately goes on to ask: "What is his fundamental project?" It is a "choice," a "substitution" of a psychology of the affections of the mind for the "unconstitutable" psychology of the mind.[43] This entails a shift from subjective introspection to objective historical analysis insofar as history is the largest possible collection of data pertaining to the affections of the mind. "Society" is what allows for the organization of history into a body of knowledge; it is that in which individuals act and also that which demands from those individuals a kind of homogeneity without which history could neither arise nor persevere. The "content of the project of the science of man," history, "has rejoined the condition that makes a knowledge [*une connaissance*] possible in general: the mind must be affected" (*ES*, 2). This is to say that a science of man is conditioned by the distinction, the specific difference, of its object (which in this case, is the subject). Man is the content of history, insofar as history is necessarily about man, but man is also the product of history—not in the sense of being its outcome, but in the sense of being given definition, a specific difference, by history. Without history, there is no content for a science of man, and without the scientific determination of man, there is no history as a body of knowledge. Where to start then? Deleuze begins by laying out a chain of equivalences: the mind is the idea in the mind, the idea in the mind is the given, and the given is experience, a collection of ideas. The mind is then a collection of ideas. What—or, better, how—is this collection determined, differentiated, given a nature? History is the content, the collection; but the subject is this collection become distinguishable.

Among the most important lines of the first chapter of *Empiricism and Subjectivity* are the following: "The essence and the destiny of empiricism are not linked to the atom, but to association. Essentially, empiricism does not pose the problem of an origin of the mind, but the problem of a constitution of the subject. What's more, it envisages the latter in the mind as the effect of transcendent principles, not as the product of a genesis" (*ES*, 15). As Wahl had argued as early as *Pluralist Philosophies*, the contemporary, neo-Humean empiricism that gets *round* Kant insists on the separation of relations and their terms.[44] This separation is crucial for the anti-Hegelian philosophical efforts of Bertrand Russell, G. E. Moore, and others because it breaks the motor of the dialectic and thereby prevents the idealist incorporation of each term into a single Whole. The dialectic relies upon the identity of a term, A, intrinsically possessing the relational and associative property of negation, of not being not-A. Dialectical negation—as Hyppolite recognizes in his reading of Hegel—is thus able to move from A to not-A without any other suppositions and then synthesize them before redeploying negation in order to obtain yet another term. This movement is poorly figured as one of "thesis, antithesis, synthesis"; such an understanding misses what is most important for both Wahl and Hyppolite (and Deleuze): the fecundity of an idealist system such as Hegel's is only possible if the relation of negation is a part of the identity of each term. When Deleuze privileges "association" over the "atom," or the term, he is making the point that what is powerful in empiricism is not the multiplicity of terms, but the fact that this multiplicity is maintained as such by a denial of any necessary association of terms. For empiricism, terms are associated differently—not according to an intrinsic relationality.

Deleuze's insistence that Hume understands the subject as an effect of "transcendent principles" and not as the result of a "genesis" marks the difference not only between Hume and phenomenological approaches to the subject, but also between Deleuze's deployment of Hume and the more traditional interpretation given by Leroy. In Leroy's book on Hume, he notes that "for Hume, the original simple qualities of human nature are not only atoms-perceptions . . . [but] are also the laws that are expressed in their [the atoms-perceptions'] organization into more or less complex systems." However, Leroy's presentation of Hume's account of human nature follows a genetic itinerary: from impressions of sensation and reflection (perceptions) and ideas, to their relations and the resulting "progress of the imagination."[45] To this "play of natural relations," Leroy then adds an account of abstract general ideas and general rules, of custom, and of the resulting formation of judgment and belief.[46] Finally, these elements are traced to the spontaneous generation of the ordered structure of nature and the mind which then studies the physical world (part 2), the mind itself (part 3), and creates a world for itself (part 4). One of the first tasks of Deleuze's book is therefore to make clear—in a somewhat polemical fashion (although, again, the targets of this polemic are revealed only obliquely)—that while the subtitle of the book may invoke Hume, it is the title of the book that indicates its central problems.

Returning to the opening lines of *Empiricism and Subjectivity*, Hume's "science of man" is defined and determined by what Deleuze calls a "choice." Hume chose the problem of formulating a "science of man," of coming to an understanding of "human nature." In order to do so, Hume found himself compelled to reject the more traditional psychological investigation of the mind itself—because such an investigation would lack the consistency and objectivity of a properly scientific study—and instead was correspondingly forced to undertake an investigation of "the affections of the mind" (*ES*, 1). Deleuze repeats or restages

Hume in a milieu dominated by phenomenological and other rationalist attempts to formulate a science of man by first arriving at a determination of the human mind.[47] The specific difference of Hume's empiricism that makes Deleuze's restaging valuable is Hume's rejection of the very possibility of a determination of the mind itself and his focus on the mind's affections. These affections can be differentiated into two kinds: the passional and the social. But each of these types of affection also implies the other: society affects the mind insofar as the mind is capable of acquiring passionate dispositions toward society and others, and passions affect the mind insofar as they determine the mind to make use of the social in order to be satisfied. History, which shows the internal unity of these affects, is therefore Hume's first concern as a moralist and also as a sociologist. What Hume describes as the condition for a valid science of man—that the mind be affected—is also, Deleuze notes, the condition for "knowledge in general." The mind cannot itself be the object of science because the mind has no intrinsic and objective nature. A science of man is made possible by, and is grounded on, the study of the affective action by which a mind acquires a (human) nature and the question of what principles can be found that give to the affections their distinctive character. One must begin with the concrete, not with the concretized.

The novelty and importance of the way that Deleuze introduces and situates his engagement with Hume is further illustrated by his prioritization of the social and political over the apparent priority of the epistemological and psychological in Hume's *Treatise*.[48] The *Treatise* is divided into three books: "Of the Understanding," "Of the Passions," and finally "Of Morals." Typical presentations of Hume's philosophy, including Leroy's, see in this order an order of priority. Thus, in Leroy's *David Hume*, the first three parts are devoted solely to the first book of Hume's *Treatise*, the fourth part treats both the second and third books, and a brief "Conclusion" discusses the relevance of Hume's empiricism to the projects of several other philosophers. The effect of such an ordering is to make Hume's empiricism appear to be a genetic account of the way that the given structures of human cognition give rise, in combination with the passions (feeling, sentiment), to morality and social action.[49] Leroy can therefore write that morality is what most interests Hume, and can insist upon Hume's role as an analyst rather than a moralist "who would want to convert his readers to the practice of virtue," while further claiming that Hume is interested "in the structure and function of the organism."[50]

Deleuze's approach to Hume questions not only whether such an "organism," human nature, is given in Hume but asserts that, in fact, it cannot be given because there is no "constant" or "universal" human mind. "The mind has no nature." Hume does, however, argue that there is a constancy to human nature and, significantly, that it is this constancy which enables history to serve as a kind of propaedeutic to moral philosophy, since the constancy of human nature entails the ongoing validity of historical moral examples. But the question is whether this constancy is that of a given entity that navigates the vicissitudes of its historical situation or whether it is instead concrete pressures, the affections, whose actions yield a particular kind of entity. According to Deleuze, Hume, in contradistinction to the dominant tradition of Western philosophy, as well as to contemporary phenomenology and idealism, argues that the only science of human nature is one that is developed on the basis of a psychology of the mind's affections.

The justification of the reversal of the traditional problem of the genesis of human nature is the subject of the brief second section of chapter 1 of Deleuze's book.[51] Like the first section, the second relies on material taken from relatively late in Hume's *Treatise*. Deleuze asks: if Hume is a sociologist, historian, and moralist prior to being a psychologist, why then does the *Treatise* begin with psychology, with the understanding? The answer is that, as an analyst, Hume breaks down the process that he is studying into its component parts without thereby rejecting or losing sight of the inseparability of those parts, similar to the way that Muybridge's film studies analyze moving bodies into their momentary poses without taking those poses to be separate entities.[52] Passion and understanding are, for Hume, two parts of the human mind and so can be treated separately by the analysis of it, but this analysis does not yield two equally constituent parts. The later sections of the *Treatise* clearly show that although Hume began the book with an analysis of the understanding, the sole function of the understanding is to "reflect interest," and this discussion therefore has the exclusive function of explaining the "meaning" of the question of how the mind becomes a human nature (*ES*, 2). The first two sections of chapter 1 of *Empiricism and Subjectivity* together provide the frame for the whole chapter which, in turn, gives an orientation to the argument of the remainder of the book.

The entirety of the first chapter of *Empiricism and Subjectivity* gives an explanation and justification for the substitution of a different kind of psychology—one of the affections of the mind—as the only kind suitable for philosophical investigation. This justification, pursued through an artful reworking of Hume, will, surprisingly, conclude in a kind of dualism. The development and analysis of this philosophically interesting dualism then occupies the remaining chapters of *Empiricism and Subjectivity*, with the central chapter, chapter 4, providing an example, a kind of case study of it. The argument of the first chapter is broken into five sections—indicated by double line breaks—that vary significantly in length. These sections can be further subdivided into two parts. In the first part, comprising the first three sections, Deleuze provides an introduction to the entirety of the project of *Empiricism and Subjectivity*. In the second part, composed of the remaining two sections of the first chapter, Deleuze justifies the separation of understanding and passions—understanding can be studied separately, but it is subordinated to the passions—in order to establish the relative priority of the latter over the former. The overall aim of the opening chapter is announced by its title: "Problem of Knowledge and Moral Problem." Deleuze aims to show that while Hume seems to prioritize the first problem, this is only because, "bizarrely," before being a psychologist, and in order to be a psychologist, one must first be a moralist, a sociologist, and a historian (*ES*, 2). In fact, it will become apparent that Hume prioritizes the latter problem, that of morality. The first two sections of the first chapter, together forming only the first two pages of the text, establish this dualism, while the remaining sections develop it and examine the relations between knowledge and morality.

The first section re-situates the very problematic of psychologism. Although transcendental phenomenology famously begins with a criticism of psychologism, it nonetheless accepts psychology's determination of the mind as an entity with a really determinable essence.[53] Hume objects to this determination as a false problem—the mind of itself has no essence and so cannot form the object of a science—and substitutes a new problematic which, he argues, is capable of scientific apprehension: a science of the affections of the mind, of those affections by which the mind acquires determination. Deleuze reminds the reader that Hume shows that the mind is affected by two kinds of principles that nonetheless implicate one another, thereby constituting a single object for scientific investigation. Again, this is the importance of Deleuze's statement that "to be a psychologist one must first be a moralist, sociologist, and historian" (*ES*, 2). The problem of psychologism remains null without the prior work of determining the forces—and their principles—that determine the mind. Hume's question, "how does the mind become human nature?" is the question that must precede any psychological investigation. Only then can psychological questions acquire scientific determinacy.

The second section, even briefer than the first, is an interjection that operates in a twofold way. First, it qualifies the argument of the preceding section. Second, it does so in a way that legitimizes Deleuze's appropriation of Hume by situating his approach in relation to a much more common reading of Hume, one that Deleuze refers to again and again in *Empiricism and Subjectivity* as he denounces various misunderstandings and misrepresentations of empiricism generally and of Hume specifically. The assertion that Hume's primary question concerns human nature risks the appearance of dispensing with what is arguably the best-known aspect of Hume's philosophy: his associationism. Does Deleuze's restaging of Hume amidst contemporary debates yield an unrecognizable Hume, one that has been distorted to meet Deleuze's own philosophical ends? Deleuze situates Hume's associationism in two ways. First, on Hume's own terms, associationism, a term which describes the operation of the understanding, is always directed to the socialization of a passion. And this implies, secondly, that passion and understanding are the component forces of the single affected mind. Insofar as the understanding is tasked specifically with the socialization of the passions, it has problems that appear to concern it alone. However, Deleuze emphasizes that the understanding always plays its part within a larger context. Associationism and the entire problematic of the understanding therefore have a secondary status in Hume's philosophy. Emphasized in this way, Deleuze simultaneously legitimates his deployment of Hume within the problematic of contemporary philosophy by privileging the question of the constitution of a science of the human mind and, conversely, legitimates the empirical project itself by reinvigorating distinctive components of Hume's philosophy such as associationism and the operation of the understanding.

The third section of the first chapter picks up the thread of the argument that Deleuze began in the first section—before the qualifying interruption—and takes up Hume's discussion of the imagination, something that, for Hume, is identical both to the mind and to ideas. But that isn't all. Deleuze goes on to identify the idea with the given, and the idea *as given* is identified with experience. Therefore, "the mind is given" (*ES*, 1). The given is the starting point for scientific investigation; the mind, as given, is "the totality [*ensemble*] of the actions and reactions [of ideas]" (*ES*, 4). "*Ensemble*" is used judiciously here by Deleuze—he writes that he means it "in the most vague sense"—as a term that names both a collection, a multiplicity, and the unity of that collection, its wholeness, without subordinating or coordinating the particularity of its elements within a pre-given framework or structure (*ES*, 3). One of the analogies here—utilized by both Hume and Deleuze—is to the theater: the mind is an ensemble of ideas, not a container for them, in the same way that a play can be put on without a theater, as in, for instance, a guerilla production. The given is the ensemble of the determinable that is as yet undetermined. It is difficult to apprehend because the "delirious and fantastic" workings of the human mind, the unrestricted linkages of ideas that constitute their determinate possibilities, overflow and surpass the regularity of the mind.[54] The given can be attained only by subtraction from the determined mind, an operation that yields not a determinate faculty or operation, but only the determinable condition(s) for such determinations. The human mind is a determinately ordered collection of ideas, an association of them, and nothing else; its condition is a multiplicity of determinable ideas, an ensemble of indifferent connections. If the imagination is the indifferent ensemble of ideas, then the mind, as its determination, is the distinct unity or association of those ideas.

According to Hume, the determination of the chaotic imaginative mind is achieved by three distinct principles that together constitute association: resemblance, contiguity, and causation. Deleuze draws from this a decisive point: what determines the imagination *surpasses* the imagination.[55] If the given is undetermined in itself—and it is so for virtually every strain of post-Cartesian philosophy—then it must acquire determination from elsewhere, and what's more, the principles that determine the given must be such as to allow the subject, itself an effect produced *in* the mind, to surpass the mind. Deleuze is anticipating here a part of his later discussion of the subject, and he is following Hume's discussion in T.1.1.3 quite closely. Deleuze's point allows him to make clear what he calls "the unique foundation of empiricism: it is because human nature in its principles surpasses the mind that nothing in the mind surpasses human nature; nothing is transcendental" (*ES*, 5). According to the empiricist, the mind acquires its specific determination from principles that give form to the specifically human mind—individual human minds are not absolutely self-determining or self-constituting—which means that the scientific study of the mind has no need or capacity to go beyond the mind and its constituting principles. Because the mind is, for Hume, the determination of the imagination by principles, and this constitutes the entirety of its determination, there is nothing in the determined mind that accounts for its determination. The mind certainly possesses a power of determining, but what it determines is in each case ideas; the mind's power of determination is in each case always already determined as the effect of the three principles. Every transcendental psychology is void from a scientific perspective.

As Deleuze explains, it might seem that the principles could or even should be grasped in their active power in order to explain and justify the determinate becoming of the imagination (*ES*, 6–7). This is the aim of every appeal to the transcendental. But empiricism understands the mind as the effect of principles on the understanding and therefore as constitutively unable to attain any transcendental purchase. The transcendental impulse of the human mind is especially apparent in judgments of belief or causality. Indeed, it is always possible for a non-empirical cause to be *thought* by way of analogy—for instance, one can believe in a transcendent God, and that God can be thought of as the cause of the harmony of the world (*ES*, 6). In each case, some element or elements of empirical knowledge serve as the model for the connection of the transcendent and the empirical. However, Deleuze continues, such a "transcendent" conception of cause, or its attendant belief, is not the proper object of "philosophy as a science of man" (*ES*, 6). Philosophy is no less determined by principles than any other activity of the human mind and these principles are known by their effects, by their power of determining the mind to have a distinctive (human) nature. When philosophy turns from the determined mind to the power that determines it, the mind attempts to go to the cause of which it is only the effect. To be the object of a science, something must be capable of being *known*, it must be rendered determinate by the action of the principles. The principles themselves, because they cannot be known as such an effect, are therefore essentially unknowable. A "science of man" must therefore eschew any analogous reasoning beyond what is given as determinate. A cause, in itself, is not capable of being known; it is known only in its effect.

What, specifically, is the effect of the three principles that determine the mind? Tendency, figured in three ways: as general ideas, as substance and mode, and as relation. When the imagination is determined, one idea guides thought to another as delirium gives way to the mind. However, the imagination persists along with the mind. Even when determined by principles, the imagination remains fantastic; it never vanishes completely. Tendency never completely abolishes novelty, and the continual possibility of delirious association necessitates the development and deployment of corrective rules whose function will be to differentiate knowledge from fantasy which has merely borrowed "nature's clothing" (*ES*, 7). If the imagination, under the determining effect of the principles, retains an active power, the determined mind is itself passive. Resemblance, causality, and contiguity are associations or tendencies that are determined not by the mind but by principles; the mind "feels," "perceives," "contemplates" these determinations, these links, but it does not constitute them for itself. Deleuze calls this the "coherent paradox" of Hume's philosophy: subjectivity surpasses itself and yet, despite this surpassing, remains passive (*ES*, 8). The thinking mind becomes a subject according to the determining action of the principles. The subject is itself therefore an effect and nothing else—it is an "impression of reflection" (*ES*, 8).

If, as Hume claims, "human nature is the sole science of man," then this science has two different "inspirations": atomism and associationism (*ES*, 9). The atomistic inspiration concerns certain determined ideas of the mind, "the ideas of space and time," which are the simplest or elemental ideas of the understanding (*ES*, 9). The associationist inspiration gives rise to a science of the practical whose object is the tendencies that are determined by principles that surpass the mind (*ES*, 9). Deleuze argues that these two inspirations, together, constitute Hume's empiricism. Of the two, associationism is the easiest to attribute to Hume insofar as it is concerned with precisely those tendencies that are the effect of principles upon the mind. But the former of the two, atomism, is less clearly justified. For Deleuze, its justification is strictly negative: the mind in itself is an atomistic collection of ideas that only acquires an objective nature under the effect of the principles. Considered apart from the associative tendencies that organize it into something with a distinctive nature, the atomized mind cannot be the object of any psychological science. Given this, Deleuze claims that "all great [*bons*] authors agree" that there can be no psychology of the mind, simply. However, there are two possible ways of accounting for the determination of the mind that can make it into an object of psychological science. The first is the path of materialism: to argue that the mind acquires determination under the effect of matter or the body. Hume is "sympathetic" toward materialism but chooses a different explanation for the mind's determinate nature.[56] Hume substitutes for matter the principles of association, "a psychic equivalent of matter," and in so doing selects what Deleuze calls "the most difficult or the most daring choice" (*ES*, 10). It is important and daring because it separates Hume both from a materialistic theory of mind and from a transcendental, Kantian account. Hume argues for principles that are external to the mind but nonetheless mental.

Quid Facti?

At the outset of the fourth section of the first chapter of *Empiricism and Subjectivity*, Deleuze declares that Hume's philosophical problem must be taken up and investigated anew (*ES*, 11). The foregoing discussion has identified the problem, but has not answered the question of what motivates Hume's question of how the mind acquires or becomes a nature. Section 4 therefore asks: *quid facti*? What are the facts that show or provide evidence for the claim that the mind does in fact have a nature? This question is an eminently empirical one, but it also provides yet another example of the way that Deleuze intends to go *round* Kant to get to Hume insofar as the *quid juris* and *quid facti* arguments are central to Salomon Maimon's critique of Kant.[57] For Maimon, Kant's account of the schemata is not sufficient to overcome the radical difference between a priori concepts and a posteriori content. This failure then casts into doubt Kant's assertion of the existence of a priori synthetic judgments in mathematics and physics. Kant's Critical philosophy thus fails to answer both questions: *quid facti?* and *quid juris?* Insofar as Kant's riposte to Hume's empiricism was predicated on the answers to both these questions—for Kant, Hume had failed to recognize the transcendental conditions that make experience possible (*quid juris?*) and had failed to recognize the existence, in mathematics and physical science, of a priori synthetic judgments (*quid facti?*)—Maimon's critique revitalizes Hume's empiricism.[58] The *quid juris* question assumes a secondary importance for Hume's philosophy since he is an empiricist; the mind is determined by principles, but this determination admits of no transcendental justification (*ES*, 11). The *quid facti* question therefore takes on a doubled importance: not only must the facts of experience justify Hume's claims, but these facts must also show the fruitlessness of the *quid juris* question. Deleuze, in *Empiricism and Subjectivity*, in effect accepts Maimon's diagnosis of the failure of Kant's system, but rather than shore up its defenses, he instead abandons the transcendental and returns to Hume's empiricism, "the most difficult or the most daring choice."

In the preceding three sections, Deleuze has shown that Hume answered the *quid juris* question by postulating principles that determine the mind to have a nature. Hume thereby dismisses the very possibility of any scientific investigation of these principles themselves in favor of an investigation into their determinate effects. It is this dismissal that motivates Kant's account of the schemata as what secures concepts and content—an answer to the *quid juris* question that Maimon found unconvincing. Maimon doubted Kant's claim that there were, in fact, a priori synthetic judgments and thought that, as was the case with the *quid juris*, Kant had not fully overcome Hume's skepticism. For Deleuze, the *quid facti* requires a recapitulation of the preceding analysis "on another level." The question is now whether there are actual judgments that "transcend or surpass" experience, and of course, there are. When I affirm, for instance, that it is a fact that the sun will rise tomorrow, this judgment asserts something that goes beyond experience, a fact that is part of a distinctive practice—"the fact of knowledge"—that is "transcendence or surpassing" (*ES*, 11). It is the activity of a subject; to be a subject for Hume requires that the imagination be determined as a faculty, to have acquired the determinate tendencies that constitute human nature.

The "fact of knowledge" is "transcendence or surpassing; I affirm more than I know, my judgment surpasses the idea. In other words: *I am a subject*" (*ES*, 11; emphasis in the original).[59] The fact of knowledge is therefore a "practice" of establishing relations between ideas, but these relations surpass the ideas of the mind (whose sources are always particular impressions). Deleuze thus describes experience as having "two inverse senses" (*ES*, 11). On the one hand, there is the experience that corresponds to an idea: the observed collision of two billiard balls. On the other hand, there is the experience of the necessity of the anticipated consequent movement of the balls. The latter aspect of experience is no less given than the first, but instead of being given in the mind it is given as a practice of the mind (*ES*, 11–12). The surpassing of the given idea in the mind, by the mind, occurs not because of a ready-made transcendental structure of the subject but because the mind is affected by principles that constitute the subject. The idea of the colliding billiard balls provides the occasion for the inevitable surpassing of that idea by principles that constitute the subject precisely through this inevitable surpassing of given ideas. Ideas in the mind have a twofold relation. Deleuze expresses this relation of ideas with corresponding impressions and general ideas (by which they are taken up) as follows: "In every case, rather than the criterion of the idea being negated, it is the negation of the idea that serves as a criterion; the surpassing is first and always grasped in its negative relation with what it surpasses. Inversely, in the structures of surpassing, the mind finds a positivity that comes to it from the outside" (*ES*, 12–13). It is the negation of a specific idea such as the colliding billiard balls— the fact that this idea is insufficient to generate the idea of a necessary causal relation between them—that allows such general ideas first to be grasped, while it is the absence of any determining idea for such general ideas that gives the principles of the mind their positivity.

This argument brings Deleuze to a brief discussion of perhaps the central reason for investigating and reinvigorating Hume's empiricism at a time when rationalism—either in the form of Hegel or Husserl—was ascendant. Hume distinguishes between impressions of sensation and impressions of reflection, both of which give rise to ideas. However, in the case of ideas—such as that of necessary connection—the corresponding idea is first given not by a pair of impressions (the billiard balls before their collision and after, for instance), but by these impressions being taken up by the mind, which is always already qualified by external principles in such a way that the impressions are thought or known as conjoined by the mind. Thus, "the proper role of the impressions of reflection, as effects of the principles, is *to qualify* in different ways the mind as a subject. What is then unveiled from the affections, is the idea of this subjectivity" (*ES*, 13; emphasis in the original). And, Deleuze emphasizes, this marks the difference between Hume's philosophy and rationalism. The latter uses representation to figure the world according to what are properly mental determinations. It externalizes the effects of the principles that give to the mind its nature as subject. In doing so, "rationalism . . . abolishes from philosophy the meaning and the comprehension of practice and of the subject" (ES, 13–14). Hume, on the contrary, preserves the distinction between mental determinations and external objects, thereby leaving to philosophy neither the task of explaining the determinative relation of one to another (Kantianism), nor the consequent task of unifying the world according to the determinations of the mind (Hyppolite's Hegel), but rather the ethical task of investigating the nature and practice of the constituted subject.

The stark separation between empiricism and rationalism also separates the former from the phenomenological problem of genesis. It is associationism, not atomism, that ultimately distinguishes the originality of Hume's empirical project. Deleuze emphasizes that, for Hume, there is little interest in the question of the origins of the mind, and Hume is instead more attentive to the impressions of reflection, to the determining effects of the principles on the mind. "The mind is not subject; it is subjected" (ES, 15). The key point here is that the question of how the mind becomes a subject is not the question of the origin of the mind. The problem of the origin of the mind would entail an (empty) inquiry into *why* the given is subject to principles that would go on to trace the development of this subjection from the ensemble of the given through the constitution of the determined and determinate mind. By taking idea and impression as qualifications rather than original determinations, empiricism avoids transcendental speculation and simultaneously opens to philosophy the practical, non-representative aspects of human nature.[60] This rejection of the phenomenological problem of genesis brings with it a new problem, however, one that was live for Hume and which Deleuze will only answer much later in *Empiricism and Subjectivity*.[61] Briefly stated, the problem is how the subjected mind acquires the capacity to affirm itself as a distinct and individual subject, as a self. The empirical self is both a mind, a collection of ideas, and a subject, the determination of those ideas by external principles.

Practice before Epistemology

The most striking—and, for Deleuze, "important and principal"—statement in Hume's *Treatise of Human Nature* is: "'Tis not contrary to Reason to prefer the destruction of the whole world to the scratching of my finger" (ES, 18). This indictment of Reason as impotent to bring about ethical communities and conclusions echoes Wahl's early dissatisfaction with the various philosophies of Wholeness. In the fifth and final section of the opening chapter of *Empiricism and Subjectivity*, Deleuze addresses the two "modalities" of human nature. He has already shown that Hume's associationist empiricism orients philosophy away from the rational speculations regarding the a priori structure of that nature. But now Deleuze argues that Hume's concern with the understanding, with reason, is only the result of his primary concern: morality. The system of the understanding and the system of the passions possess several correspondences, Deleuze notes, but these correspondences do not establish a strict parallelism between the two systems (*ES*, 16–17). As the quote about reason's inability to practically prefer a minor injury to the destruction of the world makes clear, the domain of practice, of the practical, is not determined by reason (*ES*, 17). To be sure, "Reason can always be applied, but it is applied to a preexisting world, it supposes an antecedent morality, an order of ends" (*ES*, 18). The *Treatise* may begin with the problem of reason, of theoretical knowledge, but this question acquires its importance only because theoretical knowledge is not practically effective. Hume's primary question, and the principal motivation for his philosophy, is concrete, practical. How, then, is the concrete related to the theoretical?

The practical and the rational are both forms of practice: in the latter, the function of general rules is to provide an analysis of what is known and to compose a whole from parts; in the former, the general rules determine human beings in relation to already constituted wholes (*ES*, 21–22). The rational action of a subject may operate to determine the physical system exhibited in part, for example, by the motion of colliding billiard balls. The practical action of a subject engages the world analogously, but instead of analyzing wholes—an activity that Deleuze repeatedly emphasizes cannot, of itself, yield subjective action—the subject, constituted by practical principles, engages in deliberate action. "Without a doubt, the principles of morality, that is, the original and natural qualities of the passions, surpass and affect the mind, just as the principles of association do. The empirical subject is firmly constituted in the mind by the combined effect of all principles" (*ES*, 19). Belief and influence—the subject's surpassing of the given—are, however, proper to the principles of association. The analogous surpassing of the practical by the principles of morality would be the retroactive inference of an ethical quality for a given affect. Using Hume's example, which Deleuze quotes, we feel a person to be virtuous because their actions arouse particular pleasures in us; we certainly do not draw an inference from that feeling to their character. "Morality admits the idea only as a factor of its circumstances and accepts the association as a constituted element of human nature" (*ES*, 20).

The absence of inference in practical reasoning is the reason why, for Hume, "history must be construed as a physics of humanity" (*ES*, 16–17). Moral reasoning finds its purchase only in constituted cases. "Reason can always be brought to bear, but it is applied to a preexisting world, it presupposes an antecedent morality and order of ends" (*ES*, 18). The problems of ethics are therefore different from the problems of the understanding: the latter seek to form inferences from cases; the former seek to systematize and order the affections displayed by humanity in accordance with the ends that are constitutive of human nature. The science of man is therefore a twofold task: it is concerned with properly applying the operations of the understanding, on the one hand, and properly orienting the operation of the passions on the other. This difference accounts for the merely apparent analogy between the two operations. Ethics, the science of man concerned with the passions, is "inventive" (*ES*, 21–22). There is nothing to analyze into parts in the history of human behavior. That history is instead a kind of recipe-book to be used for creating or inventing a "system of action" that will organize the passionate actions of a society's members according to ends that are judged to be good or right for that society.

* * *

Deleuze concludes the first chapter of *Empiricism and Subjectivity* by describing the dualism of Hume's science of human nature: the relation and difference between the "two species of the genus affection": the effects of passion and the effects of association.[62] These two kinds of effects form what appear to be parallel systems, one of morality and one of the understanding, with a lengthy list of correspondences that only together can explain the determination of the imagination which, without their action, "would remain fantasy" (*ES*, 16). For Deleuze, these correspondences are of less interest than the question of "which of the two determines the other as material for philosophy" (*ES*, 17). The *motive* for Hume's philosophy is moral, "Hume is above all a moralist, a political thinker, a historian" (*ES*, 17). Although the *Treatise* begins with the system of the understanding, this system only acquires its determination as the problematic object of a question insofar as something exceeds or "escapes" the domain of reason and can thereby put it into question. The strange fact that "it is not contrary to reason to prefer the destruction of the world to a cut on my finger" shows that there is "a lack of accord between ideas and the objects that they represent" (*ES*, 18).[63] Thus, reason asks about its nature only given the existence of a world; morality is established as primary through a kind of dialectic of skepticism and positivism: "the positivism of passion and morality produces a skepticism of reason; this interiorized skepticism, having become a skepticism of reason, produces in turn a positivism of the understanding, conceived *in the image* of the first, as the theory of a practice." There are therefore "two terms" of the "genus affection": "moral affection and surpassing, which is a dimension of knowledge" (*ES*, 19; emphasis in the original). Although the principles surpass the mind which they affect and determine, the subject that believes, the subject of knowledge, also surpasses the given.

It is in this kind of surpassing relation, one that is the "image" of the affective action of the principles, *inference*, that the problem of principles first arises. Association is a constituted element of human nature for morality, but it is a constituting element (the only one) for the understanding. This entails further that there are two sorts of practices, two kinds of activity that characterize determined and determining human nature. The practice of the understanding is the determination of extended Nature, the determination of the relations between objects each of which, in itself, could be linked to any other. The general rules that determine this activity are "applied" in such a way that Nature is gathered into a collection without thereby becoming a Whole. The practice of morality is a converse determination. Moral determinations are exclusive, they are partial in the sense that ideas are determined as preferable to others and therefore as exclusive. The practice of morality, then, is not the application of general rules whose determination secures a collection, but rather the invention of a different sort of determination, a "schema," that would overdetermine the exclusive determination that is given and permit exclusive determinations to be gathered into a collection, a society (*ES*, 22). General rules are therefore different in their activity according to whether they are deployed in the surpassing activity of the understanding or in the integrative activity of the moral world. Insofar as the latter has been shown to be the proper starting point for Hume's philosophy, despite the apparent priority that the *Treatise* grants to the system of the understanding, the second chapter of *Empiricism and Subjectivity* turns to an analysis of the general rules as they are deployed in the world of culture.

Conclusion

The first chapter of *Empiricism and Subjectivity* inserts Hume's empirical philosophy not only into debates surrounding the promise of Husserlian phenomenology but, more generally, into the debate between Wahl and Hyppolite concerning the possibility of a science of man. In broad strokes, Deleuze may seem to side with Wahl, and indeed, on some of the central issues he does: going round Kant (via a Maimon-inspired critique) in order to rehabilitate a system of understanding in which relations are external to their terms—an atomism—thereby preventing any dialectical ontology; separating the system of understanding from ethics, the system of practice; and, finally, insisting on the inventive character of the practical. With these arguments, Hyppolite's Hegelian dialectical unification of human knowledge—and of humanity by that same dialectic—is circumvented and put out of play. However, Deleuze rejects perhaps the key element of Wahl's own philosophy: the human drive for and experience of transcendence. In this there is an interesting echo of Hyppolite, for whom transcendence is overcome in the Absolute. Deleuze, following Hume, rejects the path of transcendence but preserves from Hyppolite the essentially ethical project of philosophy: ethics is no longer transcendent, it is concrete, multiple, historical, and inventive. "It is no longer a matter of surpassing, but of integration" (*ES*, 22). The central chapters of Deleuze's book will develop the implications of this question.

Hume, Empiricism, and the Priority of the Practical

A concept is not created and does not disappear at will, but to
the extent that new functions in new fields relatively depose it.
That is also why it is never very interesting to criticize a concept;
it is better to construct the new functions and discover the new
fields that render it useless or inadequate. . . . In this sense,
Hume marked a key moment in a philosophy of the subject . . .
—Gilles Deleuze, "Response to a Question on the Subject"

The first chapter of *Empiricism and Subjectivity* is by far the best-known
and familiar part of the book to English-language readers. It contains not
only the famous determination of the problem of empiricism—how is it
that the mind acquires a nature?—but also a number of ancillary points
that, taken together, seem to provide a comprehensive interpretation of
Hume's empiricism, especially in its difference from any form of rationalism. However, it would be a mistake not to pay attention to the way
that, already in the first chapter, Deleuze indicates that the operations of
the understanding are only one kind of practice and that human nature
is composed of two, the other being the practice of morality (*ES*, 20).
Deleuze's book, like Hume's *Treatise* as well as his work as a whole, is not
primarily an epistemology. When Deleuze states that he is seeking "the
motive of philosophy" he is echoing Hume's own concerns—stated most
starkly in Hume's statement that "'tis not contrary to Reason to prefer
the destruction of the whole world to the scratching of my finger" (*ES*,
17–18). In order for the epistemological discussion of the first chapter
to have any interest at all, it must be motivated by something other than
itself. The system of the understanding is only part of the science of
human nature which is more properly called, according to Hume, moral
philosophy. The first chapter thus does no more than allow entry into
the general problematic of Hume's philosophy. The next three chap-

ters deepen and develop Deleuze's account by extending the analysis to include the passions, thereby treating the whole of human nature. Like Hume's philosophy, *Empiricism and Subjectivity* is a book in which the practical takes primacy over the theoretical.

The first chapter of *Empiricism and Subjectivity* concluded with a transition from one type of human practice or practical activity to another. The first type of practice, which formed the central topic of chapter 1, is the exercise of the understanding that constitutes the rational aspect of the self. There, Deleuze describes what Wahl terms in *Vers le concret* an empiricism of the "second degree," a meta-empiricism, distinguished by the claim that reason does not allow for experience to serve as the starting point for the assembly of a singular Whole.[1] As Deleuze emphasizes, for Hume, the parts of the natural world are states of affairs ordered by the relative probability of their temporal and/or spatial proximity to other states of affairs. The general rules of knowledge act to determine these states of affairs and their relations, but the wholes that are discovered are never given by nature, they are instead invented through experimentation and observation. Moreover, even this invention leaves nature and its states of affairs with a thickness (*épaisseur*) that remains indissoluble. In the other domain of human nature, the "domain of morality," however, "general rules have another meaning" (*ES*, 22). Whereas the parts of nature are various states of affairs that have no intrinsic relation to one another, the parts of the moral world are defined and acquire their very natures from the relations that they have to each other. This is why Deleuze insists that, for Hume, the practical activity of morality is quite different from the activity of the understanding. While both aim to constitute general rules for their respective objects, morality finds itself unable to determine its objects in isolation: even to say of a moral entity or state of affairs that it is "independent" is to determine it in a morally significant way. Human beings are ineluctably partial in their moral judgments. Moral rules thus constantly find themselves in need of some security against those who would provide an exception for themselves. Against such a tendency, human beings have an interest in creating a system of justice that is as extensive and uniform as possible.

Kant, too, famously saw the dangers of making an exception of oneself with respect to moral rules, as did social contract theorists such as Hobbes and Rousseau. To the one who thought himself strong enough to resist the need for the social contract, Hobbes issued the chilly reminder: everyone sleeps. However, as with the argument of the first chapter, Deleuze continues to hew to James's injunction—emphasized by Wahl in *Pluralist Philosophies*—to get *round* Kant, and in the case of moral general rules, he interprets Hume to be putting forth a practical philosophy that takes sides against the rationalist and contractarian positions in moral and political philosophy that would follow in his own wake—from Kant to Rawls. Although not singled out for analysis, the moral and political theories of the most significant early authors of this tradition—Hobbes, Rousseau, and Kant—are sharply distinguished from the contractarian tradition that they helped to constitute and continue to anchor.

Instincts and Institutions

Overall insight into Deleuze's reading of Hume as a practical philosopher can be gained by reading *Empiricism and Subjectivity* in conjunction with a short text published shortly before *Empiricism and Subjectivity*: the "Introduction" to *Instincts et institutions* (*Instincts and Institutions*), a composition of texts that Deleuze edited for a series directed by Georges Canguilhem.[2] This brief introduction, as well as some of the selected texts, provide important insights into the significance of Hume's ethics and practical philosophy as it is interpreted by Deleuze in the second chapter of *Empiricism and Subjectivity*, and there is substantial overlap in their discussions.[3] Of the sixty-six selections gathered by Deleuze for publication in *Instincts and Institutions*, only two are from Hume, and both appear in the section entitled "Institution and Utility." In the first, drawn from Hume's *Treatise* and concerning the rules that determine property, Hume gives an example that Deleuze will refer to repeatedly, not only in *Empiricism and Subjectivity* but also in his 1972 essay on Hume and even in the preface to the English-language edition of *Empiricism and Subjectivity*, published more than three decades after the original French edition. In the first selection, two Greek cities, each desirous of a new residence, both hear of a nearby recently deserted city (*ES*, 38). They dispatch messengers who race to be the first to occupy and claim the city. The slower of the two messengers, seeing that he will lose the race and therefore any claim to the city, hurls his spear into the city's gates prior to the other messenger's arrival.[4] As Hume notes, it seems impossible to decide conclusively which messenger rightfully has claim to the city because—and here the quote seems to answer directly the question that Deleuze includes it under, "whether utility is enough to determine an institution"—"the whole question hangs upon the imagination" (*II*, 8 [quoting Hume]). The situation created by the spear thrown into the gate is not one foreseen by the laws governing the acquisition of property. As a result, the existing laws are shown to be both conventional, having their ground solely in human custom, and limited. What previously seemed to be and served as a suitable set of rules regarding the acquisition of property must now be expanded or revised so as to extend the rules to cover a novel situation. It is for this reason that Deleuze will emphasize in *Empiricism and Subjectivity* that for Hume "utility does not explain the institution" (*ES*, 38). Institutions are not created by a prior determination of what a particular society finds useful; they are determined according to the needs that an existing society has for regulating its activities.

In the second citation from Hume included in *Instincts and Institutions*, this one drawn from section 3 ("Of Justice") of the *Enquiry concerning the Principles of Morals*, Deleuze uses Hume to again answer—in the negative—the question of whether institutions are explained by prior human instincts. In the quote used to support this claim, Hume notes the absurdity of trying to reduce particular municipal offices to innate ideas. Human beings have passions, Hume and Deleuze will argue, and these passions are extensive but also partial. That municipal offices—such as a Recorder of Deeds—should be needed for a certain society reflects that society's particular solution to more general and extensive problems surrounding the acquisition of property. This is a solution that privileges the operation of the imagination over any determinate or "natural" constitution of the elements of civic justice.

In his introduction to *Instincts and Institutions*, Deleuze zeroes in on a problem common to both: while instincts and institutions are, at bottom, "procedures of satisfaction," it remains unclear "how . . . the synthesis of tendencies and the object that satisfies them come about" (*II*, viii, x). How is it, for instance, that property can be made to satisfy the human tendency to acquisitiveness? An instinct is a particular behavioral pattern that directly satisfies a tendency. Someone with an acquisitive tendency acts to satisfy it by taking what they please or, within society, what they are allowed to. At one extreme, then, an instinct can be understood as deeply individual: it is a "reflex," or a habit, or the operation of some individual intelligence. At the other extreme, an instinct can be understood as something that belongs to a species as what Deleuze calls a "biologically preeminent [*premiere*] finality": the instinct forms the identity of the genetically motivated actions of the member of a species. In both cases, an instinct "appears as a propulsive tendency in an organism toward specific reactions [*une tendance lancée dans un organisme aux réactions spécifiques*]" (*II*, x). The instinct to drink when an individual is thirsty is a tendency that impels the individual in a way that reacts to and satisfies their thirst. It appears species-specific the more perfect it is while, conversely, it appears increasingly to be the operation of individual intelligence when the activated tendency is more individual or idiosyncratic, as when someone chooses to satisfy their thirst only with a particular kind of drink. Deleuze notes that this creates a problem for determining how an individual could become intelligent enough to satisfy their tendencies. To resolve this problem he emphasizes, like Hume, the social nature of intelligence: the social integrates "circumstances into a system of anticipation, and internal factors into a system that regulates their appearance" (*II*, xi). To take the place of the species, which is the natural repository of instinctive powers of satisfaction, human beings invent institutions which aim in their creation and operation to provide the opportunity for the satisfaction of tendencies, and which are structured so as to permit the operation of the individual actions that they prompt and allow. This is what Deleuze means when he describes human beings as "*dépouiller*" or "sloughing off" their species (*II*, xi). Instead of relying on instincts to satisfy tendencies, human beings create both the conditions for this satisfaction and the conditions *of the tendency*, thereby substituting a social world of institutions for the natural world. The natural human species is "sloughed off" and replaced with the historico-cultural world invented by human beings.

The institution is opposed to a prevalent conception of law which may sometimes be historico-cultural—as in the case of jurisprudential systems—but is often taken to be inherent, natural, or absolute. In his discussion, Deleuze echoes Rousseau by speaking of the law as something that externally governs a social organization by limiting the "natural rights" of its members through the deployment of a "social contract" (*II*, ix). The institution as Deleuze describes it is, on the other hand, part of an "intermediate" world between natural human existence and social human existence. For example, acquisitiveness is a human tendency that is satisfied by the institution of property, which simultaneously determines the objects that might satisfy the tendency and the procedures for obtaining, transferring, recuperating, or divesting oneself of those same objects. It is the invention of the institution that provides a world in which acquisitiveness both arises and is satisfied; the natural acquisitiveness of human beings is "sloughed off" and replaced. Nonetheless, Deleuze stresses that the tendency does not "explain" its corresponding institution. This is not to say that the satisfaction of a tendency is not sufficient to give rise to a tendency, but rather that a tendency can be satisfied by multiple possible institutions. Human acquisitiveness accounts for the creation of the institution of property, but across different human societies, one can find the institutionalization of procedures for satisfying acquisitiveness taking on many forms.

The Passions and Society

Having shown in the first chapter of *Empiricism and Subjectivity* that the problem of knowledge is, for Hume, motivated by questions of practical life, the four sections of chapter 2, "The Cultural World and General Rules," argue for an empirical account of social and practical life. The chapter opens with a consideration of this practical life by asking after its formation, given the first chapter's conclusion that this formation is not due to a single principle of Reason or idea of the Whole. As Deleuze's introduction to *Instincts and Institutions* argues (in a Humean vein), practical general rules are societal rules, not governmental rules or laws. Such general rules will assume an increasing importance as *Empiricism and Subjectivity* proceeds, with Deleuze working to analyze them and to investigate how they are constituents of the human mind. As Deleuze defines them initially, general rules are systems of directed means (*ES*, 29). This definition will come to be considerably complicated both by the role of institutions developed in the second chapter and by the account of the power of imagination in the third. But Deleuze's discussion begins by explaining how, for Hume, individual interests can come to form common interests; this is the problem of sympathy, and it lays the ground for the discussion of general rules. Following this discussion, Deleuze is then able to draw explicitly on his introduction to *Instincts and Institutions* in order to explicate Hume's account of society as the community that comes into being through the creation and instantiation of general rules. Chapter 2 then concludes with Deleuze taking the example of justice as illustrative of the empirical operation of social general rules.

Deleuze's reading of Hume's practical philosophy is, in Wahl's terms, a fully immanent account of society's formation that will show its organized and purposeful character without recourse to a transcendent Whole—a recourse that is ruled out by the partiality of human beings. Nevertheless, far from preventing the formation of social bonds and groups, partiality is essential to the creation of a society, and chapter 2 of *Empiricism and Subjectivity* details the development of this society from naturally partial individuals. This is only the first part, however, of Deleuze's exposition of Hume's account of human nature. In chapter 3, the account of the socialization of human partiality will be deepened by an analysis of the faculty of imagination, which is what permits the creation of societal rules and institutions. Then, in chapter 4, Deleuze will complete his core analysis of Hume by considering the world and God as Wholes that serve as anchors for human purposiveness or finality.

Deleuze begins chapter 2 by insisting that "we must now explain these determinations of morality" (*ES*, 23).[5] The "determinations" that must be explained are the general rules that are constituted in the moral domain. In the first chapter, Deleuze analyzed the way that the understanding became a faculty and the way that the individual human mind acquires a human nature. This nature is dual: it is composed of the effects of association as well as the effects of passion (*ES*, 16). The first chapter showed that the problem of the constitution of the subject runs up against the problem of human association and, specifically, justice as the "schema" or principle of human society (*ES*, 22). The second chapter extends this discussion of the effects of passion to show the specific set of general rules that must obtain in a civil society. It begins with Hume's account of sympathy: his account of how individual, partial, and even opposed human interests can come to be conjoined into a coherent society. Hume rejects from the outset any and all claims—such as those found in Hobbes or, later, Rousseau, for instance—that human beings are naturally egotistical. They are naturally *partial*, Deleuze emphasizes, but historical and anthropological evidence overwhelmingly shows that human beings have a natural propensity to be social. They do not need to be compelled to form unions with others: the family is, after all, a natural formation. Deleuze emphasizes that Hume is not implying that humans have a moral *nature*. Such an assertion, which one finds in Kant, for instance, would imply an innate and hence universal or common morality. What a historical consideration of human communities such as Hume's finds, however, are various types of moral relationships. What appears as common or natural to human beings is the formation of various sorts of relationships on the basis of a nature that is both sympathetic and partial. "The truth is that an individual always belongs to a clan or a community" (*ES*, 25). What has been eliminated from the account of human communities is any artificial or external contractual constraint that would play the causative role in forming these communities, and what remains is the partiality of each person's sympathy, its limited extent and its differential valuation. However, simply replacing egoism with sympathy does nothing to resolve the question of how larger and larger human associations come to be formed.

Sympathy, because it is partial, creates a "contradiction" in nature insofar as there is sympathy between, for instance, family members, but this sympathy is countered by a kind of contra-sympathy toward those not included in the family or clan. Only with effort is sympathy extended beyond the family or familiar group. This contradiction of sympathy—that it both binds some individuals together and also pushes others away—presents a version of the problem faced by contractual theories that begin from single, self-interested agents: how can self-interest be developed into communal interest? With Hume's account of sympathy, the problem of creating an initial—albeit limited—extension of sympathy is solved, but the various groups bound by bonds of sympathy are not bound to each other. "The problem," Deleuze summarizes, "is how *to extend* sympathy" (*ES*, 27; emphasis in the original). According to Hume, it will be esteem that allows for more extensive human communities, *not* through a change in the partiality of sympathies but rather through a broad human agreement as to what constitutes right and wrong conduct. Only after human beings share a common understanding of praiseworthy and blameworthy actions will an extension of sympathy be possible.

The extension of esteem and the allowance given to the integration of partial sympathies make possible the constitution of a human whole. Nature provides partial sympathies which are like scattered pieces of morality, but the moral world, bound by the schema of justice, is an artificial creation. This is why Deleuze describes the constitution of the moral world in Hume as "the problem of schematism" (*ES*, 28). Different from nature, in which ends are instinctual and determined by partial sympathies and the contingencies of the natural world, the moral world is a political world that is created specifically for the orderly satisfaction of ends. Deleuze's language here echoes that of his introduction to *Instincts and Institutions*: "In short, the moral conscience is a political conscience: true morality is politics, just as the true moralist is the legislator" (*ES*, 28). Joined into a whole by common activities, matters of interest, and a common esteem for actions as either blameworthy or praiseworthy, a community is shaped by its institutions into a whole that facilitates the satisfaction of individual ends using esteem as a guide and common ground.

According to Hume, the elemental component of human societies— what brings different groups together—is property, while what facilitates the dealings of societal members with one another concerning property is conversation: the whole is secured by conversation (which replaces violence as a means for resolving disputes) and by property (which gives stability of possession to desirable commodities). The action of legislators in such a society—moral prescription—is a matter of a "general rule," by which Hume again means simply "a system of directed means" (*ES*, 29). The general rule is "general" both in the sense that it applies generally to the whole and in the sense that it guides each of the particular actions that constitute the order of the whole. With the two anchors of property and conversation, the general rule of a society is extended to create a stable point of view from which situations can be evaluated from outside of their particular occurrence. The members of a community are obligated to general rules by a "sense of duty" regarding conversation as the appropriate remedy for interpersonal disagreements and regarding the institutional assignation of property as the appropriate determination of possession (*ES*, 30). Deleuze singles out Hume's conception of property as "the political phenomenon *par excellence*" because it implicitly achieves the integration of partial sympathies by leading each person to affirm the right of others to hold private property as a condition for their own holdings. In this affirmation, "property and conversation are joined at last" by Hume, "forming the two chapters of a social science. Reason presents itself here as the conversation of proprietors." These proprietors apply general rules in conversation in a way that is both extensive and corrective: extensive insofar as the general rule replaces the individual will of particular actors with a sense of duty that is shared by everyone; and corrective insofar as conversation ensures that cases left unspecified by the general rule can be adjudicated through conversation rather than force or violence (*ES*, 30). The general rule even extends as far as a situation in which the aggrieved party does not feel the way that those sympathizing (via the application of the rule) with them do—Hume's example here is someone murdered in their sleep who therefore did not feel wronged but is nonetheless a victim that arouses others' sympathy (*ES* 31). Such an extension of sympathy is achieved because it has been institutionalized, surpassing even the combined partial interests of individual community members.

The "main question" arising from this discussion, Deleuze insists, is how the invention of the moral general rule is even possible (*ES*, 31). The contractual solution is again ruled out as impossible: partial interests cannot be compelled by force or reasoning to become general and institutionalized. Instead, Hume argues that partial interests are artificially identified with each other via the principle of sympathy. This principle secures the artifice and the artificial world of justice which are necessary for human beings to be "liberated from their natural limits." As Deleuze emphasizes, for Hume justice is therefore an extension of the passions and of partial interests; it alone "negates and constrains" partiality (*ES*, 32). For Hume, this restraint is not an external imposition or force brought to bear on partiality, but an internal "torsion" of the individual partial mind itself. And Deleuze elaborates on this, noting that "practical reason" is the natural coming to bear of impartial judgment upon partial sympathy in such a way that the mind becomes "grounded" and "calmed" (*ES*, 32). It is nature, therefore, that creates the disposition for justice by instilling human beings not only with partiality but with reflected partiality, with partiality that reflects, corrects, and thereby extends itself in the artifice of justice.

The discussion of justice brings to the fore what Deleuze calls the "real dualism" in Hume's philosophy: that between the whole of nature—which includes the artifice of the general rules—and the individual, partial mind that is "affected and determined" by nature (*ES*, 32). At issue again here is the difference between Hume's philosophy of the relation between the individual and society and the egocentric theories of the social contract theorists. Despite the fact that justice is not simply derived from some individual faculty of moral reason—that it is an artificial thing—it is nonetheless something that is naturally produced. Partial sympathy becomes a "natural obligation to justice, once the latter is constituted" (*ES*, 33). Deleuze here links Hume's claim with Bergson's argument that what is natural to human beings is that they have the habit of acquiring habits. As artifice, culture is natural—it arises naturally through the social interchange of human beings who converse and stake claims to property—and it acquires a history from which what is excluded is now determined as "nature."[6] Hume's theory is therefore opposed to both the argument that moral artifice arises solely from an individual, from some kind of individual faculty or instinct, and to the claim that moral community arises through the action of external forces such as education. Deleuze emphasizes that this sort of "egoism," found in Rousseau's *Émile*, for instance, contrasts sharply with Hume's theory that regards society and sociality as a kind of primitive something beyond which human nature cannot be reduced. Again, the social contract theorists err by reducing the fundamental social relation to the law, rather than the institution. However, "the law cannot, by itself, be the source of obligation, because legal obligation presupposes utility. Society cannot guarantee preexisting rights: if people enter society, it is precisely because they do not have preexisting rights" (*ES*, 35).

Deleuze's account of Hume here closely tracks but also amplifies his discussion from the introduction to *Instincts and Institutions*. Social utility is in fact opposed to any social contract because it is the institution that first gives human action direction. Society is first and foremost a set of conventions for satisfying needs; one based on utility, not obligation. Human beings form social groups not under any sort of compulsion but because they are useful. The "general rule is an institution" (*ES*, 36). Reprising the examples that he used in *Instincts and Institutions*, Deleuze writes that sexual and acquisitive needs are given satisfiable paths by the institutions of marriage and property, respectively (*ES*, 37). But, now going further, Deleuze makes clear that for Hume, there can be no reduction of a historically produced institution to any kind of nonhistorical instinct: "The difference between institution and instinct is this: an institution exists when the means by which a drive is satisfied are not determined by the drive itself or by specific characteristics" (*ES*, 37). To take the example of property: one institutionalized set of rules regarding property ownership and transfer bears no more intrinsic relation to acquisitiveness than another. "*Utility does not explain the institution*," Deleuze emphasizes (*ES*, 38; emphasis in the original). The utility of a particular institution, such as a particular society's determination of what can and cannot be held as property, is an artifice, unable to be completely deduced from the acquisitiveness that gave rise to it. Human history is then "the place of differences," a catalog of procedures for satisfaction that are irreducible to each other or to the instincts that gave rise to them (*ES*, 37). Hume's theory explains the institution by an instinctual drive that, operating within a particular social and historical circumstance, achieves its satisfaction through its reflection in the *imagination* (*ES*, 38). The faculty of the imagination excels at the creation of "models," of various possible social worlds within whose institutions instinctual drives would find their satisfaction (*ES*, 39). The imagination here does not become an active faculty for Hume, but it does become creative through its reflection of the drive within it. Deleuze writes that the imagination, under the effect of the drive, "*rings out*, and *resonates*," and the reflected figure this resonation produces is the institution.[7] "Thus, the satisfaction of human drives is related, not to the drive itself, but rather to the reflected drive. This is the meaning of the institution, in its difference from instinct" (*ES*, 39).

In the final part of chapter 2, Deleuze turns to the resultant problem of how Hume's theory can give to institutions, as productions of the imagination, a force that might otherwise be lacking in them. How can institutions and their practices become stabilized modes of practical life? Concerning the cultural world whose constitution forms the subject of the whole chapter, Deleuze remarks that "true morality does not address itself to children in the family but rather to adults in the state" (*ES*, 41). This is a clear jab at Rousseau's political theory, the inverse of Hume's, in which the social is a malignant and artificial growth upon the natural liberty of individual human beings. Having detailed the role of institutions, justice is now taken up and considered as an example of a moral general rule.

Considered as a general rule, justice has three dimensions: its establishment, its determination, and its correction (*ES*, 40). It is established by a shared human interest—"*that possession must be stable*"—which, reflected in the imagination, gives rise to extensive rules regarding the acquisition, transfer, and so on, of property.[8] These rules, however, are determined by the imagination; there are any number of ways in which the rules governing human acquisitiveness can be laid down. In whatever form it manifests itself, however, the determinate form of a particular system of justice will be insufficiently specified and, consequently, will yield problems—such as that illustrated by the example of the two Greek messengers—resulting from what Deleuze calls an "inadequation" between the statements stipulating the resolution of imagined possible situations and the real situations that occur. In such exceptional cases, how can the rule of justice acquire and maintain its appropriate vividness? The determinative agency of justice is only efficacious if it makes the nearest affairs appear as the most remote and the most remote affairs seem to be the most intimate and personal. Its extension ought to tend toward uniformity as an ideal. Why should an individual care if her neighbor is robbed? She ought to care if her neighbor is robbed because the function of justice as a general rule is the extension of sympathy to every other person in one's community; to steal from any person is to steal from each person, and to tolerate stealing is thus perversely to renounce one's own acquisitiveness. Similarly, the correction of the general rules takes place by addressing their distortions when applied to particular cases. Has the Greek messenger who threw his spear into the empty city's gate successfully acquired the city? The novelty of the situation demands that the existing set of extensive rules be revised—and possibly corrected—based on whether, for instance, the throwing of the spear bears a sufficient resemblance to the planting of a flag or some other accepted way of acquiring property. In such ways, justice is continually refined through reflection without losing its efficaciousness.

Deleuze emphasizes that, for Hume, justice requires a government which has as its role the "support" of the general rule: the object of the activity of the government is to ensure the regular action of justice and to work against any capricious and unintended effects. To this role of support therefore corresponds the loyalty of the citizens or members of society to the government. Loyalty is of prime importance for Hume's political philosophy and inverts and replaces the role of promises in social contract theories. For Hume, promises can only be *consequent* to the effect of the uniform extension of justice, since it is justice that secures the parties to the promise, and each to the other. The support required for justice—the matter of the particular form that a government takes (hereditary succession, representative democracy, etc.)—must also be determined, and, as with the case of justice, this support can sometimes lead to unintended and injurious situations: a hereditary title may have no legitimate heirs; a direct democratic vote may result in a tie. These call for correction by what Deleuze describes as "a right to resistance and a certain legitimacy of revolution" (*ES*, 42). The legitimacy of such revolutionary activity—and it bears noticing that this activity need not be violent—is secured by its adherence to the general rule of governmental support that was established with the institution of society. To the first series of rules that concerned justice or the content of the general rule—the stability of possession by proprietors, the laws specifying this content, and the laws specifying the correction of obscure cases and situations—a second series of rules is added that concerns government as

the support or adherence to the general rule (loyalty), the laws specifying the situations or conditions of this support, and the "legitimate"
correction of the violation of this support by a revolution that would be
more rule-governed than the illegitimate government that it seeks to
overthrow (*ES*, 42).

Finally, Deleuze turns to what he calls the "complement" to the
general rule: economic flourishing understood as the outcome of the
natural acquisitiveness of human beings that is one of the primary qualities that necessitates justice in the first place. The general rules of commerce which aim at human material flourishing, as with justice and the
government, are never sufficiently precise and never sufficiently anticipa-
tory to foresee the full effects of their determinative implementation. As
Deleuze emphasizes, for Hume, property "presents a problem of quantity: goods are scarce, and they are unstable because they are rare" (*ES*,
45). Questions arise such as: can food be rationed during times of fam-
ine? Can food be hoarded if it will only go to waste? and so on. As with
justice and government, these questions of the market require corrective
rules that respond to unforeseen situations.

The foregoing discussion of the general rule of justice—as well as
its support and complement—is summarized graphically by Deleuze at
the end of the chapter (see table 1).[9] Reading across the top two rows of
the table: the general rule of justice requires government, which, in turn,
has the function of regulating commerce. The third row of the table summarizes the determination of each of these elements; and the bottom row
of the table summarizes the means of correction for each.

Table 1. General Rules

	Justice	Government	Commerce
First step	Content of the general rule: stability of possession	Support of the general rule; loyalty to the government	Complement of the general rule: prosperity of commerce
Second step	Determination of the general rule by general rules; immediate possession, occupation, etc.	Determination of the support: length of possession, accession, etc.	Determination of the complement: monetary circulation, capital, etc.
Third step	Correction of the preceding determination by general rules: promise, transference	Correction: resistance	Correction: taxes, state service, etc.

The General Rules and Habit

The aim of the third chapter of *Empiricism and Subjectivity* is to make clear the way that the imagination acts and is acted upon by the principles of the understanding and by the passions. In this way, it takes up and expands upon the discussions of the previous two chapters, and again in this regard, one of its key claims is that the problem of the self cannot be solved at the level of the understanding—as may have seemed possible in the first chapter—but must be approached and resolved as a *practical* problem (*ES*, 59). This will lead Deleuze into a detailed discussion of the different aspects and types of general rules and the way that they determine and fix the imagination, as well as give rise to additional, corrective, general rules. While Deleuze was content to analyze the formation of the mind as a rule-governed entity in the first two chapters, in the third chapter he is concerned with the details and formation of the rules themselves. This formation is shown to hinge upon one of the fundamental features of Deleuze's reading of Hume: that relations are separate from the ideas that they relate.

   The aim of the third chapter is, however, difficult to make out at first: Deleuze opens with a continuation of his discussion of general rules, remarking that Hume sometimes speaks of them as uniting reflection and extension and, at other times, insisting that determinative rules must be separated from corrective rules. While this does continue part of the discussion begun at the end of the second chapter, Deleuze is here drawing attention to and clarifying the more general typology of rules that are at work in the description of Hume's world of culture. The general rule of justice, for example, acquires its extension by becoming reflected in the imagination in such a way as to allow for the overcoming of the partial interests of human passion and the consequent extension of sympathy. However, as the table that summarizes the final part of the second chapter shows, the general rule of justice is subject to subsequent determination by other general rules in order to create the particular set of artifices that instantiate justice for a given community. Additionally, justice has been shown to be subject to correction by still other general rules, which intervene to resolve particular cases in which the determination of the general rule produces situations that it alone cannot resolve. The upshot of this—and this is what Deleuze's discussion at the outset of the third chapter will revert to—is that general rules such as justice are sometimes depicted as created by the unification of reflection and extension (this is the linkage between the first and second cells under "Justice" in the above table), and sometimes general rules are divided into determining and corrective rules (this is the linkage between the second and third cells). How, then, are general rules to be understood?

The first aspect of general rules is relatively unproblematic: a general rule, Deleuze remarks, is the extension and reflection of a passion (*ES*, 47). The reflection of the passion of sympathy—a reflection on sympathetic partiality—leads to its necessary extension into a more expansive and uniform conception of justice, for instance. However, this extension unavoidably creates problems or "difficult cases" that are unanticipated and which require the correction of the initial general rule. It is this unavoidable creation of difficult cases that forms a kind of hinge for Deleuze's discussion: the determination and extension of the general rule is double. On the one hand, it is completely conjoined with reflection, so that it makes no sense to speak of a general rule without determination in extension—the very idea of justice, for instance, bears with it the idea of its extension to a particular society. But on the other hand, this extensive determination must always be supplemented by corrective general rules, and the origin of these rules is reflective. "Before us are two ideas in need of reconciliation: extension and reflection are identical, but they are different. Or rather: two kinds of rules are distinguished, they conflict; nevertheless they have the same origin, the same principle of constitution. We are thus led back to the principal problem: how is the rule possible?" (*ES*, 48)

A rule is possible, Deleuze begins, because passion is reflected and extended in the imagination, and this is what constitutes the general rule. Justice is the agreeableness of sympathy reflected in the imagination and extended into the world. It is the imagination that *makes the rule possible*, Deleuze emphasizes: a passion such as acquisitiveness is reflectively imagined, and imagination is passionately extended in determining a set of rules of acquisition. From this a new definition of the general rule, more fundamental than that offered in the first two chapters, is given: the general rule is "a passion of the imagination" (*ES*, 49). In other words, the imagination reflects the passion in its determination of the general rule, but does not give the extension of the rule any ground other than the imagination itself. The particular extension of the general rule is not *necessary*. This new definition of the general rule leads Deleuze to differentiate three types of rules: rules of taste, in which a passion and its object are reflected, but separated; rules of liberty, in which the individual will is distinguished but separated from its possible actions; and, finally, rules of interest and duty, in which a social cause is distinguished and held separate from its effect. In rules of taste—such as the aesthetic pleasure a spectator takes in the performance of a tragedy—disagreeable passions are reflected in the imagination, but the imagination's reflection strips these passions of their disagreeableness by holding apart the passion from its artful representation.[10] This is how pleasure can be taken in the dramatic or artful display of what is otherwise disagreeable. In the case of rules of liberty, passion itself is reflected in the imagination, which then reflects the possible actions of that passion but in a muted way, as though for contemplation, since the mind is able to imagine itself taking actions contrary to the one actually chosen. Finally, there are rules of interest and duty, such as in Hume's example of the relation between a master and a servant, in which the power of the master to compel the action of the servant is achieved through their relation rather than through the exercise of physical or direct force. It is the institution of servitude, to which is coupled an ever-possible disobedience or revolt, that bestows on the servant the obligation to display dutiful behavior that ameliorates the worry of the master: obsequiousness, meekness, eagerness, and so on. Deleuze remarks that, for Hume, "what grounds a rule in general is the *distinction* between power and its exercise, which only the imagination can make since it reflects the passion and its object, separating them from their actuality, taking them up again in the mode of the possible" (*ES*, 49, my emphasis). Only the imagination distinguishes power from its exercise—without its reflective intervention, power is simply discharged—and this distinguishing constitutes cultural realities. In each of the three types of rules, the reflection of the passion in the imagination strips the passion of its immediate connection with its object, and in the resulting distance obtained, the action of the passion is muted and interrupted, but its determination is also made possible.

This detailed typology of rules means that the earlier conception of the fixation of the imagination must be revised. According to the previous account, given in the first chapter, passions and natural principles acted on the imagination and thereby gave it a consistency. However, now, the elaboration of the three types of rules has shown that even after the imagination is fixed and rendered consistent it still retains some indeterminacy; even after acquiring the fixity of human nature, "insofar as it reflects the affections which fix it, the mind is still a fancy on another level and in a new way" (*ES*, 52). The fancy is the persistence of the undetermined imagination.

On the one hand, what determines the imagination cannot be allowed simply to be reflected because doing so would make the human world unstable, illusory, and ultimately a matter of a perpetual and perversely partial existential "choice." Passions would simply find themselves enlarged and extended. Therefore, Deleuze argues that for Hume "the fancy is reestablished in the principles of its own transformation, for at least something within the affections escapes all reflection" (*ES*, 52).

If the imagination was determined without remainder, then the mind would not be able to entertain thoughts of the possible or counterfactual and therefore no extension would be possible. That it does create and extend the general rules, as exemplified by the three types of rules highlighted by Deleuze—aesthetic, practical, and conventional—means that the imagination reflects on the very forms that give it determination and extension; it reflects on its "limits" (*ES*, 52). Such a reflection allows the imagination to "imagine power," to extend the passions while also retaining a difference between their extension and their reflection.

Returning to the original problem, then, of whether the general rule is reflected or extended, Deleuze concludes that, for Hume, the general rule "is the absolute unity of the *reflection* of the passions in the imagination and the *extension* of the passions by the imagination" (*ES*, 52–53; emphasis in the original). The fixation of the imagination by the passions, their reflection, is always accompanied by their extension in an actual rule. This also explains how reflection and extension are distinguishable, as well as the need for corrective rules. The extension of the general rule is never seamless; it requires corrections that only become apparent upon reflection—such as the question of which of the Greek messengers can rightly claim ownership of the abandoned city. Ownership is to be decided based upon a clarification and correction of the existing rules of acquisition in order to cover this case. The upshot of the discussion of general rules and the fancy is thus to reinsert the undetermined imagination, the fancy, into the heart of questions concerning practical human activity. "*How*," Deleuze then asks, "*can we explain this union of the most frivolous and the most serious?*" (*ES*, 53; emphasis in the original).

The union is the result of the principles of association being unable to fully determine the imagination. To the extent that the imagination is determined, the rules of human culture are extended by the ordered reflection of the passions; to the extent that the imagination remains undetermined, these very rules are made merely possible and, therefore, questionable. The question can always be asked: Why *these* rules and not others? Not only the rules of aesthetics, but also "rules of property, occupation, accession, and succession are determined through the principles of association." Deleuze asserts, strikingly, that "the Law is entirely associationist" (*ES*, 54). The rule or "norm" that determines the reflected passion "is the easy transition" (*ES*, 55). If the messenger's spear seems to establish ownership of the city, that is because we recognize in this case the resemblance between such an action and an existing, established means for the acquisition of territory such as the planting of a flag in unclaimed territory. The most serious matters of practical activity—indeed, the very structures that permit human activity to flourish—therefore rest upon something like a "constitutive imagination" (*ES*, 55). Furthermore, this is why disputes concerning the determinations made by the constitutive imagination can be interminable: there is no "nature" to be unearthed that will ground and absolutely decide things one way or another. Both of the Greek messengers are able to plead their case and make a plausible argument for their own position. "*This is the reason why the determination of the rule must be corrected*; it must become the object of a second reflection, of a casuistics and a theory of the accidental" (*ES*, 56; emphasis in the original). Ownership of the city cannot be ceded to both of the messengers: it must be decided in favor of one of the two, and the decision must also correct the deficiency of the existing laws that allowed for the dilemma to arise in the first place. The activity of the correction of laws and customs is interminable but neither futile nor valueless. The city will be found to belong to one faction and the corrected rule of possession— the revision of the rule or set of rules that permitted the uncertainty— obtains standing as a precedent, but not as a truth or fact of natural reason. Deleuze notes that in Hume's account, the philosopher for whom causation remains only ever hypothetical, and the historian for whom particular social customs can only be hypothetically explained, together work at an understanding of the determination of general rules that is fruitful because their "perplexity" spurs the correction of general rules that otherwise would yield counter-purposive outcomes (*ES*, 56). In the arbitration of the ownership of the city, the philosopher and the historian can, for Hume, only defer to the magistrate, since they have no body of certain knowledge from which to draw.

The criticism and correction of practical general rules has its limits, however, and Deleuze insists that the understanding is obligated not to overthrow the illusory and artificial world of culture. Its only legitimate practical employment is in the skeptical unmasking of any attempts to render general rules "real." Apart from this, the understanding can no more conceive of its principles as necessary than it can the practical actions that it analyzes, and this ought to give it a kind of essential humility. The judge who arbitrates the claims of the Greek messengers has, ultimately, no more "real" of a reason for her decision than the physical spear thrown into the gate. Deleuze writes that, for Hume, "culture is a false experience [*expérience*], but also a true experiment [*expérience*]" (*ES*, 57). It is false if it is taken to be grounded, natural, or absolutely real; but it is true insofar as its underlying principles are the same as that of the understanding.

The problem that gives the third chapter its title—"The Power of the Imagination in Ethics and Knowledge"—now becomes clear: how can the imagination be determined both by the principles of the understanding and by the passions? Deleuze observes two distinctive features of the determination of the imagination by the passions. The first of these is one that is common to both the principles of association and the principles of passion: they surpass and fix the mind (*ES*, 57).[11] The mind acquires a nature under the effect of both kinds of principles. However, the principles fix the mind in different ways. Deleuze has previously shown that, for Hume, the principles of association fix the mind in such a way that some of the elements of its ideas are placed in possible reciprocal relations. The example given of such relations is that of brotherhood, which is the same associative relation for each brother (*ES*, 57). But the relation of brotherhood nonetheless produces two very different effects on the mind of each brother insofar as the effect of the passions is partial. "The imagination passes easily from the furthest to the nearest, from my brother to me, but not from me to my brother" (*ES*, 58). Such a movement is attributed to the action of the passions, which "give the relations a direction and a meaning; they attribute to them a reality, a univocal movement, and thus a first term" (*ES*, 57). The second feature of the determining power of the passions is similar to the first: the imagination acquires a tendency "to move from the present to the future." Thus, the full picture of the imagination as determined by both kinds of principles emerges: association links ideas, while passion gives a meaning and temporal order to them. "If ideas get associated, it is according to a goal or an intention, a finality [*finalité*] that only passion can confer on human activity" (*ES*, 58). The passions therefore have both a simple effect on the imagination as well as a more complex effect. The simple effect is that they privilege certain connections by giving them a determinate meaning. Thus, in the case of the relation of one brother to another, each will feel his pole of the relationship as more vividly meaningful than the other, and will take it as the starting point for thinking through the mutual relation. Nevertheless, each brother will also be able to actualize and sympathetically understand, though less vividly, the same relation of brotherhood starting from the perspective of the other. This illustrates the complex effect of the passions: "the imagination is that in which passion, with its circumstances, is reflected across the principles of association in order to constitute general rules and to valorize the furthest, the most distant, *beyond the tendency of the imagination*" (*ES*, 59; emphasis in the original).

But, Deleuze asks, can Hume's principle *that all our perceptions are distinct experiences* be made consistent with the principle *that the mind never perceives any real connection among distinct existences*? (*ES*, 16; emphasis in the original). The account of the twofold determination of the imagination by the passions and the principles of association provides the needed means for establishing this consistency. The mind of the subject is both the simple effect of the passions—made possible by the principles of association—which gives a meaning to associated ideas; and the mind is also the complex effect of the passions, their reflective and less vivid extension to other actual relations. "The idea of subjectivity is from then on the reflection of affection in the imagination, it is the general rule itself" (*ES*, 59).

For example, one person is neighbor to another—this is an example of a relation established by the principles of association. According to the simple effect of the passions, each neighbor is, for themselves, *this* neighbor who wants, for instance, to acquire a piece of land adjacent to both persons' property. The acquisitiveness of one neighbor thereby creates the initial impetus for the general rule of justice. However, according to the complex effect of the passions, each one feels and sympathizes with—though less vividly than they feel their own acquisitiveness—their neighbor's acquisitiveness toward the same parcel of land. The general rule of justice thereby begins to acquire determination as each imagines ways of resolving the impasse. Ultimately, each neighbor can recognize the need for a determination of whether they or their neighbor has a right to acquire the land, and with the determination made based on particular criteria and reasonings, a rule of justice is first determined. "Surpassing the partiality of the subject whose idea it is, the idea of subjectivity includes in every collection that is considered both the principle and the rule of a possible agreement between the subjects. Thus, the problem of the self, insoluble at the level of the understanding, finds a moral and political solution [*dénouement*] only in culture" (*ES*, 59). The self is constituted by principles of association that determine and fix it, combined with passions that orient the resulting determinate mind and also reflect that orientation in such a way as to extend its orientation to the other terms of the associated system. As the example of the acquisitive neighbors shows, "imagination is reflective, essentially excessive, and apparently constitutive"—the acquisitive passion is reflected in the general rule of justice, which essentially includes some degree of sympathetic understanding of the other neighbor's situation and also provides the means for constituting rules of acquisition and ownership (*ES*, 60).

Deleuze characterizes the above kind of activity as that of the "*schematizing imagination*" (*ES*, 60; emphasis in the original). How, though, are the details of the resulting schematism worked out? The answer is to be found in that most eminent of Humean notions: habit. According to Deleuze, for Hume it is habit that is responsible, in the domain of general rules, for the extension of the imagination and for the correction of judgment (*ES*, 71).

Because the passions and the understanding are for Hume two different systems that operate in and on the mind, the conditions for the action of the schematism of theoretical reason will be different from those pertaining to practical reason. "Here, the schematism is no longer the principle of the construction of a whole, but the principle of the determination of parts. The role of the principles of association is to fix the imagination" (*ES*, 60). This fixity is achieved directly, without any reflection, because the principles of association organize rather than extend the imagination. Theoretical reason, however, is divided between relations of ideas and relations of objects, and corresponding to each is a distinct sort of reason: one either of certainty or of probability. This division results from the dictum that relations are external to ideas. For Hume, relations of ideas, such as that of resemblance, are relations that rely for their truth value on the ideas themselves. Thus, two people may resemble one another, but when a third person is substituted for one of them, the relation may be broken and no longer hold. On the other hand, relations of objects, such as the relation of contiguity, are relations that rely for their truth value on something other than the ideas themselves. Thus, in this case, the relation of contiguity in which one state of affairs succeeds another in time is untroubled by switching the order of the states of affairs. The difference between the two kinds is whether the relation depends upon the constituent ideas (resemblance) or not (temporal contiguity) (*ES*, 60). At the same time, reason too is divided into a kind that proceeds by certitude and another that proceeds by probability. Although certitude and probability are both based on the comparison of states of affairs, they are distinct, and Deleuze uses their distinction to get at the notion of habit.

Deleuze observes that in Hume the knowledge of causality is developed gradually, through repeated experiences, and does not come to the mind all at once; someone asserts a relation of causality only after repeated observations of a conjunction of specific states of affairs. Moreover, one's assertion becomes more and more probable or certain the more often the conjunction is observed. However, Hume insists that causality is known neither with certainty nor as the result of probabilistic reasoning. He is firm on this: the assertion of causality in the face of constant conjunction is not the result of probabilistic calculation, but is a natural disposition of human nature. However, according to Deleuze, the arguments that show why causality is not derived from probability also illustrate "the difference between the two dimensions of reason," certainty and probability (*ES*, 61). Habit is a principle of human nature, but it is also the case that particular habits are formed according to observed degrees of probability. Deleuze calls this "the paradox of habit" and again makes recourse to Bergson, arguing that "the principle is the habit of acquiring habits" (*ES*, 62). Without habit forming part of human nature, habituation—the becoming-probable of some states of affairs—would be impossible, since it is habit that makes the association of states of affairs possible. Confusion arises because causality is a natural judgment of human nature and does not admit of degrees while probability, on the other hand, does admit of degrees and develops gradually through our experience in the world. However, the causal relation is the effect of a principle that has a progressive formation: causality is not mere association, it has a direction. This brings Deleuze to the other use of reason described by Hume in which, relative to "relations of ideas," reason is immediately rather than progressively determined by principles; there is nothing that corresponds with the experiential component that leads to judgments of probability. Here, the paradigmatic example of such relations is mathematical relations, which carry certainty rather than probability.

The upshot and seemingly real interest for Deleuze of this detailed discussion of the determination of the imagination by theoretical reason is that it highlights the fact that, for Hume, both experience and habit are principles of nature (ES, 63). The essence of experience "is the repetition of similar cases," but this repetition is strictly the creation of the philosophical relation of causality. "This is how imagination turns into understanding" (ES, 64). However, the creation of the relation of causality is not enough to enable inferences to be drawn; the fact that from an initial spatial disposition of billiard balls another disposition regularly follows does not, of itself, provide the means for drawing a conclusion about the relation of the states of affairs. Again, relations are external to their terms, and in the case of human experience, it is the understanding that apprehends ideas, but it is habit that, in the case of the billiard balls, (re)constitutes the experience as one in which one state of affairs causes another. In other words, while "habit allows the understanding to reason about experience" because it introduces the real content of causality—registered by the term "always" which "cannot be constituted in experience because, in a sense, it constitutes experience—it is also the case that "habit presupposes experience" (ES, 65). Repetition achieves nothing by itself other than the determination of states of affairs; experience would be the mere "presentation of cases." Coupled with this repetition present to "the inspecting mind" is an active taking up of the presentation by the mind according to the principle of habit.

Hume's account, Deleuze continues, seems to indicate an analogous relation between the operation of "artifice" in the moral world and the operation of habit in the world of knowledge (ES, 65). However, although both artifice and habit give rise to extensive and corrective general rules within their respective spheres, they do not do so in the same way. Whereas in the moral world "the condition of the rules was the reflection of the principles of nature in general in the imagination," in the world of knowledge the condition of the rules is the constitution of experience by habit (*ES*, 66). The repetition of the motion of a set of billiard balls leads the observer to assert particular causal relations. However, because the experience of constant conjunction must be conjoined to habit in order for such an assertion to be made, a gap is left between experience and habit into which illegitimate beliefs, *fictions of the imagination*, can be introduced. These are beliefs manufactured by habit that have no corresponding experience, and they form a class of general rules that Hume calls *nonphilosophical probability*. The examples given are examples of national prejudice—"An Irishman cannot be witty, a Frenchman cannot be relied upon"—but nonphilosophical probability can extend much further (*ES*, 67). Its rectification is achieved through a renewed effort to secure habit to experience, to anchor the present to the non-fictitious past, and therefore to populate the world of knowledge with *philosophical probabilities*.

Nonphilosophical probabilities have two primary sources according to Hume: language and the fancy. Language counterfeits real experience with things heard and also gives names to indistinct or confused impressions, leading philosophers to think that there is a clear and distinct impression lurking behind the term. In this way, the deceptions of language join up with those of the fancy insofar as the fancy may seize on accidental qualities of a state of affairs and thereby distort its repetition, as when someone suffering from vertigo has a sensation of falling off a platform rather than the solidity and support of what they are standing on (*ES* 69). The result is that in both the field of knowledge and in morality, the imagination is excessive.

The case of knowledge is different, however. Habit is unavoidably plagued by fictitious repetitions engendered by language and the fancy, and this requires a set of corrective rules whereby the general can be distinguished from the accidental. "The object of philosophical probability or of the calculus of probabilities is to maintain belief within the limits of the understanding and to ensure conformity between habit and experience" (*ES*, 70). The understanding takes apart objects and states of affairs, and in seeking to infer the future from the past, must not only pay attention to the quantity of past experiences, but also to the oppositions or differences between them. For instance, in seeking to predict the motion of a billiard ball, an observer has access to all of the other past occasions on which they observed a similar ball struck in a similar way, but they must also recognize as irrelevant, for instance, the different colors of the balls seen on different occasions, the different colors of felt on which they collided, and so on. To believe is therefore "an act of the imagination" insofar as the images that are determined to be in agreement with each other by the understanding come to form a single idea in the imagination (*ES*, 70). Habit thus engenders nonphilosophical probabilities as well as their correction by philosophical ones. The "adequation of habit with experience," Deleuze concludes, "is a scientific result to be obtained, the object of a task to accomplish." It is thus that habit has opposite effects on judgment and the imagination, extending the latter and correcting this extension with the former (*ES*, 71).

God: The Whole

The guiding thread of the argument so far has been that Deleuze's book on Hume follows the prescription laid down by William James and repeated by Wahl: to use Hume's empiricism to get *round* the Critical philosophy of Kant. In the first three chapters of *Empiricism and Subjectivity*, Deleuze lays out Hume's philosophy of the formation of subjectivity. While the first chapter of the book makes the well-known epistemological argument that the mind acquires its nature from principles, it then turns to the primacy of the practical in Hume's philosophy, and this claim by Deleuze is developed in the next two chapters. By the end of Deleuze's analysis of habit, it has become apparent that there are two distinct types of principles that affect the mind: those of knowledge and those of passion, and that the imagination remains at least in part undetermined; the fancy persists. In the fourth chapter, Deleuze will bring Hume's account of subjectivity together with the other two terms of that most Kantian of trilogies: the self, the world, and God. While brief, this chapter fulfills two functions. First, as Deleuze notes in its opening lines, Hume's account of religion can serve as an example within which can be exhibited all of the general rules that have been examined in the preceding chapters. However, second, the problematics of the world and God—the extension of the discussion from subjectivity to include these—begins the concluding half of the book wherein the distinction between Hume and Kant will be brought to light.[12]

Deleuze begins by noting that, for Hume, religion presents itself, first of all, as "a dual system of extensive rules" (*ES*, 75). Polytheism is the religious pole for the passions, while theism is the pole for the extensive rules of the understanding. In polytheism, human passions are reflected and extended by the imagination such that "the gods of polytheism are the echo, the extension, and the reflection of the passions, and their heaven is only our imagination" (*ES*, 72–73). In polytheism, the gods are passions personified or otherwise made substantial. For Hume, the gods of polytheism instantiate the extraordinary rather than the everyday, and they are therefore "*cruel*" and "*capricious.*" Their worshippers mirror this, and they "willingly throw themselves into criminal ventures; for their common characteristic [*point*] is that moral acts are not sufficient for them" (*ES*, 73). Moral acts are not sufficient because they are regular, predictable, and law-governed; morality, for the polytheist, fails to attain to the essential, the divine, because it spurns the exception.

Theism, on the other hand, embraces the mundane. Also a system of extensive rules, theism is the reflective extension of the principles of the understanding. Hume emphasizes that, like polytheism, theism is also an "overstepping [*débordement*] by the imagination, a fiction, a simulation of belief" (*ES*, 74). Where the polytheist glorified the exceptional, the theist holds to written and spoken tradition—the repetition of the liturgy, for instance—and miraculous events are granted a reality appropriate to reported events: their edges are smoothed and they are fitted to the whole. A second kind of theistic argument—the argument from design—relies on an analogy between the world and machinery, but Deleuze wonders, along with Hume, what it is that makes mechanical activity—which bears only a very imperfect and superficial resemblance to the activity of the world itself—privileged over other types of activity such as "generation or vegetation." Finally, there are theistic arguments that attempt to prove the existence of God by causation, but these err either by minimizing the "disorder" and "evil" in the world—as in the case of theodicies—or by establishing what Deleuze calls "a disproportionate God," as Demea does in Hume's *Dialogues concerning Natural Religion* (*ES*, 74). In both cases, whether God acts to ensure that everything happens for the best or whether the evils of the world are atoned for by the crucifixion of Christ, it is the promise of a glorious and happy eternal life that tilts the scales decidedly in favor of the good. From Hume's perspective, all such theistic arguments are purely fanciful because they illegitimately employ the notion of causality to draw conclusions about a singular effect. Judgments of causality are always worldly because they are based on the observation of the constant conjunction of objects of the same type or "species" (*ES*, 74–75). Worldly objects can therefore provide the necessary repetition for future judgments of other worldly states of affairs, but the World itself is of a different qualitative order; its singularity prevents any repetitive experience of it.

To these extensive rules of religion—whether they tend more toward the theistic or the polytheistic—corrective rules are added. According to Hume, these rules have the function of, for instance, normalizing the miraculous by subjecting it to evidentiary scrutiny and reasoning.

Similarly, in polytheism, the exceptional case is taken as one case among others that form human worldly experience. Corrective rules operate to bind and bring the excessive into the domain of the worldly. But they do so, Deleuze emphasizes, in a way that seems to exclude religion from culture, since in the other "figures of extension" such as justice or art, the corrective rules validate the extension that they also limit. In the case of the two Greek messengers, the planting of the spear in the gates of the abandoned city occasioned a questioning and a rectification or supplementary clarification of the existing rules of acquisition; but, Deleuze emphasizes, those same rules of acquisition provided the legitimate grounds for the correction. The correction of religious extensive rules seems to strip them of everything that might be called "religious": "In short, it seems that, in extension, religion maintains only the frivolous and loses all seriousness." For Deleuze, following Hume, this is because religion is a reflection of the fancy and not of the imagination settled and fixed by the principles of association (*ES*, 76).

However, religion is not entirely dissolved or banished. God is inaccessible to knowledge and belief—is other than culture—but philosophical reasoning does not abolish religion. Moreover, this is not simply out of a case of inherent stubbornness or foolishness. The place of God that results from Hume's critique of religion is the thought of the origin of the principles—God is a "negative" thought ("negative" because God is not thought directly as an object corresponding to an impression) of the "finality" (*finalité*) of human nature. Deleuze notes that "it is in this sense that theism is valuable" for Hume: because it rests upon a formulation of the harmony between the world and each human life. After the critique of religion, finality remains as the thought of "the original agreement of the principles of human nature with Nature itself" (*ES*, 77). The idea of God lacks positivity, and "for knowledge," which seeks to determine it, "it can receive a content only by being mutilated, by being identified with such and such mode of apparition that experience manifests to us, by being determined by a necessarily partial analogy." In Hume knowledge, reason, finds no secure purchase in the idea of God; it is, Deleuze states, "beyond good and evil." Moreover, as "the original unity of origin and qualification," of origin and reflected extension, "finality [*finalité*] is more of an *élan vital* than the project or the design of an infinite intelligence." This Nietzschean and Bergsonian extravagance is parlayed into the status of the idea of the World. If the source of the World is known only negatively, and if the World as its extension is only ever known partially, then is the idea of the World "a simple fiction of the fancy"? (*ES*, 78).

Causation is a judgment founded on the experience of constant conjunction, and the discussion of religion shows "two fictitious uses of causality": one that makes gods out of extraordinary or unique experiences, and another that forms judgments about a singular object, the World, which cannot be repeated—which is like no other thing *in specie*—and is, moreover, not really an object at all (since it is never the object of an experience) (*ES*, 79).[13] But there is a third fictitious use of causality, more familiar generally but also to readers of Hume: the judgment that objects enjoy a continuous existence beyond their actual sensory perception. The continuous existence of objects is a "fiction of the imagination" that the mind has recourse to when only one of a number of previously conjoined impressions is present in a subsequent experience (*ES*, 79). It is an attribution that "surpasses" the legitimate extensive principles of the understanding. Similarly, the attribution of distinct experience to objects of experience is flatly contradictory, since the object is inaccessible save through the necessarily discontinuous medium of experience.

Deleuze notes that, for Hume, the problems associated with the belief in continuous existence and the belief in distinct existence seem to be problems of the extension of the mind. However, "contrary to extensive rules, the fiction of continuity cannot be corrected, cannot be and should not be corrected" (*ES*, 80). To do so would abolish the World. The presentation by the imagination to the understanding of the continuous and distinct existence of objects raises an objection from neither the understanding nor the imagination because these characteristics are not those of a particular object, but are rather the characteristics of the World. The World *is* what is continuously existing and distinct from the mind; "it is not a particular object, but the horizon that every object supposes" (*ES*, 81). Following from the belief in the existence of bodies comes the startling claim that "*fiction becomes a principle of human nature*" (*ES*, 82; emphasis in the original). Deleuze's presentation of Hume is quite close to Wahl and the latter's discussion of transcendence here, but, as Deleuze argues, Hume's empiricism permits the persistence of the object of transcendence only as a fiction. Because human beings cannot give up this fiction without giving up the World, Deleuze notes that the purpose of Hume's empiricism is to explain the transformation of the *multiplicity* of ideas in the mind into a *system*, and in order to accomplish this, objects must be given real existence outside of the mind. However, no faculty of the mind is sufficient to give existence the continuity that the very idea of a system entails. Quoting Hume, Deleuze writes that "the system is complete when 'an interruption in sensory appearance' is surpassed 'by the fiction of a continuous being that fills these intervals and preserves for our perceptions a perfect and entire identity'" (*ES*, 82). The source of this fiction is the imagination itself, which, with the World, finds an extension that cannot be corrected by general rules because the rules take the World as their very ground and supposition.

For Hume, the action of the imagination secures the World with principles of its own—and Deleuze stresses that continuity is not merely the illegitimate extension of resemblance, contiguity, and causality—and thereby creates a contradiction between this principle and the principles of reason (*ES*, 82–84). This threatens the entirety of the argument thus far. The imagination has been held to be fixed and determined by the principles of human nature, which obtain their reflection in the imagination but also find a new employment in the correction of the fanciful excesses of this reflection. For Deleuze, this means that "[a] new relation between extension and relation must be found" (*ES*, 85). An initial compromise is on offer if perceptions are regarded as discontinuous while objects possess continuity. Deleuze calls such a compromise a "delirium" (*délire*), by which he means to indicate a system in which neither principle—of the imagination or of the understanding—is able to win out over the other, with the result that fiction becomes constitutive of determined human nature. The fancy persists and is never solidly fixed.

As Deleuze notes, following Hume's progress in the *Treatise*, this is the conclusion at which philosophy—as opposed to nonphilosophical reflection—inevitably arrives when it takes the "first step" toward this delirium by proposing the "hypothesis of an independent existence" (*ES*, 86). Ancient and modern systems of philosophy both fail to bring the fancy to heel. The result is therefore a choice not between principles— since neither can prevail over the other—but a choice between "*contradiction and nothingness*," between philosophical thinking and its renunciation or abnegation (*ES*, 87; emphasis in the original). The delirium of a mind in which the principles of association persist alongside the principle of the imagination is the perpetual hobgoblin of modern rationalist philosophies. The upshot of the delirium diagnosed by Hume is that the understanding is powerless to correct the non-reflected imagination, the fancy, which persists alongside it. Correction is always self-correction of the understanding, and is always accomplished without a ground that might give certainty to its operation (*ES*, 88).

The implication of this, for Deleuze, is that, independent of the principles that determine the imagination, the mind is indifference and fancy. The contradiction between the principles that it submits to and the principle of the continued and continual existence of objects and the World is the dementia (*demence*) of the mind. Finally, delirium is the perpetual attempt to overcome the demented conflict between principles and fiction. However, there is no resolution in this direction. If dementedness is "human nature related to the mind" then the inverse relation, of the mind to human nature, is "good sense." The "*élan* of good sense" is discovered in the chaos of dementedness when one turns from proceeding from the mind's affections to the mind—a process that yields an unavoidable contradiction—to proceeding from the mind to its affections (*ES*, 88). This does not resolve or dissolve the philosophical contradiction, but it does set it out of play. Attending to the affections of the mind is the affair of good sense insofar as it lives the determinations of the reflections of the passions and, lacking any absolutely sure ground, ceaselessly engages in the work of correcting them. Thus, Deleuze concludes, "there is no science and no life except at the level of general rules and beliefs" (*ES*, 89).

7

Empiricism Vindicated

But empiricism has always had other secrets.
—Gilles Deleuze, "Hume"

The first four chapters of *Empiricism and Subjectivity* present a meticulously detailed analysis of Hume's philosophy, one guided by Deleuze's assertion that Hume's question can be formulated as: "how is the subject constituted within the given?" The final two chapters, as well as the "Conclusion" of the book, exhibit something of a shift from a concern with Hume's philosophical project to the use to which Hume's empiricism can be put within the frame of postwar French philosophy, and specifically to the debate between Wahl's transcendental existentialism and Hyppolite's immanent idealism. In other words, the book closes with a shift from Hume's question to that of Deleuze, which can be formulated as: "how can a practical empiricism provide assurance for knowledge claims?"

This shift in concern is marked in the text when Deleuze takes a step back from his close-in work and notes that the "specific problem of subjectivity" had previously seemed to be the key to gaining access to the "essence of empiricism." However, this now appears doubtful. "The subject is defined by and as a movement, a movement of self-development. What is developed is [a] subject. This is the sole content that can be given to the idea of subjectivity: mediation, transcendence" (*ES*, 90). This is a striking claim not only for the appearance of the term "*transcendance*," where one might expect Deleuze to continue to use the term "*se dépasser*" which he has preferred, but also for the linkage of this term with that most Hegelian of notions: mediation.[1] What Deleuze intends is to differentiate Hume's philosophy as a whole from other philosophical systems, especially those that share the rationalist project of Kant's Critical philosophy. This differentiation will set the stage not only for an analysis of what is properly distinctive to empirical philosophies, but also for the subsequent discussion of Hume's place in the history of philosophy that will open the final chapter of the book.

Transcendence and the Given

Deleuze seems to immediately retreat from his use of the term "transcendence" when he characterizes the movement through which the subject is defined. The "sole content" of the idea of subjectivity is mediation and transcendence, but the movement that constitutes the subject is that of surpassing and reflecting itself. This, for Deleuze, is a key insight of Hume's: at its root, "becoming-other" is not dialectical; it is not a single developmental path as it is portrayed in, for instance, Hegel's *Phenomenology of Spirit*. For Hume, the two "fundamental characteristics of human nature" are belief and artifice. "In short, believing and inventing makes the subject a subject" (*ES*, 90). As the analysis of Hume's philosophy has made clear, the subject is twofold. On the one hand, according to the operation of the principles of the understanding, the subject affirms more than it knows—for instance, it asserts a causal relation when what it experiences is the temporal contiguity of two states of affairs—and this naturally raises the question of the truth-value of such statements. On the other hand, according to the operation of the passions, the subject "disengages from what affects it generally a power that is independent of the present [*actual*] exercise, that is to say a pure function, and surpasses its own partiality" (*ES*, 91). From a desire to acquire a piece of land, for instance, the passion of acquisitiveness is reflected in the imagination as a desire and demand for institutions and rules that would allow for the orderly acquisition and transfer of property. "It is necessary to explain this double power, this double exercise of general rules; we must find the ground, the law, the principle of it. This is the problem" (*ES*, 91).

The beginning of the resolution of the problem can be found in the discussion of finality discussed at the end of chapter 6, above. There, Deleuze showed that for Hume, the given and the subject that surpasses it are each given in different ways. "The subject that invents and believes is constituted in the given in such a way that it makes of the given itself a synthesis, a system. This is what must be explained. In the problem thus posed, we discover the absolute essence of empiricism" (*ES*, 92). On this point, the argument of *Empiricism and Subjectivity* pivots from an articulation and defense of Hume's philosophy to a defense of empiricism now *exemplified* by Hume's philosophy, against the rationalist and transcendental philosophical lineage which runs from Kant through Hegel and Husserl to Hyppolite, but also against psychologism, which is Deleuze's worry about Wahl's adherence to the transcendental. In an essential passage, worth quoting at length, Deleuze writes:

> Of philosophy in general, one could say that it has always looked for
> a plane of analysis, from which it could undertake and put to the test

the structures of consciousness, that is to say, critique, and to justify
the whole of experience. It is thus first of all a difference of plane that
opposes the critical philosophies. We make a transcendental critique
when, situating ourselves on a methodologically reduced plane that
therefore gives us an essential certitude, a certitude of essence, we ask:
how can there be a given, how can something be given to a subject,
how can the subject be given something? Here the critical requirement
is that of a constructive logic of the type found in mathematics. The
critique is empirical when, placing itself in a purely immanent point of
view from which is possible on the contrary a description that finds its
rule in determinable hypotheses and its model in physics, one asks regarding the subject: how is it constituted in the given? The construction
of the former [transcendental critique] gives way to the latter [em-
pirical critique]. The given is no longer given to a subject, the subject is
constituted in the given. Hume's merit is to have already separated out
[*dégagé*] this empirical problem in its pure state, distancing it from the
transcendental, and also from the psychological. (*ES*, 92)

This is Deleuze's starkest demarcation of the position his exposition of
Hume's philosophy takes amidst the postwar philosophical debates in
France, and especially the debate between Wahl's transcendental existentialism and Hyppolite's immanent idealism. But it is also Deleuze's
reorganization of the historical philosophical relation between the projects of empiricism and critical rationalism.

Far from turning on the question of whether knowledge begins
from experience or not, empiricism and critical rationalism—Hume and
Kant—are distinguished according to whether one begins with a "methodically reduced" plane of analysis in which the subject and the given
are present and the question is that of their relation, or one proceeds
purely "immanently" and asks how the subject is constituted in the given.
Hyppolite's idealism rests on a methodically reduced plane of analysis
which takes the subject and the given as certain and irreducible terms
and asks about the conditions of possibility for their relation.[2] Wahl's
existentialism argues for the constitution of the subject in the given but
retains the transcendental, ecstatic experiences of individual subjects, in
particular psychological states.[3] Hume's philosophy goes further on Deleuze's analysis and, in doing so, makes possible a philosophical lineage
that might achieve James's goal of getting *round* Kant. It poses the same
question—and in this way, Deleuze is able to characterize both Kant's
and Hume's philosophies as "critical"—that animates "philosophy in
general," and certainly modern philosophy: what is the proper analytical
"plane" or ground from which the structures of consciousness can be
analyzed? However, rather than restricting the question to that of how the

subject can obtain truthful access to the given, Hume asks the prior question of the implicated constitution of the subject within the given. The resulting question is therefore: what is it that Hume means by "the given"?

Without mentioning Kant by name, the account of the empirical given offered by Deleuze implicitly criticizes and undercuts the Transcendental Aesthetic. Where Kant asks about the conditions for the possibility of experience, empiricism asks about the conditions for such conditions. And yet this does not yield an infinite regress. "Empiricism starts from [the] experience of a collection that is in flux without an organizing rule. This experience is the imagination or the mind and its principle is that of difference," Deleuze states; quoting Hume: "everything separable is discernible and everything that is discernible is different" (*ES*, 93). The succession of the discernibly different *is experience*; nothing precedes it because there is nothing *by virtue of which* the succession of the discernibly different is different. The mind does not structure experience; experience is, first of all, the differential succession of discernible perceptions. The mind is also not first of all a subject, and "if the subject is what surpasses the given, we should not first attribute to the given the faculty of surpassing itself" (*ES* 94).

Deleuze considers three challenges to Hume's claim regarding the irreducible primacy of the given. The first is a kind of Spinozistic or even Leibnizian claim that the given requires some sort of causal substrate in order to exist. However, the empiricist does not begin with the constituted experience of a subject but with experience as identical to the mind. "It is necessary to begin with *this* experience because it is *the* experience. It presupposes nothing else, nothing precedes it. It does not implicate any subject of which it would be the affection, nor any substance of which it would be the modification, the mode. If every discernible perception is a separate existence," Deleuze writes, quoting Hume, then "nothing appears necessary in order to support the existence of a perception" (*ES*, 93; emphasis in the original). The mind—which is also the imagination and experience when these terms are understood to refer to the collection of differentially discernible perceptions—requires no prior cause, no substrate, because there is no discernible perception of one; to impose such a substance by, for instance, invoking the principle of sufficient reason, is precisely to attribute to the given the capacity of surpassing itself. The given as such requires no cause to be given since it is the collection of the discernibly different; its cause would therefore also have to be discernibly different, in which case it would be part of the given, or not, in which case it is, again, either the given itself or something that is not part of experience (and is therefore a nullity). Deleuze emphasizes all this by emphatically stating: "*The mind is identical to the idea in the mind*" (*ES*, 93; emphasis in the original).

The given is not a substance underlying perceptions, nor is it "the representation of Nature" (*ES*, 94). The former argument differentiated Hume from the rationalist tradition; this argument is intended to differentiate Hume from the corpuscular theory of Locke. For Locke, primary qualities resemble the objects that they represent—they are qualities that the represented object possesses—while secondary qualities are those attributed to objects according to their influence on the faculties of perception. As in the case of Hume's rejection of rationalist metaphysics, Locke's account of primary and secondary qualities is rejected because there is no difference in our impressions that corresponds to the distinction. Like rationalist metaphysics, "the question of a determinable relation with Nature has its conditions: it does not arise from itself, it is not given, it can be posited only by a subject, a subject that asks itself about the value of its system of judgments, that is to say about the legitimacy of the transformation that it subjects the given to or the organization that it confers on it" (*ES*, 95). Both sorts of metaphysics are grounded on a plane of analysis that has already been determined. In each case the subject and the given are posited, and the questions that arise concern the relation between these essentially unquestioned entities. For Hume, however, what is given is a collection of discernibly different perceptions or ideas, and the appearance and constitution of a subject is for him a question. Thus, Deleuze states that "the true problem will be to think an accord, but only at the right [*convenable*] moment, between the unknown powers on which appearances depend that are our givens and the transcendent principles that determine the constitution of a subject in this same given, between the powers of Nature and the principles of human nature, between Nature and the subject" (*ES*, 95). This "true problem" is recognizable as Hume's, developed by Deleuze in the first chapters of *Empiricism and Subjectivity*, of how the mind becomes a subject, as well as the hope mentioned above, of an accord between the subject and the World. The superiority of Hume's empiricism is not to prematurely assume an answer to this question and thereby foreclose any inquiry into it.

Finally, Deleuze considers the relation of Hume's empiricism to the claim that the given is what affects or is present to the senses. Hume agrees with this in part—granting that there is probably a physiological basis for the operations of the mind—but also notes, again, that such a conception still begins with an already formed organism—with an organized system of sensibility. "In a word, we always return to the same conclusion: the given, the mind, collection of perceptions, cannot be identified [*se réclamer*] with something other than itself" (*ES*, 96). But this, Deleuze continues, leads Hume to the question of how the given can identify with itself if the collection of impressions is always arbitrary and capable of diminishment or augmentation without changing the identity of the given. The answer is that the identity of the given is in the quantitative rather than the qualitative character of the constituent ideas. The meaning of the principle of difference is that the mind's capacity for discerning different ideas is not unlimited. Only what can be discerned as different can be differentiated, and as Hume points out, progressively subdividing something as small as a grain of sand does not continue to produce ever-new ideas. There is a terminus to what the mind can discern; a smallest idea. "The mind, the given is not identified with [*ne se réclame pas*] such or such idea, but with the smallest idea, whether it serves to represent a grain of sand or its part." Moreover, since the smallest idea is considered only quantitatively, the problem of the status of the mind—that is, the problem of the identity of the given in Hume's empiricism—is the same as the problem of space (*ES*, 97).

Hume's argument proceeds according to two linked questions: Is extension infinitely divisible? and how is it that extension is constituted by indivisible elements? That extension is not infinitely divisible is demonstrated by the fact that the mind, in its progressive division of an idea or impression, reaches a "limit-idea," an idea which cannot be further reduced because such reductions—possible in name only—do not yield distinct and differentiable ideas or impressions. There may be smaller bodies but there are no smaller sources of experience, of impressions and ideas. The second question—as to how extension is constituted by these limit-ideas—is answered by the determination of the smallest idea or impression as "sensible." "It has no extension by itself, yet it exists" (*ES*, 97–98). The limit-impression of, for instance, a grain of sand, exists insofar as it is sensible but it cannot be said to "occupy space." If it did, it would be further divisible.

Thus, Hume's empiricism leads to the conclusion that space is the result of—rather than the condition for—the given. The same is true of time, although this is given a much more abbreviated treatment by Deleuze, who notes that while time, like space, is given in the succession of sensible limit-ideas, it is omnipresent in our sensible experience, whereas space is experienced only by sight and touch (*ES*, 99). The result of this discussion is a reversal of Kant's argument in the Transcendental Aesthetic. For Hume, the limit-ideas give objective structure to the mind and therefore also to experience. Where, for Kant, the a priori sensible forms of space and time are the conditions for any possible experience, Hume argues that it is the sensible that is required for there to be space and time. Spatial and temporal experience is always ordered, always particular, it is "an objective and spontaneous mode which owes nothing to reflection or to construction" (*ES*, 100). Again, this is the meaning of the fundamental principle of empiricism: the objectivity of the given, what constitutes the given as such, is formed by the differential relations between limit-ideas and limit-impressions.

All of this necessitates that the given itself be appropriately clarified. The given, for Hume, for empiricism, is "an eventful succession of distinct perceptions" (*ES*, 93). To proceed immanently is to resist the urge to immediately pass to the question of "what perceives the given?"[4] Instead of asking "what has this experience?" empiricism first determines the principle of experience as such, which is, again following Hume, "everything that is separable is determinable and everything that is determinable is different"; Deleuze calls this "the principle of difference." The determinate differentiation of what appears "is experience." "It supposes nothing else, nothing precedes it" (*ES*, 93). The mind, then, must be identical to the ensemble of what is determinately differentiated; it is not (the) subject. Nor is the mind representative, since "perception does not give us any difference at all between two sorts of qualities" (*ES*, 94). The relation between perception or appearance and reality can certainly be the object of speculative endeavors but these are equally always the object of skepticism. Both substance and primary qualities are postulates that "can be posed only by a subject," they are issues that arise only subsequent to the constitution of the subject, a constitution that has yet to be determined (*ES*, 95).

To these two possible counter-postulates to the empiricist account of the given can be added a third: the given "is given to the senses, . . . it supposes organs or even a brain" (*ES*, 95). Such a physiological account, however, still relies on principles: "the organism and the senses do not immediately have by themselves the characteristics of a human nature or a subject" (*ES*, 96).

All three of these possible objections to the empiricist account of the given, however, suppose what the empiricist sets out to determine. Is the given then indeterminable? "What is the constancy of the mind?" The solution to this problem is one of the most interesting discussions in all of *Empiricism and Subjectivity* and yields "the meaning" of the principle of difference, or what Deleuze calls "the fundamental principle of empiricism." It is fundamental in two ways: both as the founding point of an empirical account of the mind and experience, and as the founding point of experience itself. This founding point is quantitative, not qualitative; it is "the smallest idea" (*ES*, 96). In, for example, a progressive subdivision, Hume argues that the mind reaches an idea that is "indivisible." "This reflection that relates the idea itself or the impression to the criteria of division, we will call it *the moment of the mind*" (*ES*, 97; emphasis in the original).

The consequence of this is twofold. First, it means that the indivisible idea, the "limit-idea," gives the mind its objectivity. For the mind, there is nothing smaller than this limit-idea, regardless of whether there are smaller existing things. Second, it means that "the smallest idea . . . is neither a mathematical point, nor a physical point, but [is] a sensible point" (*ES*, 98). A mathematical point is no longer divisible, a physical point is, but the limit-idea exists as a sensible point that is also indivisible. It cannot be reduced either to mathematical nonexistence or to physical extension. In the ideas that constitute the given, "the disposition of visible and tangible objects," this disposition is not determined by some object in addition to those that are disposed, nor is it determined by something nonexistent (*ES*, 99). Every disposition of objects is able to be decomposed to a smallest, "minimum-idea," that is sensible insofar as every ensemble of objects is *determined* as having a *disposition*. Just as, in Hume's example, the smallest determinate decomposition of a grain of sand is a non-extended determinate idea that accounts for the idea of the grain of sand as a whole, so the smallest determinate decomposition of any ensemble of objects yields a non-extended determinate idea that accounts for the particularly determined ensemble.[5] The given, then, is defined "by two objective characteristics . . . : indivisibility of an element, distribution of elements; *atom and structure*." Importantly, by noting that the determining principle of the given is the smallest idea, Deleuze prevents this principle from being understood as one that is *applied to* the given: "the parts taken together are defined . . . by their temporal and sometimes spatial mode of appearance, an objective and spontaneous mode that owes nothing to reflection, nothing to construction" (*ES*, 100; emphasis in the original).

The given is differential determination, and on the basis of this determination, the question of the meaning of the subject is raised again. Deleuze presents six formulations: five that have appeared earlier in *Empiricism and Subjectivity*, and a sixth that arises from the present discussion of the determination of the given. The subject has been said to arise for Hume, first, when the imagination becomes a faculty. It has also been said to be generated when the distributed collection becomes a system, when the given is reprised by and in a movement that surpasses the given, and when the mind becomes human nature. It has furthermore been said that the subject is what invents and believes, and finally, that the subject is *synthesis, a synthesis of the mind* (*ES*, 100; emphasis in the original). From these characterizations Deleuze derives three problems that organize the remainder of chapters 5 and 6: (1) what are the characteristics of the subject in belief and invention? (2) what principles construct the subject as believing and inventing? and (3) what are the different moments of the synthesis/system?

Deleuze begins with the problem of the characteristics of the believing and inventing subject considered (1) in relation to time, (2) in relation to the sense organs, and (3) in relation to itself. In each case, Deleuze poses the question of what happens when the mind becomes a subject.

The first question is "how is time transformed when the subject is constituted in the mind?" (*ES*, 106). It has been seen that "the mind envisaged in the mode of appearance of its perceptions was essentially succession, time." Furthermore, the "constitutive root [*racine*]" of the subject is habit, "the synthesis of time, the synthesis of the present and the past in view of the future" (*ES*, 101). This synthesis is effected in two operations: belief as well as invention. Invention is exhibited by, for instance, the creation of rules of property via the creation of institutions whose objectivity makes possible an agreement between subjects by overcoming their partiality. In terms of time, now, Deleuze shows that invention rests on *anticipation*, and in the example of property, the anticipation that each person has of retaining their property in the future. Similarly, belief, "a lively idea united to a present impression by a causal relation," is, by virtue of its rootedness in causality, the "synthesis of a past and a present that constitutes the future." In both invention and belief, the past is posited as a "*rule* of the future" (*ES*, 101–3; emphasis in the original). The mind is *structured* by time; the subject is the *synthesis* of time.

But what precisely is to be understood by the synthesis of the past and the present? This question requires an account of how the past and present, determinations *of* time, are themselves determined. The past is the mind submitted to one principle, that of experience, by which the understanding (which is the mind) observes not the differentially determined elements of an ensemble but differentially determined ensembles, "a repetition of similar cases." The future is the mind submitted to a different principle, that of habit, by which the imagination (which is also the mind) fabricates both the elements of an ensemble and their differentially determined relation to other ensembles, yielding "time as a determined future filled by its [the mind as imagination] anticipations" (*ES*, 104). The relation between these two principled determinations of the mind is nothing other than habit. In terms of time, then, the mind becomes subject when it is determined by the principles of experience and habit, determinations that form between themselves the relation of habit (whereby the past becomes the rule for the present).

The second question is "how is the organism transformed when the subject is constituted in the mind?" Prior to or apart from this constitution, the biological organism, the body, is "only the mind, the collection of ideas and impressions envisaged in the mechanism of their distinct production." Under the effect of the principles of human nature, however, "the body is . . . the subject itself . . . in the spontaneity of the relations that it establishes between ideas" (*ES*, 107). Deleuze notes that the distinction between the two types of principles here follows the method of a physicist who breaks down forces into components that have no actual independent existence. The body under the effect of principles is no longer merely that which allows for differentially determined ideas, it is the determination of this differential determination itself. Deleuze calls this determination "spontaneity," remarking in a note that "the principles constitute a subject in the mind at the same time that this subject establishes relations between ideas" (*ES*, 106n2). There are two relevant kinds of spontaneity: relation and disposition. The spontaneity of relation is what makes possible the "linkage" of "neighboring" ideas, while the spontaneity of disposition—the way that a particular embodied mind is "disposed" or inclined at a particular time—is what makes possible the impressions of reflection that constitute the subject in the mind. Under the effect of the principles of human nature, the embodied mind acquires "dispositions" which account for the determination of new ideas from the same ideas of sensation. These dispositions are passions which serve as a kind of intermediary that "spontaneously provokes the appearance of an idea, an idea of the object that responds to the passion" (*ES*, 108). An embodied mind without passion has no disposition. Determined by the principles of human nature, however, which constitute impressions of reflection, passions determine the dispositions of the body as the biological correlates of the spontaneous, linked and determined, connections of ideas.

The third and final question concerning what happens when the mind becomes a subject is "how is the mind itself transformed when the subject is constituted?" The answer to this question depends upon the principles that construct and determine the subject as believing and inventing: the principles of human nature. "The subject is that instance which, under the effect of a principle of utility, pursues an end, organizes means in view of an end, and, under the effect of principles of association, establishes relations between ideas." In other words, "the collection of perceptions becomes a system . . . when they [the perceptions] are linked" (*ES*, 109). The principles of human nature—relation, contiguity, and causation—are therefore to be investigated by means of their effects: the relations between ideas. Hume's "truly fundamental proposition" is that these "relations are exterior to ideas" (*ES*, 109). According to Deleuze, there are two kinds of relation in Hume: one kind that can vary without any variation of ideas, and another that depends entirely on the related ideas.[6] The two kinds of relation are distinguished according to whether the idea is considered "distributively [or] particularly," in terms of itself or in terms of the ensemble in which it is situated (*ES*, 110).

Relations that can vary without any variation in their ideas, such as the relations of objects in space and time, are relations "of a variable object to the ensemble in which it is integrated," they are relations in which the ideas are considered distributively (*ES*, 110). In such cases, the ideas in the mind are differentially given in a "*composition*," but they acquire determination—constancy—under the effect of "an influence exterior to the mind" that fixes the idea as well as the ensemble in which it is (then) integrated. Relations that depend entirely on their component ideas, on the other hand, such as those of resemblance (the comparison of the qualities of particular objects), are relations of "the characteristics of two or several ideas considered individually." Even though these relations rely on ideas for their "material," the ideas themselves do not determine the relation. Instead, as was the case with spatiotemporal relations, relations such as that of resemblance are instances "of a normative judgment" because, in every case, "relation (pre)supposes a synthesis" that is not given in the mind (*ES*, 111; emphasis in the original). The synthesis is the "first" effect of the principles of association that gives an intersubjective constancy to the mind; "the same simple ideas are regularly grouped in complex ideas" (*ES*, 112).

However, this account does not fully solve the general problem of the origin of the determinacy of relations. It accounts for the "natural relations," but not for relations that are mediated and therefore more distant, those that Hume calls "philosophical relations." What can account for these sorts of relations? The principles of association, if they were the only determinants of relations, would yield only identical subjects. According to Hume, what accounts for the difference between different subjects (and which exists alongside their similarities) is *circumstance*. Here, as Deleuze notes, Hume rejoins Freud and Bergson, but whereas the latter two thinkers dispensed with an inquiry into the principles that determined subjects' commonality in favor of investigations into their idiosyncratic differences, Hume undertakes both projects. The principles of association determine the everyday and common forms of thought, of the subject, but, in addition to these principles, "an ensemble of circumstance always singularizes a subject since it represents a state of its passions and its needs, a repartition of its interests, a distribution of its beliefs and of its vivacities" (*ES*, 116).

The foregoing account of the principles of association throws into sharp relief the differences between the empiricism that Deleuze finds in Hume and the phenomenological account of the intentional constitution of experience found in Hyppolite. For both, the subjective phenomenological account of the intentional constitution of experience is only ever sufficient to account for a limited aspect or dimension of it. It requires supplementation in order to be sufficiently determinative and explanatory, and Hyppolite turns to Hegelian dialectics in order to account for the historically and psychologically diverse determinations of consciousness. From the standpoint of the empiricism that Deleuze finds in Hume, however, this amounts to an attempt to smuggle the principles of association onto foreign terrain. Enlisting a panoply of thinkers who will become regular touchstones in his later work—James, Freud, Bergson— Deleuze argues that Hume's philosophy offers a way to account for the concrete diversity of historical and psychological subjects that avoids the error of reducing this diversity to the effect of more general principles of association—principles that fail precisely insofar as their explanation of concrete differences recasts this difference as naturally determined.

Moreover, for Hume, "the principles of passion are no less universal and constant than the others: they define laws where circumstances only play the role of variables; they certainly concern the individual, but in the exact sense that a science of the individual can be made, and is made" (*ES*, 117). Deleuze can therefore draw the conclusion that, for Hume, the subject is constituted "in the mind under the effect of two kinds of conjoined principles": those of association and those of passion (*ES*, 116). Again, there are signs here of Deleuze's attentiveness to the contemporaneous problem engaged by Hyppolite; the difference is to be found in their respective determinations of a "science of the individual." Recalling the priority of the practical over the epistemological, Deleuze writes that "we can at least foresee how this unity [of the principles of association and passion] will be manifested in the subject: if relation cannot be separated from circumstances . . . this is because subjectivity in its essence is *practical*." Summing up Hume's claims, and sharpening their polemical force in regard to rationalist philosophical projects such as Hyppolite's, Deleuze writes that "the fundamental proposition of empiricism," that the subject is constituted in the given, can now be seen as equivalent to the claim "that there is no theoretical subjectivity" (*ES*, 117; emphasis in the original).

Empiricism and Rationalism

The final chapter of *Empiricism and Subjectivity* interrupts the detailed interpretation of Hume to begin with a discussion of what constitutes philosophical critique. Deleuze is doing two things here. On the one hand, he is juxtaposing a "proper" critique of empiricism to an improper one in order to make clear the distinction between Hume's philosophy and transcendental rationalism; this will make clear the critical import of *Empiricism and Subjectivity* in contemporary debates that are rooted in rationalist notions of subjectivity.[7] On the other hand, and more subtly, Deleuze is providing an account of his own method of engagement with contemporary philosophical debates. Deleuze emphasizes that the critique of empiricism belongs to philosophy and not to the history of philosophy. *Empiricism and Subjectivity* falls into the latter category because it offers a powerful reading of Hume's empiricism and deploys it within the contemporary problematic of postwar French philosophy. However, it shows this empirical formulation of the problem of subjectivity without specifically arguing that it is *preferable*. Deleuze's later works, on the other hand, such as *Difference and Repetition* and the *Logic of Sense*, undertake the philosophical work of developing and advocating a philosophy of difference other than rationalism.

Methodologically speaking, *Empiricism and Subjectivity* is guided by the problem of how the subject is constituted in the given. Behind this first question is a second, auxiliary one: who is posing this problem? Or, why write *Empiricism and Subjectivity*, given the prevailing currents of thought in postwar French academia? The answer is that the problem of subjectivity is at the heart of the debate between Wahl and Hyppolite and is also at the root of contemporary phenomenology. For Deleuze, the prevailing thought of the subject is properly—that is to say, philosophically— critiqued through the development of a crucially different question: how can the subject be constituted in the given *without a transcendental activity* (or one in which "relations follow from the nature of things")? (*ES*, 123; emphasis in the original). This critique is elaborated in two ways: first, by establishing the specific difference between phenomenology and empiricism; and second, by accounting for this difference historically by reference to Kant and the transcendental. Phenomenology and empiricism agree in their opposition to psychology; like every philosophy, they both have recourse to principles (*ES*, 122).[8] However, where phenomenology pursues a genetic account of experience, which necessitates a transcendental account of the accord between ideas and relations, empiricism takes relations as effects, not causes (i.e., not properties of ideas), and thereby becomes a dualistic account of subjectivity.[9] "If one wants to object to [empiricism]," Deleuze writes, "this is what it is necessary to judge, and nothing else": that "*relations are exterior to ideas*" (*ES*, 120; emphasis in the original). Empiricism prefers to speak of the "given" rather than "experience" because the given includes experience as the "collection of ideas" as well as "the subject that surpasses experience [and] the relations that do not depend on ideas" (*ES*, 122). This empirical determination of the problem of the starting point for a philosophical inquiry into subjectivity "gives empiricism a true metaphysics," and this metaphysics, in turn, makes clear the difference between transcendental rationalisms (such as phenomenology) and empiricism (*ES*, 123).

Deleuze turns to Kant's critique of Hume in order to exemplify the difference between the two philosophical approaches. Kant praises Hume for understanding that the problem of knowledge is best raised on the "terrain" of the imagination (*ES*, 124). However, Kant argues, Hume's dualism is the result of a subsequent failure to notice that the accord between the given and the subject could never be encountered as such, in a non-accidental way, if the given was not *first* submitted to the same kinds of principles that determine human nature. "Thus, for Kant, relations depend on the nature of things in the sense that, as phenomena, things suppose a synthesis whose source is the same as that of relations." For Kant, "there is the *a priori*, that is to say one must recognize a productive imagination, a transcendental activity" (*ES*, 125). The critique of empiricism by various post-Kantian rationalisms follows this general path, but "for Hume, nothing in thought surpasses the imagination, nothing is transcendental" (*ES*, 126).[10] The accord of human nature and Nature is to be found in "finality," not in any transcendental *conditions* for experience and the subject.[11]

Having made clear the philosophical stakes of the project of the revivification of Hume's empiricism, Deleuze turns his attention to an explication of the key concept of finality. Because the diverse moments of subjectivity "condition" finality, he states that "[we] must recapitulate the moments of the general action of the principles in the mind and, for each of these moments, seek the unity of the principles of passion and the principles of association, a unity that confers on the subject its successive structures" (*ES*, 126). In this account, the subject "is nothing other than the mind as *activity*": it is a "resonance" that becomes "more and more active" under the effect of principles (*ES*, 127, 126; emphasis in the original). In relation to impressions, the principles have two roles: they are selective and constitutive. As selective, it is a principle that "is inserted between the mind and the subject, between *some* impressions of sensation and *the* impressions of reflection . . . [it] is the rule of the process" (*ES*, 128; emphasis in the original). Thus, as the rule of the selection, various principles are constitutive of the impressions of reflection that are, in fact, selected, "chosen" over others. The line of Deleuze's argument leads him to set aside the issue of determining the specific principles that constitute human nature, and his account of the way that the subject is determined by principles moves on to the principles of association.[12] These principles show themselves to constitute two different kinds of relations: natural (in which impressions of reflection are determined by impressions of sensation according to the principles of association) and philosophical (in which impressions of reflection are determined, again, by impressions of sensation, but this determination is not effected by the principles of association).

In philosophical relations, the principles of association remain constitutive, but the selective operation is performed by "circumstance, affectivity." The relation of causality, however, is a special type of philosophical relation. According to Hume's account of causality as a philosophical relation, it is experience as a principle that becomes selective; habit (as a principle), on the other hand is constitutive, its effect is a natural relation. Hence the particular difficulties concerning the determination of casuality: "habit can in effect create for itself an equivalent to experience, invoking fictive repetitions that render it independent of the real" (ES, 132). The principles of passion have the same function as the principles of association, but act upon different types of impressions: those of pleasure and pain. There are two types of principles of passion: direct and indirect. Direct passions "turn the mind toward good or evil, toward the pleasure or the pain from which they proceed" and have a variety equivalent in number to the "modes of existence" of "the good and evil from which they proceed." Indirect passions, on the other hand, "turn the mind toward the idea of an object that they produce" and are therefore as numerous "as there are emotions producing the idea of an object" (ES, 133–34). The latter are "indirect" because the object that is the source of such a passion must be united to the subject by the principles of association.[13]

Hume's theory of the passions is distinctive and valuable, according to Deleuze, because the theory is not organized in a way such that relatively simple passions would be analyzed and, more geometrico, these analyses would gradually be extended to more complicated passions. Instead, it is organized in the manner of a theory in which there is "a physical decomposition of the passion, of the passionate movement" (ES, 135). And in fact, Deleuze emphasizes, "Hume's entire philosophy, and empiricism in general, should be considered as a 'physicalism' since the principles of passion are one aspect of the decomposition of the 'simple' movement whose other aspect is the understanding and the principles of association." Here again Deleuze turns to the distinctive value that empiricism acquires amidst contemporary philosophical debates dominated by rationalism: asserting the physicality of the principles of human nature is to "define the empirical problem in opposition to a transcendental deduction, and also to a psychological genesis" (ES, 136). Empiricism asserts that the subject is the effect of the principles of human nature on the mind, that "the subject is the activated mind," in two ways: "as a passivity with respect to the principles that produce it [and] as an activity with respect to the mind that undergoes [submit] it." The diverse moments of the subject are then the different effects of the principles in the mind, and yet "the subject itself is indivisible, undecomposable, active and global" (*ES*, 137).

In order for the subject to be both indivisible and divisible into the diverse effects of the principles, Deleuze continues, "one [kind of impression] must finally be absolutely subordinated to the other." Hume's response here is unequivocal: "the principles of passion are absolutely primary" (*ES*, 137). A consequence of this is that Hume's philosophy, which is often understood as a "critique of relations," is more properly understood as a critique of representation. Hume argues that "*representation . . . cannot be a criterion for relations themselves*" (*ES*, 138; emphasis in the original). The priority of the passions over the understanding entails that it is in the former, not the latter, that the meaning of relation is to be sought. Where the understanding represents relations, passion acts in and through them, and if it is nonetheless possible for the understanding to attempt the representation of relations, this is only insofar as "association gives a possible structure to the subject" (*ES*, 138). This structure is only actualized by passion.

The association of ideas, subordinate to the primacy of the passions, then defines not a "knowing subject" but "an ensemble of possible means for a practical subject in which all the real ends [*fins*] are of a passionate, moral, political, economic order" (*ES*, 138). Again, the implicit criticism of rationalism and phenomenology is clear here: the scientific attitude is a possible determination of the being-in-the-world of the existing subject—something Husserl had shown in the *Crisis of the European Sciences*, especially.[14] That this entails the constitution of the subject as primarily practical, as fundamentally determined according to a "political, economic" order, is the argument that Trân Duc Thao makes to resolve the impasse of phenomenology by utilizing dialectical materialism.[15] Finality, then, which expresses the subordination of association to passion in human nature (secondary finality) as well as the "accord" of human nature and Nature (primary finality), is intended to rectify the rational, dialectical, and still transcendental, concept of intentionality.

Intentional Finality

Finality is not Deleuze's concept. It is Hume's. But it emerges from Hume's philosophy only insofar as this philosophy is repeated, rearticulated, in a new context. To ask after a science of human nature in the middle of the twentieth century is to engage, explicitly or implicitly, with phenomenology. In such an engagement, finality is the empirical coun-terpoint to intentionality. Where intentionality accounts for the way that the transcendental subject attains access to the world that it constitutes in its proper activity, finality accounts for the implication of the subject and the world through the interaction of two types of principles that fix and determine the mind. Deleuze will conclude *Empiricism and Subjectivity* by stating that "philosophy must be constituted as the theory of what we do, not as the theory of what is. What we do has its principles; and Being can never be grasped except as the object of a synthetic relation with the very principles of what we do" (*ES*, 152). Ultimately, according to the last lines of *Empiricism and Subjectivity*, both empiricist and rationalist accounts at-tempt to describe the "conformity" of Nature and human nature, but they do so in strikingly different ways.

Taken as a unit, the final chapters of *Empiricism and Subjectivity*, together with its brief conclusion, "Finality," develop not a solution but the furthest extension of the empirical problem of how the subject is constituted in the given. Chapter 6 of the book concludes with a twofold claim. On the one hand is a more general claim: empiricism, organized by the assertion that relations are exterior to ideas, rejects the rational-ist orientation toward representation (which presumes that relations are determined by ideas). On the other hand, this claim is situated within the more specific claim that the duality of the principles of human nature, the principles of association and passion, is structured such that the latter are determinative of and for the former. This subordination, which will itself have two aspects, is what is meant by "finality."

Deleuze begins his conclusion with still another reminder of the insufficiency of the principles of association for the determination of human nature. Under their influence "the imagination becomes reason, fantasy find a consistency," but this constancy is an indifferent one. The relations that constitute reason, that link ideas into certain networks, do not provide a sufficient reason for action, for "the priority of one term over another" (*ES*, 139). Since the mind does initiate action, then, it must be determined to do so by principles other than those of associa-tion; these are the principles of passion. Deleuze contrasts the differing determinations of the mind by the principles by saying that while the principles of association fix the mind and link ideas into determined networks, the principles of passion "nail the mind down" by determining "centers of fixation" which, as centers, give direction to relations of ideas (*ES*, 140). The determination of these centers, a determination that is "ultimate" for Hume because no justification for this determination can be given, is that of pleasure and pain. Ideas that are determined as plea-surable are thereby determined as central ideas toward which the subject guides its activity in the broader network of ideas. "In making of pleasure an end, the principles of passion give action its principle, they make from the perspective of pleasure a motive for our action. . . . The essence of action is in the means-end relation. To act is to direct means in order to realize an end" (*ES*, 141).

Although this means that "causality enjoys a considerable privilege over the other relations," causality itself is not enough to determine action: "the means surpasses the cause" (*ES*, 141). It surpasses it because in utility the means is always conjoined with the end in such a way that the means is appropriated to the end. The causal relation persists as what allows for the relation of utility to be determined, but in the action of utility, a subject "unites itself" to the end, thereby determining the means as such. In utility, "the effects of the principles of affectivity, . . . the impressions of reflection, of the passions" are what determine the links between means and ends. This determination can be thought either "generically, as universal possible responses to given circumstances; [or] differentially, as traits of given characters, which do or do not agree with possible circumstances" (*ES*, 141–42). According to the first, generic, approach, one could try to draw up a list of the determinations of the passions, but in doing so, one would have said nothing about whether they were "useful or harmful." In other words, such a list would be merely representative and in itself useless. However, differentiating passions according to their efficacy—an approach that Hume favors—provides a practical account of useful action by looking to history for examples of human actors that did and did not act successfully.

The principles determine the mind, but it is the mind itself that provides the quality according to which ideas, related according to principles, enter into relations. "Our first conclusion must then be this: conjoined principles make of the mind itself a subject, of fantasy a human nature; they establish a subject in the given. For a mind capable of ends and relations, and of relations that respond to these ends, is a subject." A problem arises here, however, insofar as "the subject is constituted in the given by principles, but as the instance that surpasses the given itself" (*ES*, 143). The mind, as subject, "*advises* certain ideas rather than others" and it generates such "advisements" only if, between ideas, principles have fixed the mind into a network of related ideas (*ES*, 144; emphasis in the original). In such a network it is a quality of the ideas, that is, of the mind, that results in the passage from one idea to another, rather than a different but equally determinate passage. This quality of ideas is vivacity, and it is also determinative of the relation between ideas in the human mind. This entails the central organizing claim of the conclusion of *Empiricism and Subjectivity*: "Briefly, it is necessary to understand that the subject is simultaneously *constituted by principles* and *founded on fantasy*" (*ES*, 143; emphasis in the original).

This entails a closer look at what knowledge is according to Hume. Generally speaking, knowledge is the activity of the mind that has become a subject under the effect of the principles of association. But, under this effect, the mind, the collection of ideas, retains a determinative quality that works together with the effects of the principles. According to Hume, under the determining action of the principles of association, the activity of the mind is "to surpass, is always to go from the known to the unknown." This "schematism of the mind" is always extensive, but "in knowledge, sometimes we go from known circumstances to unknown circumstances, sometimes from known relations to unknown relations" (*ES*, 144). The former schematism, which goes from known to unknown circumstances, is causality, a "physical" schematism; the latter schematism, of relations, is a "mathematical" one, and consists in generating a new idea from a previous idea and a third idea that serves as a "rule of construction." To borrow Hume's example, the idea of 1000 is formed by taking the idea of 10 and then using the idea of the decimal system in order to construct the new idea of 1000, which thereby acquires the same certainty as the ideas used to construct it. What must not be overlooked in either schematism of knowledge is that it is extensive *both* in the sense that it goes from part to part (as determined by principles) *and* in the sense that it is surpassing (determined by the vivacity of ideas). In a way "a little like [the way that] in rationalism possibles tend toward being with all their force," "impressions tend to communicate their vivacity to every idea that is linked to them." Of course, not all of the resulting relations become legitimate beliefs, only those that are "linked in a firm and constant, invariable, way" (*ES*, 145–46). "This is why," Deleuze states, "in the schematism of knowledge, there are always excessive rules that must be corrected by other rules: the schematism of the cause must conform itself to experience, and the schematism of the general idea must conform itself to space under the double aspect that defines the latter, geometrical structure, arithmetic unity" (*ES*, 146).

To the subject is always coupled what Deleuze calls a Self. In knowledge, the subject struggles for constancy amidst the proliferation of vivacity, and this struggle forms what Deleuze calls a "polemic . . . *between the principles of human nature and the vivacity of the imagination*" (*ES*, 146; emphasis in the original). To the previous account of knowledge must now be joined an account of passion, an account that will again show that effects of the imagination are always joined to the effects of the determining action of the principles of human nature. The determination of the mind by the principles of passion fixes the mind in such a way that its relations acquire direction according to determined ends. These ends, in turn, are also determined by "the reaction of a mind that responds to the supposedly known totality of circumstances and relations" (*ES*, 147). That is, the subject pursues its ends not only according to the momentary determination of pleasure (and pain), but also according to the "general views" that situate every determination of pleasure (and pain) within a network of ends that, as such, is always thought as ultimate. The formation of general views is made possible by a reflection of both affection and the object in the imagination. Again using Hume's example, we can condemn Nero for killing his mother Agrippina not because the act is painful for the subject who judges, but because the determining action of the principles of passion is extended and reflected in the imagination. In order for Nero's act of murder to be able to be condemned by any human subject, the partiality of those subjects must be surpassed. This cannot be accomplished by the action of principles, it is only accomplished by the imagination. In imagination, "Nero" becomes "a murderer" and "Nero's killing of Agrippina" becomes a "murder," a determinate relation that can then be evaluated according to its propensity to yield pleasure or pain. Thereby "general interest is invented . . . There is a general interest only through imagination, artifice, or fantasy; nonetheless it enters into the natural constitution of the mind, as a sentiment for humanity, as culture." To the extensive schematism of knowledge there is therefore added an intensive schematism of morality in which the mind reacts "to the supposedly known totality of circumstances and relations" (*ES*, 148).

Deleuze summarizes this conclusion by borrowing from Hume another example: that of a circle. "As an object of knowledge the circle is a relation between parts, the place of points situated at an equal distance from a common point called the center" (*ES*, 149). The end of the determination of a shape (for instance) results in the determination of the center and circumference of the circle as useful for the accomplishment of the end, a determination that must be guarded against the effects of fantasy which threaten, for instance, to determine the circumference as equal to a given, rational length. "As an object of, for example, aesthetic sentiment, the figure is taken as a whole to which the mind reacts according to its natural constitution" (*ES*, 149). Here, the apprehension of the circle as useful or not for the judging subject is accompanied by an apprehension of the circle as useful or not in procuring the end of aesthetic pleasure for any human being whatsoever. "In both cases, fantasy is found at the foundation of a world, a world of culture and a world of distinct and continuous existence" (*ES*, 149).

Resonating in the imagination, the principles of association give rise, through the conjunction of vivacity and determined relations, to both licit and illicit relations whose differentiation allows for a world of distinct and continuous existence; equally resonant, the principles of passion give rise to general views, the differentiation of whose rules determines a given historical culture within the whole of universalized human nature. The function of the corrective rules in each case differs according to the different action of the excessive rules in the two cases. In the case of the rules of association, the action of the principles of association is directly contradicted, erroneous relations are prohibited, and the distinct and continuous world becomes what Deleuze calls a "general residue," the remnants of the vivacity of ideas that persists through the corrective operation of the understanding. In the case of moral rules, however, their corrective operation yields "harmony" in which it is only the partial or "limiting" effect of the passions that is checked, with the result that the fictional effect of the passions (culture) is adequate to those principles; the conflict that is manifest in the action of correction is resolved (*ES*, 149). This, according to Deleuze, again shows the primacy of passion over association: the action of the two types of principles of association yields the never-overcome contradiction between knowledge determined by causality and the belief in distinct and continuous existence; this contradiction is only "resolved" insofar as human nature is constituted by both principles of association and principles of passion. In the latter, the dual action of extensive and corrective rules achieves a result that follows from those principles even as it follows from the vivacity of ideas. "This is to say once again that association is *for* passion" (*ES*, 150; emphasis in the original). With this, Deleuze's argument, begun in chapter 5, is complete: the moments of the system of the subject (the extensive and corrective rules of association and passion) have been distinguished and their synthetic relation, the unity of the subject, has been made clear.

The closing paragraphs of *Empiricism and Subjectivity* are both summative and polemical, drawing the elements of Deleuze's account of Hume together in a concentrated form in order to make as clear as possible the difference that empiricism makes for contemporary philosophical problems. Deleuze writes that "we will call *intentional finality* the unity of a subject that functions as a whole," a term that only arises at the conclusion of the discussion, but which testifies to the fact that both empiricism and phenomenology (transcendental rationalism) take the project of the determination of a science of human nature to entail an analysis of the living, worldly subject (*ES*, 150; emphasis in the original). Phenomenology wrongly criticizes empiricism, associationism, for being a "psychology of knowledge," mistaking both the duality of the principles of human nature and, more importantly, the priority of the principles of passion over those of association. Perhaps most significant is Deleuze's claim that the subject can only be properly described by a dualism: "the mind by itself has two fundamental characteristics: *resonance* and *vivacity*" (*ES*, 150; emphasis in the original).[16] Under the effect of principles, human nature is twofold, both belief and invention: the mind becomes a subject "*when it mobilizes its vivacity in such a way that a part of which it is the characteristic (an impression) communicates it to another part (an idea), and on the other hand, when all the parts taken together resonate in producing something new*" (*ES*, 151; emphasis in the original). The subject then expects, anticipates the unknown, but also "conserves itself," that is, it invents a world of culture (or instinctually invents a natural world) that secures for the subject an identity that surpasses its own partiality.

Deleuze writes that "this is where Hume's philosophy reaches its ultimate point: this Nature conforms to Being; human nature conforms to Nature" (*ES*, 152). The corrected action of the principles of passion yields a world in which those principles are still determinative but in which the vivacity of the ideas has, in conjunction with those principles, surpassed the partiality of worldly experience. And yet, because this surpassing is the product of a resonance between the given and the principles, the resulting totalities of culture and nature, though fictional, nonetheless "agree with the hidden powers on which the given depends, and which we do not know." This agreement "that can only be thought" is finality *simpliciter*, the "agreement of intentional finality with Nature" (*ES*, 152). Against ontology, the metaphysics of Being as Being, then, Deleuze demonstrates that the duality of the given and the principles of human nature account for the worldly activity of the subject while also ruling out inquiry into any kind of determinative ground of this dual action. "Being," then, "can only ever be grasped as the object of a synthetic relation with the very principles of what we do" (*ES*, 152). The possibility of ontology is simultaneously opened and foreclosed by the action of the principles insofar as they act in concert with the vivacity of ideas, that "hidden power on which the given depends," and provide the determination that the given lacks on its own. Phenomenology therefore commits a crucial error in shifting to ontology; and here, already in Deleuze's first book, can be seen an important and decisive rejection of Heidegger's reworking of the project of transcendental phenomenology.

In agreement with a project like Thao's, which tries to address the shortcomings of transcendental phenomenology by returning to concrete historical experience, Hume's empiricism argues that a science of human nature can only be constituted by according a priority to the cultural world as the invention of the passions in their relation with the powers of the given. However, where Thao determines culture as the product of dialectical materialism, Deleuze, for reasons articulated in his review of

Hyppolite's *Logic and Existence*—reasons that form the initial kernel of what will later become his extensive work on Spinoza as a thinker of differential materialism—finds in Hume an account of culture as a fiction, an invention, determined in each case by concrete circumstances that cannot be entirely reduced to the force of the principles that determine them.[17] The subject of empiricism is, in appearance, the worldly subject of transcendental phenomenology, a subject constituted as intentional finality, but this formality is, for Hume, an invention—necessary, certainly, as the effect of principles, but an invention nonetheless—effected by the determined force of the given; it is not itself determinative. Reason is a *determined* synthesis for empiricism, for associationism, it is an invented accord of the given and the principles of human nature; for rationalism, on the other hand, reason is a *determining* synthesis that makes possible a given that the subject is tasked with representing faithfully, accurately. This determining synthesis, transcending the concrete as an unimpeachable authority, as an ideal to which the representative efforts of the subject must submit (as to a tribunal, to anticipate Deleuze's Kafkaesque reading of Kant), mistakes the task of philosophy for the rational representation of right action.[18] It fails to discover in the philosophical account of the inventive power of the primary and determinative principles of passion a "theory of what we do" that gives to the worldly subject (the subject and its circumstances) the power to determine the given, always in concert with the undetermined, multiple forces of the imagination, of the given.

Conclusion

> If you want to apply bio-bibliographical criteria to me, I confess I wrote my first book fairly early on, and then produced nothing more for eight years. I know what I was doing, where and how I lived during those years, but I know it only abstractly, rather as if someone else was relating memories that I believe but don't really have. It's like a hole in my life, an eight-year hole.
>
> —Gilles Deleuze, "On Philosophy"

The central and organizing claim of the conclusion of *Empiricism and Subjectivity* is that "the subject is *constituted by principles*, and *founded on fantasy*."[1] In what way is this a response or resolution of the original problem of the book: how does the mind acquire the regularity of human nature? Or, how does the mind become a subject? It has been shown that this is not an epistemological question; for Deleuze, Hume is, above all, a thinker of the practical. In general, knowledge is an activity of the mind that has become a subject under the effect of the principles of association. According to Deleuze's reading of Hume, under the determining action of the principles of association, the activity of the mind is "to surpass, is always to go from the known to the unknown."[2] The fantastic is the unknown, the as-yet undetermined. Importantly, although Deleuze is close to Wahl here, Hume's empiricism describes a passage from the known to another potentially known, while for Wahl, there is also an experience of transcendence in which the movement attempted or invited is from the known to the Whole, to something that essentially resists being known, something that is other than the principles of human nature.

For Hume, human nature is composed of both belief and invention: the mind becomes a subject "*when it mobilizes its vivacity in such a way that a part of which it* [vivacity] *is the characteristic (an impression) communicates it to another part (an idea), and on the other hand, when all the parts taken together resonate in producing something new*."[3] The subject expects and anticipates the unknown, but it also "conserves itself," it invents a world of culture that secures for it a general or conventional identity that surpasses its own partiality. This is what makes another—quite late—assertion by Deleuze a key passage of *Empiricism and Subjectivity*: "philosophy must be constituted as the theory of what we are doing, not as the theory of what is."[4] On the one hand, Deleuze shows in this statement that he is siding with Wahl's account of empiricism given in the preface to *Vers le concret*: for empiricism, the given is "non-deducible," and for an empiricism such as Hume's, one of the "second order," this non-deducibility, this "thickness" of the given, is a matter for philosophical thought.[5] On the other hand, this account of empiricism differs strikingly from its epistemological formulation by Hyppolite. For Hyppolite (and Hegel), empiricism is the result of a reflection in which thought still remains distinct from its content, which is therefore not securely grasped in its truth. It is overcome when language becomes speculative and is able to state the sense of the "monstration" of the content of thought.[6] In the showing of its sense, in its monstration, the content of thought is stripped of its thickness and thereby determined. This explains the importance that Deleuze attributes to Hume's claim that the subject is "founded on fantasy." Thus founded, the sense of the content of thought is never finally determined because its "thickness" always makes possible another sense. Again, epistemology gives way to the practice of "making sense" rather than allowing sense to "show itself."

According to Deleuze's reading of Hume, Nature is the product of belief and invention, the creation of a unity or whole out of disparate parts, not the coordination of parts within a primary Whole. After spending so much of his book detailing Hume's theory of subjectivity, the topic of empiricism—and its difference from rationalism—is directly engaged in the closing pages of *Empiricism and Subjectivity*. "Hume's empiricism," Deleuze writes, "reaches its ultimate point [when] Nature conforms to Being; human nature conforms to Nature." At first glance this seems all too close to Hyppolite's rationalism, but Deleuze clarifies that "in the given, we establish relations, we form totalities, [but] these do not depend on the given, [they depend on] principles that we know [and that] are purely functional."[7] The sense of Nature—worldly meaning—is constituted practically, functionally, not absolutely.

The action of the principles of passion yields a world in which those principles are determinative but in which the vivacity of the ideas has, in conjunction with these principles, surpassed the partiality of subjective worldly experience. Because this surpassing is the product of a resonance between the given and the principles rather than in contradiction with them (as was the case with the principles of association), the resulting cultural totalities, although fictional, nonetheless "agree with the hidden powers on which the given depends, and which we do not know." This agreement "that can only be thought" is finality *simpliciter,* the "agreement of intentional finality with Nature."[8] It can only be thought—and never known—because the agreement is not a relation of impressions and ideas, it is the condition of such relations. That there *is* such a condition is manifest; its characteristics, however, can only be known "deliriously."[9] The thickness of the world of experience stubbornly refuses the impulse to Wholeness even as that same world allows for the limitless possibilities of practical human activity.

It has been argued that *Empiricism and Subjectivity* is an intervention in an extensive debate between empiricism and rationalism, figured for Deleuze in terms of Wahl's existential pluralism and Hyppolite's immanent and dialectical ontology. This debate was very much alive at the beginning of the 1950s, as evidenced in part by the publication of Hyppolite's *Logic and Existence,* as well as by two essays by Wahl on empiricist aspects of Husserl's phenomenology.[10] It was Husserl, not Heidegger, whose academic fortune was on the rise in France in the early 1950s, since he was seen to be the more "scientific" of the two thinkers and so preferable for communist-inclined thinkers and others who eschewed idealism.[11] Whereas Wahl's philosophical interests placed him in the midst of this revaluation of Husserl and phenomenology, Hyppolite's interests—which, at the time, were primarily directed toward the account of the relation between Hegel's *Logic* and his *Phenomenology*—kept him on the periphery of these debates.

The publication of *Logic and Existence,* however, brought Wahl and Hyppolite into direct dialogue. Both Deleuze and Wahl reviewed Hyppolite's book: Wahl in a lengthy article for Bataille's journal *Critique* in 1953, and Deleuze in a much shorter article the following year in the *Revue Philosophique de la France et l'Étranger.*[12] A central element of both reviews is a rejection of contradictory difference and the corresponding dialectical move from one entity or conceptualization to another. Contradictory difference—as discussed above at the beginning of chapter 5—maintains that there is an inherent difference between a thing, A, and another, different, thing, not-A. This contradictory difference allows for not-A to be co-given with A, and in the speculative dialectic of Hegel, the development of thought as it follows the ramifications of this difference ultimately allows for the "monstration" or "showing" of the sense of the world. The critiques of Wahl and Deleuze can be summed up in one of the latter's comments: "can we not construct an ontology of difference which would not have to go up to contradiction, because contradiction would be less than difference and not more?"[13] In other words, isn't contradiction a particular type of difference that allows for the dialectical development of thought only by arbitrarily imposing a limitation of the concrete differentiation of things? Deleuze further wonders, again in a vein similar to Wahl, whose work insists that poetry manages to convey the irreducible "thickness" of experience and the world, whether Hyppolite's own discussion of what he calls "the ineffable," what cannot be given meaning by language, might not provide material and examples for a noncontradictory ontology. For Hyppolite, however, and for rationalism generally, the ineffable is just the not-yet-understood, what has simply not been thought through to its speculative conclusion. It is always-already rational, and because of this, speculative reason never learns anything new, it only comes to know more and more about itself.

The publication of *Logic and Existence*, and the reviews by Wahl and Deleuze, would have seemed to augur well for a rich philosophical exchange. But none came about. Instead, the middle of the 1950s saw a double transformation of the philosophical fashion in France: the waning of interest in Husserl amidst a renewal of interest in Heidegger, and the rather abrupt demise of existentialism as a philosophical project, coupled with the corresponding turn to structuralism. The ascension of Heidegger to philosophical prominence can be marked rather precisely: in August and September of 1955 Heidegger traveled to France, to Cerisy-la-Salle, for a conference devoted to his work. This marked the culmination of years of work and debate, spearheaded by Jean Beaufret, concerning not only Heidegger's philosophy but also his ties to the Nazi Party.[14] Structuralism's coming into vogue is more difficult to date, but 1955 also saw the publication of Claude Lévi-Strauss's *Tristes Tropiques*.[15] Neither Wahl nor Hyppolite played a central role in these movements, although both continued to pursue their own projects: Hyppolite publishing *Studies on Marx and Hegel* in 1955, and Wahl continuing to publish diverse works, including, importantly, his *Traité de métaphysique* [*Metaphysical Treatise*], which appeared in 1953. Retrospectively, the question of existentialism can be understood as having brought the work of Hyppolite and Wahl into philosophical proximity and, with its general abandonment, the opportunities for a renewed exchange, one that would continue the debates of the 1930s and 1940s—but now augmented by Deleuze's work—went unrealized.

As for Deleuze, contrary to the epigraph above, it is not strictly true that he produced "nothing more" for eight years after the publication of *Empiricism and Subjectivity*. Although it's true that he did not follow up on the philosophical accomplishments of his first book by continuing to author work on Hume or empiricism, perhaps due to the shifting winds of French academia mentioned above, he did author two interesting articles on Bergson in the mid-1950s. In *Empiricism and Subjectivity* Deleuze had noted similarities between Hume and Bergson, particularly their shared belief, in Bergson's words, that human beings are entities defined by the habit of acquiring habits.[16] In his two articles, as well as on subsequent occasions in his career when he again turned to Hume directly, one can see the importance that Deleuze continued to attach to Hume, to empiricism, and to the argument of *Empiricism and Subjectivity* generally.

In 1956 Deleuze published both "Bergson, 1859–1942," written for Merleau-Ponty's *Les philosophes célèbres,* and "La Conception de la différence chez Bergson" ("Bergson's Conception of Difference"), which appeared in the journal *Les Études Bergsoniennes.*[17] In the latter, more substantive, essay, Deleuze reinterprets Hume's famous discussion of causality as the question of how the new comes to appear to the mind: where "'something new' is the expectation of the thousandth time around— there you have *difference.* Hume's response [to the question of how the repetition of similar cases can nonetheless produce something new] was that if repetition produces a difference in the mind looking on, it is by virtue of the principles of human nature and especially the principle of habit."[18] In the repeated collision of billiard balls the mind "contracts," to use the Bergsonian formulation, and retains the past instances as different from the present instance. Significantly, in this same passage and subsequently, Deleuze speaks of "pure repetition" as "matter," or "what is opposed to contraction."[19] How are difference and repetition opposed? In the bare collision of the billiard balls, each "case" of collision is a repetition; there is no relation in the billiard balls themselves that binds one instance of collision to any previous one. Thus there is no possibility of newness either, since there is no mental retention, or "contraction," according to which the present could differ from the past. Only the contracting power of the mind produces difference, as in this case, each different collision of the billiard balls. "Bergson's Conception of Difference" thus shows Deleuze, again under the "cover" of the explication of another philosopher's work, working out the implications of a non-contradictory conception of difference. Over a decade later, the second chapter of *Difference and Repetition*—entitled "Repetition for Itself"—will open with a discussion of Hume and Bergson.[20]

Another significant appearance of Hume in Deleuze's work in the 1950s occurred in a course that Deleuze taught on the question "What Is Grounding?" during the academic year 1956–57, immediately following the appearance of his essays on Bergson. The primary figures considered in the course are Heidegger and Kant, but Deleuze emphasizes, near the outset of the course, that Kant's definitive formulation of the problem of the ground—that is, of what secures knowledge—ultimately derives from Hume (even if Hume did not pose this question). Much of the discussion of Hume repeats material from *Empiricism and Subjectivity,* but Deleuze focuses on how Hume prepares the way for Kant's theory of transcendental subjectivity. Hume poses the problem of what allows for knowing to go beyond the given, and answers with his conception of habit.[21] "According to him [Hume], habit involves the repetition of similar cases . . . Experience yields a repetition of similar cases."[22] Significantly, unlike his essay on Bergson, Deleuze does not invoke difference in this discussion; there is only repetition as the logical independence of each similar case. The reason for this is that, in the "What Is Grounding?" course, Deleuze is emphasizing not the epistemological fact of the emergence of difference in the mind's comprehension of a series of distinct cases, but the practical use of the regularity of cases which enables human beings to reliably go beyond the immediately given.

According to Deleuze, in Hume there is a "harmony" between Nature and the principles of human nature, but for Kant, this answer seems simply capricious, and in order to justify the harmony observed by Hume, Kant conceives of Nature as subordinate to the same principles as human nature.[23] With this re-situation of the problem and the corresponding constitution of transcendental subjectivity, Kant gives form to the question of grounding that will animate subsequent philosophies.[24] Hume is not used exclusively negatively in the course, however, and Deleuze remarks that it was Hume who "brought in something new: the analysis of the structure of subjectivity," and this structure is one of aiming at and achieving ends.[25] Although he follows a somewhat traditional presentation of the problem of grounding from Kant to Heidegger, the course exhibits Deleuze's continuing concern, broached in *Empiricism and Subjectivity*, with the difference between Hume's empiricism—and empiricism generally—and rationalist projects. For empiricism, the problem of grounding is always a practical, not an epistemological, concern.

As the foregoing shows, despite not following *Empiricism and Subjectivity* with more work devoted expressly to Hume or to empiricism, Hume continued to inform Deleuze's work in the 1950s. And he did so beyond the 1950s as well. Evidence of this can be found not only in the explicit use Deleuze makes of Hume—such as in *Difference and Repetition*—but also in the repeated inclusion of Hume when Deleuze lists important figures who constitute a kind of alternative pantheon of historical philosophers, both inside and outside of the mainstream history of philosophy. Thus, in Deleuze's 1973 "Letter to a Harsh Critic," he writes that he concentrated "on authors who challenged the rationalist tradition in this history (and I see a secret link between Lucretius, Hume, Spinoza, and Nietzsche, constituted by their critique of negativity, their cultivation of joy, the hatred of interiority, the externality of forces and relations, the denunciation of power . . . and so on.)"[26] And he gives a very similar statement in 1977, in "A Conversation: What Is It? What Is It For?": "I liked writers who seemed to be part of the history of philosophy, but who escaped from it in one respect, or altogether: Lucretius, Spinoza, Hume, Nietzsche, Bergson."[27] Even more significant are the places where—as in *Difference and Repetition*—Deleuze does more than link Hume to a particular tradition or lineage in philosophy, and returns to work more substantively on him.

The key text in this regard is his 1972 essay for a volume in François Chatelet's *History of Philosophy*.[28] However, Deleuze also returns to Hume and empiricism in his 1977 essay "On the Superiority of Anglo-American Literature," in his 1988 contribution to an issue of *Topoi* devoted to the question "Who Comes after the Subject?" and finally in his preface to the English translation of *Empiricism and Subjectivity*.[29] Surprising in all of these engagements is the consistency and near uniformity of the value attributed to Hume's philosophy by Deleuze.

Chief among the ideas that Deleuze repeatedly attributes to Hume is the exteriority of relations and their terms. As chapter 1 of this book argued, this was already a key notion in Wahl's appropriation of Russell and his conception of a radical empiricism, but Deleuze claims it as one of Hume's most important achievements. Thus, near the beginning of "Hume," Deleuze writes: "Hume's originality, one aspect of his originality, derives from the force with which he affirms: *relations are exterior to their terms*."[30] Then, in "On the Superiority of Anglo-American Literature," Deleuze writes: "What is it that the empiricists found, not in their heads, but in the world, which is like a vital discovery, a certainty of life which, if one really adheres to it, changes one's way of life? It is not the question 'Does the intelligible come from the sensible?' but a quite different question, that of relations. *Relations are external to their terms*."[31] Finally, in the "Preface" to the English edition of *Empiricism and Subjectivity*, the third (of three) concepts created by Hume is "the first great logic of relations, showing in it that all relations (not only 'matters of fact' but also relations among ideas) are external to their terms."[32] Ultimately, this is Deleuze's response to Hyppolite, just as, in Wahl's work, it was the response of Russell, James, and others to Hegel. That relations are external to their terms means that there is no Whole that can be composed or read off from the diversity of things. This is the capital importance of chapter 4 of *Empiricism and Subjectivity*, "God and the World," as discussed above in chapter 6. Against such totalizing moves, Deleuze argues that Hume plunges the mind into a "delirium" in order thereby to return it to "good sense." An echo of Wahl's sense of transcendence can be heard here, but for Deleuze, there is no movement of finite existence beyond itself, no ecstatic unity. The beyond is a fiction. But it is a fiction that returns the mind to the practical world of action, and returns the inquiry into the association of ideas from its epistemological flights to its proper task: "the association of ideas exists for the sake of law, political economy, aesthetics, and so on."[33]

To use one of Hume's examples that Deleuze never tires of quoting, empiricism asks who owns the abandoned city: the one who first touched its gate, or the one who first hurled his spear into the same gate? Rationalism can offer no answer, and yet the dispute stands. To resolve it is to rethink relations as external to their terms, to reconceive the situation. "[Hume's] empiricism is, so to speak, a kind of universe of science fiction: as in science fiction, the world seems fictional, strange, foreign, experienced by other creatures; but we get the feeling that this world is our own, and we are the creatures."[34] Association has the character of a parable in empiricism. A world is composed and exhibited without being presented as the ultimate or only World. A law is a component of a world, but is never the component of the Whole. Thus, although Deleuze denies Wahl's transcendent experience, he nonetheless sides with Wahl against Hyppolite in arguing that speculative thought, the acme of rationalism, cannot fully apprehend the sensible and the empirical.

Notes

Introduction

EPIGRAPH: Gilles Deleuze, "Letter to a Harsh Critic," in *Negotiations*, trans. Martin Joughin (New York: Columbia University Press, 1995), 11.

1. Gilles Deleuze, *Empirisme et subjectivité: Essai sur la nature humaine selon Hume* (Paris: Presses Universitaires de France, 1953), translated by Constantin V. Boundas as *Empiricism and Subjectivity: An Essay on Hume's Theory of Human Nature* (New York: Columbia University Press, 1991). While I have consulted Boundas's translation, the translations in the text are my own. I have noted significant departures from Boundas's text.

2. In 1954 Deleuze published an important review of Hyppolite's book: "Review of *Logique et existence*," *Revue Philosophique de la France et l'Étranger* (1954): 144, 457–60. The review has been translated into English and published as "Jean Hyppolite's *Logic et Existence*" in Gilles Deleuze, *Desert Islands and Other Texts*, ed. David Lapoujade, trans. Michael Taormina (New York: Semiotext(e), 2004), 15–18.

3. Deleuze, "Letter to a Harsh Critic," 14.

4. "Apart from Sartre, who remained caught none the less in the trap of the verb to be, the most important philosopher in France was Jean Wahl." Gilles Deleuze, "On the Superiority of Anglo-American Literature," in *Dialogues II*, trans. Hugh Tomlinson and Barbara Habberjam (New York: Columbia University Press, 2007), 57–58.

5. François Dosse, *Gilles Deleuze and Félix Guattari: Intersecting Lives*, trans. Deborah Glassman (New York: Columbia University Press, 2010), 89ff.

6. Dosse, *Intersecting Lives*, 95.

7. For a more extensive discussion of Sartre's lecture in its context, see below, chapter 4.

8. "The genius of the 'transcendental turn' that Kant and his heirs effected is that it seems to short-circuit the skeptical doubt that has plagued philosophy since the ancient Greeks and which assumed particular virulence with David Hume in the eighteenth century. In fact, both Kant and Husserl reckon Hume a critical force to be dealt with. . . . Admitting that we do not know the world as it is 'in itself,' the defenders of the transcendental turn argue that such naïve belief is unnecessary to justify our everyday experiences, much less to account for our scientific knowledge of the world. In fact, such an uncritical stance, they argue,

leaves us vulnerable to the skeptical objections of Hume and others." Thomas R. Flynn, *Sartre: An Intellectual Biography* (Cambridge: Cambridge University Press, 2014), 67–68.

9. Gilles Deleuze, "He Was My Teacher," in *Desert Islands and Other Texts*, ed. David Lapoujade, trans. Michael Taormina (New York: Semiotext(e), 2004), 77–80.

10. Deleuze, "He Was My Teacher," 78.

11. Dosse, *Intersecting Lives*, 110.

12. The date and location of Hyppolite's course on Hume is taken from Dina Dreyfus's brief "Avertissement" to Hyppolite's *Figures de la pensée philosophique* (Paris: Presses Universitaires de France, 1991), vi. In *Intersecting Lives*, Dosse locates the course at the University of Strasbourg (110).

13. It is worth noting that Wahl's close friend, Emmanuel Levinas, shared Deleuze's opinion of Wahl's prominent role in French intellectual life. At the outset of "Jean Wahl: Neither Having nor Being," Levinas describes his remarks as a "string of abstract terms" that will imperfectly describe "the life of the great spirit they [Wahl's wife and daughters] knew, the man who, with a nobility foreign to any academic 'mandarinate,' during over half a century of teaching and research, was the life force of the academic, extra-academic and even, to a degree, anti-academic philosophy necessary to a great culture." Levinas, "Jean Wahl: Neither Having nor Being," in *Outside the Subject*, trans. Michael B. Smith (Stanford, CA: Stanford University Press, 1993), 67.

14. See Mathias Girel, "Avant-propos à la deuxième édition," in *Vers le concret: Études d'histoire de la philosophie contemporaine, William James, Whitehead, Gabriel Marcel*, by Jean Wahl (Paris: Vrin, 2004), 5–26.

15. For information on Wahl's activities at Mount Holyoke College during the Second World War, see the essays collected in *Artists, Intellectuals, and World War II: The Pontigny Encounters at Mount Holyoke College, 1942–1944*, ed. Christopher Benfey and Karen Remmler (Amherst: University of Massachusetts Press, 2006).

16. Deleuze, "He Was My Teacher," 78.

17. Alan D. Schrift and Ian Alexander Moore, "Existence, Experience, and Transcendence: An Introduction to Jean Wahl," in *Jean Wahl, Transcendence and the Concrete: Selected Writings*, ed. Schrift and Moore (New York: Fordham University Press, 2016), 12.

18. Gilles Deleuze, "Letter-Preface to Jean-Clet Martin," in Deleuze, *Two Regimes of Madness: Texts and Interviews, 1975–1995*, trans. Ames Hodges and Michael Taormina (New York: Semiotext(e), 2006), 363.

19. Jean Wahl, *Le malheur de la conscience dans la philosophie de Hegel* (Paris: Presses Universitaires de France, 1929), 112.

20. Wahl, *Le malheur de la conscience*, 112.

21. Wahl, *Le malheur de la conscience*, 107.

22. Alexandre Koyré, "Review of Jean Wahl: *Le malheur de la conscience dans la philosophie de Hegel*," *Revue Philosophique de la France et de l'Étranger*, vol. 110 (July–December 1930): 136–43.

23. Jean Wahl, "La lutte contre hégélianisme; Appendix: Hegel et Kierke-gaard," in *Études Kierkegaardiennes* (Paris: Fernand Aubier, 1938), 166.

24. Wahl, "La lutte contre hégélianisme," 171.

25. Wahl, "La lutte contre hégélianisme," 171.

26. Jean Wahl, "Preface to *Toward the Concrete*," in *Jean Wahl, Transcendence and the Concrete: Selected Writings*, ed. Alan D. Schrift and Ian Alexander Moore (New York: Fordham University Press, 2016), 39.

27. As Alan Schrift has noted, the subjects placed on the annual *agrégation* often determine the courses taught at French universities, and indeed, Hume was included on the *agrégation* the year after Hyppolite's class and the year that Deleuze took it. Alan Schrift, "The Effects of the *Agrégation de Philosophie* on Twentieth-Century French Philosophy," *Journal of the History of Philosophy* 46, no. 3 (2008): 449–73.

28. "The true line of philosophic progress lies, in short, it seems to me, not so much *through* Kant as *round* him to the point where now we stand. Philosophy can perfectly well outflank him, and build herself up into adequate fulness by prolonging more directly the older English lines." William James, "Philosophical Conceptions and Practical Results," in *The Writings of William James*, ed. John J. McDermott (Chicago: University of Chicago Press, 1977), 361–62. Quoted by Wahl in *Les philosophies pluralistes d'Angleterre et d'Amérique* (Paris: Félix Alcan, 1920), 76, emphasis in the original.

Chapter 1

EPIGRAPH: Wahl, *Les philosophies pluralistes*, 244.

1. "We others, civilizations, we now know that we are mortal." Paul Valéry, "La Crise de l'esprit," in *Variété I et II* (Paris: Folio, 1998), 13–51.

2. While there is no shortage of accounts of the First World War and its aftermath, my thoughts have been importantly shaped by Modris Eksteins's *The Rites of Spring: The Great War and the Birth of the Modern Age* (Boston: Houghton Mifflin, 1989); Frederick Brown's *The Embrace of Unreason: France, 1914–1940* (New York: Knopf, 2014); and Enzo Traverso's *Fire and Blood: The European Civil War, 1914–1945*, trans. David Fernbach (New York: Verso, 2016).

3. By 1962—if not sooner—intellectual trends will have shifted again: when Levi-Strauss critiques Sartre in *Wild Thought*, he does so by emphasizing the latter's subjectivism and lack of interest in the unconscious forces that structure human sociability.

4. *Pluralist Philosophies* is an expansion of Wahl's 1909 thesis, "A Contribution to the Study of Pluralist Tendencies in Contemporary English and American Philosophies."

5. Levinas, "Jean Wahl: Neither Having nor Being," 83.

6. Brown, *The Embrace of Unreason*, 135.

7. For an excellent and comprehensive account of Wahl's philosophical

activities and influence, see Schrift and Moore's "Existence, Experience, and Transcendence."

8. Discussions of the "Humanism Debate" can be found in Ethan Kleinberg's *Generation Existential: Heidegger's Philosophy in France, 1927–1961* (Ithaca, NY: Cornell University Press, 2005), esp. chapter 6; and in Anson Rabinbach's interesting "Heidegger's *Letter on Humanism* as Text and Event," *New German Critique*, no. 62 (Spring/Summer 1994): 3–38. In *An Atheism That Is Not Humanist Emerges in French Thought*, Stefanos Geroulanos notes the important role Wahl had both in teaching Heidegger's work after the Second World War and in publicizing information about Heidegger's involvement with the Nazis. See *An Atheism That Is Not Humanist Emerges in French Thought* (Stanford, CA: Stanford University Press, 2010), esp. 230–31. For an excellent statement of Wahl's philosophical position, see his essay "Freedom and Existence in Some Recent Philosophies," *Philosophy and Phenomenological Research* 8, no. 4 (June 1948): 538–56. There, Wahl writes: "The fact that our freedom is never completed, that it always fails by my limitation, which are finally my faults, makes us relate ourselves to transcendence" (539).

9. Jean Hyppolite, *Logic and Existence*, trans. Leonard Lawlor and Amit Sen (Albany: State University of New York Press).

10. Leonard Lawlor's work has engaged and investigated the implications of Hyppolite's claim. As Lawlor succinctly states in his essay "The End of Phenomenology: Expressionism in Deleuze and Merleau-Ponty," "the challenge of immanence eliminates transcendence," *Continental Philosophy Review* 31 (1998): 15. Important expansions of this claim can be found in Lawlor's *Thinking Through French Philosophy: The Being of the Question* (Bloomington: Indiana University Press, 2003) and his *The Implications of Immanence: Toward a New Concept of Life* (New York: Fordham University Press, 2006).

11. Hyppolite's translation of Hegel's *Phenomenology of Spirit* was published in two parts, the first in 1939 and the second in 1941. His epochal study of the *Phenomenology, Genesis, and Structure of Hegel's Phenomenology of Spirit* appeared in 1946, and his *Introduction to Hegel's Philosophy of History* appeared in 1948.

12. For details of Wahl's escape from France, see Schrift and Moore's "Existence, Experience, and Transcendence," especially 2–10.

13. In *Origins of the Other: Emmanuel Levinas between Revelation and Ethics* (Ithaca, NY: Cornell University Press, 2005), Samuel Moyn refers to Wahl's 1937 presentation to the *Société Française de Philosophie*, "Subjectivity and Transcendence," as "a turning point in twentieth-century intellectual history" (182). A translation of Wahl's presentation, as well as the discussion that followed, can be found in Jean Wahl, *Human Existence and Transcendence*, trans. and ed. William C. Hackett with Jeffrey Hanson (Notre Dame, IN: University of Notre Dame Press, 2016).

14. Wahl uses the term "transcendental empiricism"—the very term that Deleuze will use to characterize his own philosophy—for the first time in the preface to *Human Existence and Transcendence*. There, he writes: "From the starting point of the Kantian affirmation that being is position, we could pass to a positive philosophy analogous to Schelling and to the highest empiricism. In this

way we could have a transcendental empiricism, as Schelling demonstrated, seeking the conditions by which experience is not merely possible but real, and this realism would be founded on the critique of the idea of the possible and on the reality of contingency (which goes hand in hand with the contingency of the necessary)." Jean Wahl, *Existence humaine et transcendance* (Geneva: La Baconnière, 1944), 18. In *Vers le concret*, Wahl had spoken in similar terms about empiricism and Schelling: "One could certainly distinguish two degrees of empiricism: the empiricism that does not pose the problem, which refuses to pose it, and from the beginning takes being as given; . . . But there would also be the empiricism that would have passed through [*par*] rationalism, and would have surpassed it; such is that of the later Fichte and the later Schelling; . . . This empiricism of the second degree is certainly that of Gabriel Marcel, certainly influenced on this point by the meta-empirical empiricism, if one can call it that, of Schelling." Wahl, *Vers le concret*, 33.

15. In the middle of a long footnote in the preface to *Human Existence and Transcendence*, Wahl writes: "Since the Greeks, philosophy has been oriented by the *logos* which expresses, and by the *eidos* which is essentially expressible, the form inasmuch as it is expressible. Man, a being which speaks and sees, weaves a world of words and spectacles. But the real world is not a world of propositions and perspectives. This world of words and spectacles has been modeled on perception and production. Everything is imagined under the form of the produced and the perceived" (19).

16. The tension between Wahl and Hyppolite lies just beneath the surface of Deleuze's review of *Logic and Existence*, in its repeated references to the empirical (and its distinction from the absolute), and particularly in Deleuze's valorization of the first part of Hyppolite's book, entitled "The Ineffable." See Deleuze, "Jean Hyppolite's *Logic and Existence*," in *Desert Islands*, 18.

Leonard Lawlor's work has shown that Deleuze, as well as Derrida and Foucault, did not think that phenomenology overcame metaphysics successfully or fully; and, according to Lawlor, Derrida, Deleuze, and Foucault can be linked by the claim that phenomenology retains a problematic conception of lived experience which echoes Wahl's concerns. Lawlor, *Implications of Immanence*, 8.

17. Although G. E. Moore is not traditionally associated with a neutral monist position, Wahl explicitly links Moore's and Russell's philosophical positions in *Pluralist Philosophies*. For Wahl, both arrive at theories that are roughly pluralist in outlook, but they do so in different ways: "The theory at which Moore had arrived, starting from the study of moral questions, is reached by Russell mainly through reflection on mathematical data; just as in the case of Moore morality cannot be understood without the affirmation of multiple terms and of relations external to these terms, so, without these terms and relations, mathematics, science in general, are incapable of being understood, according to Russell." Wahl, *Les philosophies pluralistes*, 215. Wahl relies on *Principia Ethica* (1903) for Moore's position. Russell published a number of essays during the decade preceding Wahl's book and outlined his position for the Société Française de Philosophie in a lecture in 1911 that was subsequently published as "Le Réalisme analytique," *Bulletin de la Société Française de Philosophie*, vol. 11 (March 1911): 282–

91. Russell's explicit embrace of a neutral monist philosophy is apparent in his 1919 essay "On Propositions: What They Are and How They Mean," *Proceedings of the Aristotelian Society*, supplementary volume 2 (1919): 1–43.

18. Levinas, "Neither Having nor Being," 80. Levinas quotes the last entry in "Building and Destroying" from Wahl's *Poésie, pensée, perception*. The full entry reads:

> To build a house in flames.
> This would be something perverse and barbarous.
> To consent to the annihilation of the most precious values. (248)
>   [translation altered]

19. Wahl, "La lutte contre hégélianisme," *Études Kierkegaardiennes*, 157.

20. Wahl's 1932 book *Vers le concret* became a touchstone for a generation of French thinkers, including existentialists such as Sartre and Beauvoir, but also phenomenologists such as Gaston Berger, Levinas, and Merleau-Ponty. It also had a decisive effect on the generation of thinkers coming of age in the 1930s. In a 1990 letter to Jean-Clet Martin, Deleuze writes: "I therefore have only one thing to say to you: don't lose the concrete, return to it constantly." Deleuze, "Letter-Preface to Jean-Clet Martin," in *Two Regimes of Madness*, 363. Despite its manifest importance, the "concrete" was taken up in so many different ways—by so many different figures—that there was no tangible accretion of thought around Wahl's book. Even its author would devote much of the next decade not to the "concrete" directly but to one of its exponents, Kierkegaard.

21. Wahl, "La lutte contre hégélianisme," *Études Kierkegaardiennes*, 130.

22. The so-called "French Hegel" has been the object of a great deal of commentary since Wahl and others reintroduced him to the philosophical scene in the 1920s. Anglo-American evaluations and reevaluations of the impact of Hegel on French philosophy largely began with a pair of books, *Subjects of Desire: Hegelian Reflections in Twentieth-Century France* by Judith Butler (1987), and *Knowing and History: Appropriations of Hegel in Twentieth-Century France* by Michael S. Roth (1988). Both of these books gave pride of place to the work of Alexandre Kojève—often occluding the important and influential work of other figures such as Wahl, Alexandre Koyré, and Jean Hyppolite. Essays such as Mark Poster's "The Hegel Renaissance," in *Telos*, vol. 16 (1973): 109–27; John Heckman's "Hyppolite and the Hegel Revival in France" in the same volume of *Telos*; Michael Kelly's "The Post-War Hegel Revival in France," in the *Journal of European Studies* 13, no. 51 (1983): 199–216; as well as, importantly, Bruce Baugh's book *French Hegel: From Surrealism to Postmodernism* (2003) did much to correct this overemphasis on Kojève, elaborating the wide diversity of arguments and positions taken in France toward Hegel's work. Other more recent works, such as Alan D. Schrift's *Twentieth-Century French Philosophy: Key Themes and Thinkers* (London: Wiley-Blackwell, 2006) and Geroulanos's *An Atheism That Is Not Humanist* (2010) provide more measured and nuanced accounts of the role of Hegel in twentieth-century French thought.

23. This weakness of human beings is on early display in the *Meditations* when, at the start of the Second Meditation, Descartes recollects the results of the

previous day's work: "So serious are the doubts into which I have been thrown as a result of yesterday's meditation that I can neither put them out of my mind nor see any way of resolving them." René Descartes, *Meditations on First Philosophy*, in *The Philosophical Writings of Descartes*, trans. John Cottingham, Robert Stoothoff, and Dugald Murdoch (Cambridge: Cambridge University Press, 1984), 2:16. Descartes here makes no mention of the uncertainty of memory itself.

24. Moreover, because the Cartesian theory of movement depends upon the Cartesian theory of God, all natural differences reduce to movement. Moreover, "since all the phenomena of nature are reduced to movement, all of physics depends upon metaphysics." Jean Wahl, *Du rôle de l'idée de l'instant dans la philosophie de Descartes* (Paris: Félix Alcan, 1920), 32. The succession of instants is also "the negation of all the possibilities that are not realized possibilities, the slow destruction of everything that is not real and present. History is the slow destruction of everything not present and real. . . . History itself becomes the negation of the importance of history." Wahl, *Du rôle de l'idée de l'instant*, 43.

25. Wahl here makes use of William James's discussion of the role that a philosopher's "personal vision" plays in his or her philosophical outlook. As James writes in "The Types of Philosophic Thinking": "All philosophers, accordingly, have conceived of the whole world after the analogy of some particular feature of it which has particularly captivated their attention." And "every [philosopher] is nevertheless prone to claim that his conclusions are the only logical ones, that they are necessities of universal reason, they being all the while, at bottom, accidents more or less of personal vision which had far better be avowed as such; for one man's vision may be much more valuable than another's, and our visions are usually not only our most interesting but our most respectable contributions to the world in which we play our part." In *The Writings of William James*, ed. John J. McDermott (Chicago: University of Chicago Press, 1977), 484–85.

26. Sterling Lamprecht, "Review of Jean Wahl's *Les philosophies pluralistes d'Angleterre et d'Amérique*," *Journal of Philosophy* 18, no. 26 (December 22, 1921): 718. Indeed, it is a photo of William James, not Wahl, that graces the frontispiece of the book's English translation.

27. While no doubt drawing the importance of the idea of the exteriority of relations and their terms to empiricism from Wahl's work, Deleuze repeatedly attributes this idea to Hume, whereas Wahl does not. In *Empirisme et subjectivité*, Deleuze writes that "as relations of ideas or as relations of objects, relations are always external to their terms" (63). In 1972, he writes in the entry on "Hume" for Francois Châtelet's *Histoire de la philosophie*, that "Hume's originality, one aspect of his originality, derives from the force which he affirms: *relations are exterior to their terms*." Gilles Deleuze, "Hume," in *Desert Islands*, 163 (emphasis in the original). And in 1989, in the "Preface to the English-Language Edition" of *Empirisme et subjectivité*, Deleuze writes that Hume "created the first great logic of *relations*, showing in it that all relations (not only 'matters of fact' but also relations among ideas) are external to their terms" (x; emphasis in the original).

28. In his essay "Philosophy of Logical Atomism," Russell describes his position as that of a "neutral monism," to be distinguished from Spinoza's "dual

aspect monism" as well as from Hegel's substantial monism. Russell's monism is irreducible to either idealism or materialism. Bertrand Russell, *The Philosophy of Logical Atomism* (New York: Routledge, 2010).

29. Wahl notes that "the theory of internal relations has never been proved; neither the doctrine of sufficient reason, nor the idea that a change in relations would bring about a change in terms, suffices to prove it." Wahl, *Les philosophies pluralistes*, 216.

30. The English translation adds: "finally, it is neither." This phrase is not in the French.

31. It is worth emphasizing that in *Pluralist Philosophies,* Wahl already sees the issue of the relation of immanence and transcendence—an issue that will only grow more prominent in his later work—at work in James.

32. In the following section, section 7, Wahl describes the contemporary development in monism. Section 8 then goes on to discuss the several ideas that are common to both monism and contemporary pluralism: (1) the rejection of abstract reasoning as inadequate for thinking the particular; (2) the importance of starting from pure experience; (3) a common effort to bring together immanence and transcendence; and (4) a moral conception of the tragic character of life. Wahl, *Les philosophies pluralistes*, 270.

33. For an overview of works on Hegel in France prior to—and immediately subsequent to—Wahl's *Le malheur,* see Michael Kelly's excellent and thorough article, "Hegel in France to 1940: A Bibliographical Essay," *Journal of European Studies* 11, no. 41 (1983): 29–52. Although sometimes referred to as *The Unhappy Consciousness in Hegel's Philosophy,* a more accurate rendering of Wahl's title is *The Unhappiness of Consciousness,* since Wahl's focus is on the unhappy striving of consciousness rather than on a particular stage of Hegel's *Phenomenology of Spirit.*

34. Bud Burkhard's excellent and exhaustively researched *French Marxism between the Wars* (Amherst, NY: Humanity Books, 2000) remains the best English-language introduction to the Philosophies group.

35. "When they first coalesced as a group in 1924, they were searching for a philosophic and religious solution to the *inquiétude* plaguing French intellectuals after the Great War." Burkhard, *French Marxism,* 14. In a strikingly personal section of "On Space and Time" in *Human Existence and Transcendence,* Wahl seems to be looking back to his time as a fellow-traveler with the Philosophies group. Wahl writes: "I cannot help thinking that these reflections call attention to the decadence of philosophy. It is curious, since the idea of decadence has a stronger grip on me than the idea of progress. . . . Here things are equally easy for the Marxist, Thomist, and Critical Idealist. They call me petty bourgeois, unbeliever, realist. They speak of a philosophy or poetry of despair, even though it is completely the reverse." Wahl, *Existence humaine et transcendance,* 69.

36. "Breton and the Surrealists suggested Hegel to the Philosophies during the fusion talks of 1924–1925. Yet the first systematic introduction they received came from Jean Wahl, whose reading of Hegel was tinged with Kierkegaardian religious overtones." Burkhard, *French Marxism,* 70. See also Henri Lefebvre's *Les temps des méprises* [*The Time of Misunderstandings*] (Paris: Stock, 1975), 48–50; and his article "1925" in the *Nouvelle Revue Française,* no. 172 (April 1967).

37. Burkhard, *French Marxism*, 62.

38. F. W. J. Schelling, *Recherches philosophiques sur l'essence de la liberté humaine et sur les problemes qui s'y rattachent*, trans. Georges Politzer (Paris: F. Rieder, 1926).

39. In his "Commentaire d'un passage de la 'Phénoménologie de l'esprit' de Hegel," Wahl stresses the contemporary relevance of the Hegelian account of the unhappiness of consciousness: "The signification of the chapter [of the *Phenomenology*] has an even more general bearing, or, at least, another kind of generality, if it is true that consciousness has for its nature to be divided before being reassembled, to be torn apart before being sewn up again into a nevertheless indissoluble unity, where consciousness and its essence, consciousness and its object, come to coincide. Whence, not only the unhappiness of consciousness but of the world in general, divorced from what makes its unity, by a sort of cosmic rending, a gulf that reason fills in." Jean Wahl, "Commentaire d'un passage de la 'Phénoménologie de l'esprit' de Hegel," *Revue de Métaphysique et de Morale* 34, no. 4 (1927): 471. Both the translation of Hegel's *Phenomenology* on the unhappiness of consciousness and Wahl's commentary are reprinted in *Le malheur*. There would not be a full translation of Hegel's *Phenomenology of Spirit* until Jean Hyppolite's was published more than a decade after Wahl's book.

40. Wahl, "La lutte contre hégélianisme," *Études Kierkegaardiennes*, 157.

41. Roth, *Knowing and History*, 95. Some of the notes from Koyré's course have been reprinted in *De la mystique à la science: Cours, conférences et documents, 1922–1962*, ed. Pietro Redondi (Paris: Éditions de l'École des Hautes Études en Sciences Sociales, 1986).

42. The exclusion of religion from Wahl's account reflects his interest in the contemporary attempts by Heidegger and Jaspers to discuss the phenomenon of anxiety outside of a religious frame. All of these connect to the larger problem of whether and how Kierkegaard's work and thought might be dissociated from the vocabulary and concepts of Christianity.

43. Koyré, "Review of Jean Wahl: *Le malheur de la conscience dans la philosophie de Hegel*," 136–37.

44. These include Leon Brunschvicg's *Le progrès de la conscience dans la philosophie occidentale* [*The Progress of Consciousness in Western Philosophy*] (Paris: Alcan, 1927); and the first volume of Theodor Haering's *Hegel, sein Wollen und sein Werk* [*Hegel: His Aims and Work*] (Berlin: B. G. Teubner, 1929). It is also worth noting that in the academic year 1930–31, Heidegger taught a course on Hegel, now published as *Hegel's Phenomenology of Spirit*, trans. Parvis Emad and Kenneth Maly (Bloomington: Indiana University Press, 1988).

45. Wahl, "Commentaire d'un passage de la 'Phénoménologie de l'esprit' de Hegel," 471.

46. For an informative account of the status of Hegel research in France at the time of Wahl's book, one can consult Wahl's own bibliography to *Le malheur*. More recently, Bruce Baugh provides an excellent and nuanced account of the twentieth-century reception of Hegel in France in his "Limiting Reason's Empire: The Early Reception of Hegel in France." *Journal of the History of Philosophy* 31, no. 2 (April 1993): 259–75, as well his more extended discussion in *French Hegel: From Surrealism to Postmodernism* (New York: Routledge, 2003). For a broader account

that includes the nineteenth century as well as postwar developments, see Gwen-doline Jarczyk and Pierre-Jean Labarriere, "Cent cinquante années de 'récep-tion' hégélienne en France" ["150 Years of the French Hegelian 'Reception'"], *Genèses*, vol. 2 (1990): 109–30; as well as John Russon, "Dialectic, Difference, and the Other: The Hegelianizing of French Phenomenology," in *The History of Con-tinental Philosophy*, ed. Alan D. Schrift, vol. 4, *Phenomenology: Responses and Develop-ments*, ed. Leonard Lawlor (Chicago: University of Chicago Press, 2019), 17–42.

47. Particularly important for Wahl's claim are three books: Nohl's edition of *Hegel's Theologische Jugendschriften* [*Hegel's Youthful Theological Writings*] (Tübin-gen: J. C. B. Mohr, 1907), Rosenkranz's *Hegel's Leben* [*Hegel's Life*] (Berlin, 1844), and Thaulow's *Hegel's Ansichten uber Erziehung und Unterricht* [*Hegel's Views on Edu-cation and Teaching*], vol. 3 (Kiel, 1854). In the bibliography to *Le malheur*, Wahl emphasizes that Rosenkranz's and Thaulow's volumes contain material by Hegel that is unavailable elsewhere. In his 1930 review of *Le malheur*, Koyré will criticize Wahl's reliance on the writings of Hegel's youth.

48. Only a very brief section of the book, pages 119–23, contains an ex-tended discussion of other sections of the *Phenomenology*.

49. This is significant for two related reasons. First, because it means that Wahl's book is concerned with the instance of a more general problem as it ap-pears and is developed in Hegel's work. Second, because Wahl's book served as an introduction—or reintroduction—of Hegel to a generation of French thinkers, these thinkers developed a somewhat idiosyncratic Hegel. Jean Hyppolite notes the importance of Wahl's book in his essay "La 'Phénoménologie' de Hegel et la pensée française contemporaine" ["Hegel's *Phenomenology* and Contemporary French Thought"], a lecture originally presented in 1957 and included in his *Figures de la pensée philosophique* [*Figures of Philosophical Thought*] (Paris: Quadrige, 1991), 1:231–41. See also the informative discussion in Rodolphe Gasché's "One Coming before the Other? On Jean Wahl and Jacques Derrida," *CR: The New Cen-tennial Review* 15, no. 1 (Spring 2015): 1–23.

50. Wahl foregrounds the religious aspect by dividing his "Commentary" into five sections: an introduction, "The Unhappy Consciousness in Judaism," "Christianity," "The Unhappy Consciousness in Christianity," and "The Unhappy Consciousness and Spirit." Jean Wahl, *Le malheur*, 119–47.

51. It is well known that the French Revolution exerted a profound influ-ence over Hegel and his intellectual circle. For an account of the role of the Revo-lution in Hegel's thought that is roughly contemporary with Wahl, see Jean Hyp-polite's "Preface aux les 'Principes de la philosophie du droit'" ["Preface to the *Principles of the Philosophy of Right*"], originally published in 1940 and reprinted in *Figures de la pensée philosophique*, vol. 1, 73–91. More recently, see Rebecca Comay's excellent *Mourning Sickness: Hegel and the French Revolution* (Stanford, CA: Stan-ford University Press, 2010), which moves the Revolution toward the center of Hegel's preoccupations.

52. G. W. F. Hegel, *Phenomenology of Spirit*, trans. A. V. Miller (Oxford: Ox-ford University Press, 1977), 496.

53. Hegel, *Phenomenology of Spirit*, 590.

54. Wahl emphasizes that the immanent activity of the *Aufheben* is what dis-tinguishes Hegel's philosophy from Schelling's: "From the Jena period on, Hegel

saw that it is necessary to oppose the idea of immanence to the 'transcendence' of the Schellingian principle, that for the passivity of the *Aufgehobensein*, it is necessary to substitute the activity of the *Aufheben*, a destructive restlessness of realities that it in a sense allows to subsist." Wahl, *Le malheur*, 96.

55. In *Le malheur*, Hegel's philosophy is elaborated as the solution to two intertwined problems: the idealist systems put forward by Fichte and Schelling, and Christianity. For Hegel, the first problem was, specifically, to overcome the opposition between Fichte's pluralism and Schelling's monism: "The unhappy consciousness is then the bad infinity as conceived by Fichte's philosophy; and it is also the indifferent absolute of Schelling's philosophy. Both of these belong to the beyond; both of these are abstractions, they are products of a rending [*déchirure*]." Wahl, *Le malheur*, 66.

56. This passage, as well as others found throughout *Le malheur*, show the degree to which Wahl's reading of Hegel cannot be reduced to one of "thesis-antithesis-synthesis." As Wahl writes in the concluding section of his "Commentary on a Passage from Hegel": "Each of the stages through which consciousness passes is a deepening—or if you prefer, an elevation—of the preceding stage. The deepening or elevation consists of the fact that we are heading toward an ever greater unity." Wahl, *Le malheur*, 144.

Chapter 2

1. Koyré, "Review of Jean Wahl: *Le malheur de la conscience dans la philosophie de Hegel*," 136–43. Rory Jeffs stresses the continuing importance of Koyré's reading not only for Kojève's interpretation, but also for Catherine Malabou in his "The Future of the Future: Koyré, Kojève, and Malabou Speculate on Hegelian Time," *Parrhesia*, no. 15 (2012): 35–53.

2. Some of Hegel's writings from his Jena period had appeared before the First World War in volume 7 of Hegel's Sämtliche Werke: *Hegels Schriften zur Politik und Rechtsphilosophie* [*Hegel's Political and Legal Writings*], ed. Georg Lasson (Leipzig: F. Meiner, 1913). Volume 18a of the complete works, *Jenenser Logik, Metaphysik und Naturphilosophie* [*The Jena Logic, Metaphysics, and Philosophy of Nature*], ed. Georg Lasson (Leipzig: F. Meiner), appeared in 1923.

3. See Victor Delbos, "La méthode de démonstration chez Hegel" ["Hegel's Method of Demonstration"], *Revue de Métaphysique et de Morale*, vol. 35 (1928): 529–51. Koyré would have been familiar with Delbos from his student years at the Sorbonne. For more on the importance of Delbos's reading of Hegel, see Bruce Baugh's comparison of Delbos and Derrida in "Subjectivity and *Begriff* in Modern French Philosophy," *Owl of Minerva*, 23, no. 1 (Fall 1991): 65. A revised and expanded version of this essay appears as the second chapter of Baugh's *French Hegel*.

4. Koyré, "Review of Jean Wahl: *Le malheur de la conscience dans la philosophie de Hegel*," 142.

5. In the previous year, Koyré delivered an address to the First International Hegel Congress at The Hague on the status of Hegel research in France. Of

special interest is the fact that in his address, Koyré lamented the fact that, with the notable exception of Wahl's book, there was not much interest in Hegel in France at the time. Much of the substance of Koyré's address consisted of material culled from his review of *Le malheur*. In addition to the Congress, two special journal issues devoted to Hegel were published in 1931: *Revue Philosophique de la France et de l'Étranger* 112, no. 11–12 (November–December 1931), and *Revue de Métaphysique et de Morale*, vol. 38 (1931). The former included articles by Koyré, Victor Basch, and Wahl. The latter included articles by Benedetto Croce, Nicolai Hartmann, Charles Andler, Victor Basch, Martial Gueroult, René Berthelot, and Edmond Vermeil. For further information on the state of Hegel studies in France at the time of the centenary of his death, see again Michael Kelly, "Hegel in France to 1940: A Bibliographical Essay," 29–52.

6. See Andler's *Le pan-germanisme philosophique* [*Philosophical Pan-Germanism*] (Paris: Conard, 1917), as well as his essay—contemporaneous with Koyré's—"Le Fondement du savoir dans la *Phénoménologie de l'esprit* de Hegel" ["The Ground of Knowledge in Hegel's *Phenomenology of Spirit*"] in the *Revue de Métaphysique et de Morale*, vol. 38 (1931): 317–40.

7. Alexandre Koyré, "Note sur la langue et la terminologie Hégéliennes," *Revue Philosophique de la France et de l'Étranger*, 112, no. 11–12 (November–December 1931): 410.

8. For the importance of time and temporality to Koyré's interpretation of Hegel, see, again, Jeffs's "The Future of the Future," as well as Baugh's *French Hegel*.

9. As will be shown, Wahl's notion of the secret—a key notion in his reading of Kierkegaard—is an objection to precisely this linguistic clarity and transparency of thought. He discussed the theme of the secret in Kierkegaard in his address to the Hegel Congress in Rome in 1933, published as "Hegel et Kierkegaard" in *Kierkegaard: L'un devant l'autre* [*Kierkegaard: The One before the Other*] (Paris: Hachette, 1998), 97–118, and translated as "Hegel and Kierkegaard," in Wahl, *Jean Wahl, Transcendence and the Concrete*, 90–106. At the end of "On the Idea of Being" in *Human Existence and Transcendence*, Wahl notes Koyré's reading of Hegel and affirms that for Hegel, language is the life of Spirit. Wahl, *Existence humaine et transcendance*, 56.

10. Compare Koyré's claims about a "bacchanal in which no one is sober" with Gillian Rose's explication of "*the movement of the Absolute as comedy*" in her "The Comedy of Hegel and the *Trauerspiel* of Modern Philosophy," *Bulletin of the Hegel Society of Great Britain* 15, no. 1 (1994): 14–22.

11. The topic of philosophical language would be of especial importance for the atheistic interpretation of Hegel offered by Koyré's successor at the *École Pratique des Hautes Études*, Alexandre Kojève, and for the young Jean Hyppolite, who would begin publishing his own work on Hegel shortly after Koyré left Paris for the University of Cairo. Their work, in turn, would influence the generation of philosophers who came of age during and immediately after the Second World War. For an excellent discussion of the place of the atheistic interpretation of Hegel in France from the 1920s to the 1940s, see Stefanos Geroulanos's *An Atheism That Is Not Humanist Emerges in French Thought*.

12. Alexandre Koyré, "Hegel à Iéna (À propos de publications récentes)," *Revue Philosophique de la France et de l'Étranger* 118, no. 9 / 10 (1934): 239.

13. For an account of the impact of this book, see Alan D. Schrift's introduction to Leonard Lawlor's translation of the book's preface in *Jean Wahl, Transcendence and the Concrete*, 32–34.

14. For a concise but informative account of Marcel's work in its context, see Edward Baring's *Converts to the Real: Catholicism and the Makings of Continental Philosophy* (Cambridge, MA: Harvard University Press, 2019), 155–61. Baring's book is an important and exhaustively researched account of the important role played by religiously oriented philosophy in the constitution of the various programs of interwar French philosophy.

15. For a bibliography of the works by Kierkegaard as well as the major secondary literature available to Wahl, see the editorial note at the beginning of Wahl, *Kierkegaard: L'Un devant l'autre*.

16. As Schrift points out in his introduction to the translation of the book's preface, the three chapters of the book, as well as the preface, had all been published separately. "Vers le concret" appeared in the inaugural issue of Koyré's journal, *Recherches Philosophiques*, vol. 1 (1931–32): 1–20. The first part of "William James d'après sa correspondence" appeared in the *Revue Philosophique de la France et de l'Étranger*, vol. 93 (May–June 1922): 381–416, and the second part appeared in vol. 94 (September–October 1922): 298–347. The first part of "La Philosophie spéculative de Whitehead" appeared in the *Revue Philosophique de la France et de l'Étranger*, vol. 111 (January–June 1931): 341–78, and the second part appeared in vol. 112 (July–December 1931): 108–43. "Le Journal métaphysique de Gabriel Marcel" appeared in the *Revue de Métaphysique et de Morale* 37, no. 1 (January–March 1930): 75–112.

17. In a note to the preface of *Vers le concret*, Wahl writes that he will be referring to Heidegger many times and describes his project as an attempt "to join the feeling of individual existence as Kierkegaard experienced it with the feeling of our existence in the midst of things as it is brought to light in contemporary philosophy." Wahl, *Vers le concret*, 31n1, and 36. Wahl undertakes a more extensive analysis of the relations between Kierkegaard and Heidegger in his article "Heidegger et Kierkegaard: Recherche des éléments originaux de la philosophie de Heidegger" ["Heidegger and Kierkegaard: An Investigation of the Original Elements of Heidegger's Philosophy"], *Recherches Philosophiques*, vol. 2 (1932–33): 349–70. For a more general account of the influence of Heidegger on French philosophy in the 1930s, especially as it was transmitted through Kojève's work, see Ethan Kleinberg's *Generation Existential*. For a broader account of the impact and influence of Heidegger's philosophy in France, see the two volumes of Dominique Janicaud's *Heidegger en France*, which include interviews with many of the philosophers who participated in bringing Heidegger to a French audience.

18. Repetition—and temporality more generally—are an important topic in Wahl's subsequent work on Kierkegaard. See especially the essay "A la conquête du temps perdu (*Crainte et Tremblement*)" ["For the Conquest of Lost Time (*Fear and Trembling*)"] in *Études Kierkegaardiennes*, 184–209. More important for Wahl is the "instant," which not only links together several of his essays on Kierkegaard,

especially "Kierkegaard: L'angoisse et l'instant" ["Kierkegaard: Angst and the Instant"] and "Kierkegaard: Le paradoxe," but also links his concern for Kierkegaard generally with his early essay on Descartes. Both of these essays on Kierkegaard have been collected in *Kierkegaard: L'un devant l'autre*, 43–68 and 187–204.

19. Wahl, *Vers le concret*, 37–38. As Samuel Moyn notes, such conceptions of transcendence exerted a profound impact on the work of Emmanuel Levinas. Referring to Wahl's work on Kierkegaard, Moyn writes that it is "Wahl's naturalization of Kierkegaard's insistence on the infinite qualitative difference between God and man, as well as his sense of the philosophical relevance of that theme for understanding the self, that now seem like his most important contribution" to Levinas's philosophy. Moyn, *Origins of the Other*, 179. The above illustrates that such ideas are more pervasive in Wahl's work and are not confined to his work on Kierkegaard.

20. The "itself" here refers to the subject that remains unquestioned.

21. Wahl had already published several articles on Kierkegaard prior to this address. *Études Kierkegaardiennes*, a collection of Wahl's work on Kierkegaard in the 1930s, appeared in 1938. See also note 15 above.

22. Kierkegaard's "Fragments du Journal," trans. Jean-Jacques Gateau, appeared in the August 1, 1927 issue of the *Nouvelle Revue Française;* his *Le Journal du Séducteur*, trans. Jean-Jacques Gateau (Paris: Stock), appeared in 1929; and translations by Gateau as well as Paul-Henri Tisseau, the primary translator of Kierkegaard into French, followed throughout the 1930s.

23. Wahl, "Hegel et Kierkegaard," in *Kierkegaard: L'un devant l'autre*, 160.

24. At the time, there were many French readers of Heidegger who sought to understand him within a religious context, despite Heidegger's protestations. See Baring, *Converts to the Real*, chapter 3, "An Ecumenical Atheism: Martin Heidegger's Existential Philosophy," which treats Heidegger's early religious aspirations and interests (and their dissipation), as well as the discussion of Heidegger in chapter 7, "The Secular Kierkegaard."

25. Jaspers's philosophy was readily received in French existentialist circles, and Wahl authored several works that dealt at length with Jaspers's work. These include the early essay "Le Nietzsche de Jaspers," in *Recherches Philosophiques*, vol. 6 (1936–1937): 346–62, as well as important discussions of Jaspers within the larger context of existentialism in books such as *Tableau de la philosophie française [An Overview of French Philosophy]* (Paris: Fontaine, 1946) and *Petite histoire de l'existentialisme [A Short History of Existentialism]* (Paris: Club Maintenant, 1947). In 1950, Wahl taught a course at the Sorbonne entitled, "Le Théorie de la vérité dans la philosophie de Jaspers" ["The Theory of Truth in Jaspers' Philosophy"].

26. This language echoes the situation of the man from the provinces seeking entrance to the Law in Kafka's parable, "Before the Law."

27. Jean Wahl, "Kierkegaard et le mysticisme," in *Kierkegaard: L'un devant l'autre*, 39.

28. Wahl, "Kierkegaard et le mysticisme," 38–39.

29. An experience that can be explicated only by a philosophy of difference. See also Baugh, *French Hegel*, 40.

30. Wahl, "Hegel et Kierkegaard," 110.

31. Wahl, "Hegel et Kierkegaard," 102–3.

32. For an interesting and comprehensive overview of interpretations of the secret, see Arild Christensen's essay "Kierkegaard's Secret Affliction," *Harvard Theological Review* 42, no. 4 (October 1949): 255–71.

33. Jean Wahl, "La Lutte contre le hegelianisme" ["The Struggle against Hegelianism"], in *Études Kierkegaardiennes*, 111. Later in this same essay, in section 4 entitled "Critique du hégélianisme comme 'philosophie historique de l'identité'" ["Critique of Hegelianism as a 'Historical Philosophy of Identity'"] Wahl writes that "to this philosophy of identity, Kierkegaard, like Fichte, like Renouvier, like James, opposes a philosophy of difference. The moral element supposes a difference. The interior can never be completely expressed." While these figures hardly constitute a Deleuzian pantheon, Wahl's use not only of the term but of the *idea* of a philosophy of difference clearly anticipates Deleuze's own philosophical project.

34. "System means: a closed and complete totality, immanence. Existence is quality, discontinuity, transcendence." Wahl, "La Lutte contre le hegelianisme," 115. Reviewing Deleuze's *Nietzsche and Philosophy* almost three decades later, one of Wahl's criticisms of the book will be that Deleuze makes use of a dialectical method: "Is there not in Deleuze, adversary of the dialectic, a dialectic; and also even in Nietzsche." Jean Wahl, "Review: *Nietzsche et la philosophie* par Gilles Deleuze," *Revue de Métaphysique et de Morale* 68, no. 3 (July–September 1963): 374.

35. Wahl, "La Lutte contre le hegelianisme," 106.

36. Wahl, "Hegel et Kierkegaard," 107.

37. Henri Delacroix, "Søren Kierkegaard, le christianisme absolu à travers le paradoxe et le désespoir," *Revue de Métaphysique et de Morale*, vol. 8 (1900): 459–84.

38. Wahl was a last-minute replacement for Ernst Leroux, who was scheduled to speak but who was unable to attend because his wife was ill.

39. Jean Wahl, "Subjectivité et transcendance," *Bulletin de La Société Française de Philosophie* 37, no. 5 (October-December 1937): 161.

40. Wahl's presentation, as well as an account of the subsequent discussion, was originally published in the *Bulletin de la Société Française de Philosophie*, 161–211. This publication also included letters from several people unable to attend and Wahl's responses to those letters. Wahl's essay "Subjectivity and Transcendence" then appeared in *Human Existence and Transcendence* in 1944, and a transcript of the 1937 discussion, as well as the letters and Wahl's responses to them, are included as an appendix to that book. After the war, in 1946, Wahl again convened a colloquium and discussion, this time concerned with existentialism and the variety of philosophical authors and themes grouped under that label. The written record of this colloquium appeared as *A Short History of Existentialism*. For an account of the 1946 meeting, see Moyn, *Origins of the Other*, 202–5.

41. These commitments would continue to be present in the works that Wahl published during and just after the war, not only *Human Existence and Transcendence* (1944) and *A Short History of Existentialism* (1946), but also the many essays Wahl contributed to various publications concerning the state of French philosophy after the war.

42. This was primarily due, as explained below, to the growing influence of Jean Hyppolite's reading of Hegel. However, as several authors have noted, the

philosophical situation in France in the years following the Second World War were exceptionally turbulent. See especially the discussion in "Settling Accounts with Phenomenology: Husserl and His Critics," in Kleinberg's *Generation Existential*; the chapter "Marxism and Humanism" in Warren Montag's *Althusser and His Contemporaries* (Durham, NC: Duke University Press, 2013); and part 2, "The Postwar Decade," in Geroulanos's *An Atheism That Is Not Humanist.*

43. This neutral monism is adapted from the neo-realist positions of G. E. Moore and Bertrand Russell discussed in *Pluralist Philosophies.* See above, chapter 1, note 17.

44. In *Intersecting Lives,* François Dosse describes Deleuze and his lifelong friend, the author Michel Tournier, attending Sartre's lecture, "Existentialism Is a Humanism," in 1945: "Deleuze was in the crowd. He had just passed his baccalaureate exam, as had Tournier, and both were disturbed by their guru's performance; they never forgave him for trying to rehabilitate the old notion of humanism." Dosse, *Intersecting Lives,* 94–95. Dosse then quotes directly from Michel Tournier's account in *Le vent Paraclet [The Wind Spirit]* (Paris: Gallimard, 1977): "We were floored. So our master had had to dig through the trash to unearth this worn-out mixture reeking with sweat and of the inner life of humanism" (160). That humanism could already be thought of as out of fashion testifies to the turbulence in French philosophy at the time.

45. This line is repeated toward the end of the chapter "On Space and Time" in *Human Existence and Transcendence.* Wahl writes: "The theory of the discontinuity of time is often found linked to a theory of the exteriority of relations (explicated by Russell) and to a theory of the possible. . . . In Descartes, the idea of discontinuity, thanks to the idea of the instant, leads to a certain conception of eternity. Or rather, it supposes this conception of eternity. Today I realize that this idea of the instant is only an *ersatz* of the idea of eternity, a phantom." Wahl, *Existence humaine et transcendance,* 73.

46. Herbert Spencer regarded the ultimate nature of things as "the Unknowable." Marcel's point appears to be that Spencer's conception of the Unknowable is not something that human beings strive for but is, rather, a necessary presumption of the scientific inquiry into nature. For a useful overview of Spencer's notion, see Elijah Jordan's article "The Unknowable of Herbert Spencer," *Philosophical Review* 20, no. 3 (May 1911): 291–309.

47. Wahl taught a course on Hartmann—"The Theory of the Fundamental Categories in Nicolai Hartmann"—at the Sorbonne in 1952, and would also include a section on Hartmann's philosophy of nature in another course, on "The Qualitative Aspects of the Real," taught in 1954.

48. The choice of subject was on the one hand unsurprising, given Wahl's philosophical interests, but it was also scandalous, given what was then known of Heidegger's Nazi affiliation. See chapter 5 of Kleinberg's *Generation Existential* on the fate of Heidegger in postwar France. The text of Wahl's course was published the following year as *Introduction á la pensée de Heidegger* (Paris: Centre de Documentation Universitaire, 1946).

49. See Russell Ford, "Against Negativity: Wahl, Deleuze, and Postwar Existentialism," *Symposium: Canadian Journal of Continental Philosophy* 20, no. 1 (Spring 2016): 107–28.

50. Wahl, *A Short History of Existentialism,* 32.

51. Wahl, *Existence humaine et transcendance,* 10.

52. The exemplary text in this regard is Trân Duc Thao's *Phénoménologie et matérialisme dialectique* (Paris: Éditions Minh-Tân, 1951), translated by D. Herman and D. Morano as *Phenomenology and Dialectical Materialism* (Boston: D. Reidel, 1986). For an overview of Thao's work and influence during the war and immediately afterward, see Russell Ford, "Trân Duc Thao: Politics and Truth," *Philosophy Compass* 15, no. 2 (January 2020), doi.org/10.1111/phc3.12650.

Chapter 3

EPIGRAPH: Jean Hyppolite, "Les travaux de jeunesse de Hegel d'après des ouvrages récents (suite et fin)" ["Hegel's Youthful Works in Light of Recent Works"], *Revue de Métaphysique et Morale* 42, no. 4 (October 1935): 566.

1. See chapter 1, note 36, above.

2. For an excellent overview of Hyppolite's life and work, see Giuseppe Bianco, "Introduction: Jean Hyppolite, intellectuel-constellation," in *Jean Hyppolite, entre structure et existence,* ed. Bianco (Paris: Éditions Rue d'Ulm, 2013).

3. Hyppolite, "La "Phénoménologie" de Hegel et la pensée française contemporaine," [Hegel's *Phenomenology* and Contemporary French Thought], *Figures de la pensée philosophique,* 236.

4. Hyppolite, "La "Phénoménologie" de Hegel et la pensée française contemporaine," 236.

5. Hyppolite's *Genesis and Structure* was almost immediately understood to be a major intervention in the ongoing philosophical conversation which remained extensively concerned with Hegel. Evidence for this can be seen in the numerous reviews both of *Genesis and Structure* and Hyppolite's *Introduction to Hegel's Philosophy of History,* which appeared shortly after their publication. Among the reviews were important ones by major figures such as Georges Canguilhem, "Hegel en France," *Revue de l'Histoire et de Philosophie Religieuses* 28/29, no. 1 (1948–49): 282–97; Alphonse de Waelhens, "Review: Jean Hyppolite: Introduction à la philosophie de l'histoire de Hegel," *Revue Philosophique de Louvain* 47, no. 13 (1949): 147–50; and Mikel Dufrenne, "À propos de la thèse de Jean Hyppolite," *Fontaine* 11, no. 61 (1947): 461–70.

6. By contrast, interest in the development of Hegel's philosophy had been a topic of interest in German philosophy since the beginning of the century. Notable works include Dilthey's *Die Jugendgeschichte Hegels* [*The Young Hegel*] (1st edition 1905; 2nd edition 1921), Nohl's anthology (1907), and Ehrenberg and Link's *Hegels Erstes System* [*Hegel's First System*] (1915).

7. These include Rosenzweig's *Hegel und der Staat* [*Hegel and the State*] (1920), Kroner's two part *Von Kant bis Hegel* [*From Kant to Hegel*] (1921 and 1924), and Hartmann's *Die Philosophie der deutschen Idealismus 2: Hegel* [*The Philosophy of German Idealism 2: Hegel*] (1929).

8. For an excellent survey of the plethora of works published during this time, again see Michael Kelly's "Hegel in France to 1940: A Bibliographical Essay."

9. Gunnar Aspelin, *Hegels Tubinger Fragmente, eine psychologischideen-geschichtliche Untersuchung* [*Hegel's Tübingen Fragment: A Psychological-Historical Study*] (Lund: Ohlssons Buchdruckerei, 1933). For further discussion of the Fragment, see H. S. Harris, *Hegel's Development: Towards the Sunlight, 1770–1801* (Oxford: Clarendon, 1972).

10. Baugh, *French Hegel*, 39.

11. Koyré, "Hegel à Iéna (À propos de publications récentes)," 276.

12. Fichte is mentioned frequently by Wahl, although he never devotes an extended discussion to him. Deleuze mentions Fichte briefly in his final essay, "Immanence, A Life," where he writes that "it is to the degree that he goes beyond the aporias of the subject and the object that Johann Fichte, in his last philosophy, presents the transcendental field as *a life*, no longer dependent on a Being or submitted to an Act—it is an absolute immediate consciousness whose very activity no longer refers to a being but is ceaselessly posed in a life." Deleuze, *Pure Immanence: Essays on A Life*, trans. Anne Boyman (New York: Zone Books, 2001) 27; emphasis in the original. Schelling is another important figure for Wahl, to whom the latter attributes the idea of a "transcendental empiricism." In 1933, Vladimir Jankélévitch completed his *doctorat ès lettres* with a thesis on "The Odyssey of Consciousness in Schelling's Late Philosophy," supervised by Wahl.

13. Alongside the academic debate being conducted primarily in journals and conferences, Alexandre Kojève took over the seminar of Koyré at the École Pratique des Hautes Études. Kojève's seminar is the stuff of legend: he presented a highly idiosyncratic reading of Hegel and his reading was spellbinding for the seminar's participants, for whom participation in the seminar would have lasting consequences for their philosophical developments. The bifurcation in the French reading of Hegel would only begin to be stitched together again after the Second World War, when Kojève's anthropological Hegel would be pitted against Hyppolite's ontological reading. In general, Kojève faired poorly in this debate, although part of the reason for this may be that he assumed a position with the French Ministry of Foreign Affairs shortly after the war. The history of this contest can be gleaned from the review essays cited in note 5, above. For an excellent intellectual biography of Kojève, see *The Black Circle: A Life of Alexandre Kojève* by Jeff Love (New York: Columbia University Press, 2018).

14. Hyppolite, "Les travaux des jeunesse de Hegel d'après des ouvrages récents," 400.

15. Hegel's *Life of Jesus*, written in Berne, is included in the youthful works published by Nohl in 1907.

16. In *Le malheur*, Wahl focuses on the importance of Jesus as an individual mediator between the human and the divine. In "Les travaux des jeunesse de Hegel d'après des ouvrages récents," Hyppolite argues that there is also a tendency, carried over from Hegel's Tübingen period, to look for the socially relevant teachings of Jesus.

17. Compare Brady Bowman, "Spinozist Pantheism and the Truth of 'Sense Certainty': What the Eleusinian Mysteries Tell Us about Hegel's *Phenomenology*," *Journal of the History of Philosophy* 50, no. 1 (2010): 85–110.

18. Wahl will give central importance to Hyppolite's conception of Hegelian

negation in his lengthy review essay on *Logic and Existence*. See Jean Wahl, "Une Interpretation de la *Logique* de Hegel," *Critique* 73 (December 1953): 1050–71.

19. "Above all, Hegel is the philosopher of spirit; Schelling, the philosopher of nature." Hyppolite, "Les travaux de jeunesse de Hegel d'après des ouvrages récents (suite et fin)," 577.

20. "The problem of the Nature-Spirit synthesis is posed for each of them [Schelling and Hegel] in a more complex fashion. Schelling's solution, completely new for Hegel, appears to have been the idea of a development. Nature would be an inferior form of spirit. In the 1801 text [*The Difference between Fichte's and Schelling's Systems of Philosophy*], Hegel, adopting his friend's thesis, does not abandon his own; there results a certain obscurity that will be found, much later, in Hegelian philosophy." Hyppolite, "Les travaux de jeunesse de Hegel d'après des ouvrages récents (suite et fin)," 575.

21. "In the *Phenomenology*, only the order is new." Hyppolite, "Les travaux de jeunesse de Hegel d'après des ouvrages récents (suite et fin)," 578.

22. "The difference between the youthful works and the first system of Jena seems to the first commentator on this system, to Ehrenberg, to be 'a mystery.' Until this time, Hegel lived the passage from the finite to the infinite; now he is forced to think it. Philosophy succeeds religion. Cf. Ehrenberg's preface to *Hegels erstes System*." Jean Hyppolite, "Vie et prise de conscience de la vie, dans la philosophie hégélienne d'Iéna," *Revue de Métaphysique et de Morale* 45, no. 1 (1938): 46, note 1.

23. Jean Hyppolite, "Vie et prise de conscience de la vie, dans la philosophie hégélienne d'Iéna," 51–52, note 3.

24. "The problem of relation was the very problem of knowledge from Descartes to Kant." Hyppolite, "Vie et prise de conscience," 50.

25. See note 13, above.

26. At the end of his "Hegel, Marx, et le christianisme," a review of Henri Niel's book *De la mediation dans la philosophie de Hegel* (Paris: Aubier, 1945), Kojève famously declares: "It can then be said that, for the moment, every interpretation of Hegel, if it is more than chatter [*un bavardage*], is only a program of conflict and work (one of these programs is called *Marxism*). And this is to say that the work of an interpreter of Hegel has the meaning of a work of political propaganda." Alexandre Kojève, "Hegel, Marx, et le christianisme," *Critique* 1, no. 3/4 (1946): 366. See chapter 4, below, for an extended discussion of this important essay.

27. Pierre Macherey, "Between Philosophy and History of Philosophy: Hyppolite's Hegel," in *Jean Hyppolite, entre structure et existence*, ed. Giuseppe Bianco (Paris: Éditions Rue d'Ulm, 2013), 33.

28. Jean Hyppolite, *Genesis and Structure of Hegel's "Phenomenology of Spirit,"* trans. Samuel Cherniak and John Heckman (Evanston, IL: Northwestern University Press, 1979), 10.

29. Hyppolite relies on Hegel's introduction to the *Phenomenology*—rather than the more famous preface—for this assertion. He writes: "The preface is an hors d'oeuvre . . . The introduction, on the contrary, is an integral part of the book." Hyppolite, *Genesis and Structure*, 10.

30. See Tom Rockmore, "Hyppolite's Hegel Reconsidered," *Pli*, vol. 24 (2013): 167–81.

31. Hyppolite is referring to the "Proceedings of the Estates Assembly in the Kingdom of Württemberg, 1815–1816," which Hegel published in 1817 in the *Heidelbergische Jahrbücher*.

32. See note 5, above, for an indication of the interest shown in Hyppolite's interpretation immediately following the war.

33. Both Merleau-Ponty and Sartre, it should be noted, were at least occasional attendees at Kojève's seminars. Merleau-Ponty's *The Structure of Behavior* appeared in 1942, and his *Phenomenology of Perception* appeared in 1945. Sartre's *Being and Nothingness* appeared in 1943. Kojève's seminars, edited by Raymond Queneau, were published in 1947.

34. See Karl Löwith's *From Hegel to Nietzsche* (New York: Columbia University Press, 1964). Löwith was one of the philosophers invited to Wahl's presentation in 1937.

35. Again, though Wahl's thinkers hardly form a Deleuzian pantheon, the idea of a subterranean lineage of thinkers pursuing a project that is shut out of mainstream thought is one that Deleuze will adopt as central to his own project. In the infamous "Letter to a Harsh Critic," Deleuze writes: "I see a secret link between Lucretius, Hume, Spinoza, and Nietzsche, constituted by their critique of negativity, the hatred of interiority, the externality of forces and relations, the denunciation of power . . . and so on." Deleuze, *Negotiations*, 6. Also, like Wahl, Deleuze does not view these linkages as unique to philosophy; Deleuze opens his essay "Helene Cixous, or Writing in Strobe," by observing that she "has pursued a subterranean body of work." *Desert Islands*, 230.

36. Jean Wahl, *Existence humaine et transcendence* (Geneva: La Baconnière, 1944), 57.

37. This is one of the clearest passages for noting the distinction between Wahl's interpretation and that developed by Hyppolite. For Wahl, the essential unhappiness of consciousness means that the human striving after transcendence cannot be eliminated; for Hyppolite, following Koyré's work, the rational system of Hegel's *Logic* achieves precisely this elimination. See Leonard Lawlor, "'L'immanence est complete,' ou l'héritage de la pensée de Jean Hyppolite" ["'Immanence Is Complete,' or the Legacy of Jean Hyppolite's Thought"], in *Jean Hyppolite, entre structure et existence*, ed. Giuseppe Bianco (Paris: Rue d'Ulm, 2013), 143–56.

38. In his 1956 essay "Bergson's Conception of Difference," Deleuze makes the same distinction when he argues that Bergson's philosophy is opposed to dialectics generally: "Internal difference will have to distinguish itself from contradiction, alterity, and negation. This is precisely where Bergson's method and theory of difference are opposed to the other theory, the other method of difference called dialectic, whether it's Plato's dialectic of alterity or Hegel's dialectic of contradiction, each of which imply the presence and power of the negative." Deleuze, *Desert Islands*, 38.

39. It is strange to see Wahl reduce the Hegelian dialectic to "thesis-antithesis-synthesis," given his more sophisticated account in *Le malheur*. See chapter 1, note 56, above.

40. In a note to "On Existence," Wahl writes: "The philosophy of existence is a philosophy of transcendence. Existence is ecstasy, in the primitive sense of the word, an exit outside of the self; the human being is such inasmuch as it is standing outside of itself, in order to be in proximity to what is manifested. In this way the phenomenon of intentionality is most deeply understood. *Dasein* itself is outside of itself, is projected beyond. Existence transcends. The two ideas of existence and transcendence are reconnected in the idea of being-in-the-world, in the idea of being-with" (Wahl, *Existence humaine et transcendance*, 21). This note makes clear how close Wahl feels his own thinking is to Heidegger's. However, the feeling is not mutual. As Heidegger makes clear in his response to Wahl's 1937 letter, *Dasein* cannot be equated with "human being."

41. In *Human Existence and Transcendence* existence is always ek-stasis, not being.

42. Reading "subjective" for the last "objective."

43. The necessarily unconscious character of transcendence is a theme developed at length by Pierre Klossowski in his reading of Nietzsche. See in particular "Nietzsche, Polytheism, and Parody," as well as the translator's afterword, "Klossowski's *salto mortale*," in Klossowski's *Such a Deathly Desire*, trans. Russell Ford (Albany: State University of New York Press, 2007), 99–122. See also Klossowski's *Nietzsche and the Vicious Circle*, trans. Daniel W. Smith (Chicago: University of Chicago Press, 1997). Wahl and Klossowski were both fellow travelers in Georges Bataille's circle in the late 1930s.

44. This problem is central to the exchange between Wahl and Gabriel Marcel following Wahl's 1937 lecture. Wahl concludes the exchange by insisting that the argument could be resolved only "by studying the mode of reflection that you [Marcel] are calling philosophy." Wahl, *Existence humaine et transcendance*, 124.

45. The idea and language here are very close to the contemporaneous work of Bataille and his circle.

46. Again, Wahl stresses the philosophical value of "non-philosophical" works and thinkers, while Marcel wants to insist on a distinctive value of philosophers and philosophical texts.

47. This thought of the absolute is the ecstatic sensible converse of Hegel's absolute knowing.

48. See the discussion in chapter 5 of Baugh's *French Hegel*, "Bataille: Negativity Unemployed."

49. Quoting the Schlegel and Tieck edition of Novalis, 271.

Chapter 4

EPIGRAPH: Deleuze, *Dialogues II*, 57–58.

1. "I pity us all, oh swirlings of dust!" Paul Valéry, "La jeune parque," in *The Collected Works of Paul Valéry, Volume 1: Poetry*, trans. David Paul (Princeton, NJ: Princeton University Press, 1971), 86 (translation altered).

2. Jean Hyppolite, "Note sur Paul Valéry et la crise de la conscience," *La Vie Intellectuelle* 14, no. 3 (1946): 122. Valéry's "man of spirit," exemplified by Leo-

nardo da Vinci, combines both artistic and intellectual virtues. See Paul Valéry, *Introduction à la méthode de Léonard da Vinci* (Paris: Gallimard, 1992).

3. Hyppolite, "Note sur Paul Valéry," 122–23.

4. "This crisis, linked then to human reality, has first been thought in the poems of Paul Valéry, especially [*singulièrement*] in *Cimitière marin* and in *Jeune Parque*; it has become, with all the transformations implicated in this becoming, a crisis for everyone, and contemporary existentialism is the living evidence of it." Hyppolite, "Note sur Paul Valéry," 122.

5. Arthur Rimbaud, *A Season in Hell and The Drunken Boat*, trans. Louise Varèse (New York: New Directions, 1961), 36–37.

6. Hyppolite, "Note sur Paul Valéry," 126.

7. "Here it would again be necessary to take up, regarding the despair of consciousness, Péguy's philosophy of hope." Hyppolite, "Note sur Paul Valéry" 126. See Charles Péguy, *The Portal of the Mystery of Hope* (New York: Continuum, 1996).

8. Hyppolite, "Note sur Paul Valéry," 126.

9. Hyppolite's conclusion to his 1949 essay, "Du bergsonisme à l'existentialisme" ["From Bergsonism to Existentialism"], echoes this sentiment: "From Bergsonism to existentialism an entire spiritual evolution can now be discerned. If Bergson defined philosophy with this formula: 'philosophy ought to be an effort to surpass the human condition,' we should now say to the contrary that existentialism shows itself powerless to surpass this condition, except by a faith that philosophy could never justify alone. This is why an existentialism linked to an indefinite analysis of human reality (and on this point this analysis perpetually rejoins a literature that seems to be an integral part of the existential philosophy) implies a crisis of philosophy itself. We can no longer seek greater lucidity about this human reality that we ourselves are and that we ourselves make; a philosophical system that would allow us to surpass this existence, to refer it to something other than itself, seems impossible. So-called vertical transcendence is accessible only to faith. It is true that there remains the meaning of the historicity of this existence, and the enlargement of this historicity in history. How can we understand the link between human existents, historical becoming, how can we envisage the problem of the *meaning* of this history which in certain ways is given to us, but which we must also constitute? The ultimate problem that existentialists, Marxists, and Christians confront today appears to us to be that of this '*meaning* of history.'" Hyppolite, *Figures de la pensée philosophique*, 458; emphasis in the original.

10. Hyppolite, "Note sur Paul Valéry," 126.

11. For recent assessments of Hyppolite's influence and importance, see the final chapter of Geroulanos's *An Atheism That Is Not Humanist*, "Man in Suspension: Jean Hyppolite on History, Being, and Language," as well as the essays collected in *Jean Hyppolite, entre structure et existence*, and an issue of the journal *Pli* devoted to Hyppolite's work (vol. 24 [2013]).

12. Michel Foucault, "The Discourse on Language," in *The Archaeology of Knowledge*, trans. A. M. Sheridan Smith (New York: Pantheon, 1972), 235.

13. Gilles Deleuze, "A Conversation: What Is It? What Is It For?" in *Dialogues II*, 12.

14. Wahl's *Tableau de la philosophie française* (Paris: Fontaine, 1946) is an overview of French philosophy from the seventeenth century to the twentieth, with appendixes on "French Philosophy in 1939" and another on "French Philosophy in 1946." Upon returning to Paris after the war, Wahl taught a course on Heidegger's philosophy, based almost entirely on the latter's "Introduction to Philosophy" course taught in Freiburg in 1928, now published as volume 27 of Heidegger's Gesamtausgabe, *Einleitung in die Philosophie* (Winter semester 1928/29), ed. O. Saame and I. Saame-Speidel, 1996, 2nd edition. Wahl's *A Short History of Existentialism* (1947) consists of a brief account of existentialism and its roots, followed by a longer conversation with several other philosophers.

15. Jean Wahl, *A Short History of Existentialism*, trans. Forrest Williams and Stanley Maron (New York: Philosophical Library, 1949), 34.

16. Wahl, *A Short History of Existentialism*, 33.

17. Wahl, *A Short History of Existentialism*, 31; 33.

18. Wahl, *A Short History of Existentialism*, 33. For a brief but comprehensive account of Wahl's activity and work in the postwar years, see Frédéric Worms, *La philosophie en France au XXe siècle: Moments* (Paris: Gallimard, 2009), 315.

19. Wahl opens *A Short History of Existentialism* with an anecdote about being confronted by a student on the streets who states that Wahl is "surely" an existentialist. Wahl uses this story to introduce his considerations of various problematic definitions of existentialism, as well as of the promise that its various adherents and fellow travelers show. Wahl, *A Short History of Existentialism*, 1.

20. See Mark Poster, *Existential Marxism in Postwar France: From Sartre to Althusser* (Princeton, NJ: Princeton University Press, 1975); Tony Judt, *Past Imperfect: French Intellectuals, 1944–1956* (Berkeley: University of California Press, 1992); the second part of Frédéric Worms's *La philosophie en France* (2009); and the essays collected in *Situating Existentialism: Key Texts in Context*, ed. Jonathan Judaken and Robert Bernasconi (New York: Columbia University Press, 2012).

21. For the career of Sartre, see Thomas R. Flynn's *Sartre: A Philosophical Biography*. An excellent biography of Beauvoir is available in Kate Kirkpatrick's *Becoming Beauvoir: A Life* (New York: Bloomsbury, 2019). Biographical work on Camus is somewhat less even, but see Olivier Todd's *Albert Camus: Une vie* (Paris: Gallimard, 1996). For a penetrating discussion of the French "heroes" formed in and by the Second World War and what such formations meant for philosophy, see "Le héros et le philosophe: Un problème philosophique partagé dans le moment de la guerre," in Worms, *La philosophie en France au XXe siècle: Moments*, 439–55.

22. Hyppolite, "Du Bergsonisme à l'existentialisme," *Figures de la pensée philosophique*, 444.

23. At the beginning of his 1963 essay "Sens et existence dans la philosophie de Maurice Merleau-Ponty," Hyppolite writes: "In 1961 we lost a great French philosopher of whom I had the honor of being a friend. We belonged to the same generation, to the same region of France, and our thoughts developed in parallel; we fell under the same influences, lived the same historical dramas. Happy people, Hegel said, have no history, but we, we have faced [*rencontré*] history, with the German Occupation, the Liberation, and more recently the Algerian drama. All of these events have marked us, they have helped us understand the philosophical movement, known by the name "existentialism," in which we have par-

ticipated, Sartre, Merleau-Ponty, and myself; this movement is inseparable from our individual and collective history, it is born of a keen conscious grasp of the real conditions of thought." Hyppolite, *Figures de la pensée philosophique*, 731–32.

24. Hyppolite, "Du Bergsonisme à l'existentialisme," 445.

25. For an excellent account of the fortunes of Bergsonian philosophy in the first half of the twentieth century, see Giuseppe Bianco, *Après Bergson: Portrait de groupe avec philosophe* (Paris: Presses Universitaires de France, 2015).

26. Hyppolite, "Vie et philosophie de l'histoire chez Bergson," *Figures de la pensée philosophique*, 459.

27. It's worth quoting this passage in full to make clear Hyppolite's critique of Bergson's statement: "Perhaps there is too much given to this fundamental orientation of his [Bergson's] thought: "Philosophy should be an effort to surpass the human condition," going from biological man to the overman without stopping for very long at the characters of this historical human existence that are situated between the two." Hyppolite, "Vie et philosophie de l'histoire chez Bergson," 467.

28. Hyppolite, "Vie et existence d'après Bergson (Faiblesse et grandeur de l'intelligence)," *Figures de la pensée philosophique*, 490. In his Inaugural Lecture to the Collège de France, Hyppolite describes his lifelong philosophical project as "studying what constitutes this thought [philosophy], what it adds to lived experience when it reflects it, what it perhaps destroys of it or what it recuperates from it." Hyppolite, "Leçon inaugurale au Collège de France," *Figures de la pensée philosophique*, 1005. Deleuze's philosophical work, beginning with his work on Hume, is, like Wahl's, a challenge to the philosophical necessity of reflecting concrete life.

29. Hyppolite, "Du Bergsonisme à l'existentialisme," *Figures de la pensée philosophique*, 453.

30. Hyppolite, "Du Bergsonisme à l'existentialisme," 454, emphasis in the original.

31. "Fabulation," sometimes translated into English as "the myth-making function," is an especially important Bergsonian concept for Deleuze. In response to a question of, in part, how a minority can attain power, Deleuze responds: "Utopia isn't the right concept: it's more a question of a 'fabulation' in which a people and art both share. We ought to take up Bergson's notion of fabulation and give it a political meaning." Gilles Deleuze, "Control and Becoming," in *Negotiations*, 174.

32. Hyppolite, "Du Bergsonisme à l'existentialisme," *Figures de la pensée philosophique*, 454; 458.

33. Hyppolite, "Du Bergsonisme à l'existentialisme," 458. Hyppolite describes both Christian and atheist existentialism as implying "a certain renunciation of the philosophical system." Hyppolite, "Du Bergsonisme à l'existentialisme," 452.

34. Hyppolite, "Du Bergsonisme à l'existentialisme," 458.

35. See Jean Wahl, "Poetry and Metaphysics," in *Existence humaine et transcendance*, 78–97.

36. Hyppolite, "Du Bergsonisme à l'existentialisme," *Figures de la pensée philosophique*, 458, emphasis in the original.

37. Hyppolite, *Genesis and Structure*, 34.

38. Hyppolite, *Genesis and Structure*, 43.

39. Hyppolite, *Genesis and Structure*, 44.

40. Hyppolite, *Genesis and Structure*, 42.

41. "It is the *Phenomenology of Spirit* which has drawn most of the attention, although an article by A. Koyré is devoted to time in Hegel in a more general fashion. Koyré shows that, in the Hegelian conception of time, the future is the determining moment and plays, so to speak, the [role of] precedent." Jean Wahl, *Tableau de la philosophie française* (Paris: Gallimard, 1962), 170.

42. Koyré, "Hegel à Iéna," 239.

43. See chapter 3, above.

44. For a critical reading of this inescapability of Hegel, see Louis Althusser's 1950 essay, "The Return to Hegel: The Latest Word in Academic Revisionism," in *The Spectre of Hegel*, trans. G. M. Goshgarian (New York: Verso, 1997), 173–84.

45. Hyppolite paid tribute to both men in his Inaugural Address to the Collège de France. His chair in the History of Philosophical Thought succeeded Gueroult's chair in the History and Technology of Philosophical Systems.

46. Hyppolite, "Ruse de la raison et histoire chez Hegel," *Figures de la pensée philosophique*, 151–52.

47. Hyppolite, "Ruse de la raison et histoire chez Hegel," 150.

48. Hyppolite, "La "Phénoménology" de Hegel et la pensée française contemporaine," *Figures de la pensée philosophique*, 240.

49. Hyppolite, "Essai sur la 'Logique' de Hegel," *Figures de la pensée philosophique*, 158.

50. Hyppolite, "Hegel à l'Ouest," and "Leçon inaugurale au Collège de France," *Figures de la pensée philosophique*, 264; 1013. In 1963, when he took up his chair at the Collège de France, Hyppolite notes that what he and some other existentialists "refused in Hegelian thought, was the pretension to a final and definitive judgment upon history, on philosophical systems." Hyppolite, "Leçon inaugurale au Collège de France," 1015.

51. Hyppolite, "Projet d'enseignement d'histoire de la pensée philosophique," *Figures de la pensée philosophique*, 999.

52. Hyppolite, "Projet d'enseignement d'histoire de la pensée philosophique," 1001.

53. Hyppolite, "Projet d'enseignement d'histoire de la pensée philosophique," 1001.

54. Hyppolite, "Projet d'enseignement d'histoire de la pensée philosophique," 1001–2.

55. For details of Hyppolite's philosophical career, see Giuseppe Bianco's "Introduction: Jean Hyppolite, intellectual-constellation," in *Jean Hyppolite, entre structure et existence*, 9–29.

56. See Bianco, "Introduction: Jean Hyppolite, intellectual-constellation" 13; Alphonse de Waelhens, "Jean Hyppolite, *Introduction a la philosophie de l'histoire de Hegel*," *Revue Philosophique de Louvain* 47, no. 13 (1949): 147–50; and Émile Brehier, "Jean Hyppolite, *Introduction a la philosophie de l'histoire de Hegel*," *Revue Philosophique*, nos. 4–6 (1950).

57. Dosse, *Intersecting Lives*, 91–92. Deleuze was a regular attendee at these gatherings.

58. Étienne Fouilloux, "'Intellectuels catholiques?' Réflexions sur une naissance différée," *Vingtième Siècle*, vol. 53 (1997): 13–24. See also Hyppolite, *Genesis and Structure*, xxx.

59. Niel's book receives a passing mention in the introduction to *Genesis and Structure*, xxx.

60. Alexandre Kojève, "Hegel, Marx, et le christianisme," *Critique* 1, no. 3/4 (1946): 40.

61. This is roughly the same time period during which Hegel was working in Jena. See chapter 3, above, for Hyppolite's discussion of Hegel's Jena writings.

62. Sartre's wartime activity has been the subject of several debates, including two important ones following his death in 1980. Recently, the "Affaire de Lycée Condorcet" focused on Sartre's acceptance of a position in 1941 from which a Jewish professor had been forcibly removed, an acceptance that would be strikingly at odds with Sartre's own theory of engagement according to which each person bears responsibility for the actions of a state. (See Sartre's 1946 lecture to UNESCO at the Sorbonne, "The Writer's Responsibility," where he went so far as to state that German teachers and professors should have resigned their positions when their Jewish colleagues were forced to surrender theirs.) In fact, as Jonathan Judaken has noted, further research shows that it was Ferdinand Alquié who assumed Dreyfus-Le Foyer's position, not Sartre. This "affaire" was initially triggered by Ingrid Galster's book *Sartre sous l'Occupation et après: Nouvelles mises au point* (Paris: L'Harmattan, 2014), but the true facts were uncovered and published in *Le Nouvel Observateur* by Jacques Lecarme and Michel Contat. Earlier, in an interview published posthumously in *Liberation* in 1985, Vladimir Jankélévitch, a close friend of Jean Wahl, described Sartre's wartime activity as arising more from guilt than from the deliberate refocusing of his thought that Sartre describes. Invoking Primo Levi's "grey zones," Jonathan Judaken states that "the time has come to situate Sartre beyond the dichotomies of guilt or innocence, armed resistance or collaboration." (Judaken, *Jean-Paul Sartre and the Jewish Question* [Lincoln: University of Nebraska Press, 2007], 50–51). In the immediate aftermath of the war, it bears emphasizing, Sartre's wartime actions were not questioned or challenged.

63. See Flynn, *Sartre: An Intellectual Biography*, 236.

64. Jean-Paul Sartre, *Existentialism Is a Humanism*, trans. Carol Macomber (New Haven, CT: Yale University Press, 2007), 18.

65. Sartre, *Existentialism Is a Humanism*, 22. Sartre's strategy is to begin with the criticisms that implicitly deny existentialism's humanism, then to develop an account of existentialism by responding to these criticisms in detail, in order then to return at the end of the essay to declare that existentialism, as described in the essay, is a humanism but in a different sense than that sort of humanism that considers "man as an end," which, Sartre emphasizes, ultimately leads to fascism. Sartre, *Existentialism Is a Humanism*, 52.

66. Sartre, *Existentialism Is a Humanism*, 42–44, 52–54.

67. Sartre, *Existentialism Is a Humanism*, 51. Baring, *The Young Derrida*, 40.

68. Geroulanos's *An Atheism That Is Not Humanist* provides a detailed and insightful account of the philosophical debates around humanism both before and after the war. Particularly important for the present discussion is his discussion (in the second part of his book) of the "postwar negotiation of antihumanism" and the constitution of its three competing camps: communist, Catholic, and existential atheist. Chapter 5 of Ethan Kleinberg's *Generation Existential* contains an excellent discussion of the complexities surrounding the French reception of Heidegger's "Letter on Humanism." Finally, the first chapter of Edward Baring's *The Young Derrida* contains a very clear discussion of the influence and importance of Catholic philosophy immediately following the war.

69. For an excellent and thorough discussion of the Catholic strains of philosophy in France in the early twentieth century, see Edward Baring's *Converts to the Real*.

70. See Tony Judt's *Past Imperfect* as well as his *The Burden of Responsibility: Blum, Camus, Aron and the French Twentieth Century* (Chicago: University of Chicago Press, 2007).

71. Geroulanos, *An Atheism That Is Not Humanist*, 113.

72. Baring, *The Young Derrida*, 29–30.

73. Baring, *The Young Derrida*, 42ff.; Janicaud, *Heidegger en France*, 140–46.

74. This is not to say, however, that Marx or Marxism have been relegated to the dustbin. Compare Derrida's *Specters of Marx: The State of the Debt, the Work of Mourning, and the New International*, trans. Peggy Kamuf (New York: Routledge, 1994), as well as the philosophical projects of thinkers such as Slavoj Žižek and Alain Badiou. Deleuze famously told Didier Eribon in 1995 that he was then at work on a book about "the grandeur of Marx." Eribon, "Le 'Je me souviens' de Gilles Deleuze," interview, *Le Nouvel Observateur*, November 16–22, 1995, 114–15.

75. See Baring, *The Young Derrida*, 40–42.

76. See Baring, *The Young Derrida*, 41.

77. See Baring, *The Young Derrida*, 41. Both disavowals took place in 1949.

78. Merleau-Ponty's *Humanism and Terror* first appeared in 1947, and Lukács's *Existentialism or Marxism* appeared in 1948. Lukács's book was a political challenge to Sartre's RDR (Rassemblement Démocratique Révolutionnaire), and following its publication, there was a public exchange between Sartre and Lukács in *Combat*. Lukács argued that, after the French Revolution and the collapse of idealism, there was no "third way" between the materialism of Hegel and Marx and the "theological-mystical" (irrational) path of Schelling and Kierkegaard.

79. Jean-François Lyotard, *Phenomenology*, trans. Brian Beakley (Albany: State University of New York Press, 1991), 31

80. Lyotard, *Phenomenology*, 33; cited by Baring, *The Young Derrida*, 42.

81. Lyotard, *Phenomenology*, 55.

82. Lyotard, *Phenomenology*, 61.

83. Lyotard, *Phenomenology*, 67.

84. Baring, *The Young Derrida*, 41.

85. Baring, *The Young Derrida*, 94.

86. Baring, *The Young Derrida*, 103.

87. Leonard Lawlor, *Derrida and Husserl*; Paola Marrati, *Genesis and Trace: Derrida Reading Husserl and Heidegger* (Stanford, CA: Stanford University Press, 2005); Baring, *The Young Derrida*.

88. See Ludwig Landgrebe's "Editor's Foreword to the 1948 Edition," in Edmund Husserl, *Experience and Judgment*, trans. James S. Churchill and Karl Ameriks (Evanston, IL: Northwestern University Press, 1973), 3–8.

89. The two essays by Wahl referred to here are "Notes sur la première partie de *Erfahrung und Urteil* de Husserl," *Revue de la Métaphysique et de Morale* 56, no. 1 (1951): 6–34, and "Notes sur quelques aspects empiristes de la pensée de Husserl," *Revue de la Métaphysique et de Morale* 57, no. 1 (1952): 17–45. Husserl's former assistant, Ludwig Landgrebe, who had edited *Experience and Judgment* for publication, responded favorably to Wahl's first essay in a letter published in the *Revue de la Métaphysique et de Morale* 57, no. 2 (1952): 282–83. See also Baring, *The Young Derrida*, 124ff., for a discussion of Wahl and the counter-idealist reading of Husserl.

90. Edmund Husserl, *Experience and Judgment*, trans. James Spencer Churchill and Karl Ameriks (Evanston, IL: Northwestern University Press, 1975), 3–4.

91. Husserl, *Experience and Judgment*, 172–73.

92. Jean Wahl, "La Situation présente de la philosophie française," in *L'activité philosophique contemporaine en France et aux États-Unis*, ed. Marvin Farber (Paris: Presses Universitaires de France, 1950), 40, 41. See also Russell Ford, "Against Negativity," *Symposium* 20, no. 1 (2016): 107–28.

93. Jean Wahl, "Notes on the First Part of *Experience and Judgment*," trans. Laurence E. Winters, in *Apriori and World: European Contributions to Husserlian Phenomenology*, ed. William McKenna, Robert M. Harlan, and Laurence E. Winters (The Hague: Martinus Nijhoff, 1981), 179.

94. Husserl, *Experience and Judgment*, §24, 112–21.

95. Husserl, *Experience and Judgment*, 133–34.

96. Husserl, *Experience and Judgment*, 134.

97. Wahl, "Notes on the First Part of *Experience and Judgment*," 174.

98. Husserl, *Experience and Judgment*, 149–51.

99. Husserl, *Experience and Judgment*, 150.

100. Wahl, "Notes on the First Part of *Experience and Judgment*," 181.

101. Husserl, *Experience and Judgment*, 150.

102. Wahl, "Notes on the First Part of *Experience and Judgment*," 182.

103. In addition to being-in-the-world, which is a pervasive concern of *Experience and Judgment*, Wahl notes seven links between Husserl's analytic-descriptive investigations and Heidegger's ontological project: (1) Heidegger's contention that there are no self-evident truths; all truths are founded on experience; (2) the Heideggerian idea of truth, which arises from the idea that the real presents itself as it is; (3) Heidegger's demand for regional ontologies insofar as intuition never gives detached objects; (4) form as the non-a priori character that is the possibility of an intuitive unity; (5) the identification of this most universal form as time; (6) the importance and conception of the pre-predicative; and (7) the similar roles played by others, the world, and objectivity.

104. Wahl, "Notes on the First Part of *Experience and Judgment*," 192.

105. Ludwig Landgrebe, "A Letter from Ludwig Landgrebe to Jean Wahl," in *Apriori and World: European Contributions to Husserlian Phenomenology*, ed. William McKenna, Robert M. Harlan, and Lawrence E. Winters (The Hague: Martinus Nijhoff, 1981), 198–99 (emphasis in the original). This letter originally appeared in the *Revue de Métaphysique et de Morale* 57, no. 2 (April–June 1952): 282–83.

106. A French translation of *Ideas I* by Paul Ricoeur had appeared in 1950.

107. Landgrebe, "A Letter from Ludwig Landgrebe to Jean Wahl," 198–99 (emphasis in the original).

108. Landgrebe, "A Letter from Ludwig Landgrebe to Jean Wahl," 199.

109. Landgrebe, "A Letter from Ludwig Landgrebe to Jean Wahl," 199.

110. Landgrebe, "A Letter from Ludwig Landgrebe to Jean Wahl," 199.

111. Wahl, "Notes sur quelques aspects empiristes de la pensée de Husserl," 19.

112. Wahl may be referring here to an appendix of *Experience and Judgment* entitled "The Self-Evidence of Assertions of Probability—Critique of the Humean Conception."

113. Ludwig Landgrebe, "Correspondance," *Revue de Métaphysique et de Morale* 57, no. 2 (1952): 282.

114. Wahl, "Notes sur la première partie de *Erfahrung und Urteil* de Husserl," 6.

115. Wahl, "Une Interpretation de la *Logique* de Hegel," 1050–71.

116. In the context of Deleuze's work, *Empiricism and Subjectivity* is most frequently referenced, when it is discussed at all, as a precursory work to Deleuze's major works of the 1960s. Such an approach is exemplified by, for instance, Jon Roffe, who writes, in his essay on Hume in *Deleuze's Philosophical Lineage*: "I would like to indicate the extent to which this work provides an implicit foundation for what comes after, and in particular the metaphysics of *Difference and Repetition*." Graham Jones and Jon Roffe, eds. *Deleuze's Philosophical Lineage* (Edinburgh: Edinburgh University Press, 2009), 67.

Chapter 5

EPIGRAPH: Deleuze, "A Conversation: What Is It? What Is It For?" 12.

1. Michel Foucault, "Structuralism and Poststructuralism," in *The Essential Foucault*, ed. Paul Rabinow and Nikolas Rose (New York: New Press, 2003), 84.

2. In the interview, Foucault is speaking of the broader move from a search for the essence of the subject to the development of historical interest in the origins of the contemporary problem of the subject.

3. For biographical details of Deleuze's life, I have relied primarily on Schrift, *Twentieth-Century French Philosophy*, and Dosse, *Intersecting Lives*.

4. According to Dina Dreyfus, the editor of Hyppolite's posthumous *Figures de la pensée philosophique*, Hyppolite taught a course on Hume in the 1946–47 academic year. Hyppolite, *Figures*, vi.

5. See the information available at http://rhe.ish-lyon.cnrs.fr/?q =agregsecondaire_laureats&nom=&annee_op=%3D&annee%5Bvalue%5D=& annee%5Bmin%5D=&annee%5Bmax%5D=&periode=4&concours=14&items _per_page=100&page=6.

6. See Dosse, *Intersecting Lives*, 91ff.; and Bianco, *Jean Hyppolite, entre structure et existence*, 13.

7. The *Décades* were an annual series of ten-day meetings organized by the philosopher Paul Desjardins and held at the abbey at Pontigny which regularly attracted the best minds of Europe—philosophers, but also authors and other intellectuals. For an account of Wahl's conferences—or *Décades*—at Mount Holyoke, see Laurent Jeanpierre, "Pontigny-en-Amerique," in *Artists, Intellectuals, and World War II*, ed. Benfey and Remmler, 19–36.

8. Heidegger's course that Wahl followed was entitled *Einleitung in die Philosophie* (*Introduction to Philosophy*) and is volume 27 of his *Gesamtausgabe*.

9. Dosse, *Intersecting Lives*, 97.

10. This lecture was subsequently published in the *Revue de Métaphysique et de Morale* 55, no. 1 (January–March 1950): 1–15. It appears in English as part 4, chapter 8, of *Russell on Metaphysics*, ed. Stephen Mumford (New York: Routledge, 2003).

11. Hyppolite, *Figures de la pensée philosophique*, vi.

12. Schrift, *Twentieth-Century French Philosophy*, 117.

13. Schrift, "The Effects of the *Agrégation*," 449–73.

14. Schrift, "The Effects of the *Agrégation*," 453ff.

15. Davy "served for almost thirty years as a member of the *jury de agrégation de philosophie*, including serving as president of the jury from 1940 to 1956." Schrift, *Twentieth-Century French Philosophy*, 117.

16. Gilles Deleuze, "Bergson: 1859–1941," in *Les Philosophes célèbres*, ed. Maurice Merleau-Ponty (Paris: Éditions d'Art Lucien Mazenod, 1956), 292–99; Gilles Deleuze, "La Conception de la différence chez Bergson," *Les Études Bergsoniennes*, vol. 4 (1956): 77–112; and Gilles Deleuze, *What Is Grounding? From Transcripted Notes Taken by Pierre Lefebvre*, ed. and trans. Arjen Kleinherenbrink, Tony Yanick, Jason Adams, and Mohammed Salemy (Grand Rapids, MI: &&&, 2015).

17. Deleuze, *Empirisme et subjectivité*, 152.

18. Hyppolite, *Logic and Existence*, 26.

19. Hyppolite, *Logic and Existence*, 125. In his review of *Logic and Existence*, Deleuze asks, in a passage worth quoting at length:

How can absolute knowledge still be distinguished from empirical knowledge? . . . Absolute knowledge must simultaneously comprehend all empirical knowledge and comprehend nothing else, since there is nothing else to comprehend, and yet comprehend its radical difference from empirical knowledge. Hyppolite's idea is the following: despite appearances, essentialism was not what safeguarded us from empiricism and permitted us to overcome it. In the vision of essence, reflection is no less external than in empiricism or in pure critique. Empiricism posited determination as purely subjective; essentialism only goes as far as the ground of this limitation by opposing determinations among themselves and by opposing determinations to the Absolute. One is on the same side as the other. In contrast, the ontology of sense is the total Thought knowing itself only in its determinations, which are the moments of form. In the empirical and in the absolute, it is the same being and the same thought; but the external, empirical difference of thought and being has given way to the difference identical with Being, to the difference internal to the Being which thinks itself. Thereby, absolute knowledge actually distinguishes itself from empirical knowledge, but it distinguishes itself only by also negating the knowledge of indifferent essence. In the *Logic*, there is no longer therefore, as in the empirical, what I say on the one side and on the other side the sense of what I say—the pursuit of one by the other which is the dialectic of the *Phenomenology*. On the contrary, my discourse is logical or properly philosophical when I say the sense of what I say, and when in this manner Being says itself. (Gilles Deleuze, "Jean Hyppolite's *Logic and Existence*," in *Desert Islands*, 17)

20. Wahl, *Vers le concret*, 29.

21. Wahl, *Vers le concret*, 30.

22. Wahl, *Vers le concret*, 33.

23. See the extensive comparison of these two sections with sections from *Empiricism and Subjectivity* in David Scott's "Gilles Deleuze's Contributions to David Hume, sa vie, son oeuvre," *Angelaki* 16, no. 2 (June 2011): 175–80.

24. Gilles Deleuze and David Scott, "On the Work of David Hume," *Angelaki* 16, no. 2 (2011): 181.

25. For a detailed account of French readings of Hume, see Michel Malherbe's essay "Hume's Reception in France," in *The Reception of David Hume in Europe*, ed. Peter Jones (New York: Thoemmes Continuum, 2005).

26. Wahl, *Les philosophies pluralistes*, 76. The quote from James comes from "Philosophical Conceptions and Practical Results," in *The Writings of William James*, 361–62, emphasis in the original.

27. Prior to Leroy's book, and the book Deleuze coauthored with Cresson, the most recent comprehensive treatments of Hume in France were a pair of book-length surveys published over fifty years previously: Gabriel Compayré's, *La hilosophie de D. Hume* (Paris: Thorin, 1873) and Georges Lechartier's *David Hume, sociologue et moraliste* (Paris: Alcan, 1900).

28. André-Louis Leroy, *David Hume* (Paris: Presses Universitaires de France, 1953).

29. The other sections of Leroy's book are, in order, "Knowledge of the Physical World," "Human Nature and Academic Skepticism," and "Customs and Human Institutions."

30. Leroy, *David Hume*, 17.

31. Boundas translates *finalité* as "purposiveness" according to the standard French translation of Kant's *Zweckmassigkeit*. This is accurate, given the importance of Kant to Deleuze's argument in *Empiricism and Subjectivity*. However,

I have preferred the more literal translation of "finality," since it includes the Kantian resonance but also has a broader resonance that is important, given that the project of *Empiricism and Subjectivity* is to get *round* Kant and back to Hume.

32. Deleuze later writes that "we know that a philosophical theory involves psychological and, above all, sociological factors." Deleuze, *Empirisme et subjectivité*, 120.

33. Translation significantly modified.

34. "The imagination is not a factor, an agent, a determinant determination; it is a place, where it is necessary to localize, that is to say to fix, a determinable. Nothing is made *by* the imagination, everything is made *in* the imagination." Deleuze, *Empirisme et subjectivité*, 3 (emphasis in the original).

35. "In any case, Kant does not doubt that the imagination is, effectively, the better ground on which one can pose the problem of knowledge. Of the three syntheses that he distinguishes, he himself presents the synthesis of the imagination to us as being the ground of the two others." Deleuze, *Empirisme et subjectivité*, 124.

36. Husserl, *Experience and Judgment*, Appendix II (to §76), "The Self-Evidence of Assertions of Probability—Critique of the Humean Conception."

37. Husserl, *Experience and Judgment*, 393.

38. Husserl gives the example of a die that is blank on two faces and has a figure on the other four. The probability of the claim that "there will be a figure on the top face of the die when it is thrown" is "given" by the "weight" of previous experiences with throwing such a die. The general formulation of this is: "an empirical assertion is justified . . . if [its] principle guarantees the ideal possibility of its verification." Such judgments are rational and are like judgments of relations of ideas because the relation and the related terms are not independent. To deny the validity of such a judgment, for Husserl, would be to deny its terms—a denial that can be overcome by verifying the ideal possibility of the probability in question—that is, by merely inspecting the die and its faces. Husserl, *Experience and Judgment*, 395.

39. On the phenomenological problem of genesis, see Eugen Fink, "The Phenomenological Philosophy of Edmund Husserl and Contemporary Criticism," in *The Phenomenology of Husserl*, ed. R. O. Elveton (Chicago: Quadrangle Books, 1970), 73–147. For that problem's importance to French philosophy in the early 1950s, especially the work of the young Derrida, see Paola Marrati, *Genesis and Trace*, and Leonard Lawlor, *Derrida and Husserl*.

40. Gaston Berger published a short essay, "Husserl et Hume," in the *Revue Internationale de Philosophie* 1, no. 2 (January 15, 1939): 342–53. Elements of Berger's essay were later incorporated into his *Le cogito dans la philosophie de Husserl* (Paris: Aubier, 1941), translated by Kathleen McLaughlin as *The Cogito in Husserl's Philosophy* (Evanston, IL: Northwestern University Press, 1972).

41. See note 39, above, for further resources concerned with the phenomenological problem of genesis. Lawlor's book makes the strongest claim: that the problem of genesis is the "basic" problem of phenomenology. See Lawlor, *Derrida and Husserl*, chapter 1.

42. Leroy, *David Hume*, 15. Leroy will later specify the importance of psy-

chology for Hume: "But this psychology does not have its end in itself, it prepares a philosophy; it is already this philosophy." Leroy, *David Hume*, 40.

43. Deleuze's language here echoes Sartre's in the introduction to *Being and Nothingness.*

44. See chapter 1, above.

45. Leroy, *David Hume*, 19. The title of part 1, chapter 3, of Leroy's book is "The Progress of the Imagination."

46. Leroy, *David Hume*, 64.

47. For critical assessments of Deleuze's idiosyncratic repetition and restaging of Hume and other philosophers, see David Neil, "The Uses of Anachronism: Deleuze's History of the Subject," *Philosophy Today* 42, no. 4 (1998): 418–31; and Jay Conway, "Deleuze's Hume and Creative History of Philosophy," in *Current Continental Theory and Modern Philosophy* (Evanston, IL: Northwestern University Press, 2006), 197–209; as well as Deleuze's own "La Méthode de dramatisation," *Bulletin de la Société Française de Philosophie* 61, no. 3 (July–September 1967): 89–118.

48. References to Hume's *A Treatise of Human Nature* will be made to the text included in the Clarendon Edition of the Works of David Hume. Specific citations will be made using the standard parenthetical notation in which, for instance, (T 1.4.3.2) indicates the first book, fourth chapter, third section, and second paragraph.

49. Leroy, *David Hume*, 211.

50. Leroy, *David Hume*, 206.

51. These section breaks are marked by double returns in the French. The breaks were not preserved in the English translation.

52. For an interesting presentation of Hume that highlights this cinematic character of his thinking, see Davide Panagia, *Impressions of Hume: Cinematic Thinking and the Politics of Discontinuity* (Lanham, MD: Rowman and Littlefield, 2013).

53. See the selections in part 1, section 1 of *The Essential Husserl: Basic Writings in Transcendental Phenomenology*, ed. Donn Welton (Bloomington: Indiana University Press, 1999), 3–22.

54. See the later discussion in *Empiricism and Subjectivity* of the "delirium of the mind."

55. The verb translated here as "surpass" is *dépasser*. In his translation of *Empirisme et subjectivité*, Constantin Boundas translates this term (and its cognates) as "transcend." In his *Gilles Deleuze's Empiricism and Subjectivity*, Roffe agrees with this choice, arguing that, at one point in *Empirisme et subjectivité*, Deleuze treats the terms as equivalent (Jon Roffe, *Gilles Deleuze's Empiricism and Subjectivity: A Critical Introduction and Guide* [Edinburgh: Edinburgh University Press, 2016], 36n2). However, this choice of translation occludes the places where Deleuze does use the term "*transcendance*." More importantly, it renders confusing or unintelligible an important passage of *Empirisme et subjectivité* where Deleuze explicitly contrasts the terms. See the discussion in chapter 7, below.

56. This sympathy helps to explain Deleuze's affection for thinkers as outwardly different as Hume and Spinoza. Compare "A Conversation: What Is It? What Is It For?" in *Dialogues II*, 14–15. This is only one of many places where Deleuze places both Hume and Spinoza in a group of philosophers who are both

"part of the history of philosophy, but who escaped from it in one respect, or all together."

57. This is a critique that Deleuze may have been familiar with from Martial Gueroult's 1929 *La philosophie transcendentale de Salomon Maimon* (Paris: Alcan, 1929). Maimon's solution is not to return to Hume, but to rectify Kant through recourse to a Spinozistic-Leibnizian dogmatism.

58. Again, Maimon's own solution, in his *Essay on Transcendental Philosophy*, does not fall back on a kind of Humean skepticism, but attempts to rehabilitate the Kantian system with an original form of dogmatic rationalism that owes much to Leibniz and Spinoza.

59. Again, Boundas—and Roffe in his commentary—use "transcendence" to translate *dépasser,* even though Deleuze uses *dépasser* consistently throughout this section.

60. Deleuze concludes this discussion by indicating the presence of an antinomy: if the subject is only the constitution of a collection of ideas, how can this collection grasp itself as a self? How do the mind and the subject become one? His answer is that there is a synthesis that conjoins origin and qualification, but he notes that this is something only hoped for by Hume. See chapter 7, below, for how Deleuze hopes to "fulfill" this hope.

61. See chapter 7, below.

62. The importance of this section is not only that it shows that there are two systems, but it also shows that the empirical critique of rationalism reveals that the problems of rationalism only acquire their sense and force through the prior, primary problem of morality. Deleuze, *Empirisme et subjectivité*, 16.

63. This discussion closely follows T 3.3.1.1, "Moral distinctions not deriv'd from reason."

Chapter 6

EPIGRAPH: Deleuze, "Response to a Question on the Subject," in *Two Regimes of Madness*, 349 (translation altered).

1. See the discussion of this issue in chapter 4 of *Empiricism and Subjectivity*, below.

2. As noted in chapter 5 above, Canguilhem, along with Hyppolite, directed Deleuze's 1947 thesis on Hume.

3. See Roffe's excellent discussion of the relation of *Instincts and Institutions* to the argument of *Empiricism and Subjectivity*. Roffe, *Gilles Deleuze's Empiricism and Subjectivity*, 48ff.

4. The passage cited by Deleuze comes from Hume's *Treatise*, 3.2.3: "Of the Rules, Which Determine Property."

5. Boundas's English translation, "We must now explain some issues pertaining to ethics," obscures the link between the conclusion of the first chapter and the beginning of the second. Deleuze, *Empirisme et subjectivité*, 23.

6. Deleuze emphasizes that a "convention" is not equivalent to a "contract." Deleuze, *Empirisme et subjectivité*, 36.

7. Leroy's translation has "*instrument à percussion*" for Hume's "stringed instrument." Deleuze follows Leroy's translation in *Empiricism and Subjectivity*, but Boundas corrects the relevant cited passages in his English translation. See Roffe, *Gilles Deleuze's Empiricism and Subjectivity*, 116–18.

8. Hume writes, in a passage quoted by Deleuze: "Justice in her decisions, never regards the fitness or unfitness of objects to particular persons . . . the general rule, that *possession must be stable*, is not apply'd by particular judgments, but by other general rules, which must extend to the whole society, and be inflexible either by spite or favour." Deleuze, *Empirisme et subjectivité*, 40 (emphasis in the original).

9. Deleuze, *Empirisme et subjectivité*, 46. The translation of this table has been significantly altered.

10. Deleuze is relying here on the argument of Hume's essay "Of Tragedy," in *Essays, Moral, Political, and Literary: Volumes 1 and 2*, ed. Tom L. Beauchamp and Mark A. Box (Oxford: Oxford University Press, 2021). This is one of the few times in *Empiricism and Subjectivity* that Deleuze makes use of any of Hume's work other than the *Treatise*.

11. As Roffe notes, Hume never uses the phrase "the principles of the passions"; it is Deleuze's coinage. Roffe, *Gilles Deleuze's Empiricism and Subjectivity*, 13.

12. In the first section of the chapter, which is devoted entirely to religion, Deleuze departs from his steady use of Hume's *Treatise* and makes use almost exclusively of Hume's *Dialogues concerning Natural Religion* and the *Enquiry concerning the Principle of Morals*.

13. At this point in his argument, Deleuze turns back from the *Dialogues concerning Natural Religion* and the *Enquiry concerning the Principle of Morals* to the *Treatise*.

Chapter 7

EPIGRAPH: Deleuze, "Hume," in *Desert Islands*, 226.

1. For a discussion of the reasons for translating "*dépasser*" as "surpassing" rather than "transcendence," as Boundas does in the English translation of *Empiricism and Subjectivity*, see above, chapter 5, note 55. The present passage illustrates the importance of this terminological choice, and the translation has been substantially modified from Boundas's one in order to track the distinction that Deleuze is making.

2. It is true that the task of the dialectic is the overcoming of this situation, but for Deleuze, the solution requires the additional supposition that relations are internal to ideas, that negation—the not-A contained in every A—is productive of new knowledge.

3. See Wahl's essay "La Poésie comme union des contraires," in *Poésie, pen-*

sée, perception (Paris: Calmann-Lévy, 1948), 20–27, which concludes: "At the same time that he can become aware of himself as knowing, the poet is conscious of himself as existent. For, in man, knowledge is existence and existence, knowledge. And existence implies transcendence; man exists insofar as he feels things and beings beyond himself. Likewise, knowledge implies the transcendence of its object."

4. For Hume, it seems that nothing is necessary to support the existence of a perception. Thus, as noted above, he rejects the law of sufficient reason, since it can never adequately explain causality.

5. Deleuze touches on time only briefly here. Extension is a property only of the impressions of sight and touch; time is a quality or disposition of any impression whatsoever.

6. Examples of relations that can vary without any variation of ideas include relations of contiguity and distance whose variation can involve identical ideas. Examples of relations that can depend entirely on ideas that we compare with one another include resemblance and contrariety. In his critique of Hume's account of mathematical reasoning, Kant argues that the second type of relation means that some relations are intrinsic to ideas.

7. It is no accident that the two examples appealed to in this section are Descartes and Kant.

8. Thinking that empiricism is defined by the claim that all knowledge derives from experience mistakes empiricism for being concerned with knowledge when it is properly concerned with practice.

9. Deleuze is employing two definitions of "experience" here: experience as a "collection of distinct perceptions" (so relations do not derive from it) and as "diverse conjunctions of objects in the past" (this past produces the present/future and therefore acts as a principle; principles do not derive from it).

10. Again, translating "*se dépasser*" as "surpass" rather than "transcend." See chapter 5, note 55, above.

11. "Finality" is thus a concept that Deleuze defines over against the transcendental concept of intentionality.

12. Deleuze notes in passing that the specific principles that constitute human nature are relatively few in number, since they make possible a science of human nature, and that "even Kant" does not provide a full accounting of such principles.

13. According to Hume, this is why the quality of our own possessions makes us vain or humble, while the possessions of others do not.

14. "*Objectification* is a matter of *method*, founded upon prescientific data of experience. Mathematical method 'constructs,' out of intuitive representation, ideal objects and teaches how to deal with them operatively and systematically." Edmund Husserl, *The Crisis of European Sciences and Transcendental Phenomenology*, trans. David Carr (Evanston, IL: Northwestern University Press, 1970), 348 (emphasis in the original).

15. "We end with *dialectical materialism* as the *truth of transcendental idealism*. Since the naïve attitude has been definitively suppressed by the reduction, the *practice* of the description of pure lived experience is necessarily *absorbed* within

a dialectical materialism that *suppresses* it in its properly phenomenological sense in order to preserve it in its resultant form and *to elevate it to a superior level.*" Thao, *Phenomenology and Dialectical Materialism*, 129 (emphasis in the original).

16. Deleuze clarifies that although resonance and vivacity are characteristics of the mind itself, "these two modes are presented as the original modifications of the mind by the principles, as the effect of principles in the mind, principles of association and principles of passion." Deleuze, *Empirisme et subjectivité*, 150–51.

17. Deleuze, "Jean Hyppolite's *Logic et Existence*," in *Desert Islands*, 15–18.

18. See Deleuze's preface to *Kant's Critical Philosophy*, "On Four Poetic Formulas That Might Summarize the Kantian Philosophy." Gilles Deleuze, *Kant's Critical Philosophy*, trans. Hugh Tomlinson and Barbara Habberjam (Minneapolis: University of Minnesota Press, 1984), vii–xiii.

Conclusion

EPIGRAPH: Gilles Deleuze, "On Philosophy," in *Negotiations 1972–1990*, trans. Martin Joughin (New York: Columbia University Press, 1995), 138.

1. Deleuze, *Empirisme et subjectivité*, 143 (emphasis in the original).

2. Deleuze, *Empirisme et subjectivité*, 144.

3. Deleuze, *Empirisme et subjectivité*, 151 (emphasis in the original).

4. Deleuze, *Empirisme et subjectivité*, 152.

5. Wahl, *Vers le concret*, 38–39.

6. Hyppolite, *Logic and Existence*, 36, 141–44. It should be noted that while this reference to *Logic and Existence* may seem to court anachronism, Hyppolite's course on Hume, in 1946–47, certainly contained at least *in statu nascendi* the account of empirical knowledge elaborated in *Logic and Existence*.

7. Deleuze, *Empirisme et subjectivité*, 152.

8. Deleuze, *Empirisme et subjectivité*, 152.

9. Deleuze, *Empirisme et subjectivité*, 86.

10. See above, chapter 4, note 89, for information on Wahl's articles dealing with *Experience and Judgment*.

11. One sign of the reassessment of phenomenology and the growing importance of Husserl in particular was the number of introductions to German as well as French phenomenology (especially Sartre and Merleau-Ponty) that appeared in the early 1950s. Among the most important of these introductions were Pierre Thévenaz's three-part essay, "Qu'est-ce que la phénoménologie?" ["What Is Phenomenology?"] in the *Revue de Théologie et de Philosophie*, vol. 2 (1952): 9–30, 126–40, 294–316; and Lyotard's *La phénoménologie*. Also important was Paul Ricoeur's 1950 translation of Husserl's *Ideas I* into French.

12. See Wahl, "Une Interpretation de la *Logique* de Hegel," 1050–71; and Deleuze's review in *Revue Philosophique de la France et l'Étranger* 144, no. 7–9 (July–September 1954): 457–60.

13. Hyppolite, *Logic and Existence*, 195.

14. See Janicaud, *Heidegger en France*, especially chapter 5, "L'Embellie des années 1950" ["The Calm of the 1950s]. Wahl, among others, did not attend the conference at Cerisy because of Heidegger's Nazi ties. Some of Wahl's reasons for not participating in the conference can be found in his introduction to *Vers la fin de l'ontologie: Étude sur l'introduction dans la métaphysique par Heidegger* [*Toward the End of Ontology: An Essay on Heidegger's Introduction to Metaphysics*] (Paris: Sedes, 1956).

15. For accounts of structuralism in France, see chapter 2, "Structuralism in France," of Peter Caws's *Structuralism: A Philosophy of the Human Sciences* (New York: Humanity Books, 2000); and chapter 4 of Schrift's *Twentieth-Century French Philosophy*, "Structuralism and the Challenge to Philosophy." Schrift gives 1960 as the year that existentialism ceased to be a vigorous philosophical project in France.

16. Deleuze, *Empirisme et subjectivité*, 33.

17. Gilles Deleuze, "Bergson, 1859–1941," in *Les Philosophes célèbres*, ed. Maurice Merleau-Ponty (Paris: Éditions d'Art Lucien Mazenod, 1956); and Deleuze, "La Conception de la différence chez Bergson," in *Les Études Bergsoniennes*, vol. 4 (1956): 77–112.

18. Gilles Deleuze, "Bergson's Conception of Difference," in *Desert Islands*, 46 (emphasis in the original).

19. Deleuze, "Bergson's Conception of Difference," 45.

20. Gilles Deleuze, *Difference and Repetition* (New York: Columbia University Press, 1994), 70ff.

21. Deleuze, *What Is Grounding?* 24–26.

22. Deleuze, *What Is Grounding?* 27.

23. Deleuze, *What Is Grounding?* 28.

24. For Deleuze's account in *Empiricism and Subjectivity* of the relation between Hume's philosophical project and Kant's, see chapter 5, above.

25. Deleuze, *What Is Grounding?* 24.

26. Deleuze, "Letter to a Harsh Critic," in *Negotiations*, 6.

27. Deleuze, "A Conversation: What Is It? What Is It For?" in *Dialogues II*, 14–15.

28. Deleuze, "Hume," in *Desert Islands*, 162–69.

29. Gilles Deleuze, "Response to a Question on the Subject," in Deleuze, *Two Regimes of Madness: Texts and Interviews, 1975–1995*, trans. Ames Hodges and Michael Taormina (New York: Semiotext(e), 2006), 349–51; Gilles Deleuze, "Preface to the English-Language Edition," in *Empiricism and Subjectivity*, trans. Constantin V. Boundas (New York: Columbia University Press, 1991), ix–x.

30. Deleuze, "Hume," 163 (emphasis in the original).

31. Gilles Deleuze, "On the Superiority of Anglo-American Literature," in *Dialogues II*, 55 (emphasis in the original).

32. Deleuze, "Preface to the English-Language Edition," x.

33. Deleuze, "Preface to the English-Language Edition," ix.

34. Deleuze, "Hume," 162.

Bibliography

Alquié, Ferdinand. *Le désir d'éternité*. Paris: Presses Universitaires de France, 1947.

Althusser, Louis. *Écrits philosophiques et politiques*, vol. 1. Paris: Le Livre de Poche, 1999.

———. *L'avenir dure longtemps*. Paris: Stock / IMEC, 1992. Translated by Richard Veasey as *The Future Lasts Forever: A Memoir* (New York: New Press, 1994).

———. *The Spectre of Hegel: Early Writings*. New York: Verso, 2014.

Andler, Charles. "Le Fondement du savoir dans la *Phénoménologie de l'esprit* de Hegel." *Revue de Métaphysique et de Morale*, vol. 38 (1931): 317–40.

———. *Le pan-germanisme philosophique*. Paris: Conard, 1917.

Antonioli, Manola. *Deleuze et l'histoire de la philosophie*. Paris: Éditions Kimé, 1999.

Aspelin, Gunnar. *Hegels Tübinger Fragmente, eine psychologischideen-geschichtliche Untersuchung*. Lund: Ohlssons Buchdruckerei, 1933.

Badiou, Alain. *The Adventure of French Philosophy*. Translated by Bruno Bosteels. New York: Verso, 2012.

Baring, Edward. *Converts to the Real: Catholicism and the Making of Continental Philosophy*. Cambridge, MA: Harvard University Press, 2019.

———. *The Young Derrida and French Philosophy, 1945–1968*. Cambridge: Cambridge University Press, 2012.

Bataille, Georges. *Guilty*. Translated by Stuart Kendall. Albany: State University of New York Press, 2011.

———. *Inner Experience*. Translated by Stuart Kendall. Albany: State University of New York Press, 2014.

———. *Oeuvres complètes*. 12 vols. Edited by Denis Hollier et al. Paris: Gallimard, 1970–88.

———. *On Nietzsche*. Translated by Stuart Kendall. Albany: State University of New York Press, 2016.

———. *Visions of Excess: Selected Writings, 1927–1939*. Edited by Allan Stoekl, translated by Allan Stoekl with Carl R. Lovitt and Donald M. Leslie Jr. Minneapolis: University of Minnesota Press, 1985.

Bataille, Georges, Roger Caillois, Pierre Klossowski, and Michel Leiris. *The Sacred Conspiracy: The Internal Papers of the Secret Society of Acéphale and Lectures to the College of Sociology*. Edited by Alastair Brotchie and Marina Galletti. Translated by John Harman and Natasha Lehrer. London: Atlas Press, 2018.

Baugh, Bruce. *French Hegel: From Surrealism to Postmodernism*. New York: Routledge, 2003.

————. "Jean Hyppolite and the French Kierkegaard." *Pli: The Warwick Journal of Philosophy* 24 (2013): 40–68.

————. "Limiting Reason's Empire: The Early Reception of Hegel in France." *Journal of the History of Philosophy* 31, no. 2 (April 1993): 259–75.

Beaulieu, Alain. "La Réforme du concept phénoménologique de 'monde' par Gilles Deleuze." *Studia Phaenomenologica: Romanian Journal of Phenomenology* 3, no. 3–4 (January 1, 2003): 257–87.

Beauvoir, Simone de. *Philosophical Writings.* Edited by Margaret A. Simons, Marybeth Timmermann, and Mary Beth Mader. Urbana: University of Illinois Press, 2005.

————. *Pour une morale de l'ambiguïté.* Paris: Folio, 2003. Translated by Bernard Frechtman as *The Ethics of Ambiguity* (New York: Open Road Media, 2018).

Bell, Jeffrey A. "Charting the Road of Inquiry: Deleuze's Humean Pragmatics and the Challenge of Badiou." *Southern Journal of Philosophy* 44, no. 3 (September 1, 2006): 399–425.

————. *Deleuze's Hume: Philosophy, Culture, and the Scottish Enlightenment.* Edinburgh: Edinburgh University Press, 2008.

Bell, Martin. "Transcendental Empiricism? Deleuze's Reading of Hume." In *Impressions of Hume*, edited by Marina Frasca-Spada and P. J. E. Kail. Oxford: Oxford University Press, 2005.

Bellantone, Andrea. *Hegel en France.* 2 vols. Paris: Hermann, 2011.

Benfey, Christopher E. G., and Karen Remmler, editors. *Artists, Intellectuals, and World War II: The Pontigny Encounters at Mount Holyoke College, 1942–1944.* Amherst: University of Massachusetts Press, 2006.

Benoist, Jocelyn, and Michel Espagne. *L'itinéraire de Trân Duc Thao: Phénoménologie et transferts culturels.* Paris: Armand Colin, 2013.

Berger, Gaston. "The Different Trends of Contemporary French Philosophy." *Philosophy and Phenomenological Research* 7, no. 1 (1946): 1–11.

————. "Husserl et Hume." *Revue Internationale de Philosophie* 1, no. 2 (1939): 342–53.

————. *Le cogito dans la philosophie de Husserl.* Paris: Aubier. 1941. Translated by Kathleen McLaughlin as *The Cogito in Husserl's Philosophy* (Evanston, IL: Northwestern University Press, 1972).

————. "The Main Themes of Husserl's Phenomenology." *Études de Métaphysique et de Morale* 49 (1944): 22–43.

Bergson, Henri. *Creative Evolution.* Translated by Arthur Mitchell. Mineola, NY: Dover, 1998.

————. *Les deux sources de la morale et de la religion: Édition critique sous la direction de Frédéric Worms.* 11th edition. Paris: Presses Universitaires de France, 2013.

————. *L'évolution créatrice: Édition critique dirigée par Frédéric Worms.* 12th edition. Paris: Presses Universitaires de France, 2013.

————. *Matière et mémoire: Essai sur la relation du corps à l'esprit. Édition critique dirigée par Frédéric Worms.* Paris: Presses Universitaires de France, 2012.

————. *Matter and Memory.* Translated by Nancy Margaret Paul and W. Scott Palmer. New York: Zone Books, 1990.

————. *The Two Sources of Morality and Religion.* Translated by R. Ashley Audra. Notre Dame, IN: University of Notre Dame Press, 1977.

Bernet, Rudolf, Iso Kern, Eduard Marbach, and Lester E. Embree, editors. *Introduction to Husserlian Phenomenology.* Evanston, IL: Northwestern University Press, 1993.

Bianco, Giuseppe. *Après Bergson: Portrait de groupe avec philosophe.* Paris: Presses Universitaires de France, 2015.

————. "Experience vs. Concept? The Role of Bergson in Twentieth-Century French Philosophy." *European Legacy* 16, no. 7 (2011): 855–72.

————, editor. *Jean Hyppolite, entre structure et existence.* Paris: Rue d'Ulm, 2013.

Bident, Christophe. *Maurice Blanchot: A Critical Biography.* Translated by John McKeane. New York: Fordham University Press, 2018.

Blanchot, Maurice. *La part du feu.* Paris: Gallimard, 1949. Translated by Charlotte Mandell as *The Work of Fire* (Stanford, CA: Stanford University Press, 1995).

————. *Lautréamont et Sade.* Paris: Éditions de Minuit, 1949. Translated by Michelle Kendall and Stuart Kendall as *Lautréamont and Sade* (Stanford, CA: Stanford University Press, 2004).

Bojanic, Petar. "La violenza come origine dell'Istituzione (Deleuze con Hume e Saint-Just)." Translated by Mario Autieri. *Iride: Filosofia e Discussione Pubblica* 25, no. 65 (April 1, 2012): 79–90.

Bourdieu, Pierre. *Homo Academicus.* Translated by Peter Collier. Stanford, CA: Stanford University Press, 1988.

Bourgeois, Bernard. "Jean Hyppolite et Hegel." *Les Études Philosophiques* 2 (June 1993): 145–59.

Bowman, Brady. *Hegel and the Metaphysics of Absolute Negativity.* Cambridge: Cambridge University Press, 2013.

————. "Spinozist Pantheism and the Truth of 'Sense Certainty': What the Eleusinian Mysteries Tell Us about Hegel's *Phenomenology.*" *Journal of the History of Philosophy* 50, no. 1 (2010): 85–110.

Braidotti, Rosi, Claire Colebrook, and Patrick Hanafin, editors. *Deleuze and Law: Forensic Futures.* New York: Palgrave Macmillan, 2009.

Bréhier, Émile. *Les thèmes actuels de la philosophie.* Paris: Presses Universitaires de France, 1956.

Brown, Frederick. *The Embrace of Unreason: France, 1914–1940.* New York: Knopf, 2014.

Brunschvicg, Leon. *Le progrès de la conscience dans la philosophie occidentale.* Paris: Alcan, 1927.

Bryant, Levi R. *Difference and Givenness: Deleuze's Transcendental Empiricism and the Ontology of Immanence.* Evanston, IL: Northwestern University Press, 2008.

Burkhard, Bud. *French Marxism between the Wars: Henri Lefebvre and the Philosophies.* Amherst, NY: Humanity Books, 2000.

Butler, Judith. *Subjects of Desire: Hegelian Reflections in Twentieth-Century France.* New York: Columbia University Press, 2012.

Caeymaex, Florence. "Bergson, Sartre, Merleau-Ponty: Les Phénoménologies existentialistes et leur heritage Bergsonien." In *Annales Bergsoniennes II:*

Bergson, Deleuze, La Phénoménologie, 409–25. Paris: Presses Universitaires de France, 2004.

Caillois, Roger. *L'homme et le sacré.* Paris: Folio, 1988. Translated by Meyer Barash as *Man and the Sacred* (Urbana: University of Illinois Press, 2001).

Canguilhem, Georges. "Hegel en France." *Revue d'Histoire et de Philosophie Religieuse* 28–29 (1949): 282–97.

Canguilhem, Georges, and Michel Foucault. "Jean Hyppolite (1907–1968)." *Revue de Métaphysique et de Morale* 74, no. 2 (1969): 129–36.

Caws, Peter. *Structuralism: A Philosophy of the Human Sciences.* New York: Humanity Books, 2000.

Chestov, Leon. *Kierkegaard et la philosophie existentielle: Vox clamantis in deserto.* Translated by T. Rageot and B. Schoelzer. Paris: Vrin, 2000.

Christensen, Arild. "Kierkegaard's Secret Affliction." *Harvard Theological Review* 42, no. 4 (October 1949): 255–71.

Clark, Christopher. *The Sleepwalkers: How Europe Went to War in 1914.* New York: Harper, 2013.

Comay, Rebecca. *Mourning Sickness: Hegel and the French Revolution.* Stanford, CA: Stanford University Press, 2010.

Compayré, Gabriel. *La philosophie de David Hume.* Paris: Thorin, 1873.

Conway, Jay. "Deleuze's Hume and Creative History of Philosophy." In *Current Continental Theory and Modern Philosophy,* edited by Stephen H. Daniel. Evanston, IL: Northwestern University Press, 2005.

Cranaki, Mimica. "Review of Jean Hyppolite: *Logique et existence.*" *Revue de Métaphysique et de Morale* 59, no. 2 (1954): 202–5.

Croce, Benedetto. "Un cercle vicieux dans la critique de la philosophie hégélienne." *Revue de Métaphysique et de Morale* 38, no. 3 (1931): 277–84.

Cutler, Anna, and Iain Mackenzie. "Critique as a Practice of Learning: Beyond Indifference with Meillassoux, towards Deleuze." *Pli: The Warwick Journal of Philosophy* 22 (2011): 88–109.

De Coster, Sylvain. "La crise de l'existentialisme." Review of *Études Kierkegaardiennes* by Jean Wahl. *Revue Internationale de Philosophie* 1, no. 2 (1939): 398–402.

De Martelaere, Patricia. "Gilles Deleuze, interprète de Hume." *Revue Philosophique de Louvain* 82, no. 54 (1984): 224–48.

De Sutter, Laurent. *Deleuze: La pratique du droit.* Paris: Michalon, 2009.

De Waelhens, Alphonse. Review of *Études Kierkegaardiennes* by Jean Wahl. *Revue Neo-Scolastique de Philosophie* 41, no. 58 (1938): 302–8.

———. Review of *Existence humaine et transcendance* by Jean Wahl. *Revue Philosophique de Louvain* 44, no. 2 (1946): 328.

———. Review of *Existentialisme ou Marxisme* by Georges Lukács. *Revue Philosophique de Louvain* 46, no. 12 (1948): 500–504.

———. Review of *Introduction à la philosophie de l'histoire de Hegel* by Jean Hyppolite. *Revue Philosophique de Louvain* 47, no. 13 (1949): 147–50.

Delacroix, Henri. "Søren Kierkegaard, le christianisme absolu à travers le paradoxe et le désespoir." *Revue de Métaphysique et de Morale,* vol. 8 (1900): 459–84.

Delbos, Victor. "La méthode de démonstration chez Hegel." *Revue de Métaphysique et de Morale*, vol. 35 (1928): 529–51.

Deleuze, Gilles. *Critique et clinique*. Paris: Éditions de Minuit, 1993. Translated by Daniel W. Smith and Michael Greco as *Essays Critical and Clinical* (Minneapolis: University of Minnesota Press, 1997).

———. *Deux régimes de fous: Textes et entretiens, 1975–1995*. Edited by David Lapoujade. Paris: Éditions de Minuit, 2003. Translated by Ames Hodges and Michael Taormina as *Two Regimes of Madness: Texts and Interviews, 1975–1995* (Cambridge, MA: Semiotext(e), 2007).

———. *Différence et répétition*. Paris: Presses Universitaires de France, 1968. Translated by Paul Patton as *Difference and Repetition* (New York: Columbia University Press, 1994).

———. *Empirisme et subjectivité*. Paris: Presses Universitaires de France, 1953. Translated by Constantin Boundas as *Empiricism and Subjectivity: An Essay on Hume's Theory of Human Nature*. New York: Columbia University Press, 1991.

———. *Instincts et institutions*. Paris: Hachette, 1953.

———. "La méthode de dramatization." *Bulletin de la Société Française de Philosophie* 61, no. 3 (July–September 1967): 89–118.

———. *La philosophie critique de Kant*. Paris: Presses Universitaires de France, 1963. Translated by Hugh Tomlinson and Barbara Habberjam as *Kant's Critical Philosophy* (Minneapolis: University of Minnesota Press, 1984).

———. *Le bergsonisme*. Paris: Presses Universitaires de France, 1966. Translated by Hugh Tomlinson and Barbara Habberjam as *Bergsonism* (New York: Zone Books, 1990).

———. *Lettres et autres textes*. Edited by David Lapoujade. Paris: Les Éditions de Minuit, 2015. Translated by Ames Hodges as *Letters and Other Texts* (Cambridge, MA: Semiotext(e), 2020).

———. *L'île déserte et autres textes: Textes et entretiens, 1953–1974*. Paris: Éditions de Minuit, 2002. Translated by Michael Taormina as *Desert Islands, and Other Texts, 1953–1974* (Cambridge, MA: Semiotext(e), 2004).

———. "L'immanence: Une vie." *Philosophie* 47 (September 1, 1995): 3–7. Translated as "Immanence: A Life," in *Two Regimes of Madness: Texts and Interviews, 1975–1995* (Cambridge, MA: Semiotext(e), 2007).

———. *Logique du sens*. Paris: Éditions de Minuit, 1969. Translated by Mark Lester and Charles Stivale as *The Logic of Sense*, edited by Constantin V. Boundas (New York: Columbia University Press, 1990).

———. *Nietzsche et la philosophie*. Paris: Presses Universitaires de France, 1962. Translated by Hugh Tomlinson and Barbara Habberjam as *Nietzsche and Philosophy* (New York: Columbia University Press, 2006).

———. *Pourparlers*. Paris: Éditions de Minuit, 1990. Translated by Martin Joughin as *Negotiations, 1972–1990* (New York: Columbia University Press, 1995).

———. "Supplement: On the Work of David Hume." Translated by David Scott. *Angelaki: Journal of the Theoretical Humanities* 16, no. 2 (June 1, 2011): 181–88.

———. *What Is Grounding? From Transcripted Notes Taken by Pierre Lefebvre*. Edited and translated by Arjen Kleinherenbrink, Tony Yanick, Jason Adams, and Mohammed Salemy. Grand Rapids, MI: &&&, 2015.

Deleuze, Gilles, and Claire Parnet. *Dialogues*. Paris: Flammarion, 1977. Translated by Hugh Tomlinson and Barbara Habberjam as *Dialogues II* (New York: Columbia University Press, 2007).

Deleuze, Gilles, and Leopold von Sacher-Masoch. *Présentation de Sacher-Masoch: Le froid et le cruel*. Paris: Les Éditions de Minuit, 1967. Translated by Jean McNeil and Aude Willm as *Masochism: Coldness and Cruelty and Venus in Furs* (Cambridge, MA: Zone Books, 1991).

Depraz, Natalie. "L'empirisme transcendental: De Deleuze à Husserl." *Revue Germanique Internationale* 13 (2011): 125–48.

Derrida, Jacques. *Le problème de la genèse dans la philosophie de Husserl*. Paris: Presses Universitaires de France, 1990. Translated by Marian Hobson as *The Problem of Genesis in Husserl's Philosophy* (Chicago: University of Chicago Press, 2003).

———. *Specters of Marx: The State of the Debt, the Work of Mourning, and the New International*. Translated by Peggy Kamuf. New York: Routledge, 1994.

Desanti, Jean-Toussaint. "Merleau-Ponty et la decomposition de l'idealisme." *La Nouvelle Critique* 37, no. 1 (1952): 63–82.

Descartes, René. *Meditations on First Philosophy*. In *The Philosophical Writings of Descartes*, vol. 2, translated by John Cottingham, Robert Stoothoff, and Dugald Murdoch (Cambridge: Cambridge University Press, 1984).

Descombes, Vincent. *Modern French Philosophy*. Translated by L. Scott-Fox and J. M. Harding. Cambridge: Cambridge University Press, 1980.

Dilthey, Wilhelm. *Die Jugendgeschichte Hegels*. Berlin: Reimer, 1905.

Dosse, Francois. *Gilles Deleuze et Félix Guattari: Biographie croisee*. Paris: La Decouverte, 2009. Translated by Deborah Glassman as *Gilles Deleuze and Félix Guattari: Intersecting Lives* (New York: Columbia University Press, 2011).

Dosse, François, Michael Behrent, David Berry, Lucia Bonfreschi, Warren Breckman, Michael Scott Christofferson, and Stuart Elden, et al. *After the Deluge: New Perspectives on the Intellectual and Cultural History of Postwar France*. Edited by Julian Bourg. Lanham, MD: Lexington Books, 2004.

Dufrenne, Mikel. "À propos de la thèse de Jean Hyppolite." Review of *Genèse et structure de la Phénoménologie de l'esprit de Hegel* by Jean Hyppolite. *Fontaine* 11 (1947): 461–70.

———. "Actualité de Hegel." *Esprit* 148, no. 9 (1948): 396–408.

———. "Existentialism and Existentialisms." *Philosophy and Phenomenological Research* 26, no. 1 (September 1965): 51.

Dupont, Christian. *Phenomenology in French Philosophy: Early Encounters*. New York: Springer, 2013.

Duvernoy, Russell J. "Commentary on Jean Wahl: Reckoning with 'Poetry as Spiritual Exercise' in Times of Duress." *Philosophy Today* 64, no. 3 (2020): 797–807.

École Normale Supérieure. Bibliothèque des Lettres et Sciences Humaines et Sociales. Fonds Hyppolite.

Ehrenberg, Hans, and Herbert Link. *Hegels Erstes System*. Heidelberg: Carl Winters, 1915.

Eilenberger, Wolfram. *Time of the Magicians: Wittgenstein, Benjamin, Cassirer, Heidegger, and the Decade That Reinvented Philosophy.* New York: Penguin, 2020.

Eksteins, Modris. *Rites of Spring: The Great War and the Birth of the Modern Age.* Boston: Mariner Books, 2000.

Enretiens de Pontigny Records. Mount Holyoke College Archives and Special Collections. South Hadley, MA. https://aspace.fivecolleges.edu/repositories/2/resources/280.

Eribon, Didier. "Le 'Je me souviens' de Gilles Deleuze." Interview. *Le Nouvel Observateur*, November 16–22, 1995, 114–15.

Farber, Marvin. *L'activité philosophique contemporaine en France et aux États Unis: Études,* vol. 2, *Philosophie française.* Paris: Presses Universitaires de France, 1950.

Ferrell, Robyn. "Rival Reading: Deleuze on Hume." *Australasian Journal of Philosophy* 73, no. 4 (December 1, 1995): 585–93.

Fink, Eugen. "The Phenomenological Philosophy of Edmund Husserl and Contemporary Criticism." In *The Phenomenology of Husserl,* edited by R. O. Elveton, 73–147. Chicago: Quadrangle Books, 1970.

———. "The Problem of the Phenomenology of Edmund Husserl." In *Apriori and World: European Contributions to Husserlian Phenomenology,* edited by William McKenna and Laurence E. Winters, translated by Robert M. Harlan, 21–55. Dordrecht: Springer, 1981.

Flynn, Thomas R. *Sartre: A Philosophical Biography.* Cambridge: Cambridge University Press, 2014.

Fondane, Benjamin. *Existential Monday: Philosophical Essays.* Edited and translated by Bruce Baugh. New York: New York Review Books Classics, 2016.

Ford, Russell. "Against Negativity: Deleuze, Wahl, and Postwar Existentialism." *Symposium* 20, no. 1 (2016): 107–28.

———. "Trân Duc Thao: Politics and Truth." *Philosophy Compass* 15, no. 2 (2020): e12650. https://doi.org/10.1111/phc3.12650.

Foucault, Michel. "The Discourse on Language." In *The Archaeology of Knowledge,* translated by A. M. Sheridan Smith. New York: Pantheon, 1972.

———. "Structuralism and Poststructuralism." In *The Essential Foucault,* edited by Paul Rabinow and Nikolas Rose. New York: New Press, 2003.

———. "Theatrum Philosophicum." In *Language, Counter-Memory, Practice: Selected Essays and Interviews,* edited and translated by Donald F. Bouchard and Sherry Simon. Ithaca, NY: Cornell University Press, 1980.

Fouilloux, Etienne. "'Intellectuels catholiques?' Réflexions sur une naissance différée." *Vingtième Siècle*, vol. 53 (1997): 13–24.

Galster, Ingrid. *Sartre sous l'Occupation et après: Nouvelles Mises au point.* Paris: L'Harmattan, 2014.

Gandillac, Maurice de. *Le Siècle traversé.* Paris: Albin Michel, 1998.

Gasché, Rodolphe. "One Coming before the Other? On Jean Wahl and Jacques Derrida." *CR: The New Centennial Review* 15, no. 1 (2015): 1–23.

Geroulanos, Stefanos. *An Atheism That Is Not Humanist Emerges in French Thought.* Stanford, CA: Stanford University Press, 2010.

Goldhammer, Jesse. *The Headless Republic: Sacrificial Violence in Modern French Thought.* Ithaca, NY: Cornell University Press, 2005.

Gordon, Peter E. *Continental Divide: Heidegger, Cassirer, Davos.* Cambridge, MA: Harvard University Press, 2010.

Guéhenno, Jean. *Diary of the Dark Years, 1940–1944: Collaboration, Resistance, and Daily Life in Occupied Paris.* Translated by David Ball. Oxford: Oxford University Press, 2016.

Gueroult, Martial. *La philosophie transcendentale de Salomon Maimon.* Paris: Alcan, 1929.

Gurvitch, Georges. "La philosophie phénoménologique en Allemagne: I. Edmund Husserl." *Revue de Métaphysique et de Morale* 35, no. 4 (1928): 553–97.

Gurwitsch, Aron. Review of *Husserl et Hume* by Gaston Berger. *Philosophy and Phenomenological Research* 2, no. 1 (1941): 127–29.

———. Review of *Le cogito dans la philosophie de Husserl,* by Gaston Berger. *Philosophy and Phenomenological Research* 7, no. 4 (1947): 649–54.

———. Review of *Recherches sur les conditions de la connaissance: Essai d'une théorétique pure,* by Gaston Berger. *Philosophy and Phenomenological Research* 8, no. 2 (1947): 287–94.

Gutting, Gary. *Thinking the Impossible: French Philosophy since 1960.* Oxford: Oxford University Press, 2013.

Haering, Theodor L. *Hegel, sein Wollen und sein Werk.* Berlin: B. G. Teubner, 1929.

Halévy, Élie. *The Growth of Philosophic Radicalism.* Eastford, CT: Martino Fine Books, 2013.

Hardt, Michael. *Gilles Deleuze.* Minneapolis: University of Minnesota Press, 1993.

Harris, H. S. *Hegel's Development: Towards the Sunlight, 1770–1801.* Oxford: Clarendon, 1972.

Hartmann, Nicolai. *Die Philosophie der deutschen Idealismus 2: Hegel.* Berlin: Walter de Gruyter, 1929.

Havet, J. "Philosophie de l'absolu et philosophie de l'action," review of *Logique de la philosophie* by Eric Weil. *Revue de Métaphysique et de Morale* 61, no. 3/4 (1956): 283–302.

Heckman, John. "Hyppolite and the Hegel Revival in France." *Telos* 16 (1973): 128–45.

Hegel, G. W. F. *The Difference between Fichte's and Schelling's System of Philosophy.* Translated by H. S. Harris and Walter Cerf. Albany: State University of New York Press, 1977.

———. *Early Theological Writings.* Translated by T. M. Knox and Richard Kroner. Philadelphia: University of Pennsylvania Press, 1971.

———. *Hegels Schriften zur Politik und Rechtsphilosophie.* Edited by Georg Lasson. Leipzig: F. Meiner, 1913.

———. *Hegel's Theologische Jugendschriften.* Edited by Herman Nohl. Tübingen: J. C. B. Mohr, 1907.

———. *Jenenser Logik, Metaphysik und Naturphilosophie.* Edited by Georg Lasson. Leipzig: F. Meiner, 1923.

———. *La Phénoménologie de l'esprit,* vol. 1. Translated by Jean Hyppolite. Aubier Montaigne, 1939.

———. *La Phénoménologie de l'esprit,* vol. 2. Translated by Jean Hyppolite. Aubier Montaigne, 1941.

———. *The Phenomenology of Spirit.* Translated by A. V. Miller. Oxford: Oxford University Press, 1977.

Heidegger, Martin. *Basic Writings.* Edited and translated by David Farrell Krell. New York: Harper and Row, 2008.

———. *Being and Time.* Translated by Joan Stambaugh and Dennis J. Schmidt. Albany: State University of New York Press, 2010.

———. *Einleitung in die Philosophie* (Winter semester 1928/29). 2nd edition. Edited by O. Saame and I. Saame-Speidel. *Gesamtausgabe* 28. Frankfurt am Main: Vittorio Klostermann, 1996.

———. *Hegel's Phenomenology of Spirit.* Translated by Parvis Emad and Kenneth Maly. Bloomington: Indiana University Press, 1988.

———. *Kant and the Problem of Metaphysics.* Translated by Richard Taft. 5th enlarged edition. Bloomington: Indiana University Press, 1997.

———. *Off the Beaten Track.* Translated by Julian Young and Kenneth Haynes. Cambridge: Cambridge University Press, 2002.

———. *Pathmarks.* Edited and translated by William McNeil. Cambridge: Cambridge University Press, 1998.

Hering, Jean. "La phénoménologie d'Edmund Husserl il y a trente ans." *Revue Internationale de Philosophie* 1, no. 1 (1939): 366–73.

Herrick, Tim. "'A Book Which Is No Longer Discussed Today': Trân Duc Thao, Jacques Derrida, and Maurice Merleau-Ponty." *Journal of the History of Ideas* 66, no. 1 (2005): 113–31.

Houle, Karen, and Jim Vernon, editors. *Hegel and Deleuze: Together Again for the First Time.* Evanston, IL: Northwestern University Press, 2013.

Hughes, Joe. *Deleuze and the Genesis of Representation.* New York: Bloomsbury, 2011.

Hume, David. *David Hume: A Treatise of Human Nature, Volume 2: Editorial Material.* Edited by David Fate Norton and Mary J. Norton. Oxford: Clarendon, 2011.

———. *A Dissertation on the Passions; The Natural History of Religion.* Edited by Tom L. Beauchamp. Oxford: Oxford University Press, 2009.

———. *An Enquiry concerning Human Understanding.* Edited by Tom L. Beauchamp. Oxford: Clarendon, 2006.

———. *An Enquiry concerning the Principles of Morals: A Critical Edition.* Edited by Tom L. Beauchamp. Oxford: Clarendon, 2006.

———. *Essays, Moral, Political, and Literary: Volumes 1 and 2.* Edited by Tom L. Beauchamp and Mark A. Box. Oxford: Oxford University Press, 2021.

———. *A Treatise on Human Nature: Volume 1, Texts.* Edited by David Fate Norton and Mary J. Norton. Oxford: Oxford University Press, 2007.

Husserl, Edmund. *Cartesian Meditations: An Introduction to Phenomenology.* Translated by Dorion Cairns. Dordrecht: Martinus Nijhoff, 1977.

———. *The Crisis of European Sciences and Transcendental Phenomenology: An Introduction to Phenomenological Philosophy.* Translated by David Carr. Evanston, IL: Northwestern University Press, 1970.

———. *Experience and Judgment.* Translated by James Spencer Churchill and Karl Ameriks. Evanston, IL: Northwestern University Press, 1975.

———. *Ideas directrices pour une phénoménologie.* Translated by Paul Ricoeur. Paris: Gallimard, 1950.

———. *Ideas for a Pure Phenomenology and Phenomenological Philosophy: First Book: General Introduction to Pure Phenomenology.* Translated by Daniel O. Dahlstrom. Indianapolis, IN: Hackett, 2014.

———. *Méditations Cartésiennes: Introduction a la phénoménologie.* Translated by Emmanuel Levinas. Paris: Vrin, 1931.

———. *The Paris Lectures.* Dordrecht: Martinus Nijhoff, 1964.

Hyppolite, Jean. *Études sur Marx et Hegel.* Paris: Éditions Marcel Riviere et Cie., 1955. Translated by John O'Neill as *Studies on Marx and Hegel* (New York: Harper, 1973).

———. *Figures de la pensée philosophique.* Paris: Presses Universitaires de France, 1991.

———. *Genèse et structure de la Phénoménologie de l'esprit de Hegel (Tomes I et II).* Paris: Aubier Montaigne, 1946. Translated by Samuel Cherniak and John Heckman as *Genesis and Structure of Hegel's "Phenomenology of Spirit"* (Evanston, IL: Northwestern University Press, 1979).

———. *Introduction à la philosophie de l'histoire de Hegel.* Paris: Éditions Marcel Riviere et Cie., 1948. Translated by Bond Harris and Jacqueline B. Spurlock as *Introduction to Hegel's Philosophy of History* (Gainesville: University Press of Florida, 1996).

———. "La Signification de la Révolution Française dans la 'Phénoménologie' de Hegel." *Revue Philosophique de la France et de l'Étranger* 128, no. 9/12 (1939): 321–52.

———. "Les travaux de jeunesse de Hegel d'après des ouvrages récents." *Revue de Métaphysique et de Morale* 42, no. 3 (1935): 399–426.

———. "Les travaux de jeunesse de Hegel d'après des ouvrages récents (suite et fin)." *Revue de Métaphysique et de Morale* 42, no. 4 (1935): 549–78.

———. *Logique et existence.* Paris: Presses Universitaires de France, 1952. Translated by Leonard Lawlor and Amit Sen as *Logic and Existence* (Albany: State University of New York Press, 1997).

———. "Note sur Paul Valery et la crise de la conscience." *La Vie Intellectuelle* 14, no. 3 (1946): 121–26.

———. "Vie et prise de conscience de la vie dans la philosophie hégélienne d'Iéna." *Revue de Métaphysique et de Morale* 45, no. 1 (1938): 45–61.

James, William. *The Writings of William James: A Comprehensive Edition.* Edited by John J. McDermott. Chicago: University of Chicago Press, 1978.

Janicaud, Dominique. *Heidegger en France, tome 1: Récit.* Paris: Albin Michel, 2001.

———. *Heidegger en France, tome 2: Entretiens.* Paris: Albin Michel, 2001.

———. *Heidegger in France.* Translated by François Raffoul and David Pettigrew. Bloomington: Indiana University Press, 2015.

Jankélévitch, Vladimir. "Mystique et dialectique chez Jean Wahl." *Revue de Métaphysique et de Morale* 58, no. 4 (1953): 423–31.

Jarczyk, Gwendoline, and Pierre-Jean Labarrière, editors. "Alexandre Kojève et Trân Duc Thao: Correspondance inédite." *Genèses* 2 (December 1990): 131–37.

———. *De Kojéve à Hegel: Cent cinquante ans de pensée hégélienne en France.* Paris: Albin Michel, 1996.

Jaspers, Karl. *Philosophy of Existence*. Translated by Richard F. Grabau. Philadelphia: University of Pennsylvania Press, 1971.

———. *Way to Wisdom*. Translated by Ralph Manheim. New Haven, CT: Yale University Press, 1968.

Jones, Graham, and Jon Roffe, editors. *Deleuze's Philosophical Lineage*. Edinburgh: Edinburgh University Press, 2009.

———. *Deleuze's Philosophical Lineage II*. Edinburgh: Edinburgh University Press, 2019.

Jordan, Elijah. "The Unknowable of Herbert Spencer." *Philosophical Review* 20, no. 3 (May 1911): 291–309.

Judaken, Jonathan. *Jean-Paul Sartre and the Jewish Question*. Lincoln: University of Nebraska Press, 2007.

Judaken, Jonathan, and Robert Bernasconi, editors. *Situating Existentialism: Key Texts in Context*. New York: Columbia University Press, 2012.

Judt, Tony. *The Burden of Responsibility: Blum, Camus, Aron, and the French Twentieth Century*. Chicago: University of Chicago Press, 2007.

———. *Past Imperfect: French Intellectuals, 1944–1956*. Berkeley: University of California Press, 1992.

Kelly, Michael. "Hegel in France to 1940: A Bibliographical Essay." *Journal of European Studies* 11, no. 41 (1981): 29–52.

———. "The Post-War Hegel Revival in France: A Bibliographical Essay." *Journal of European Studies* 13, no. 51 (September 1983): 199–216.

Kerslake, Christian. *Immanence and the Vertigo of Philosophy: From Kant to Deleuze*. Edinburgh: Edinburgh University Press, 2009.

Kierkegaard, Søren. *The Concept of Anxiety: A Simple Psychologically Orienting Deliberation on the Dogmatic Issue of Hereditary Sin*. Edited by Reidar Thomte and Albert B. Anderson. Princeton, NJ: Princeton University Press, 1981.

———. *Either/Or, Part I*. Translated by Howard V. Hong and Edna H. Hong. Princeton, NJ: Princeton University Press, 1987.

———. *Either/Or, Part II*. Translated by Howard V. Hong and Edna H. Hong. Princeton, NJ: Princeton University Press, 1987.

———. *Fear and Trembling/Repetition*. Translated by Edna H. Hong and Howard V. Hong. Princeton, NJ: Princeton University Press, 1983.

———. *The Sickness unto Death: A Christian Psychological Exposition for Upbuilding And Awakening*. Edited by Howard V. Hong and Edna H. Hong. Princeton, NJ: Princeton University Press, 1983.

Kirkpatrick, Kate. *Becoming Beauvoir: A Life*. New York: Bloomsbury, 2019.

Kisiel, Theodore. *The Genesis of Heidegger's Being and Time*. Berkeley: University of California Press, 1993.

Kleinberg, Ethan. *Generation Existential: Heidegger's Philosophy in France, 1927–1961*. Ithaca, NY: Cornell University Press, 2007.

Klossowski, Pierre. *Nietzsche et le cercle vicieux*. Paris: Mercure de France, 1967. Translated by Daniel W. Smith as *Nietzsche and the Vicious Circle* (Chicago: University of Chicago Press, 1997).

———. *Sade mon prochain*. Paris: Éditions du Seuil, 1947. Translated by Alphonso

Lingis as *Sade My Neighbor* (Evanston, IL: Northwestern University Press, 1991).

―――. *Tableaux vivants: Essais critiques 1936–1983.* Paris: Le Promeneur, 2001.

―――. *Un si funeste désir.* Paris: Gallimard, 1963. Translated by Russell Ford as *Such a Deathly Desire* (Albany: State University of New York Press, 2007).

Kockelmans, Joseph, editor. *Phenomenology: The Philosophy of Edmund Husserl and Its Interpretation.* New York: Anchor Books, 1967.

Kojève, Alexandre. "Hegel, Marx, et le christianisme." *Critique* 1, no. 3/4 (1946): 339–66.

―――. *Introduction à la lecture de Hegel: Leçons sur la Phénoménologie de l'ésprit professées de 1933 à 1939 à l'École des Hautes Études.* Edited by Raymond Queneau. Paris: Gallimard, 1947. Translated by James H. Nichols as *Introduction to the Reading of Hegel: Lectures on the "Phenomenology of Spirit,"* edited by Allan Bloom (Ithaca, NY: Cornell University Press, 1980).

―――. *Le concept, le temps, et le discours: Introduction au système du savoir.* Edited by Bernard Hesbois. Paris: Gallimard, 1990.

―――. *The Notion of Authority.* Edited by François Terré, translated by Hager Weslati. New York: Verso, 2020.

―――. *Outline of a Phenomenology of Right.* Edited by Bryan-Paul Forst, translated by Bryan-Paul Forst and Robert Howse. Lanham, MD: Rowman and Littlefield, 2000.

Koyré, Alexandre. *De la mystique à la science: Cours, conférences et documents, 1922–1962.* Edited by Pietro Redondi. Paris: Éditions de l'École des Hautes Études en Sciences Sociales, 1986.

―――. *Études d'histoire de la pensée philosophique.* Paris: Éditions Gallimard, 1971.

―――. "Hegel à Iéna (À propos de publications récentes)." *Revue Philosophique de la France et de l'Étranger* 118, no. 9/10 (1934): 274–83.

―――. "Note sur la langue et la terminologie Hégéliennes." *Revue Philosophique de la France et de l'Étranger* 112 (1931): 409–39.

―――. "Present Trends of French Philosophical Thought." *Journal of the History of Ideas* 59, no. 3 (1998): 521–48.

―――. Review of *Le malheur de la conscience dans la philosophie de Hegel* by Jean Wahl. *Revue Philosophique de la France et de l'Étranger* 110 (1930): 136–43.

Kroner, Richard. *Von Kant bis Hegel.* Tübingen: Verlag von J. C. B. Mohr, 1921/24.

Lalande, André. "Philosophy in France, 1931." *Philosophical Review* 42, no. 1 (1933): 1–30.

Lamprecht, Sterling. Review of *Les pluralistes philosophies d'Angleterre et d'Amérique* by Jean Wahl. *Journal of Philosophy* 18, no. 26 (December 22, 1921): 717–20.

Landgrebe, Ludwig. "Correspondance." *Revue de Métaphysique et de Morale* 57, no. 2 (1952): 282–83.

―――. "Regions of Being and Regional Ontologies in Husserl's Phenomenology." In *Apriori and World: European Contributions to Husserlian Phenomenology,* edited by William McKenna, Robert M. Harlan, and Laurence E. Winters, 132–51. Dordrecht: Martinus Nijhoff, 1981.

Lapoujade, David. *Deleuze, les mouvements aberrants.* Paris: Les Éditions de Minuit, 2014.

———. *William James: Empiricism and Pragmatism*. Translated by Thomas Lamarre. Durham, NC: Duke University Press Books, 2019.

Lawlor, Leonard. *Derrida and Husserl: The Basic Problem of Phenomenology*. Bloomington: Indiana University Press, 2002.

———. "The End of Phenomenology: Expressionism in Deleuze and Merleau-Ponty." *Continental Philosophy Review* 31 (1998): 15–34.

———. *The Implications of Immanence: Toward a New Concept of Life*. New York: Fordham University Press, 2006.

———. *Thinking through French Philosophy: The Being of the Question*. Bloomington: Indiana University Press, 2003.

Lechartier, Georges. *David Hume, sociologue et moraliste*. Paris: Alcan, 1900.

Leclercq, Stéfan, Manola Antonioli, Alain Beaulieu, Giuseppe Bianco, Collectif, Anne Sauvagnargues, and Didier Bazy. *Aux sources de la pensée de Gilles Deleuze*, vol. 1. Paris: Sils Maria, 2005.

Lefebvre, Henri. *Les temps des meprises*. Paris: Stock, 1975.

———. "1925." *Nouvelle Revue Française*, no. 172 (April 1967).

Lemieux, René. "Hume et Bergson, une pratique de la méthode chez Deleuze: Réflexions pour une éthique de la lecture." *Symposium: Canadian Journal of Continental Philosophy* 13, no. 2 (September 1, 2009): 68–96.

Leroy, André-Louis. *David Hume*. Paris: Presses Universitaires de France, 1953.

Lévi-Strauss, Claude. *Wild Thought*. Translated by Jeffrey Mehlman and John Leavitt. Chicago: University of Chicago Press, 2021.

Levinas, Emmanuel. *Basic Philosophical Writings*. Edited by Adriaan T. Peperzak, Simon Critchley, and Robert Bernasconi. Bloomington: Indiana University Press, 2008.

———. *Collected Philosophical Papers*. Translated by Alphonso Lingis. Pittsburgh, PA: Duquesne University Press, 1998.

———. *De l'évasion*. Montpellier: Fata Morgana, 1982. Edited by Jacques Rolland, translated by Bettina Bergo as *On Escape* (Stanford, CA: Stanford University Press, 2003).

———. *De l'existence à l'existant*. 2nd edition. Paris: Vrin, 1947. Translated by Alphonso Lingis as *Existence and Existents* (The Hague: Martinus Nijhoff, 1988).

———. *Discovering Existence with Husserl*. Translated by Richard A. Cohen and Michael B. Smith. Evanston, IL: Northwestern University Press, 1998.

———. *En découvrant l'existence avec Husserl et Heidegger*. Paris: Vrin, 2002.

———. "Jean Wahl: Neither Having nor Being." In *Outside the Subject*, translated by Michael B. Smith. Stanford, CA: Stanford University Press, 1993.

———. "Le temps et l'autre." In *Le choix, le monde, l'existence*, edited by Jean Wahl. Grenoble: Arthaud, 1947. Translated by Richard A. Cohen as *Time and the Other* (Pittsburgh: Duquesne University Press, 1987).

———. "L'oeuvre d'Edmund Husserl." *Revue Philosophique de la France et de l'Étranger* 129, no. 1/2 (1940): 33–85.

———. "L'ontologie, est-elle fondamentale?" *Revue de Métaphysique et de Morale* 56, no. 1 (1951): 88–98. Translated as "Is Ontology Fundamental?" in *Basic Philosophical Writings*, translated and edited by Adriaan Peperzak, Simon

Critchley, and Robert Bernasconi, 1–10 (Bloomington: Indiana University Press, 2008).

———. *Théorie de l'intuition dans la phénoménologie de Husserl.* Paris: Vrin, 1963. Translated by Andre Orianne as *Theory of Intuition in Husserl's Phenomenology,* 2nd edition (Evanston, IL: Northwestern University Press, 1995).

Levinas, Emmanuel, Xavier Tilliette, and Paul Ricoeur. *Jean Wahl et Gabriel Marcel.* Éditions Beauchesne, 1976.

Love, Jeff. *The Black Circle: A Life of Alexandre Kojève.* New York: Columbia University Press, 2018.

Löwith, Karl. *From Hegel to Nietzsche.* Revised edition. New York: Columbia University Press, 1964.

Lubac, Henri de. *Le drame de l'humanisme athée.* Paris: Les Éditions du Cerf, 1999. Translated by Mark Sebanc as *The Drama of Atheist Humanism,* revised edition (San Francisco: Ignatius, 1995).

Lukács, Georg. *Existentialisme ou marxisme.* Translated by E. Kelemen. Paris: Nagel, 1948.

———. *History and Class Consciousness: Studies in Marxist Dialectics.* Translated by Rodney Livingstone. Cambridge, MA: MIT Press, 1972.

Lyotard, Jean-Francois. *La phénoménologie.* Paris: Presses Universitaires de France, 1954. Translated by Brian Beakley as *Phenomenology* (Albany: State University of New York Press, 1991).

Maimon, Salomon. *Essay on Transcendental Philosophy.* Translated by Nick Midgley, Henry Somers-Hall, Alistair Welchman, and Merten Reglitz. London: Continuum, 2010.

Malherbe, Michel. "Hume's Reception in France." In *The Reception of David Hume in Europe,* edited by Peter Jones, 43–97. New York: Continuum, 2005.

Marcel, Gabriel. *Essai de philosophie concrète.* Paris: Gallimard, 1999.

———. *Gabriel Marcel: Être et avoir.* Paris: Aubier, 1935.

———. *Gabriel Marcel: Homo Viator, prolégomènes à une métaphysique de l'espérance.* Paris: Aubier, 1945. Translated by Emma Craufurd and Paul Seaton as *Homo Viator: Introduction to the Metaphysic of Hope* (South Bend, IN: St. Augustine's Press, 2010).

———. *Journal métaphysique.* Paris: Gallimard, 1928.

———. "Le drame de l'humanisme athée." *La Vie Intellectuelle* 13 (1945): 141–48.

———. *The Philosophy of Existentialism.* New York: Citadel, 2002.

———. "Schelling fut-il un précurseur de la philosophie de l'existence?" *Revue de Métaphysique et de Morale* 62, no. 1 (1957): 72–87.

Marrati, Paola. *Genesis and Trace: Derrida Reading Husserl and Heidegger.* Stanford, CA: Stanford University Press, 2005.

Martin, Jean-Clet. *Variations: La philosophie de Gilles Deleuze.* Paris: Payot, 1993.

McGee, Kyle. "Machining Fantasy: Spinoza, Hume and the Miracle in a Politics of Desire." *Philosophy and Social Criticism* 36, no. 7 (September 1, 2010): 837–56.

McGrath, Larry. "Bergson Comes to America." *Journal of the History of Ideas* 74, no. 4 (2013): 599–620.

McKeon, Richard. "A Philosophy for UNESCO." *Philosophy and Phenomenological Research* 8, no. 4 (1948): 573–86.

McMahon, Darrin M., and Samuel Moyn, editors. *Rethinking Modern European Intellectual History*. Oxford: Oxford University Press, 2014.

Menand, Louis. *The Metaphysical Club: A Story of Ideas in America*. New York: Farrar, Straus and Giroux, 2002.

Merleau-Ponty, Maurice. *Humanisme et terreur: Essai sur le problème communiste*. Paris: Gallimard, 1947. Translated by John O'Neill as *Humanism and Terror: An Essay on the Communist Problem* (Boston: Beacon, 1969).

———. *La structure du comportement*. Paris: Presses Universitaires de France, 1942. Translated by Alden Fisher as *The Structure of Behavior* (Boston: Beacon, 2000).

———. *L'Union de l'âme et du corps chez Malebranche, Biran et Bergson*. Paris: Vrin, 2000.

———. *Phénoménologie de la perception*. Paris: Gallimard, 1945. Translated by Donald Landes and Taylor Carman as *Phenomenology of Perception* (New York: Routledge, 2013).

———. *Sens et non-sens*. Paris: Gallimard, 1996. Translated by Hubert Dreyfus and Patricia Allen Dreyfus as *Sense and Non-Sense* (Evanston, IL: Northwestern University Press, 1992).

Monique, Jutrin, editor. *Benjamin Fondane: Entre philosophie et littérature*. Paris: Parole Silence, 2015.

Montag, Warren. *Althusser and His Contemporaries: Philosophy's Perpetual War*. Durham, NC: Duke University Press, 2013.

Moore, A. W. *The Evolution of Modern Metaphysics: Making Sense of Things*. Cambridge: Cambridge University Press, 2011.

Moore, G. E. *Principia Ethica*. New York: Dover, 2004.

Moran, Dermot. *Edmund Husserl: Founder of Phenomenology*. Cambridge: Polity, 2005.

Moyn, Samuel. *Origins of the Other: Emmanuel Levinas between Revelation and Ethics*. Ithaca, NY: Cornell University Press, 2005.

———. "Transcendence, Morality, and History: Emmanuel Levinas and the Discovery of Søren Kierkegaard in France." *Yale French Studies*, no. 104 (2004): 22–54.

Mudimbe, V. Y., and A. Bohm. "Hegel's Reception in France." *Journal of French and Francophone Philosophy* 6, no. 3 (March 3, 1994): 5–33.

Neil, David. "The Uses of Anachronism: Deleuze's History of the Subject." *Philosophy Today* 42, no. 4 (December 1, 1998): 418–31.

Panagia, Davide. *Impressions of Hume: Cinematic Thinking and the Politics of Discontinuity*. Lanham, MD: Rowman and Littlefield, 2013.

Patton, Paul, editor. *Deleuze: A Critical Reader*. Oxford: Wiley-Blackwell, 1991.

Peden, Knox. *Spinoza contra Phenomenology: French Rationalism from Cavaillès to Deleuze*. Stanford, CA: Stanford University Press, 2014.

Péguy, Charles. *The Portal of the Mystery of Hope*. New York: Continuum, 1996.

Pinkard, Terry. *German Philosophy, 1760–1860: The Legacy of Idealism*. Cambridge: Cambridge University Press, 2002.

Pinto, Louis. "(Re)Traductions (Phénoménologie et 'Philosophie Allemande' dans les années 1930)." *Actes de La Recherche en Sciences Sociales* 145 (December 2002): 21–33.

Politzer, Georges. *Contre Bergson et quelques autres: Écrits philosophiques 1924–1939.* Paris: Flammarion, 2013.

Poster, Mark. *Existential Marxism in Postwar France: From Sartre to Althusser.* Princeton, NJ: Princeton University Press, 1976.

———. "The Hegel Renaissance." *Telos,* vol. 16 (1973): 109–27.

Rabinbach, Anson. "Heidegger's 'Letter on Humanism' as Text and Event." *New German Critique,* no. 62 (1994): 3–38.

Rauch, Leo, and David Sherman. *Hegel's Phenomenology of Self-Consciousness: Text and Commentary.* New York: State University of New York Press, 1999.

Ravaisson, Felix. *Of Habit.* Translated by Clare Carlisle and Mark Sinclair. New York: Continuum, 2009.

Reed, Joel. "Althusser and Hume: A Materialist Encounter." In *Current Continental Theory and Modern Philosophy,* edited by Stephen H. Daniel, 210–21. Evanston, IL: Northwestern University Press, 2005.

Rimbaud, Arthur. *A Season in Hell and The Drunken Boat.* Translated by Louise Varèse. New York: New Directions, 1961.

Rockmore, Tom. "Aspects of French Hegelianism." *Owl of Minerva* 24, no. 2 (Spring 1993): 191–206.

———. *Heidegger and French Philosophy: Humanism, Antihumanism, and Being.* New York: Routledge, 1995.

———. "Hyppolite's Hegel Reconsidered." *Pli: The Warwick Journal of Philosophy* 24 (2013): 167–81.

Roffe, Jon. *Gilles Deleuze's Empiricism and Subjectivity: A Critical Introduction and Guide.* Edinburgh: Edinburgh University Press, 2016.

Romano, Claude, J.-L. Chretien, J.-F. Courtine, J.-L. Marion, and J.-F. Spitz. *Philosophie 47: Gilles Deleuze.* Paris: Éditions de Minuit, 1995.

Rome, Sydney, and Beatrice Rome, editors. "Interrogation of Jean Wahl." In *Philosophical Interrogations,* 179–200. New York: Holt, Rinehart and Winston, 1964.

Rose, Gillian. "The Comedy of Hegel and the *Trauerspiel* of Modern Philosophy." *Bulletin of the Hegel Society of Great Britain* 15, no. 1 (1994): 14–22.

Rosenkranz, Karl. *Hegels Leben.* Berlin: Duncker und Humblot, 1844.

Rosenzweig, Franz. *Hegel und der Staat.* Berlin: R. Oldenbourg, 1920.

Roth, Michael S. *Knowing and History: Appropriations of Hegel in Twentieth-Century France.* Ithaca, NY: Cornell University Press, 1988.

Roudinesco, Elisabeth. *Histoire de la psychanalyse en France.* 2 vols. Paris: Fayard, 1994.

———. *Jacques Lacan.* Translated by Barbara Bray. New York: Columbia University Press, 1997.

Russell, Bertrand. "Analytic Realism [1911]." In *The Collected Papers of Bertrand Russell,* vol. 6, *Logical and Philosophical Papers, 1909–1913,* 132–46. New York: Routledge, 1992.

———. "La philosophie anglaise contemporaine: Le principe d'individuation." *Revue de Métaphysique et de Morale* 55, no. 1 (1950): 1–15.

———. "On Propositions: What They Are and How They Mean." *Proceedings of the Aristotelian Society*, supplementary vol. 2 (1919): 1–43.

———. *The Philosophy of Logical Atomism.* New York: Routledge, 2010.

Russon, John. "Dialectic, Difference, and the Other: The Hegelianizing of French Phenomenology." In *The History of Continental Philosophy*, edited by Alan D. Schrift, vol. 4, *Phenomenology: Responses and Developments*, edited by Leonard Lawlor, 17–42. Chicago: University of Chicago Press, 2019.

Saint-Just, Louis-Antoine-Léon. *Oeuvres.* Edited by Anne Kupiec and Miguel Abensour. Paris: Gallimard, 2004.

Sartre, Jean-Paul. *Existentialism and Human Emotion.* New York: Citadel, 1987.

———. *La nausée.* Paris: Gallimard, 1938. Translated by Lloyd Alexander as *Nausea* (Provo, UT: New Directions, 2013).

———. *La transcendance de l'ego et autres textes phénoménologiques.* Paris: Vrin, 2003.

———. *L'être et le néant.* Paris: Gallimard, 1943. Translated by Sarah Richmond as *Being and Nothingness* (New York: Atria Books, 2021).

———. *L'existentialisme est un humanisme.* Paris: Gallimard, 1996. Translated by Carol Macomber as *Existentialism Is a Humanism* (New Haven, CT: Yale University Press, 2007).

———. *Situations I.* Paris: Gallimard, 2010.

———. *Situations II.* Paris: Gallimard, 2012.

———. *Situations III.* Paris: Gallimard, 2013. Translated by Chris Turner as *The Aftermath of War* (London and New York: Seagull Books, 2008).

———. *The Transcendence of the Ego: An Existentialist Theory of Consciousness.* New York: Hill and Wang, 1991.

———. *"What Is Literature?" and Other Essays.* Edited by Steven Ungar. Cambridge, MA: Harvard University Press, 1988.

Schelling, F. W. J. *Recherches philosophiques sur l'essence de la liberté humaine et sur les problemes qui s'y rattachent.* Translated by Georges Politzer. Paris: F. Rieder, 1926.

Schrift, Alan D. "The Effects of the *Agrégation de Philosophie* on Twentieth-Century French Philosophy." *Journal of the History of Philosophy* 46, no. 3 (2008): 449–73.

———. *Nietzsche's French Legacy.* New York: Routledge, 1995.

———. *Twentieth-Century French Philosophy: Key Themes and Thinkers.* London: Wiley-Blackwell, 2006.

Scott, Charles E. *The Language of Difference.* Atlantic Highlands, NJ: Prometheus Books, 1989.

Scott, David. "Gilles Deleuze's Contributions to 'David Hume, Sa Vie, Son Oeuvre': Translator's Introduction." *Angelaki: Journal of the Theoretical Humanities* 16, no. 2 (June 1, 2011): 175–80.

Sealey, Kris. *Moments of Disruption: Levinas, Sartre, and the Question of Transcendence.* Albany: State University of New York Press, 2014.

Simont, Juliette. "Hegel et Deleuze: La statut de la différence en dialectique." In

Hegel und die Geschichte der Philosophie, 2:298–303. Hegel-Jahrbuch. Berlin: Akademie Verlag, 1998.

Smith, Daniel W. *Essays on Deleuze.* Edinburgh: Edinburgh University Press, 2012.

Smith, Daniel W., and Henry Somers-Hall, editors. *The Cambridge Companion to Deleuze.* Cambridge: Cambridge University Press, 2012.

Somers-Hall, Henry. *Hegel, Deleuze, and the Critique of Representation: Dialectics of Negation and Difference.* Albany: State University of New York Press, 2012.

Spiegelberg, Herbert. *The Context of the Phenomenological Movement.* Dordrecht: Martinus Nijhoff, 1981.

———. *The Phenomenological Movement: A Historical Introduction.* Dordrecht: Martinus Nijhoff, 1981.

Surya, Michel. *Georges Bataille: An Intellectual Biography.* Translated by Krzysztof Fijalkowski and Michael Richardson. New York: Verso, 2002.

Tally Jr., Robert T. "Nomadography: The 'Early' Deleuze and the History of Philosophy." *Journal of Philosophy: A Cross-Disciplinary Inquiry* 5, no. 11 (December 1, 2010): 15–24.

Terzi, Pietro. "Wrestling with the Shadow: The Panlogism Controversy in Hegel's French Reception (1897–1927)." *Modern Intellectual History* 17, no. 4 (2020): 1–28.

Thao, Trân Duc. "Existentialisme et matérialisme dialectique." *Revue de Métaphysique et de Morale* 54, no. 3/4 (1949): 317–29.

———. "Le 'Phenomenologie de l'esprit' et son contenu reel." *Les Temps Modernes* 4, no. 36 (1948): 492–519.

———. "Les origines de la reduction phénoménologique chez Husserl." *Deucalion* 3 (1950): 128–42.

———. "Les relations Franco-Vietnamese." *Les Temps Modernes* 2, no. 18 (1947): 1053–67.

———. *Phénoménologie et matérialisme dialectique.* Paris: Éditions Minh-Tân, 1951. Translated by D. J. Herman and D. V. Morano as *Phenomenology and Dialectical Materialism* (Dordrecht: D. Reidel, 2011).

———. "Sur l'interpretation Trotskiste des événements du Viet-Nam." *Les Temps Modernes* 2, no. 21 (1947): 1697–1705.

Thaulow, Gustav. *Hegels Ansichten uber Erziehung und Unterricht*, vol. 4. Glashütten: Kiel, 1854.

Thévenaz, Pierre. "Qu'est-ce que la phénoménologie?" *Revue de Théologie et de Philosophie* 2 (1952): 9–30, 126–40, 294–316.

Todd, Olivier. *Albert Camus: Une vie.* Paris: Gallimard, 1996.

Tournier, Michel. *Le vent Paraclet.* Paris: Gallimard, 1977.

Traverso, Enzo. *Fire and Blood: The European Civil War, 1914–1945.* Translated by David Fernbach. New York: Verso, 2016.

Valéry, Paul. *Introduction à la méthode de Léonard da Vinci.* Paris: Gallimard, 1992.

———. "La crise de l'esprit." In *Variété I et II.* Paris: Folio, 1998.

———. "La jeune parque." In *The Collected Works of Paul Valéry*, vol. 1, *Poetry.* Translated by David Paul. Princeton, NJ: Princeton University Press, 1971.

van Buren, John. *The Young Heidegger: Rumor of the Hidden King.* Bloomington: Indiana University Press, 1994.

Wahl, Jean. "Commentaire d'un passage de la 'Phénoménologie de l'esprit' de Hegel." *Revue de Métaphysique et de Morale* 34, no. 4 (1927): 441–71.

———. *Du rôle de l'idée de l'instant dans la philosophie de Descartes*. Paris: Felix Alcan, 1920.

———. "Edmund Husserl 1859–1959." *Revue de Métaphysique et de Morale* 65, no. 3 (1960): 327–38.

———. *Esquisse pour une histoire de "l'existentialisme."* Paris: L'Arche, 2001.

———. *Études Kierkegaardiennes*. Paris: Fernand Aubier, 1938.

———. *Existence humaine et transcendance*. Geneva: La Baconnière, 1944. Translated by William C. Hackett as *Human Existence and Transcendence* (Notre Dame, IN: University of Notre Dame Press, 2016).

———. Fonds Jean Wahl. Institut Mémoire de l'Edition Contemporaine (IMEC). Caen.

———. "Freedom and Existence in Some Recent Philosophies." *Philosophy and Phenomenological Research* 8, no. 4 (1948): 538–56.

———. "Hegel et Kierkegaard." In Jean Wahl, *L'un devant l'autre*, ed. Vincent Delecroix and Frederic Worms, 97–118. Paris: Hachette, 1998.

———. "Heidegger et Kierkegaard: Recherche des éléments originaux de la philosophie de Heidegger." *Recherches Philosophiques* 2 (1932–33): 349–70.

———. "Husserl et la pensée moderne." *Revue de Métaphysique et de Morale* 65, no. 3 (1960): 339–43.

———. *Introduction à la pensée de Heidegger*. Paris: Centre de Documentation Universitaire, 1946.

———. *Kierkegaard: L'un devant l'autre*. Paris: Hachette, 1998.

———. "La situation présente de la philosophie française." In *L'activité philosophique contemporaine en France et aux États-Unis*, edited by Marvin Farber, 34–63. Paris: Presses Universitaires de France, 1950.

———. *Le malheur de la conscience dans la philosophie de Hegel*. Paris: Presses Universitaires de France, 1929.

———. "Le Nietzsche de Jaspers." *Recherches Philosophiques*, vol. 6 (1936–37): 346–62.

———. *Les philosophies pluralistes d'Angleterre et d'Amérique*. Paris: Felix Alcan, 1920. Translated by Fred Rothwell as *The Pluralist Philosophies of England and America* (London: Open Court, 1925).

———. "A Letter to Marvin Farber." *Philosophy and Phenomenological Research* 11, no. 3 (1951): 401–5.

———. "L'introduction à la métaphysique de M. Heidegger." *Revue de Métaphysique et de Morale* 61, no. 2 (1956): 113–30.

———. "Note sur la métaphysique." *Revue de Métaphysique et de Morale* 52, no. 3/4 (1947): 228–32.

———. "Notes sur la première partie de *Erfahrung und Urteil* de Husserl." *Revue de Métaphysique et de Morale* 56, no. 1 (1951): 6–34. Translated by Laurence E. Winters as "Notes on the First Part of *Experience and Judgment*," in *Apriori and World: European Contributions to Husserlian Phenomenology*, edited by William McKenna, Robert M. Harlan, and Laurence E. Winters (The Hague: Martinus Nijhoff, 1981), 172–97.

———. "Notes sur quelques aspects empiristes de la pensée de Husserl." *Revue de Métaphysique et de Morale* 57 (1952): 17–45. Translated by Laurence E. Winters as "A Note on Some Empiricist Aspects of the Thought of Husserl," in *Apriori and World: European Contributions to Husserlian Phenomenology*, edited by William McKenna, Robert M. Harlan, and Laurence E. Winters, 202–25 (The Hague: Martinus Nijhoff, 1981).

———. *Petite histoire de l'existentialisme*. Paris: Club Maintenant, 1947. Translated by Forrest Williams and Stanley Maron as *A Short History of Existentialism* (New York: Philosophical Library, 1949).

———. *Poésie, pensée, perception*. Paris: Calmann-Lévy, 1948.

———. "Poetry as Spiritual Exercise." Translated by Russell J. Duvernoy. *Philosophy Today* 64, no. 3 (2020): 793–96.

———. Review of *Encounter with Nothingness: An Essay on Existentialism* by Helmut Kuhn. *Ethics* 60, no. 3 (1950): 215–17.

———. Review of *Nietzsche et la philosophie* by Gilles Deleuze. *Revue de Métaphysique et de Morale* 68, no. 3 (July–September 1963): 352–79.

———. "Subjectivité et transcendance." *Bulletin de La Société Française de Philosophie* 37, no. 5 (December 1937): 161–211.

———. *Tableau de la philosophie française*. Paris: Gallimard, 1962.

———. *Transcendence and the Concrete: Selected Writings*. Edited by Alan D. Schrift and Ian Alexander Moore. New York: Fordham University Press, 2016.

———. "Une interpretation de la *Logique* de Hegel." *Critique*, no. 73 (December 1953): 1050–71.

———. *Vers la fin de l'ontologie*. Paris: Sedes, 1956.

———. *Vers le concret: Études d'histoire de la philosophie contemporaine (William James, Whitehead, Gabriel Marcel)*. Paris: Vrin, 1932.

Weil, Eric. *Hegel et l'état*. Paris: Vrin, 1950. Translated by Mark A. Cohen as *Hegel and the State* (Baltimore: Johns Hopkins University Press, 1998).

———. *Logique de la philosophie*. Paris: Vrin, 1950.

Welton, Donn, editor. *The Essential Husserl: Basic Writings in Transcendental Phenomenology*. Bloomington: Indiana University Press, 1999.

Worms, Frédéric. "La conscience ou la vie? Bergson entre phénoménologie et metaphysique." In *Annales bergsoniennes II: Bergson, Deleuze, la phénoménologie*, 191–206. Paris: Presses Universitaires de France, 2004.

———. *La philosophie en France au XXe.siècle: Moments*. Paris: Folio, 2009.

Yolton, John W. Review of *Logique et existence: Essai sur la logique de Hegel* by Jean Hyppolite. *Philosophy and Phenomenological Research* 14, no. 2 (December 1953): 273–75.

Zourabichvili, François. *Deleuze: Une philosophie de l'évènement*. Paris: Presses Universitaires de France, 1996.

———. *Le vocabulaire de Deleuze*. Paris: Ellipses, 2003.

Index

Critic," 197; *Logic of Sense*, 181; "On the Superiority of Anglo-American Literature," 198. See also *Empiricism and Subjectivity* (*Empirisme et subjectivité*)
De Lubac, Henri, 97; *Drame de l'humanisme athée* (*The Drama of Atheist Humanism*), 97
Derrida, Jacques, 100
Descartes, René, 4, 16, 72, 80, 83; cogito of, 20, 52, 118; doubt of, 53, 118–19; idea of God in, 20–21; instantaneous knowledge in, 51; *Meditations*, 20, 206n23; mortal and divine knowledge in, 18; as the paradigmatic figure of the French philosophical tradition, 118; *Principles of Philosophy*, 20; reconciliation of finite time and eternity of, 31; securing of personal and scientific knowledge for, 20; two different conceptions of time in, 19
dialectic: as arising from a subjective experience of transcendence for Wahl, 51; existential, 75–77; Hegelian, 68, 75, 77, 93–95; ontological, 93; as perpetual and inescapable, 75; philosophical, 51, 79; Platonic, 75, 77; rational, 48; of recognition in Hegel, 93–94; of sensibility, 77; of transcendence, 75–77
dialectical materialism, 56, 184, 190
Dilthey, Wilhelm, 58–60; *Die Jugendgeschichte Hegels* (*The Young Hegel*), 59, 65
Dosse, François: *Gilles Deleuze and Felix Guattari: Intersecting Lives*, 4–5, 109, 216n44
Dostoevsky, Fyodor, 74, 97

École Normale Supérieure, 58–59, 91, 100, 109
École Pratique des Hautes Études, 27, 36, 61, 218n13
Éditions de la Baconnière, 72
egoism, 149
Ehrenberg, Hans: *Hegels erstes System* (*Hegel's First System*), 61, 67, 219n22
empiricism: associationist Humean, 136; of Bradley, 102; as a dualism for Deleuze, 119; of Hume, 3, 10, 13, 111–13, 120–21, 126–29, 132–35, 140–75, 180, 192, 197; of Husserl, 12, 101; between

immanence and transcendence, 108–39; of James, 22, 24, 102–5; Kant's critique of, 120; knowledge both begins from and is derived from experience in Deleuze's concept of, 120; neo-Humean, 124; opposition to psychology of phenomenology and, 181; phenomenological justification for, 101; and phenomenology, 181, 189; radical, 3; and rationalism, 119–21, 123, 134–35, 170, 180–85, 199; realist, 103; relations exterior to ideas in, 119–20, 124, 138–39, 153, 160–61, 178–81, 185, 197–98, 207n27; and subjectivity, 106–7; transcendental, 17, 35, 57, 78; two kinds of, 9, 42–43; vindication of, 116, 169–91. See also associationism
Empiricism and Subjectivity (*Empirisme et subjectivité*) (Deleuze), 3–5, 7, 12, 107–84; causality itself not enough to determine action in, 186; constitution of the mind as subject in, 190; critique of rationalism and phenomenology in, 184; deployment of Hume's account of causality in, 160–66; determination of the imagination by the principles of human nature in, 131, 155–56, 160, 167; empiricism and rationalism in, 180–85, 193–94, 197; general rules and habit in, 153–63; God and the Whole in, 163–68; Hume's philosophy of the formation of subjectivity as deployed by Deleuze in, 163, 172–74; identity of the mind with the idea in the mind in, 172–74; importance of Kant to the argument of Deleuze in, 231n31; Kant's critique of Hume as deployed by Deleuze in, 182; philosophy as the theory of what we are doing, not as the theory of what is in, 193; as a precursory work to the major works of Deleuze of the 1960s, 229n116; principles of association in, 182–85, 188–89, 193; principles of passion in, 185–89, 193; subject constituted by principles and founded on fantasy for Deleuze in, 186–88; transcendence and the given in, 170–84
Erdman, Johann Eduard, 65

de la vie dans la philosophie hégélienne d'Iéna" (Life and Consciousness
of Life in Hegel's Jena Philosophy"),
67–69

idealism, 5, 112, 115; aporias of, 48;
collapse of, 227n78; constructive,
102; Hegel's system of, 125; Husserl's
phenomenology as an, 103; incorporation of each term into a single Whole
by, 124; rational, 113. *See also* German
idealism
imagination: constitutive, 157; in the
creation of various possible social
worlds according to Hume, 150; determination according to principles
for Deleuze's interpretation of Hume
regarding the, 131, 155–56, 160, 167;
general rule for Deleuze's interpretation of Hume as a passion of the,
154–55; Husserl's relationality of free,
102; illegitimate beliefs for Deleuze's
interpretation of Hume as fictions of
the, 162–63, 166; rules of taste (aesthetics) for Deleuze's interpretation of
Hume as passions that are reflected in
the, 154–55; schematizing, 159; as the
undetermined ensemble of ideas for
Hume, 120, 130. *See also* mind
immanence: completeness in Hegel's
mature system of, 10; Deleuze's conception of, 4; rupture of the interjection of transcendence into, 24. *See also*
concrete, the; transcendence
intentional finality, 184–91. *See also* intentionality
intentionality: evidence and, 104; of
judgment, 101; phenomenological
account of, 122, 179. *See also* intentional finality

James, William, 9, 13, 15, 21–23, 41,
112, 180; on Kant, 114–15, 120, 141,
203n28; on the "personal vision" of
philosophers, 207n25; pluralism of,
114, 123; radical empiricism of, 22, 24,
102–5; response to Hegel of, 198
Jaspers, Karl, 6, 42, 46–47, 50–53, 73, 75,
99; aporias of, 88; existence and transcendence for, 47; in French existen-

tialist circles, 214n25; as philosopher
of existence, 54; transcendental hope
for, 86
Jeunesse Étudiantes Chrêtiennes, 100
Journal of Philosophy, 22
justice: as the agreeableness of sympathy
reflected in the imagination and extended into the world for Hume, 154;
as extension of the passions and of
partial interests for Hume, 148–51; as
extensive and uniform as possible, 141,
151–63; as general rule of morality for
Hume, 150–63. *See also* morality; social
contract theory

Kant, Immanuel, 13, 65, 83, 116–22,
141–42, 181, 196–97; account of the
schemata as what secures concepts and
content of, 133; assertion of the existence of a priori synthetic judgments
in mathematics and physics of, 133;
conditions for the possibility of experience for, 172, 74; critical rationalism
of, 121; critique of empiricism of, 120–
22, 133; critique of Hume's account of
mathematical reasoning of, 236n6; on
moral rules, 141, 146; self, world, and
God in, 163; theory of transcendental
subjectivity of, 196–97; Transcendental
Aesthetic of, 172, 74; "transcendental
turn" of, 201n8
Kierkegaard, Søren, 6, 9, 15, 72–75;
account of anxiety of, 52–53; concrete
universal for, 45; criticism of Hegel
of, 43–49; dialectic of subjective existence for, 48; *Diary of a Seducer*, 44;
as existential philosopher, 54, 75, 83;
experience of the death of God for,
74; French translations of, 44; and the
other dialectic, 41–43; qualitative dialectic of, 19; revolt of, 27
Kleinberg, Ethan: *Generation Existential*,
227n68
Klossowski, Pierre, 221n43
knowledge: complete system of, 7–8;
conceptual, 82; empirical, 82, 112, 116;
judicative, 104; and morality in Hume,
128, 145, 162; partial and complete
human, 7; philosophical work of Hegel
completes the work of, 94; practical

philosophy (*continued*)
81; experience of transcendence as the
origin of, 76; French, 3, 12, 17–19, 27,
48–50, 55–56, 81–89, 94–97, 107–14,
169, 181, 195; French Catholic, 97,
213n14, 227n69; Hegel as a particularly important touchstone for, 89, 94–
95; history of, 90, 108; post-Cartesian,
18, 130. *See also* existentialism; phenomenology; philosophy of science
philosophy of science, 36. *See also* philosophy
Plato, 16, 73–75, 83; *Parmenides*, 25, 47,
51, 73–74
pluralism, 8, 21–29; as the absolute unity
of the diverse, 73; Anglo-American,
16, 19, 23–24; identification for Russell of realism with, 23; Jamesian, 18;
nineteenth-century debates beween
monism and, 19; objective and materialist, 33; radical empiricism of, 24,
35; Wahl's interest in, 22–27. *See also*
monism
poetry: truth-character of nonconceptual
and ecstatic existence communicable
by, 90; as the unity of the subjective
and the objective, 77; Wahl on the irreducible "thickness" of experience and
the world in, 195
Politzer, Georges, 26
polytheism, 163–65. *See also* religion
pragmatism, 22
Proust, Marcel, 75
psychologism, 122–23; empiricist critique
of, 170; phenomenological critique
of, 128

Queneau, Raymond, 11

Rassemblement Démocratique Révolutionnaire, 227n78
rationalism: critical, 171; Descartes
as the forefather of contemporary,
118; Descartes as the forefather of
phenomenological, 118; difference
between Hume's philosophy and, 134–
35, 171–73, 180–81; empiricism and,
119–21, 123, 134–35, 170, 180–85, 199;
existential critique of, 111; Hyppolite's, 180; Kantian, 13, 121, 169, 171;
neo-Kantian, 60; orientation toward

representation of, 185; relations determined by ideas in, 180–85; vindication
of empiricism over, 4
Rawls, John, 142
realism: apprehension of the world for,
112–13; empirical, 78, 106, 113; as
immanent and transcendent for Wahl,
103, 113; problem of the exteriority of
relations in Anglo-American philosophy against monism in pluralist position of, 23; subjectivity inheres in the
world for, 42
Recherches Philosophiques, 5, 27
religion: as a dual system of extensive
rules for Hume, 163; irrationality as
an aspect of the experience of, 65;
and religious history, 67. *See also* God;
polytheism
Renaissance, 19
Revue de Métaphysique et de Morale, 26
*Revue Philosophique de la France et de
l'Étranger*, 8, 27–28, 38, 69, 194
Rilke, Rainer Maria, 78
Rimbaud, Arthur, 17, 54, 72–74, 76–77,
81, 90
Romanticism, 28, 46, 63, 71, 73, 86
Rousseau, Jean-Jacques, 64, 141–41, 144,
146, 150; *Émile*, 149
Russell, Bertrand, 6, 18–19, 23, 55,
124, 205n17; "Philosophy of Logical
Atomism," 207n28; "The Principle of
Individuation," 109; response to Hegel
of, 198

Sartre, Jean-Paul, 4–7, 55, 58, 72, 91, 95,
201n4; *Being and Nothingness*, 4, 95,
220n33; decline of interest in, 100;
"Existentialism Is a Humanism," 4, 6–
7, 84, 95–97, 216n44; existentialism of,
7, 52, 81, 83–86, 88, 226n65; *Nausea*,
96; *The Transcendence of the Ego*, 5; wartime activity of, 226n62
Scheler, Max, 73
Schelling, Friedrich Wilhelm Joseph, 31,
33–34, 62–67, 77–78, 204n14, 211n55;
*Philosophical Inquiries into the Essence
of Human Freedom*, 26; philosophy of
nature of, 67; transcendental empiricism of, 218n12
Schiller, Friedrich, 65
Scholasticism, 19